Social Outsiders in Nazi Germany

Social Outsiders in Nazi Germany

Edited by Robert Gellately and Nathan Stoltzfus

PRINCETON UNIVERSITY PRESS

PRINCETON AND OXFORD

Copyright © 2001 by Princeton University Press
Published by Princeton University Press, 41 William Street,
Princeton, New Jersey 08540
In the United Kingdom: Princeton University Press,
3 Market Place, Woodstock, Oxfordshire OX20 1SY
All Rights Reserved

Library of Congress Cataloging-in-Publication Data

Social outsiders in Nazi Germany / edited by Robert Gellately
and Nathan Stoltzfus
p. cm.
Includes bibliographical references and index.
ISBN 0-691-00748-9 (cloth: alk. paper)—
ISBN 0-691-08684-2 (pbk: alk. paper)
1. National socialism. 2. Germany—Social conditions—1933–1945.
3. Minorities—Germany—History—20th century. 4. Gays—
Nazi persecution. 5. Jews—Persecutions—Germany. 6. Germany—
Ethnic relations. 7. Gypsies—Nazi persecutions.
I. Gellately, Robert, 1943– II. Stoltzfus, Nathan.
DD256.5. S579   2001
323.1′43′09043—dc21   00-059827

This book has been composed in Galliard

The paper used in this publication meets
the minimum requirements of
ANSI/NISO Z39.48-1992 (R 1997)
(*Permanence of Paper*)

www.pup.princeton.edu

Printed in the United States of America

1 2 3 4 5 6 7 8 9 10
       3 4 5 6 7 8 9 10
                    (pbk.)

ISBN-13: 978-0-691-08684-2 (pbk.)

ISBN-10: 0-691-08684-2 (pbk.)

Contents

Social Outsiders in Nazi Germany

CHAPTER 1

Social Outsiders and the Construction of the Community of the People

ROBERT GELLATELY AND
NATHAN STOLTZFUS

THE NAZI Party began as a collection of right-wing radicals on the fringes of German society. Once the Great Depression hit Germany, however, the party rapidly became the largest, and certainly the most active, of all those competing for power. Shrewdly tailoring their propaganda and election activities to fit local and regional differences, the Nazis were able to win support from across the social spectrum. At the same time, they took every opportunity to denounce liberal democracy and were particularly vociferous in both their anti-Communism and their antisemitism.[1] To those who joined the party, Nazism was especially attractive because of its promise to create a conflict-free "community of the people."[2] Soon after Hitler was appointed chancellor on 30 January 1933, he made it clear that he would not retreat from the nationalist and racist elements of his vision of this "community." Within a week after his appointment, he told leading military men he wanted to remove "the cancer of Democracy" and create the "tightest authoritarian state leadership." He even ruminated about the "conquest of new living space in the east and its ruthless Germanization."[3]

At the end of February Hitler was able to take advantage of an arsonist's attack on the Reichstag building. He immediately obtained an emergency-measure act in the name of stopping an alleged Communist coup and used it effectively to begin the establishment of the Gestapo and concentration camps. Less than a month later, he secured the two-thirds majority in the Reichstag he needed for a constitutional change and an Enabling Law that in effect made it possible for him to become a law-giving dictator.[4]

The major questions facing the new dictatorship were where to begin establishing a racially pure "community of the people" and what to do about Hitler's call for a "moral purification of the body politic."[5] Clearly

3

it was going to take time to get the economy going, to mobilize an army, and to throw off the shackles of the peace treaty of Versailles. In the meantime it was necessary to deal with the economic crisis in the country and with other problems, such as the political opposition. Hitler tended to frame all domestic policies around preparing the nation for war; even the idea of creating the racially pure and internally harmonious "community of the people" was discussed in terms of the next war. He began constructing that community—as well as preparing it for war—by way of a negative-selection process. That process involved eliminating or at least confining certain groups and individuals, especially the Communists and others who were already hated, feared, or envied by many German citizens.[6]

In Germany at the end of the Weimar Republic there were deep worries about Communism, but there was also a pronounced antiliberal tide that rejected the freedoms offered by Weimar and yearned for the restoration of old values. Many citizens worried about crime and what they viewed as the disintegration of society. Under these circumstances, the Nazis saw a winning strategy in their law-and-order platform. Hitler's personal convictions, Nazi ideology, and what he deemed to be the wishes and hopes of many people came together in deciding where it would be politically most advantageous to begin. The Nazis knew what they shared with many other Germans, and most of their targets were individuals and groups long regarded as outsiders, nuisances, or "problem cases." The identification, the treatment, and even the pace of their persecution of political opponents and social outsiders illustrated that the Nazis attuned their law-and-order policies to German society, history, and traditions.

The Nazi ideal of a "community of the people" tapped into German traditions that lauded social harmony over conflict and in addition valued hard work, clean living, and law and order. For the Nazis, this idealized community could never see the light of day unless it was based on racial purity.[7] To this end, the new regime set out to mobilize the nation around certain missions, including the elimination of recognizable social types (and stereotypes) who disturbed the peace or who did not conform to well-established German values, but also those who did not fit into the white "Aryan" race.[8] The Nazi version of the struggle between "us" and "them," between the "community of the people" and the "enemies of the community," was not just hostile, but vehement and full of language that dripped with war and images drawn from the Darwinian struggle for survival. In the kind of total-war rhetoric the Nazis used,

4

it followed that mercy and compassion toward all enemies was portrayed as a vice, while intolerance and fanaticism were transformed into virtues.[9]

Once social enemies were targeted, the police, the judges, and any number of civil servants were quick to take the initiative and swing into action, even trying to outdo one another in their fealty to the cause of making the new order. The authorities in state and society "below," in the cultural realm, medicine, welfare, the penal system, and so on, showed they were pleased that Hitler allowed them the flexibility and freedom to implement measures that many of them had only dared to contemplate in earlier years.

Hitler and to some extent other leaders like Heinrich Himmler did not draw up their far-reaching goals or their tactical plans in a social or historical vacuum. Therefore, to understand what happened to social outsiders we cannot ignore the pre-1933 era. Almost all the contributions in this volume make more than casual reference to pre-Nazi times. As Richard Evans shows in his survey of the preceding three centuries, many of the same kinds of victims of the Third Reich had been pilloried and persecuted for generations. Nazi exclusionary theories built on so-called scientific theories as well as on social traditions and phobias about social outsiders from the pre-Nazi era. What set the Third Reich apart from its predecessors were the radical and murderous practices that issued from the theory and teachings of contempt.

In early 1933 the Communists were the first group attacked. Until then Communism had been growing rapidly in Germany, and after the Depression hit the Communist Party was invariably the third largest in the country. Many citizens were driven into the arms of the Nazis in part because of their flight from and anxieties about this development.[10] The Communists were inimical to the Nazis and to many Germans because of their political behavior, not their social identity or genetic makeup. The Nazis, however, came to view political convictions, especially deeply rooted ones, in social and even in semibiological terms. According to Nazi propaganda, the die-hard Communists in the concentration camps could be recognized by their deformed head shapes and the twisted features of their faces.[11] Beginning the Third Reich with an anti-Communist crusade certainly paid political dividends for the Nazis.

What should happen to the Jews? Hitler downplayed his antisemitism in the very last elections before his appointment so that the Nazi Party could focus on other topics to win more votes.[12] However, by then he and his party were already well known for their stance on the Jews, and

5

few could doubt that from Hitler's point of view the Jews were enemies to be eliminated one way or another. Whatever else citizens might have thought about the Nazis before 1933, it would be hard to imagine they did not know that Hitler's party was a proponent of the most radical antisemitism.

In 1933 the German Jews were not really "social outsiders." Since gaining their full legal emancipation in 1871, they had become increasingly well integrated. Antisemitism by no means disappeared, but spread during and after the First World War and particularly in the last years of the Weimar Republic. Nazi violence aimed at the Jews was already under way even before Hitler was appointed chancellor.[13] But while German Jews still suffered social discrimination, on the whole they were well represented at the universities, in the arts and sciences, and in the professions. Most were proud of their Fatherland, many had served with distinction in the First World War, and they were often quite nationalistic, much like the Jewish community in Italy.[14] Jews in Germany exhibited all the middle-class values that were generally lauded. As cultured and law-abiding citizens, they embodied the ideals of hard work, long study, and clean living.

At the start of the Third Reich, therefore, Hitler's government softpeddled its antisemitism, and Hitler carefully steered a course between what he would like to do and what was possible, given public opinion at home and abroad. Instead of an open assault on the Jews, the government opted for less ostentatious steps to begin the reversal of Jewish emancipation. Another consideration was that forcing out the Jews would have disrupted the already crisis-ridden economy. But if the national government proceeded cautiously, Nazi hotheads at the local level used selective violence and intimidation against the Jews. Germans may have been upset by the lawlessness of these persecutions, but in time many yielded to the appeals of antisemitism or at the very least ignored it. As the months passed, pushing the Jews out became easier for many Germans to stomach, especially when they saw that doing so made available Jewish jobs, businesses, and property.

The Jews in Germany were a small minority, but given Nazi definitions of who counted as Jewish, they were potentially one of the largest groups of social outsiders in the country. According to official figures for January 1933, approximately 525,000 Jews lived in Germany.[15] The percentage of these "believing Jews" in the total population, at under 1 percent, was small and had been declining well before Hitler came to power. But vigilant racists, like those in the new German Christian movement, which strove to unite Christianity and Nazism, worried that the published statistics missed **300,000** or more "Jews" who did not practice their faith and who were not counted as Jews by the statisticians. At the very least, the German Christians wanted to expel them from Protestantism. The Ministry of the Interior's document from April 1935, to which the German Christians alluded with alarm, also recorded that there were an estimated additional 750,000 "Jewish-Germans" of mixed race in the country.[16] Although Jews of mixed race were not subject to the full scope of Nazi antisemitism, they suffered various kinds of discrimination.[17] Even when some of them applied for and were granted special legal certification to show they were not "Jews" as defined in the laws, their lives remained precarious, not least because decisions about ancestry could always be reversed.[18]

A law of 7 April 1933 made it easy to purge Jews and others from the civil service. Called the Law for the Restoration of a Professional Civil Service to avoid the impression that the Nazis were tampering, this law had enormous implications.[19] It not only applied to the federal civil service, but also reached down to the village level. It pertained to all kinds of officials, judges, the police, university professors, and schoolteachers. The public was told that the law aimed at "the elimination of Jewish and Marxist elements."[20]

Millions of people were affected by the notorious questionnaires about family background that were part of the law, and follow-up investigations dragged on, guaranteeing lots of snooping. Informers rushed in to settle old scores or to gain some personal advantage from the process.[21] Above and beyond the considerable direct effects these proceedings had on Jews and/or on people with some association with "Marxism," the process undoubtedly made the entire civil service aware of the new rules of the game, and in case anyone did not yet know, it was guaranteed to spread the word that official antisemitism was now government policy.

Nazi hotheads out in the provinces were impatient with these legalistic measures, but such antisemitic violence as developed generally did not look like the pillage and plunder, for example, seen recently in the Balkans. Instead the Nazis tempered their persecutions to accommodate public opinion that did not wish to see street violence or property destruction.

Historians continue to debate how Germans responded to what happened. However, most would now agree that although citizens generally did not want violence, by the end of the prewar era many came to

accept the Nazi point of view, that there was a "Jewish question."[22] By
then the Jews had been turned into social outsiders, and most non-Jews
in Germany came to the self-righteous conclusion that it would be better for all concerned if the Jews, driven to the margins of society, would
leave the country. Underground Socialist observers, highly critical of
Hitler's dictatorship, noted that while some people sympathized with
the persecuted Jews, others took the view that "these Jews must have
been up to something," for otherwise "the state would not have
pounced."[23] According to one detailed study, even before the war,
"there is conclusive evidence that on the whole the population con-
sented to attacks on the Jews as long as these neither damaged non-Jews
nor harmed the interests of the country, particularly its reputation
abroad."[24]

Frank Bajohr investigates in this volume what was euphemistically
called "Aryanization," that is, taking over Jewish businesses and property. The gradual impoverishment of the Jews made it difficult for them
to emigrate, and it became a struggle for many who remained in the
country to maintain themselves. Bajohr shows elsewhere how, in Hamburg, the public auction of goods that had been stolen from the local
Jews or from Jews in eastern Europe became almost a daily occurrence
from early 1941 until the end of the war. These auctions turned citizens
into accomplices who profited directly from the persecution and murder
of the Jews.[25]

Marion Kaplan investigates how the Jews reacted when the country
and people they loved turned on and rejected them. Although in the
post-Holocaust world one may wonder why the Jews did not leave Germany in greater numbers, in fact the regime's intentions were not immediately clear. At least until 1938, persecution was halting and sporadic,
and in many parts of the country, even in Berlin, as Peter Gay has testified, Jews could live a relatively "normal" existence.[26] What struck
most Jews, according to Kaplan, were these ambiguities, the mixed mes-
sages, and not least their own ambivalent feelings about leaving. Looking back, however, the survivors testify to how quickly they began to feel
like outsiders.

The situation of the Jews who stayed, often because they had no-
where to go, deteriorated with the pogrom in November 1938 and grew
worse after the coming of the war in 1939. The desolate status of the
Jews, who were the subject of endless hate-filled speeches from the
country's leaders and the recipients of shabby treatment by most of their
neighbors, was formally symbolized when they were forced to wear the

yellow star (from 15 September 1941). The deportations soon began, and as if to cut Jews off from all contact with other citizens, shortly thereafter (24 October 1941) it became a serious crime for any "German-blooded person" to be seen in public with a Jew.

We have to be aware, of course, that there was no such thing as a "German-blooded person," and that the Nazis used this kind of language, along with an arsenal of laws and other measures, to turn Jewish citizens into social outsiders.[27] It is precisely because of what the Nazis did to language that historians are driven to use quotation marks around so many words, whose meanings were utterly twisted out of shape and at times turned on their head. Victor Klemperer, whose recently published diaries have become famous, partly because of his philological observations, was the first (in 1947) to publish a study of Nazis' corruption of the German language.[28]

As part of their political and racial mission, Hitler and the Nazis set out to restore what they termed the "wholesomeness" to Germany's cultural life, and to remove the "poison." Alan Steinweis indicates some of the ways the Nazis led a kind of cultural revolution of their own, one that was bound up with and reinforced by the policies of persecution and marginalization that targeted the groups studied in this volume. Jews suffered disproportionately as the Third Reich's culture victims, for they could be driven out on the basis of racist teachings and also on the grounds that all cultural fields and artistic endeavors were by definition reserved for non-Jewish Germans only. The purges of the Jews from the civil service inspired follow-up dismissals from the arts and the press, and even from the free professions. Such steps were necessary—according to press reports—to placate the "outrage of the entire German-blooded population" at Jewish professionals.[29] Steinweis maintains that the "vast majority" of non-Jewish artists who were allowed to continue their work found little difficulty in adjusting to Nazi practices, including censorship.

One of the groups who suffered both state-sponsored discrimination and enormous social pressure were the couples who lived in what the Nazis called "mixed marriages," that is, those involving Jewish and non-Jewish partners. Whereas in earlier times "mixed marriages" loosely referred to a marriage between people of different religions, now the Nazis transformed the term and applied it to their definition of different "races." Nathan Stoltzfus traces the history of those living in such unions. He shows that many "Aryan" Germans remained loyal to their spouses, even though the regime did everything possible to break the ties. The non-Jewish spouses in these marriages had social-outsider status thrust upon them at every turn. They were despised by the regime and also by many people who knew them. As they were continually reminded, all they had to do to avoid further difficulty and to be welcomed back into the fold was to divorce their Jewish spouse, a process that the authorities tried to bring about. Many who lived in these "mixed marriages" refused to go along and, as Stoltzfus shows, rescued their spouses from deportation to a concentration camp.

Victor Klemperer's diaries provide testimony from the inside of such a "mixed marriage." Stoltzfus indicates that in contrast to most citizens, intermarried Germans refused to yield to the advancement of Nazi anti-Jewish policies with regard to their family members. For its part, the Nazi regime was surprisingly timid when it came to dissolving these marriages even into the war years, and was also slow to encroach on the sanctity of private property, because these moves might have made many Germans uncomfortable.[30]

Even as they perpetrated the Holocaust and other unspeakable crimes all over Europe, the Nazis fussed and worried about marriage certificates and property deeds. The regime also steered a careful course when it came to excluding and destroying Germans who suffered from various hereditary diseases and infirmities. As Henry Friedlander shows, older German and European theories about heredity, race, "degeneration," and criminality merged to form a racist ideology that was taken up, advanced, and translated into murderous practices by the Nazis. Until 1933 sterilization had been illegal, much to the frustration of race and medical experts, some of whom had been arguing for it from as early as the turn of the century. In the Third Reich, those in many branches of medicine and "racial hygiene" were pleased that the dictatorship finally untied their hands to deal with people whose "defects"—whether mental, physical, or merely ones of appearance—were thought (often on dubious grounds) to be hereditary.[31] The participation of race scientists, medical specialists, and learned judges in the massive sterilization campaign helped to assure good citizens that proper procedures were being followed. Far from being appalled at the sterilization program the Nazis brought in, medical officials greeted it.[32] The Nazis expended an enormous amount of time and energy to "sell" this program to the German people,[33] and they won at least their "tacit support."[34] However, because the Nazis ran up against deep-seated religious convictions when it came to what they called "euthanasia," they were more secretive and circumspect in pushing it.[35]

10

We know from other sources that Nazi medical officials who toured some parts of the country wanted to sterilize whole villages when the people (all "ordinary Germans") did not appear well-kept or tidy enough.[36] At the very least sterilization, forced and otherwise, would mean that the people who had "infirmities" and other problems would not be able to pass them on. In the event, an estimated 400,000 people were sterilized in Germany.[37]

The exclusionary polices that aimed to cleanse the Fatherland of chronic-care cases and the mentally ill became more radical with the coming of the war. Hitler backdated to 1 September 1939 his authorization (not order) for doctors to begin the "mercy killing" operation, as if to symbolize that war made it possible at last to put aside mere civilian considerations in the creation of the "community of the people." When the public got wind of what was happening there was some unrest, but no open protest. Some, but not all, local residents near the killing sites were appalled. One woman wrote to the hospital where her two siblings reportedly died within a few days of each other. She said she accepted the Third Reich, and hoped to "find peace again" if doctors could assure her that her siblings had been killed by virtue of some law that made it possible to "relieve people from their chronic suffering."[38]

People who had been tried by the courts and sent to prison as criminals were regarded as social outsiders in Germany and most other countries long before the Third Reich, and dealing with them more radically than ever seemed almost inevitable for a "law-and-order" dictatorship like Hitler's. Thus in mid-1933, at about the same time that the Nazis promulgated the first important measures against the Jews and introduced what would become their massive sterilization program, they also proceeded against criminals. As Nikolaus Wachsmann makes clear, during the Weimar Republic criminologists, prison officials, and the police had all called for the kinds of steps the Nazis were soon to permit. For example, in Weimar the authorities sought the preventive arrest of repeat offenders, but those demands did not get very far until after Hitler's appointment. From the Nazi point of view, arresting people before they committed new crimes not only fitted the new approach to "law and order" but was consistent with popular demands for an end to what was widely perceived in 1933 to be a crime wave. Wachsmann shows what happened, and especially how the war led to a radicalization in the persecution of certain criminals.

Nazi theory and practice toward convicted criminals reflected what happened to the "asocials," a loosely defined group that was much

11

discussed in welfare and police circles well before the Nazi era. We do not have a specific contribution focusing on people who were labeled asocials by the Nazis, but this vaguely and quite arbitrarily defined group is studied at some length in several of the essays. The concept was used to describe anyone who did not act according to what the Nazis defined as a "good citizen," and who avoided what were held to be one's proper social responsibilities. Asocials were usually described in emotional terms as the "dregs of society," with weak characters, loose morals, and poor work habits. The Nazis took many steps to deal with them, and carried out some curious experiments in social engineering, like one attempt in the mid-1930s to establish a "family colony" of asocials near Bremen, ostensibly to see if they could be resocialized. Pictures of the camp make it look like a modern suburb, but it did not last, mainly because the Nazis ultimately concluded that "asociality," like most social ills, was hereditary.[39]

The Nazis wanted to rid society of all people whose way of life did not conform to the new ideals. They moved quickly against anyone who would not take up a regular job, and even in mid-1933 various authorities went after beggars and others, like the Gypsies, the "work-shy," and the homeless for (what a local ordinance called) "bothering the population."[40] By mid-September 1933 the police ordered a nationwide end to the "plague of the beggars" in the streets. Citizens were asked to cooperate by reserving their funds for proper charities, and were reminded that Germany was too poor to afford "full-time beggars, work-shy, drinkers, and fraud artists."[41]

Annette Timm focuses on the prostitutes, yet another asocial group toward whom the Nazis adopted an ambivalent stance. Certainly prostitutes offended traditional morality, lived outside the law, avoided regular work, were an affront to family values, and perhaps worst of all, spread fertility-threatening venereal disease. Women even vaguely suspected of being prostitutes were sent to variously defined "work camps," and for a time mere failure to pay health insurance premiums could be used as a pretext to send "loose women" to a camp. Any woman treated by a doctor for a sexually transmitted disease also risked being classed by a health or welfare official as a "work-shy welfare recipient" and sent to a camp.[42] However, Nazi attitudes toward prostitution changed over time, and as the war approached, the regime that had presented itself as a moral and health crusader began to tolerate officially registered prostitutes in what became state-run brothels. It is difficult to quantify prostitution over the centuries, as much of it was part time or occasional, but the Third Reich may well have fostered more prostitution in state-sanctioned brothels than any comparable period in German history.

The war marked a dramatic and a deadly turn in the persecution of the Roma and Sinti, usually referred to as the "Gypsies." As Sybil Milton shows, social prejudice and state hostility toward these people had a long history in Germany and the rest of Europe, reaching back well before the Third Reich. German society was not alone among European nations in regarding the Roma and Sinti as problem cases who could not, or would not, fit in. In the modern era of state- and nation-making, such people were often seen as a group apart, and in addition they were considered to be prone to crime, socially inferior, and utterly outside "normal" society. In Germany the Roma and Sinti constituted a very small minority, but under Hitler's dictatorship they caught the official eye. The Third Reich offered local officials and citizens the prospect of dealing with "their Gypsies" more fundamentally than ever, and there were plenty of suggestions for actions from "below." Milton points to parallels in the definition, registration, confinement, and deportation of the Jews and the Roma and Sinti. Michael Zimmermann recently and quite rightly has insisted that "racially motivated genocide formed the essence of National Socialist Gypsy policy, when compared to the earlier German variety."[43] Milton reminds us of the fate of these people and how greatly they suffered.

Social prejudices against homosexuality in Germany were also very old, and they found their way into the German criminal code in 1871. Neither the law nor the social prejudices entirely disappeared over the years. Under the liberal Weimar Republic, there was the widespread perception that homosexuality was on the increase. Geoffrey Giles suggests that Hitler may not have been as obsessed by homophobia as is often supposed, but nevertheless when he addressed the topic he sounded murderous enough, and at the very least the kind of leader who would support any of his followers who wanted to wipe out homosexuality. As it happened, Himmler was as keen to deal with homosexuals as he was determined to solve many other "problem cases." He wanted them not just out of the SS and the police, but stamped out of German society.

The identification and persecution of gay men was very much on the police agenda in the new Reich. The Nazis sharpened the laws and centralized enforcement. Both the Gestapo and the criminal police (Kripo) had special sections to track down and prosecute gay men. Like many of the policies and practices aimed at other social outsiders, the persecution of gay men was noticeably radicalized during the war. Although lesbianism also offended what the Nazis called "wholesome popular senti-ment," it evoked no systematic campaign, partly because it was not re-garded as a serious "danger to the nation's survival."[44]

The war brought home a stunning new fact of life for everyone in the country: Germany could not cope with the war without using hundreds of thousands, and then millions, of foreign laborers. In the autumn of 1939 Polish prisoners of war and then civilian Poles became the first to arrive. These were the new social outsiders, and Robert Gellately dis-cusses them in his essay. The Poles are studied as a "representative" ex-ample of the millions of others who came from eastern and western Eu-rope, many of them against their will.

Anti-Polish attitudes and traditions in Germany were and still are leg-endary, going back for generations. A study of the citizenship law of 1913 (until quite recently, still in force) shows that it was drawn up in such a way as to keep German citizenship from the Poles and the Jews coming into the country from the East. The law restricted citizenship to lineage and blood, and would not confer it when a person simply lived in Germany, even for a long time. The law made it possible to keep citizen-ship away from at least any newly arriving Poles and Jews, and they could be permanently excluded.[45]

The anti-Polish sentiments that were part and parcel of German tradi-tion were magnified many times in the Third Reich, so that it was a bit-ter pill for the Nazis to have to import these foreigners they despised so much into their midst. At the very moment the Nazis were taking un-precedented steps to form a racially pure community by killing "defec-tives" and deporting the Jews, they were creating a dilemma for them-selves insofar as they began to import "racially foreign people." To limit the damage, the Nazis established an apartheid system inside Germany. Poles were forced to wear a badge with a "P" on their clothing and were told that any sexual relations with Germans was a capital offense. In-deed, the offending foreign workers were initially hanged in the street. Many Germans were not as hostile toward the Poles as the authorities wished. Farmers were happy to have help on their farms, and many ordi-nary people were pleased to have cheap hired hands, including young women, to help out around the house.[46]

Doris Bergen focuses on "ethnic Germans," another group of new outsiders in wartime Germany. They were gathered up from various re-gions across eastern Europe, but some thrust themselves forward with tenuous proof of their German origins. In one sense these people were insiders, or at least had this potential from the Nazi point of view, and they certainly wanted to be counted in the "master race." Supposedly

14

their ethnicity (or blood) made them "Aryans." However, as Bergen shows, the pseudoscientific and arbitrary nature of the "theories" on which Nazi racism and ethnic cleansing rested became clear when the experts tried to examine such borderline cases. The ethnic Germans, often having lived for generations outside Germany, had their own backgrounds and strange accents and customs that caused them to stand out in the eyes of ordinary Germans and officialdom and made them seem barely distinguishable from their east European neighbors. Nazi race "science" revealed itself as quackery, but often very deadly quackery.

During the conference on which this book is based, we all became aware that there were other groups we would like to have included in this book. We especially regret not having a study of the Jehovah's Witnesses, religious outsiders who in the end resisted Nazi pressure to conform. Many of them paid with their lives in concentration camps.[47]

The examination of social outsiders also raises many theoretical issues. During the conference some of us decided to work on another follow-up volume to address those issues and to deal with the comparative study of social outsiders in other times and places. It is also true that the persecution of social outsiders inside Nazi Germany led into theories and practices of genocide in eastern Europe. A theoretical framework for the comparative study of social outsiders in twentieth-century Europe and their links to genocide can be seen in Omer Bartov's provocative essay. He explores the wider implications of the Nazis' apocalyptic vision of the idyllic and harmonious future that was to be attained by selectively forgetting the past and proposing all kinds of "final solutions" to social and political questions. Bartov's analysis brings us back to the centrality of antisemitism in the Third Reich as he focuses mainly on the Jews and the Holocaust. What he has to say more generally also elucidates the context in which a series of social outsiders were singled out, stigmatized, and slated for elimination. As he puts it, modern war and totalitarianism "necessitate and devise final solutions in which humanity is perceived as a mass of matter to be molded, controlled, moved, purged, and annihilated. This conceptualization of the world biologizes society and sociologizes biology; humanity becomes an organism in need of radical surgery, or a social construct in need of sociological reordering. Hence the vast population transfers, brutal operations of ethnic cleansing, eradication of whole social classes, and ultimately outright genocide, the most final solution of all."

This book began as a conference on social outsiders in Nazi Germany, organized by Robert Gellately and Nathan Stoltzfus, supported by the

15

Harry Frank Guggenheim Foundation, and held in Madrid in December 1998. Most of the essays presented here began as papers for that conference. Some were extensively revised, and we have added a number of others to round out the picture.[48] We would like to thank the Guggenheim Foundation and, for their useful suggestions to improve this volume, also the two anonymous readers of the manuscript for Princeton University Press, as well as Kevin Mason for technical assistance in manuscript preparation. It is our hope that through this work we can stimulate discussion and debate about the social and political construction of social outsiders and their fate inside Nazi Germany.

NOTES

1. See Michael H. Kater, *The Nazi Party: A Social Profile of Members and Leaders, 1919–1945* (Cambridge, Mass., 1983); and Thomas Childers, *The Nazi Voter: The Social Foundation of Fascism in Germany, 1919–1933* (Chapel Hill, 1983).

2. A classic account is Theodore Abel, *Why Hitler Came to Power* (1938; Cambridge, Mass., 1986).

3. For General Liebmann's notes of the meeting, see Jeremy Noakes and Geoffrey Pridham, eds., *Nazism, 1919–1945: A Documentary Reader* (Exeter, 1988), 3:628–29.

4. This and other relevant documents can be found in ibid.,1:142.

5. See Max Domarus, ed., *Hitler Reden und Proklamationen, 1932–1945* (Leonberg, 1973), 1:229–37, here 232–33.

6. See Martin Broszat, *Der Staat Hitlers*, 2 ed. (Munich, 1971), 434.

7. For an excellent introduction, see Jeremy Noakes, "Social Outcasts in the Third Reich," in *Life in the Third Reich*, ed. Richard Bessel (New York, 1987), 83–96.

8. For an interesting overview, see Uli Linke, *German Bodies: Race and Representation after Hitler* (New York, 1999), esp. 37–54.

9. For a convenient collection of the relevant documents, see Wolfgang Ayaß, ed., *"Gemeinschaftsfremde": Quellen zur Verfolgung von "Asozialen," 1933–1945* (Koblenz, 1998), 366–82.

10. For the statistics, critique of the literature, and latest analysis, see Jürgen W. Falter, *Hitlers Wähler* (Munich, 1991).

11. See the book by Camp Commandant Werner Schäfer of Oranienburg, *Konzentrationslager Oranienburg: Das Anti-Braunbuch über das erste deutsche Konzentrationslager* (Berlin, 1934), 25, 31.

12. For an interesting analysis, see Anthony Kauders, *German Politics and the Jews: Düsseldorf and Nuremberg, 1919–1933* (Oxford, 1996), here 183.

16

13. For a convincing recent account of antisemitism and violence aimed at the Jews, see Dirk Walter, *Antisemitische Kriminalität und Gewalt: Judenfeindschaft in der Weimarer Republik* (Bonn, 1999).

14. See the remarkable study by Alexander Stille, *Benevolence and Betrayal: Five Italian Jewish Families under Fascism* (New York, 1991), esp. 17–90.

15. See, for example, Ino Arndt and Heinz Boberach, "Deutsches Reich," in *Dimension des Völkermords: Die Zahl der jüdischen Opfer des Nationalsozialismus*, ed. Wolfgang Benz (Munich, 1996), 23.

16. See Doris L. Bergen, *Twisted Cross: The German Christian Movement in the Third Reich* (Chapel Hill, 1996), 83–84.

17. See Saul Friedländer, *Nazi Germany and Jews,* vol 1: *The Years of Persecution, 1933–1939* (New York, 1997), here 157.

18. For a detailed recent analysis, see Beate Meyer, *'Jüdische Mischlinge': Rassenpolitik und Verfolgungserfahrung, 1933–1945* (Hamburg, 1999), 162–259.

19. For a copy of the law and others applying to the civil service, see Ingo von Münch, ed., *Gesetze des NS-Staates*, 3 ed. (Paderborn, 1994), 26–28.

20. "Nur deutschblütige Beamte dürfen die Staatsautorität verkörpern," in *Völkischer Beobachter* (4 April 1933); "Säuberung des Beamtentums," in *Völkischer Beobachter* (13 April 1933).

21. Jane Caplan, *Government without Administration: State and Civil Society in Weimar and Nazi Germany* (Oxford, 1988), 143–46. For a local examination, see Karl Teppe, *Provinz, Partei, Staat* (Münster, 1977), 36–68.

22. See Ian Kershaw, *Popular Opinion and Political Dissent in the Third Reich: Bavaria, 1933–1945* (Oxford, 1983), 224–77.

23. See the July report of *Deutschland-Berichte der Sozialdemokratischen Partei Deutschlands (Sopade)* (Frankfurt am Main, 1980), here (1938), 763.

24. David Bankier, *The Germans and the Final Solution: Public Opinion under Nazism* (Oxford, 1992), 73–74.

25. Frank Bajohr, *"Arisierung" in Hamburg: Die Verdrängung der jüdischen Unternehmer, 1933–1945* (Hamburg, 1997), 331–38.

26. Peter Gay, *My German Question: Growing Up in Nazi Berlin* (New Haven, 1998), 57–83.

27. These laws and others are discussed in Robert Gellately, *The Gestapo and German Society: Enforcing Racial Policy, 1933–1945* (Oxford, 1990).

28. His classic study is now available in English as Victor Klemperer, *The Language of the Third Reich*, trans. M. Brady (New York, 1999). See also the remarkable account by George Steiner, *Language and Silence: Essays, 1958–1966* (Harmondsworth, 1969).

29. The phrases are from government officials as cited in Horst Göppinger, *Juristen jüdischer Abstammung im "Dritten Reich,"* 2 ed. (Munich, 1990), 59; see also "Aufbruch zum Recht," in *Völkischer Beobachter* (6 April 1933).

30. For the testimony of a Jewish survivor of a "mixed marriage" who

refused to sign over the property of her "Aryan" husband after his death and her immediate deportation, see Donald L. Niewyk, ed., *Fresh Wounds: Early Narratives of Holocaust Survival* (Chapel Hill, 1998), 268–72, here 271.

31. See Robert N. Proctor, *Racial Hygiene: Medicine under the Nazis* (Cambridge, Mass., 1988), 95–117.

32. For more on this theme, see Götz Aly, Peter Chroust, and Christian Pross, *Cleansing the Fatherland: Nazi Medicine and Racial Hygiene*, trans. B. Cooper (Baltimore, 1994).

33. See Christine Charlotte Makowski, *Eugenic, Sterilisationspolitik, "Euthanasie" und Bevölkerungspolitik in der nationalsozialistischen Parteipresse* (Husem, 1996).

34. See Noakes, "Social Outcasts," 86.

35. For a study of the propaganda films used to "sell" euthanasia, see Michael Burleigh, *Death and Deliverance: "Euthanasia" in Germany, 1900–1945* (Cambridge, 1994), 183–219.

36. For local details, see Paul Sauer, *Württemberg in der Zeit des Nationalsozialismus* (Ulm, 1975), 146–54.

37. See Gisela Bock, *Zwangssterilisation im Nationalsozialismus: Studien zur Rassenpolitik und Frauenpolitik* (Opladen, 1986), 238.

38. Correspondence is reprinted in *Der Prozess gegen die Hauptkriegsverbrecher vor dem Internationalen Militärgerichtshof, Nürnberg*, vol. 35 (Nuremberg, 1949), here 689.

39. See Lisa Pine, *Nazi Family Policy, 1933–1945* (Oxford, 1997), 117–46.

40. The phrase is from a Bremen law of 11 August 1933, reprinted Ayaß, ed., *"Gemeinschaftsfremde,"* 33. See also the excellent study of Wolfgang Ayaß, *"Asoziale" im Nationalsozialismus* (Stuttgart, 1995). By "Gypsies" we mean the two distinct groups of Roma and Sinti, many of whom do not accept the collective term "Gypsies" that was used pejoratively over many years to stereotype them negatively. Instead, throughout the book we try to use Roma and Sinti, the terms they prefer. For additional information see chapter 10.

41. The *Völkischer Beobachter* (Munich) printed the call of the Bavarian government (18 September 1933); see Ayaß, ed., *"Gemeinschaftsfremde,"* 42–43.

42. See Wolfgang Ayaß, *Das Arbeitshaus Breitenau* (Kassel, 1992), 282–83.

43. Michael Zimmermann, "Die nationalsozialistische 'Lösung der Zigeunerfrage,'" in Ulrich Herbert, ed., *Nationalsozialistische Vernichtungspolitik, 1939–1945: Neue Forschungen und Kontroversen* (Frankfurt am Main, 1998), 225–62, here 261.

44. See the 1937 speech of Dr. Josef Meisinger in J. Noakes, *Nazism, 1919–1945*, vol. 4: *The German Home Front in World War II* (Exeter, 1998), 391. For an analysis, see Claudia Schoppmann, "National Socialist Policies towards Female Homosexuality," in Lynn Abrams and Elizabeth Harvey, eds., *Gender Relations in German History* (Durham, 1997), 177–87.

45. See Rogers Brubaker, *Citizenship and Nationhood in France and Germany* (Cambridge, Mass., 1992), 114–37.

46. For a recent oral history, see Annekatrein Mendel, *Zwangsarbeit im Kinderzimmer: "Ostarbeiterinnen" in deutschen Familien von 1939 bis 1945. Gespräche mit Polinnen und Deutschen* (Frankfurt, 1994).

47. For a major study, see Detlev Garbe, *Zwischen Widerstand und Martyrium: Die Zeugen Jehovas im "Dritten Reich"* (Munich, 1994). He shows that this religious community counted between 25,000 and 30,000 members in Germany at the start of the Third Reich. Eventually many were sent to camps, where they were mistreated and sometimes shot out of hand when they would not renounce their faith, show loyalty to Nazism such as by giving the Hitler greeting, or serve in the armed forces after the draft was reintroduced in 1935.

48. For studies that deal with a wide range of social outsiders and provide extensive additional reading, see Michael Burleigh and Wolfgang Wippermann, *The Racial State: Germany, 1933–1945* (Cambridge, 1991); Michael Berenbaum and Abraham J. Peck, eds., *The Holocaust and History: The Known, the Unknown, the Disputed, and the Reexamined* (Bloomington, 1998).

CHAPTER 2

Social Outsiders in German History

FROM THE SIXTEENTH CENTURY TO 1933

RICHARD J. EVANS

I

There is now a substantial literature on social outsiders in the Third Reich. Much of it is the product of a realization that Nazism had many categories of "forgotten victims" whose fate had previously been little studied by historians. Although the Jews undoubtedly bore the main brunt of Nazism's policies of hatred and destruction of various forms of human life, other groups suffered too. They included "Gypsies" (Roma and Sinti), homosexuals, the mentally and physically handicapped, "habitual criminals," "asocials," the "work-shy," the homeless and itinerants, and Slavic and other subject peoples (both within Germany, as forcibly imported slave laborers, and beyond its borders). All these groups were subjected by the Nazis, in varying proportions and with varying degrees of severity, to arrest, imprisonment, brutal maltreatment in concentration camps, sterilization, and murder.[1]

The impulses of discovery and documentation which have driven this research have inevitably meant that it has concentrated almost exclusively on the years 1933 to 1945. To be sure, many authors have traced back at least some of the roots of Nazi policies in this area to the social thought and practice of the Weimar Republic, or to racial and eugenic theories which came to the fore in the 1890s. But in sharp contrast to the immense literature on German antisemitism, which has given exhaustive coverage to the social, economic, ideological, cultural, and political origins of the Nazi persecution of the Jews from the Middle Ages onward, there is next to nothing on the long-term historical background to the Nazi persecution of other minorities in German society. German attitudes to the Slavs, and the history of foreign workers in nineteenth-century Germany, have been well documented.[2] Yet this is mainly because of the impulse given to historical research on these topics by two major problems of West German politics in the 1970s and 1980s, namely the status and condition of millions of disfranchised Gastarbeiter in the country and the ever-present challenge of peaceful coexistence with the Soviet Union and the Warsaw Pact. By contrast, there has been very little debate on the long-term history of other social outsiders in modern Germany.

Yet it is on the face of it surprising that historians have not so far asked the same kind of questions in this area as they have in the history of German Jews and antisemitism. Did social outsiders play a particularly prominent role in German society from the Middle Ages onward? Were the Germans particularly hostile to them? Did their situation improve or deteriorate over time? Do we have examples of their being made scapegoats in periods of trouble? Did they become more integrated or less into German society in the course of industrialization? Did German liberals champion the cause of their emancipation during the political struggles of the nineteenth century? What difference did the coming of Weimar democracy make to their status and position? All these, and many other, similar questions that spring to mind can be summed up by asking whether German society, as some historians of culture and ideas have supposed, was particularly conformist, regimented, and hostile to outsiders. Did the Nazi persecution of social outsiders, in other words, meet with a ready response from the broader, conforming German population because the latter had always been hostile to social outsiders, to a degree perhaps unusual in other countries?

II

A start can be made by looking at the substantial literature which now exists on social outsiders in the early modern period, that is, from roughly the Reformation to the French Revolution and Napoleonic Wars. German society in this period was organized into status-based orders, or *Stände*, whose rights and duties were enforced by law and custom. All the elements of the social order were sustained by the notion that they possessed, in differing measure and in different ways, social honor (*Ehre*).

Outside this elaborate structure of honorable society, however, stood the heterogeneous group of the "dishonorable" (*unehrliche Leute*), whose outsider status derived from five major sources: it could be inherited, it could be attached to an occupation, or it could be the

21

consequence of deviant conduct, especially (and above all for women) sexual, it could result from membership in a religious or ethnic minority, or it could follow from a criminal conviction. Distinctions between honorable and dishonorable groups were in part underwritten by the state, but it was above all the craft guilds that insisted on disqualifying a variety of social groups from membership by labeling them as infamous.[3]

Thus the dishonorable in early modern Germany included those who plied trades which brought them into contact with dirty or polluting substances: millers, shepherds, tanners, street cleaners, and, most dishonorable of all, skinners, knackers, molecatchers, and public executioners. A second larger and more amorphous group consisted of itinerants, people with no fixed abode: peddlers, Gypsies, traveling entertainers (bear-keepers, conjurers, and the like), mountebanks, knifegrinders, and so on. Third, there were women who had lost their honor through sexual misconduct, above all, prostitutes and unmarried mothers. Fourth, infamy also attached to non-Christians, which in the German context meant above all the Jews, and subject linguistic-cultural groups such as the Wends. And finally, anyone, whatever his prior status, who had received a criminal conviction and suffered at the polluting hands of the public hangman at the pillory (called in German the *Schandpfahl*, or pillar of shame) was also considered dishonorable.[4]

Stigmatization as dishonorable made it impossible to enter a guild to acquire a citizen's rights, to buy most kinds of landholding, and in general to carry on a decent existence above the poverty line. So concerned were guildsmen to distance themselves from the dishonorable that the merest accidental physical contact could provoke serious rioting, as in Berlin in 1800, when an executioner's assistant manhandled a journeyman spectator during a public execution, resulting in disturbances that only subsided when a senior and thus extremely honorable city official formally restored the journeyman's honorable status by shaking his hand (while at the same time calling out the troops just to make sure).[5] Executioners, indeed, were one of the few dishonorable trades where a decent living could be made and substitutes appointed to do the most dishonorable kinds of work. Even they had to drink in the local inn out of special mugs which nobody else was allowed to touch. Any guildsman who married an executioner's daughter was liable to find himself summarily expelled from his guild and deprived of his living.[6]

The guilds and other "honorable" groups in urban and rural society excluded the "dishonorable" in the teeth of growing opposition from the territorial state, which considered such restrictive practices harmful to the interests of the majority and productive of poverty and disorder among those whom it affected. It was not least its desire to reduce the power of the guilds that impelled the eighteenth-century absolutist state in repeated promulgations to attempt to reintegrate many of the dishonorable into society. The state's main concerns with social outsiders in the early modern period were to repress disorder and encourage industriousness. Thus it deployed a range of repressive strategies against those it regarded as disruptive or idle, such as bandits, beggars, confidence tricksters, and some classes of itinerants such as traveling musicians, Gypsies, mountebanks, and bear-keepers, but it could not see why hardworking trades that contributed to the national wealth should be regarded as dishonorable.

In 1731 the Holy Roman Empire formally declared all trades apart from that of skinner/knacker/executioner (the three were usually combined) to be honorable, and in 1772 it extended this provision to the last-named group as well. In 1775 King Friedrich II of Prussia, followed in 1783 by Joseph II of Austria, reversed the previous policy of trying to drive out or exterminate the Gypsies and attempted instead to promote their integration into society. Numerous legal reforms drastically reduced the number of offenses punishable by death, including sodomy (for which a young man had been burned at the stake in Prussia as late as 1730), and effectively decriminalized a wide variety of offenses such as witchcraft and blasphemy. The replacement of Christian codes of conduct by Enlightenment rationalism led to the law codes of the late eighteenth and early nineteenth centuries which effectively abandoned sanctions against many consensual sexual acts including homosexuality and bestiality.[7]

These laws, like so many of the proclamations of Enlightened monarchs, had a very limited effect on social attitudes and behavior. Thus knackers and executioners continued to be excluded from respectable society and to form inbred dynasties of their own well into the nineteenth century.[8] Guilds continued to defy authority in enforcing a strict interpretation of the notion of honor. Moreover, the provisions of late eighteenth-century edicts ordering the integration of the Gypsies into German society in some ways merely amounted to novel forms of persecution. Gypsies were ordered to find a permanent residence, forbidden to marry each other, ordered to give all their children to German peasants to bring up, and banned from using their own language. These measures too proved impossible to enforce.[9]

The boundaries of honor and dishonor were often shifting and vague in the early modern period. Trades which were regarded as infamous in some areas were widely accepted as capable of forming guilds in others.

23

RICHARD J. EVANS

Some kinds of conduct became less dishonorable as time went on, others more so. A particularly important example of the latter is prostitution, which suffered increasing discrimination and state regulation in the course of the sixteenth and seventeenth centuries. In almost all cases in early modern society, the ostracization of the dishonorable was mitigated by the fact that they performed useful social functions of one kind or another. In an era when communications were poor, roads unmade or nonexistent, resources limited, and manufacturing often located many days' or even weeks' journey from the villages, small towns, and farmsteads where the vast majority of people lived, itinerants such as knife-grinders, peddlers, and the like were a necessary part of the rural economy. In a different way, knackers and skinners, millers, and shepherds also came into frequent contact with the population and were generally recognized as important to it. Traveling entertainers, mountebanks, quacks, and tooth-pullers brought spectacle and diversion at fair-time.

Moreover, mental or physical handicap was not, on the whole, a cause for dishonor. Life was neither long nor pleasant for village idiots or town fools, but on the whole they remained within the care of their family and were not social outsiders. Violent and disruptive mental disorder was likely to lead to confinement in a city prison, where the small number of criminal offenders who were imprisoned rather than whipped, branded, or executed were also kept. Even here, however, honorable families would do their best to cope rather than resorting to such a drastic measure. Duke Wilhelm the Younger of Braunschweig-Lüneburg, for instance, was accustomed to run half-naked around the streets of Celle giving people presents and gesticulating wildly, but it was not until he attacked his wife with a pair of tailor's shears that the ducal council agreed to confine him, and he continued to rule, subject to periodic bouts of madness, without being replaced by a regent, for another seven years, until his death in 1589.[10]

Just as madness led to total exclusion only when it became dangerous, so too itinerants only aroused the complete hostility of the population when poverty spilled over into destitution and they took to begging, thieving, and banditry. Itinerant occupations provided an even more precarious existence than those of settled people. It was not surprising that the great robber bands which roamed many parts of Germany during the early modern period, above all in times of war and upheaval, were drawn mostly from the ranks of social outcasts, including not only itinerants, peddlers, beggars, and Gypsies but also poor yet settled communities of outsiders such as Jews. When sweeping the countryside for suspicious characters, robbers, and criminals, therefore, the early modern state paid special attention to the wandering trades. By stigmatizing them in this way, the organs of the state thus reinforced their marginalization.[11]

III

The eighteenth century saw not a general improvement in the position of social outsiders in Germany, but the beginnings of a restructuring of the notion of who was and was not an outsider, and the proclamation— though only to a limited extent the actual enforcement—of a new policy designed at integrating them into society. These processes were accelerated by the disintegration of the social order in the course of population growth, economic change, and the impact of British industrialization on the Continent. The French and Napoleonic Wars lent new urgency to the reforming zeal of Enlightened monarchs and bureaucrats struggling to modernize their states and make them more effective in the face of the threat from France. A new bourgeois public sphere was emerging, whose educated members believed in equality before the law and the spread of civic freedoms and responsibilities in a free market and a liberal political order. Most important of all was the drastic reduction of the power of the guilds in the first decades of the nineteenth century, undermined by industrialization on the one hand and attacked by the reforming state on the other. The transition from a "society of orders" to a "class society," from a *Ständegesellschaft* to a *Klassengesellschaft*, brought a new situation for social outsiders in the nineteenth century.

Many groups which had been excluded from society by custom and law were gradually, if in some cases imperfectly, integrated in the course of the liberal reforms which characterized the middle decades of the century. The Jews were the most obvious example, gaining civil equality by 1871 and abandoning their social isolation and religious identity in increasing numbers in the years up to the outbreak of the First World War. Of course they were still excluded from elite positions of power in the army, the civil service, and politics. But while they continued to suffer discrimination, this did not make them social outsiders. Jews were integrated into German society before the First World War in a wide variety of ways. Even Kaiser Wilhelm II had a number of close personal friends who were Jewish, despite his occasional outbursts of antisemitic

25

RICHARD J. EVANS

rhetoric. The same goes for other groups excluded from elite positions in the government and society of the Bismarckian and Wilhelmine Empire. The most numerous of these were women, who lacked even the vote, and only slowly gained a modicum of basic civil rights during this period. The feminists who tried to improve their lot were frequently subjected to petty acts of bullying by the police. More strikingly, the two largest political movements of the day, the Social Democrats and political Catholicism, were ostracized by the state political and administrative apparatus and subjected to wide-ranging legal discrimination and police harassment. In the end, however, these groups were a disadvantaged part of society, not excluded from it altogether; taken all together they formed the vast majority of people living in Germany at this time.

However, their predicament is not without relevance to the later history of state policy toward social outsiders. In particular, Bismarck's policy of labeling Social Democrats and Catholics as "enemies of the Reich" and persecuting them in a variety of ways, from imprisonment on petty or trumped-up charges to wholesale proscription of many of their activities, set an ominous precedent for the future. At various points in the nineteenth century, conservative rhetoric had bracketed crime and revolution and argued for political radicals to be treated as common criminals. As heirs to this tradition, Bismarck and his successors used the criminal law to combat threats to the social and political order of the Reich in a manner which was still very much present in the minds of the many judges and penal administrators who survived the collapse of imperial Germany in 1918 and continued in their posts through the Weimar Republic.[12] In other countries too, some political movements—most notably anarchism, responsible for a wave of political assassinations in late nineteenth-century Europe and America—was also subjected to police and legal repression, but in few countries west of tsarist Russia did such repression reach so wide or penetrate so deeply.

Political repression became enmeshed with criminal law and policing at a time when the state in Germany was rationalizing its approach to social exclusion. As the power of the guilds dwindled, many trades, from milling to linen weaving, became more respectable. Others, such as shepherding, declined to marginal importance. Honor lost its significance as a means of sustaining the social order, and correspondingly dishonoring lost its significance as a means of punishment by the law and the state. On the other hand, steady work and a fixed abode, already prioritized by the Enlightened administrations of the eighteenth century, gained a more exclusive significance as criteria of social belonging

26

in the nineteenth. Industrialization and urbanization brought rapid communication, mass production and distribution, and the demise of the majority of itinerant trades. The remaining itinerants, like the remaining journeymen artisans, found it increasingly difficult to make a living and had to resort to a growing degree to begging. At the same time, by the late nineteenth century, economic growth meant a high demand for labor in the towns and cities. Many workers traveled the land looking for employment, and the instability and rapid fluctuations of industrial production often meant periods when they were unable to find it. Finally, the landed estates of the north and east were increasingly replacing settled with seasonal labor, which in turn attracted large groups of traveling agricultural laborers (often from Poland) looking for employment at various times of the year.

All this contributed to what contemporary social observers described as a growing problem of vagrancy in the late nineteenth century. Attempts to solve it ranged from the establishment of labor colonies to the beginnings of provisions of cheap lodging houses for the homeless, funded by charitable foundations, often religious in their inspiration. All the while, however, the basic experience of the itinerant remained that of continual harassment by the police and the courts, who punished begging, failure to carry papers, and tramping the land (*Landstreicherei*) with repeated short periods of incarceration in a workhouse or prison.[13] Poor relief in this period, under the influence of the so-called Elberfeld system, changed from a matter of indiscriminate charity to a project of closely supervising the destitute and forcing them to find employment either in a workhouse or in a poorly paid job, on pain of losing their entitlement. A similar policy was adopted toward the Roma and Sinti, who were constantly harassed by the police using legal instruments such as the requirement to carry identity papers, the tax law, the law against concubinage, and the requirement to register with the police on taking up residence in a district. In the context of virtually full employment and a growing elaboration of state and voluntary provision for the unemployed, vagrancy, begging, and tramping the countryside were seen not as responses to unemployment but as matters of personal choice by the "work-shy" and the deviant. Such policies had their limitations, however. The absence of a national police force, and the responsibility of local officials for such matters, meant that the authorities were frequently satisfied by simply expelling Gypsies and vagrants from their district and abandoning responsibility for them to another. Often enough, indeed, local authorities would issue them with legitimation

27

papers certifying that they were bona fide journeymen simply to get rid of them.[14]

The same kind of policy was applied to prostitution, which commentators tended to see, not as what it very often was, a temporary strategy for dealing with loss of income of employment by young women, or a means of dealing with the consequences of illegitimate motherhood and the consequent social stigmatization, but as the expression of personal social and sexual deviance on the part of its practitioners. As a consequence prostitutes continued to be subject to police harassment if they resisted joining the small minority who were confined in state-regulated "public houses" or bordellos. Most, however, were able to escape the attentions of the police.[15] At the same time the state was increasingly insistent upon the need to care for the mentally and physically handicapped in specially created institutions. The nineteenth century was the age of the great mental hospitals and lunatic asylums, when medicine and the law elaborated a series of medical definitions of deviant behavior. With urbanization and the relative decline of the proportion of the community living in rural communities, it became more difficult for the majority of families to support their mentally and physically handicapped members. The medical profession also increasingly intervened to enforce the committal of the mentally handicapped to institutions, even when the family of the person concerned resisted.[16]

It would be wrong to see such medical intervention in an entirely negative light. No doubt there were some kinds of mental disturbance which could be treated medically; and the situation of the mentally and physically handicapped in the poor quarters of Germany's great cities in the later nineteenth and early twentieth centuries was certainly not to be envied. Medical intervention and institutionalization may well have prolonged the lives of some of them; in a few cases, indeed, they even saved a life by persuading the courts to avoid applying the death penalty on the grounds of a murderer's insanity.[17] However, the growth of the medical profession in the course of the nineteenth century undoubtedly led to a growing stigmatization of certain kinds of mental and physical handicap as medically determined. The doctors were increasingly able to enlist the support of the state in compulsory certifications of insanity and mental incapacity.

What all this amounts to is the fact that social and sexual deviance in the nineteenth century was dealt with in the first place not by government policies and initiatives but in the everyday activities of what might be called low-level policing and administration. In some instances applying specific provisions of the criminal law, in others merely operating local regulations or police ordinances, the police harassed and harried itinerants, beggars, vagrants, Roma and Sinti, and prostitutes in much the same way as they harassed and harried recalcitrant Catholic priests during the *Kulturkampf* or Social Democratic activists under the *Sozialistengesetz* and indeed for long after. The illegality of male (though not female) same-sex relations according to Paragraph 175 of the Reich criminal code of 1871 was a further instrument in the hands of the police, who used it to harass homosexual men in big cities such as Berlin.[18]

The results were almost predictable. The lack of any coordinated national policy, coupled with inadequate police resources to deal with the numbers of people involved, meant that social outsiders such as these were stigmatized as deviants, identified and identifiable to the authorities through their numerous convictions, and subject to frequent and arbitrary interference with their way of life. There was no chance of police intervention actually reducing the numbers of the social outsiders or bringing about their integration into society. On the contrary, police harassment actually strengthened their identity as outsiders by arousing their resentment against society and forcing them to create and strengthen protective subcultures of their own. Thus a homosexual subculture grew up in Berlin just as a Catholic subculture grew up in the south and west; a subculture of vagrants, with its own jargon, its own meeting places, and its own language of chalked signs on houses and street corners, paralleled the organizational subculture of German Social Democracy.[19] The culture of the Roma and Sinti, though little studied by serious historians, was similarly in all probability further cemented by such irregular but inescapable petty persecution.[20]

The same may be said of the criminal subculture in nineteenth-century Germany. As imprisonment replaced public physical punishment as the main penal sanction, so commentators began to note that the majority of prison inmates were persistent offenders who had been there many times before. Prison seemed to be a vehicle for the creation of criminals, not their reformation. Providing them with criminal records barred the way to regular employment had they wished to take it, while the company of other prisoners cemented their sense of criminal identity. Attempts to remedy this situation failed. Solitary confinement, the rule of silence, religious instruction, and prison education, as advocated by reformers, were implemented too patchily to have any general effect. Voluntary associations for the care of released prisoners were too few to have more than a marginal influence, just as charitable "Magdalen homes" for the reform of prostitutes, philanthropic labor colonies, and charitable lodging houses for vagrants barely touched the fringes of the problem they were respectively trying to address.

The stigmatization of these social outsiders indeed helped perpetuate the social threat which respectable society feared they posed. It reminded the bourgeoisie and the respectable working class alike of the fate that would await those who seriously deviated from social, sexual, or legal norms. In a somewhat different category were Prussia's, and later imperial Germany's, ethnic minorities, principally Alsatians and Lorrainers, Danes, and above all Poles. Here too the overwhelming drive was toward assimilation. Local German authorities attempted to suppress the use of Polish, French, Danish, and Alsatian patois in official contexts, including state schools, encouraged German-speaking settlers, and used the law in a variety of ways to the disadvantage of the local, non-German-speaking population. The result was as predictable as it was in other contexts, namely the growth of nationalist movements and the emergence of a strong regional or nationalist subculture which regarded the Germans as little better than an occupying power.[21]

Finally, the physically and mentally handicapped were in a different category again. The extent to which they were able to fashion subcultures of their own within the institutions to which they were confined is difficult to assess; isolated from their family and community and cut off to a large extent from the world beyond the asylum walls, they were the most vulnerable of all among nineteenth-century Germany's social outsiders.

IV

Despite the varied and changing kinds of discrimination outlined above, the history of social outsiders in eighteenth- and nineteenth-century Germany does not, on the whole, suggest that German society was particularly rigidly defined, or that it excluded larger numbers of people than other societies did, or that the German state persecuted deviants and outcasts more ruthlessly than other states did. In general, and with some qualifications, the processes which were taking place in the redefinition, investigation, isolation and stigmatization of social outsiders in Germany were the same as those described by the French philosopher-historian Michel Foucault for England and France.[22] It was in the late nineteenth century that significant differences began to emerge. Eugenics, "racial hygiene," and the theory and rhetoric of "degeneration," though increasingly influential in many countries including Italy, France, and the United States, seem to have struck a particular chord among German intellectuals from the 1890s on. By the eve of the First World War, increasing numbers of Germany's social outsiders were being regarded by growing numbers of those who wrote and thought about them in the light of theories of this kind.[23]

What this reflected was the growing influence of the medical profession in German society. At a time when it was gaining immense prestige through the triumphs of its research into the causes of tuberculosis, cholera, diphtheria, and other major afflictions of the nineteenth century, German medicine was also gaining an all-pervasive social influence through the creation and rapid expansion of the medical and social insurance systems in which Germany was the undoubted pioneer. German doctors began to conceive the ambition of bringing other areas of society into their remit.[24] Among these were crime and social deviance. The German school of criminology, founded by figures such as Franz von Liszt, and developed by figures such as Gustav Aschaffenburg, gradually took the study of crime and deviance out of the hands of lawyers and moralists and placed it in the purview of psychiatrists and eugenicists. Adapting the ideas of the Italian criminologist Cesare Lombroso, himself also a medical man, they were arguing by the early 1900s that persistent, recidivist criminals were primarily the product of hereditary degeneracy, activated under particular social and economic circumstances. Other deviants, such as alcoholics, prostitutes, vagrants, and tramps were placed in the same category of the hereditarily degenerate and eugenically vulnerable.[25]

Behind these arguments was a wider belief that with the decline in the German birth rate that set in around the turn of the century, and which was most marked among the upper and middle classes, "less valuable" members of society were reproducing themselves faster than the "fully valuable." This language of *Minderwertigkeit* and *Vollwertigkeit* became almost universal among medical and other professionals involved in discussions of "the social problem" by the eve of the First World War. However neutral and "scientific" it may have seemed, it inevitably involved the moral and political judgment that some human beings were less than fully human; the very terminology broke down barriers to the abandonment of time-honored liberal principles such as equality before the law and freedom of the individual. Eugenics could of course be applied in a positive sense, and was one of the factors behind efforts by the medical profession to improve standards of hygiene, nutrition, infant care, and general public health; but the more the institutional network of health provision spread among the population, the more obvious it seemed to many of those involved in it that the minority who persisted in rejecting the benefits of a regular, sober, hard-working, law-abiding life must be doing so because of some innate hereditary defect such as the mentally and physically handicapped seemed to suffer from. Thus negative eugenics—the reduction or elimination of the "less valuable" sectors of the population—followed as an almost inevitable consequence of the spread of positive eugenics—the improvement of the mental and physical state of the population as a whole.

By the eve of the First World War, the language of eugenics and racial hygiene was being widely used by criminal lawyers, state prosecutors, penal administrators and social commentators in Germany as well as by those involved in Germany's rapidly growing profession of social welfare administrators. International organizations devoted to the application of medical ideas to criminal and penal policy were dominated by Austrians and Germans. Well before the outbreak of the First World War, penal reformers were arguing for the indefinite detention, castration, or even execution of persistent offenders whose conduct over the years had in their view demonstrated their hereditary degeneracy and their unfitness to live in human society or pass on their character defects to the next generation.[26] In other countries such as the United States, eugenicists put forward similar views; but in Germany, the movement was far more dominated by the medical and psychiatric professions, who applied the concept of degeneracy as a diagnostic tool to an increasing variety of social outsiders, including alcoholics, homosexuals, and prostitutes.[27]

Even before the First World War, these new ideas were already having a discernible impact on attitudes toward serious and violent offenders, and in a popularized form were used in the legal profession, the press, and political life as a means of justifying the death penalty. But it was only under the Weimar Republic that they became linked to two other sets of ideas in a new and fateful mixture. First, after Germany's defeat in the war, the idea of Nordic supremacy, along with its corollaries, belief in the inferiority of Jews, Slavs, and other races, was adopted by increasing numbers of racial hygiene specialists, above all in the younger generation. Those eugenicists who opposed antisemitism and racism became a minority. Second, the medical model began to be applied to political deviance. In the mid-nineteenth century, revolutionary activity and belief had been regarded by many commentators as a form of criminality. From the First World War, the idea began to gain hold that it was the product of a diseased or degenerate mind. Already in 1916–1918, indeed, Jehovahs Witnesses who refused military service on ethical grounds were being put into lunatic asylums after being diagnosed as suffering from "religious mania." During the Weimar Republic they were widely regarded on the political right as deluded revolutionaries manipulated by Jews, with whom they were thought to share a number of religious beliefs.[28] The 1918 Revolution itself was seen by one leading criminologist as the product of psychic disturbance brought on by cosmic and climatic change which caused a reversion of the masses to an atavistic state of primitive bestiality not dissimilar to that diagnosed in criminals by the Italian theorist Lombroso.[29]

Racial hygiene became an established academic discipline under the Weimar Republic. The founding of the first chair in the subject, at Munich University in 1923, was followed in the next nine years by no fewer than forty courses on the subject at German universities in general. A variety of research institutes opened, criminological-biological collection stations were established to collect data on the personalities and families of offenders, and publications began to appear arguing for eugenically defective people to be killed because as "ballast existences" they were imposing a financial burden on society at a time when economic crisis was making life difficult for those who did contribute to national production. Indeed, already during the First World War, the deliberate withholding of supplies from lunatic asylums had led to a rise in the death rate among inmates so drastic that it is not much of an exaggeration to claim that tens of thousands of mentally ill patients met an untimely death at the hands of officials who knew well enough what they were doing and had few qualms about it.[30]

The elaboration of welfare services and the rise of the social work profession in the Weimar Republic accelerated this process rather than slowing it down. Whatever else they might have disagreed about, welfare workers were increasingly agreed on the need for legislation to replace outmoded policing measures and obsolete institutions such as the workhouse with modern homes in which tramps, vagrants, prostitutes, and other "asocials," as they were now widely known, could be interned without limit until they were judged fit to be integrated into society. All parties right of the Communists agreed on the introduction of a law decriminalizing offenses such as vagrancy and prostitution and introducing instead measures providing for the forcible and indefinite confinement of "asocials" in secure homes of various kinds run by the welfare system.[31] A parallel debate took place in the case of habitual or "incorrigible" offenders against the criminal law, who, many lawyers, criminologists, and psychiatrists argued, should similarly be detained in "security confinement" without limit of time, and for much the same reasons.[32] Thus they would be prevented from reproducing themselves and endangering the future health of the German race.

The spread of ideas drawn from eugenics and racial hygiene also affected other social outsiders in the Weimar Republic. Gypsies, for example, presented the welfare system with many of the same problems as "asocials." They were vagrants, they avoided laws about educating their children, they were thought to be involved in petty crime, and in addition they were clearly from a racial background altogether different from that of the Germans. As with persistent offenders and "asocials," policy in the Weimar Republic was still largely a matter of policing, but the growth of the welfare system had an impact too in cementing their exclusion from society and prompting welfare agencies to argue more strongly than ever for their integration. "Criminal biology" found it easy to describe them as "primitive" and undeveloped human beings, racially inferior to the Germans. The idea of integrating them into society, therefore, came to be replaced in the minds of a significant number of policy makers, by the idea of cordoning them off from it altogether, in case they contaminated it through intermarriage, which indeed was occurring on an increasing scale in this period. A Bavarian law of 1926 sought to restrict their movements to designated sites, tried to prevent their forming "bands," and threatened them with two years in a workhouse "on grounds of public security" if they failed to prove regular employment. Officials began to compile a comprehensive register of Gypsies, with a view to keeping track of them in the criminal and welfare files as a separate racial group.[33]

The influence of medical and racial-biological thinking also made itself felt in discussions of homosexuality under the Weimar Republic. Already the sexologists of the turn of the century had classified homosexuality as a psychological disorder. As the birth rate declined, so worries among eugenicists about the contribution made to the decline by a possible spread of homosexuality began to grow. This was thought to be a disorder where, in the view of medical commentators, heredity, for obvious reasons, played only a subordinate role. Medical intervention could thus, in theory at least, effect a "cure". On the far right of the political spectrum, priority thus came to be given to the restriction and, if possible, elimination of the flourishing homosexual subculture of cities such as Berlin, in order to prevent young men who (it was thought) would otherwise have contributed to the reproduction of the race from being corrupted and seduced. In addition criminologists pointed to the criminal connections of the subculture (inevitable because of the illegality of male homosexuality under the criminal law). Finally, there were widespread worries on the right about the "effeminacy" of male homosexuals and the effect this might have—in the eyes of some, was already having—on the masculinity of German men, their willingness to fight in a future war, and the manly vigor they should be transmitting to future generations. The sexologist Magnus Hirschfeld, a pioneering campaigner for equal rights for homosexuals, probably only fueled such irrational anxieties by portraying homosexual men as neither masculine nor feminine but a "third sex" somewhere between the two.[34]

Under the Weimar Republic the issue of social exclusion became heavily politicized. On the one hand, counterrevolutionaries and the political right increasingly lumped all kinds of social, political, and religious deviants together in a single category of subversives thought to be undermining the German race. In this they were supported by at least some eugenicists and racial hygienists, although others resisted the political appropriation of the issue by the racist and antisemitic forces of extreme nationalism. More broadly, the burgeoning welfare apparatus of the Weimar period itself entered the political arena by demanding legislative action to take a variety of minorities, from the mentally ill to the persistent offender, from the vagrant and tramp to the alcoholic and the drug addict, out of the criminal justice and penal systems and into the realm of compulsory institutionalization under medical supervision for an indefinite period of time.

Some groups of social outsiders became politicized too. During the 1920s the Jehovah's Witnesses won massive new support in Germany; by 1926 there were more members of the sect in Dresden than there were in New York, and they became more thoroughly and uncompromisingly pacifist than they had been during the First World War, when a high proportion of them had agreed to serve in the German armed forces. Their forthright opposition to the growing menace of antisemitism enraged the far right and cemented the belief of ultranationalists that Jehovah's Witnesses were stooges of the Jews, hell-bent on preventing the resurgence of the German race after the catastrophe of 1918.[35] Homosexuals campaigned vigorously, and far more openly than under the Wilhelmine Empire, for the abolition of Paragraph 175 of the criminal code and the legalization of homosexuality.[36] Anarchists such as Erich Mühsam and Gregor Gog attempted to politicize vagrants, although Gog's Vagabundentreffen in Stuttgart in 1929 had only a limited success, and the idea of organizing tramps in a *Verein* was a predictable failure.[37]

Social outsiders also came to have a heavily symbolic political function under the Weimar Republic, when the forces of extreme nationalism were demanding that all right-thinking Germans should combat the Treaty of Versailles and fight subversive forces holding back national resurgence. Of no group was this more true than of the so-called Rhineland bastards. During the 1920s, the left bank of the Rhine was under Allied military occupation, and in the French zone this meant colonial troops from Senegal, Madagascar, and other parts of the French overseas empire. Virtually all German political parties including the Social Democrats protested against this policy of using what they openly declared to be racially inferior troops in the occupation, and particularly during the French invasion of the Ruhr in 1923, racist propaganda of this kind reached almost hysterical proportions, accusing the black troops of numerous rapes of German women. In *Mein Kampf*, indeed, Hitler ascribed this policy to a deliberate Jewish conspiracy to degrade and corrupt the German race. In fact, the colonial troops seem to have behaved with courtesy and consideration and the "Rhineland bastards" were the offspring of entirely voluntary relationships with German women. Others so categorized were the children of older, entirely legitimate relationships between German colonists in Africa before the First World War and native African men or women. These distinctions, however, were ignored in the furor over the French occupation, and all mixed-race Germans were categorized as "Rhineland bastards," a symbol of German humiliation so potent that officials in the Bavarian Ministry of the Interior were already asking the Reich government to subject them to forcible sterilization in 1927.[38]

V

Despite all these ominous developments it would be wrong to view the treatment of social outsiders in the Weimar Republic simply in terms of growing state discrimination and persecution. The 1920s also witnessed a widespread movement of social reform in the welfare, penal, and policing apparatus of the state. Even those who believed in a strong hereditary element in social deviance of one kind or another generally considered that the majority of deviants were still capable of reintegration into society. Liberal and Socialist ideas had some influence, and proposals to sterilize deviants or subject them to a policy of involuntary "euthanasia" met with overwhelming rejection on all sides.

However, this situation did not last. The economic depression of 1929–1933 exacerbated the problem of social outsiders in a number of ways. Mass unemployment on an unprecedented scale meant a huge increase in the numbers of homeless and vagrants. Benefits were cut, and were removed altogether from the long-term unemployed, nearly a million and a quarter of whom were receiving no benefits of any kind by the beginning of 1933. The number of people sleeping rough and living on the streets in Germany was estimated at between 200,000 and 500,000 by the early 1930s. Cutbacks in state expenditure during the crisis fueled the arguments of those who regarded the mentally and physically handicapped as "social ballast." Prostitution became once more a common means for young, mostly working-class women to earn a living when regular jobs were hard to obtain. And while crime rates did not increase as much as they had done during the hyperinflation of 1922–23, youth gangs or "cliques" were particularly noticeable during the Depression and perceived as a serious threat to public order by many people in the middle classes.[39]

In this situation the boundaries between respectable society and its outcasts became vaguer and more fluid than ever. Even in normal times prostitution, for example, was generally a temporary expedient adopted by women who subsequently had little difficulty in reintegrating themselves into the working class. Vagrancy was less a permanent way of life than an unavoidable makeshift for the hundreds of thousands of mostly young men who were unable to afford a roof over their heads in the early 1930s; at other times it was little more than a phase for many who engaged in it. Theft, embezzlement, and petty crime were a temptation to many in a period of mass unemployment and bankruptcy. In the longer run, too, an ethnic minority such as the so-called Rhineland bastards managed to find a role in society, above all in the circus and entertainment business. While some forms of mental and physical handicap were undeniably extreme and made it impossible for those who suffered from them to live a normal life integrated into society at large, others were ill-defined, and dependent on the whims of diagnostic procedures that were as vague as they were arbitrary.[40]

In normal times, as we have seen, policy and policing tactics could often harden these boundaries and turn what for many was a part-time or temporary role outside society into a more or less permanent condition. The medicalization of penal policy and the rise of social welfare had extended social exclusion in this way to increasing numbers of people who had previously escaped the net, while in no way diminishing the impact of everyday policing on identifying and perpetuating the world of the "asocial," the petty criminal, and the repeat offender. The collection of statistics on Gypsies, the creation of elaborate card indices by the "criminal-biological collection stations" of social outsiders thought to be hereditarily impaired and therefore to pose a threat to coming generations, the information-gathering activities of the social welfare system, all this provided the basis long before the coming of the Third Reich for the reassertion of boundaries between society and its outcasts which the Depression in many ways threatened to obscure.[41]

The Nazi regime sought to re-create these boundaries in an extreme form. In doing so, it fused all the various elements which had previously been present in official, medical-psychiatric, administrative, and criminological thinking about social outsiders. Dividing their world into "racial comrades" and "community aliens," *Volksgenossen* and *Gemeinschaftsfremde*, the "ins" and the "outs," the Nazis defined almost any kind of refusal to contribute to their goals as deviant, sick, racially motivated, or degenerate. German society was probably, historically speaking, no more hostile to outsiders than other European societies; even in the age of the *Ständegesellschaft*, the boundaries between the "honorable" and the "dishonorable" had been changeable and fluid, and in any case these had largely been wiped away by the middle of the nineteenth century. Industrial society had created new categories of social outsider, notably among the physically and mentally handicapped, while partly perpetuating, partly transforming others, such as itinerants and vagrants. Social and to some extent official attitudes toward socially deviant acts such as sodomy and prostitution and outsider groups such as the Gypsies became more lenient in the course of the eighteenth and nineteenth centuries. Petty police harassment was the lot of outsiders such as these until the turn of the nineteenth century or thereabouts. It may have cemented their deviant identity but it did not entirely sever their links with society.

Three factors changed this situation in the period from about 1890 to about 1930. The first was the medicalization of penal and welfare policy, coupled with a vast expansion of the state welfare system. Increasingly, and above all from the First World War onward, a significant proportion of social outsiders were categorized by those who dealt with them as hereditarily tainted, degenerate, a threat to the future of the German race. The second, related factor was the rise of racial hygiene, the tendency to view German society and its relations with other societies in Europe and beyond in racial terms. This led to a gradual, if uneven, link between the discourse on social outsiders and the discourses of antisemitism and the fitness of the German race to survive in the struggle for supremacy with other races such as the Latins and the Slavs. The third factor was the increasing politicization of the discourse on social outsiders, indeed the increasing politicization of German society as a whole, above all under the Weimar Republic, when to many on the extreme right, drastic remedies seemed necessary to overcome the trauma of defeat in the First World War and regenerate the German nation as a virile, energetic, committed, and united entity ready to reestablish on the world stage the world power it had failed to grasp in 1914–1918.

These were the criteria which the Nazis applied to social outsiders in Germany from 1933 onward. They often did so as much by riding roughshod over the careful distinctions drawn by the experts as by adopting their ideas and utilizing the data they had so painstakingly collected under the Weimar Republic. As Nazism radicalized, above all during the war, so too did its policy toward the socially excluded. In this situation, distinctions between political, racial, and social deviance more or less vanished. By 1944 the definition of the "community alien" had become a totally arbitrary instrument in the hands of the SS and police apparatus. According to the Nazi criminologist Edmund Mezger, a "community alien" was "anyone who, by his personality and way of life, and particularly through unusual deficiencies in understanding and character, shows himself unable to satisfy the minimal demands of the racial community by his own efforts."[42] This encompassed far more than the categories of social outsider which had borne the brunt of the Nazis' repression and extermination previously. It gave the enforcement agencies a practical carte blanche to arrest, incarcerate and kill almost anybody they wanted to. The biological term *Volksschädling* (damager of the "racial" people), commonly used in Nazi legislation against wartime offenses such as looting, testified to the permeation of Nazi thinking by the biological metaphor. Justice was explicitly proclaimed by leading Nazi jurists such as Roland Freisler and Otto-Georg Thierack to be an instrument of eugenic cleansing.

This was the end of a long road. It had begun, not with the survival of premodern forms of social exclusion inherited from the early modern

Ständegesellschaft, but with the long-term autonomy and wide-ranging powers that the police in the majority of German states had inherited from the era of absolutism, powers which they used to harass and perpetuate the social exclusion of a variety of categories of deviant and outcast. The failure of penal reform in the nineteenth century, though far from unique to Germany, had played its part too. But it was the eruption of racist, Social Darwinist and eugenic modes of thought into judicial, penal, and social administration around the turn of the century, the medicalization of these areas of thought and practice, and their politicization during the Weimar Republic that set Germany on the fateful path toward the indefinite incarceration, sterilization, and eventually mass extermination of deviant groups. Of these, only the most radical step, that of mass murder, would probably not have been taken had the Nazis not come to power in 1933. For repressive policies toward a variety of social outsiders were undertaken in other countries too, from Sweden to the United States, in the interwar years, all the way up to forcible sterilization, though on a much smaller scale than was involved in Germany. It was only in Germany that mass killing became state policy; and it began, not with the Jews, but with the mentally and physically handicapped, in 1939.

Thus seen in a longer historical perspective, the confinement, sterilization, and extermination of social outsiders in Nazi Germany were the product of modernity, of political mobilization and scientific advance, or what was held to be such, in the half century from around 1890 to 1940.[43] The process was not a regression into barbarism. To describe it as such is to use barbarism in a moral rather than in a historical sense, and hence to bar the way to an informed, historical understanding of the nature of Nazi exterminism. Instating barbarism as the central conceptual tool for understanding the Third Reich is to mistake moral condemnation for thought. Thinking of Nazi extermination instead as an aspect of the Janus-faced phenomenon of modernity involves recognizing that there could be a dark side to modernization, that—as Marx and Engels saw long ago—modernization could have its victims as well as its beneficiaries. It does not mean rewriting the concept of modernization until it is emptied of all positive connotations altogether.[44] It means recognizing that science, in certain places and at certain times, and most notably of all perhaps in Germany between 1890 and 1940, could be a destructive as well as a constructive force, and that what some saw as social progress, others experienced as discrimination, oppression, suffering, and death.

NOTES

1. For a useful overview, see Michael Burleigh and Wolfgang Wippermann, *The Racial State: Germany, 1933–1945* (Cambridge, 1991); the authors' general approach to the subject is discussed at the end of this chapter. A useful local collection was produced in 1986 by the Projektgruppe für die vergessenen Opfer des NS-Regimes: Klaus Frahm et al., eds., *Verachtet-Verfolgt-Vernichtet: zu den "vergessenen" Opfern des NS-Regimes* (Hamburg, 1986).

2. Ulrich Herbert, *A History of Foreign Labor in Germany, 1880–1980* (Ann Arbor, 1990), is the most useful overview; the broader question of German attitudes toward the Slavs is beyond the scope of the present chapter.

3. Richard van Dulmen, "Der infame Mensch: Unehrliche Arbeit und soziale Ausgrenzung in der Frühen Neuzeit," in idem, ed., *Arbeit, Frömmigkeit, und Eigensinn: Studien zur historischen Kulturforschung* (Frankfurt am Main, 1990), 106–140.

4. Wolfgang von Hippel, *Armut, Unterschichten, Randgruppen in der Frühen Neuzeit* (Munich, 1995), 32–43.

5. Richard J. Evans, *Rituals of Retribution: Capital Punishment in Germany, 1600–1987* (Oxford, 1996), 193–201.

6. Ibid., 56–64; see also Jutta Nowosadtko, *Scharfrichter und Abdecker: Der Alltag zweier "unehrlicher Berufe" in der Frühen Neuzeit* (Paderborn, 1994); Gisela Wilbertz, *Scharfrichter und Abdecker im Hochstift Osnabrück: Untersuchungen zur Sozialgeschichte zweier "unehrlicher" Berufe im nordwestdeutschen Raum vom 16. Bis zum 19. Jahrhundert* (Osnabrück, 1979).

7. Evans, *Rituals*, 122–23; Hippel, *Armut*, 96–101; Isabel V. Hull, *Sexuality, State, and Civil Society in Germany, 1700–1815* (Ithaca, N.Y., 1996), 349–50.

8. Evans, *Rituals*, 372–83.

9. K. Bott-Bodenhausen, ed., *Sinti in der Grafschaft Lippe: Studien zur Geschichte der "Zigeuner" im 18. Jahrhundert* (Munich, 1988); H. Lemmermann, *Zigeuner und Scherenschleifer im Emsland* (Sögel, 1986).

10. H. C. Erik Midelfort, *Mad Princes of Renaissance Germany* (Charlottesville, 1994), 60–70.

11. Carsten Küther, *Menschen auf der Strasse: Vagierende Unterschichten in Bayern, Franken und Schwaben in der zweiten Hälfte des 18. Jahrhunderts* (Göttingen, 1983); idem, *Räuber und Gauner in Deutschland: Das organisierte Bandenwesen im 18. Jahrhundert* (Göttingen, 1976); Uwe Danker, *Räuberbanden im Alten Retch um 1700: Ein Beitrag zur Geschichte von Herrschaft und Kriminalität in der Frühen Neuzeit* (Frankfurt am Main, 1988).

12. The best coverage of this process is still that of Klaus Saul, "Der Staate und die 'Mächte des Umsturzes': Ein Beitrag zu den Methoden antisozialistischer Repression und Agitation vom Scheitern des Sozialistengesetzes bis zur

Jahrhundertwende," *Archiv für Sozialgeschichte* 12 (1972): 293–350; and Alex Hall, "'By Other Means': The Legal Struggle against the SPD in Wilhelmine Germany," *Historical Journal* 17 (1974): 365–80. For the Weimar years, see the classic by Heinrich and Elisabeth Hannover, *Politische Justiz, 1910–1933* (Frankfurt am Main, 1966).

13. Jürgen Scheffler, "Die Vagabundenfrage: Arbeit statt Almosen: Herbergen zur Heimat, Wanderarbeitsstätten, und Arbeiterkolonien," in *Wohnsitz: Nirgendwo. Vom Leben und Überleben auf der Strasse*, ed. Michael Haerdter (Berlin, 1982), 59–70.

14. See Richard J. Evans, *Death in Hamburg: Society and Politics in the Cholera Years, 1830–1910* (Oxford, 1987), 99–100, for a brief description of the Elberfeld system; for police policy toward Gypsies in this period, see Michael Zimmermann, *Verfolgt, vertrieben, vernichtet: Die nationalsozialistische Vernichtungspolitik gegen Sinti und Roma* (Essen, 1989).

15. See Richard J. Evans, *Tales from the German Underworld: Crime and Punishment in the Nineteenth Century* (London, 1998), 166–212.

16. Dirk Blasius, *Der verwaltete Wahnsinn: Eine Sozialgeschichte des Irrenhauses* (Frankfurt am Main, 1980); see also idem, *"Einfache Seelenstörung": Geschichte der deutschen Psychiatrie, 1800–1945* (Frankfurt am Main, 1994).

17. For one such example from shortly before the First World War, see Evans, *Rituals*, 477–84.

18. Anon., ed., *Eldorado: Homosexuelle Frauen und Männer in Berlin 1850 bis 1950. Geschichte, Alltag, und Kultur* (Berlin, 1984); Magnus Hirschfeld, *Berlins Drittes Geschlecht* (Berlin, 1905).

19. H. Stümke, *Homosexuelle in Deutschland: Eine politische Geschichte* (Munich, 1989); Angelika Kopecny, *Fahrende und Vagabunden: Ihre Geschichte, Überlebenskünste, Zeichen, und Strassen* (Berlin, 1980).

20. J. S. Hohmann, *Verfolgte ohne Heimat: Geschichte der Zigeuner in Deutschland* (Frankfurt am Main, 1990).

21. Martin Broszat, *Zweihundert Jahre deutsche Polenpolitik* (Frankfurt am Main, 1972), is still the best overview of the Polish question. For imprisonment, see Evans, *Tales from the German Underworld*, esp. 61–64.

22. Michel Foucault, *Discipline and Punish: The Birth of the Prison* (London, 1975).

23. See Daniel Pick, *Faces of Degeneration: A European Disorder, c. 1848–c. 1918* (Cambridge, 1989).

24. Evans, *Death in Hamburg*, 528–39; and Ute Frevert, *Krankheit als politisches Problem: Soziale Unterschichten in Preussen zwischen medizinischer Polizei und staatlicher Sozialversicherung* (Göttingen, 1984).

25. Richard F. Wetzell, "The Medicalization of Criminal Law Reform in Imperial Germany," in *Institutions of Confinement: Hospitals, Asylums, and Prisons in Western Europe and North America, 1500–1950*, ed. Norbert Finzsch and Robert Jütte (Cambridge, 1996), 275–83.

26. Evans, *Rituals*, 434–45.

27. Henry Friedländer, *The Origins of Nazi Genocide: From Euthanasia to the Final Solution* (Chapel Hill, 1995), 9; for prostitutes, see Evans, *Tales from the German Underworld*, 209, citing Kurt Schneider, *Studien über Persönlichkeit und Schicksal eingeschriebener Prostituierter* (Berlin, 1921), a work based on research carried out before the First World War.

28. Detlev Garbe, *Zwischen Widerstand und Martyrium: Die Zeugen Jehovas im "Dritten Reich"* (Munich, 1982), 45–46.

29. Hans von Hentig, *Über den Zusammenhang zwischen den kosmischen, biologischen, und sozialen Ursachen der Revolution* (Tübingen, 1920).

30. Michael Burleigh, *Death and Deliverance: "Euthanasia" in Germany, 1900–1945* (Cambridge, 1994), chap. 1.

31. Wolfgang Ayaß, *"Asoziale" im Nationalsozialismus* (Stuttgart, 1995), 13–18. See also Klaus Scherer, *"Asoziale" im Dritten Reich* (Münster, 1990).

32. Nikolaus Wachsmann, "Reform and Repression: Prisons and Penal Policy in Germany, 1918–1945" (Ph.D. diss., University of London, 1999), chap. 1.

33. Joachim S. Hohmann, *Robert Ritter und de Erben der Kriminalbiologie: "Zigeunerforschung" im Nationalsozialismus und in Westdeutschland im Zeichen des Rassismus* (Bern, 1991); Burleigh and Wippermann, *The Racial State*, 113–17; Rainer Hehemann, *Die "Bekämpfung des Zigeunerunwesens" im Wilhelminischen Deutschland und in der Weimarer Republik, 1871–1933* (Frankfurt am Main, 1987).

34. Günter Grau, ed., *Homosexualität in der NS-Zeit: Dokumente einer Diskriminierung und Verfolgung* (Frankfurt am Main, 1993); Burkhard Jellonnek, *Homosexuelle unter dem Hakenkreuz: Die Verfolgung vom Homosexuellen im Dritten Reich* (Paderborn, 1990), 37–50; Richard Plant, *The Pink Triangle: The Nazi War against Homosexuals* (New York, 1986).

35. Garbe, *Zwischen Widerstand und Martyrium*, chap.1.

36. See Stümke, *Homosexuelle in Deutschland*, for details.

37. Künstlerhaus Bethanien, ed., *Wohnsitz: Nirgendwo von Leben und vom über Leben auf der Strasse* (Berlin, 1982), 179–232.

38. Burleigh and Wippermann, *The Racial State*, 128–30; Sally Marks, "Black Watch on the Rhine: A Study in Propaganda, Prejudice, and Prurience," *European Studies Review* 13 (1983): 297–334; Gisela Lebeltzer, "Die 'Schwarze Schmach': Vorurteile–Propaganda–Mythos," *Geschichte und Gesellschaft* 11 (1985): 37–58; Reiner Pommerin, *"Sterilisierung der Rheinlandbastarde": Das Schicksal einer farbigen deutschen Minderheit, 1918–1937* (Düsseldorf, 1979).

39. Wolfgang Ayaß, "Vagrants and Beggars in Hitler's Reich," in *The German Underworld: Deviants and Outcasts in German History*, ed. Richard J. Evans (London, 1988), 210–37; Detlev Peukert, "The Lost Generation: Youth Unemployment at the End of the Weimar Republic," in *The German Unemployed: Experiences and Consequences of Mass Unemployment from the Weimar*

Republic to the Third Reich, ed. Richard J. Evans and Dick Geary (London, 1987), 172–93; Eve Rosenhaft, "Organising the 'Lumpenproletariat': Cliques and Communists in Berlin during the Weimar Republic," in *The German Working Class, 1888–1933: The Politics of Everyday Life*, ed. Richard J. Evans (London, 1982), 174–219.

40. Lynn Abrams, "Prostitutes in Imperial Germany, 1870–1918: Working Girls or Social Outcasts?" in Evans, ed., *The German Underworld*, 189–209; Pommerin, *Sterilisierung der Rheinlandbastarde*; and, for examples of the arbitrariness of diagnosis, Evans, *Rituals*, 526–36.

41. Karl Heinz Roth, ed., *Erfassung zur Vernichtung: Von der Sozialhygiene zum "Gesetz über Sterbehilfe"* (Berlin, 1984).

42. Preamble to a never promulgated law of 1944 on the treatment of "community aliens," quoted in Norbert Frei, *Der Führerstaat: Nationalsozialistische Herrschaft, 1933 bis 1945* (Munich, 1987), 202–208.

43. Detlev Peukert, "The Genesis of the 'Final Solution' from the Spirit of Science," in *Reevaluating the Third Reich*, ed. Thomas Childers and Jane Caplan (New York, 1993), 234–52.

44. For these various arguments, criticized here, see Burleigh and Wippermann, *The Racial State*, 2.

No "Volksgenossen"

JEWISH ENTREPRENEURS IN THE THIRD REICH

FRANK BAJOHR

I

Before the National Socialists took power in 1933, the Hamburg entrepreneur Edgar Eichholz, as joint proprietor of Messrs. Eichholz & Loeser, was one of the largest importers of grain and animal feed in Germany.[1] He belonged to the economic elite of the Hanseatic city, who set the tone both economically and socially. Born in 1880, he reached the peak of his entrepreneurial success during the years of the Weimar Republic. Eichholz—like his father before him—did not belong to the Jewish community and was married to a non-Jew, not atypical for Hamburg where the number of so-called mixed marriages was far above the Reich average.[2]

Nevertheless the new regime categorized him as a "full Jew" in 1933. This foreign definition had an immediate effect on the economic wellbeing of his company: previous business partners dropped their contacts with him, partly voluntarily, partly under pressure from National Socialist institutions. In 1934, the company's quotas for the import of grain were drastically reduced. This step was taken within the scope of the National Socialist currency control, which first affected Jewish grain importers; Jewish companies in other sectors were not affected by these reductions until 1937. In order to save at least part of his quotas for the import of grain, Eichholz transferred this sector of his company's business to an "Aryan" executive who then set up his own operation. This partial sale of the company had to be authorized by the Nazi Party *Gauwirtschaftsberater* (economic advisor of the region), who changed the conditions of sale so much to the detriment of the Jewish owner that Eichholz described the result as a "dictatorship on the part of the National Socialist rulers."

After 1933 there were also changes in the social environment surrounding Edgar Eichholz—even though these were very gradual. Some
neighbors started avoiding him, and friends who had invited him out to
dinner sometimes asked their service staff beforehand whether they felt
that too much was expected of them when having to serve a "Jew."

On the other hand Eichholz, who always kept an obvious distance
from the Jewish community, maintained a circle of "Aryan" friends and
acquaintances during the whole period of National Socialist rule. With
his own company, villa, servants, and car, for a long time he had all the
insignia of a well-situated businessman, which disguised the creeping
process of economic and social exclusion. Eichholz was also spared any
experiences of deep humiliation and antisemitic violence, acts which
since 1933 had become part of everyday life, in particular for poorer
Jews. For this reason, the pogrom night in November 1938 constituted
a significant turning point for Eichholz. On 11 November 1938 he was
arrested in his office and imprisoned for several weeks in the police
prison in Fuhlsbüttel. After his release he reported to his son about his
experiences during his term of imprisonment:

> At 1 o'clock I was just about to leave the office [when] two civilians en-
> tered and asked me whether the company is purely Aryan. No, you're the
> owner, then you must come with us. Empty all your pockets and take a
> maximum of M 10.- with you. Your watch, pencils, leave all that here. Off
> to the city hall. There a long wait, inquisition, you must stay in prison,
> down into a dark hole with a bench and a urinal. Half an hour later ap-
> peared a fairly unpleasant type of a junior petty cash clerk.[3] Another half
> hour and we were joined by Herr Clavier, who had once furnished every-
> thing for us and is the same age as I am. Then gradually came the trans-
> port in the green police van. In the yard of the city hall, two SS officers, as
> tall as trees. And then came the maltreatment. Move, move along there,
> you Judenschweine, can't you pick up your feet? You guys, that's what
> we're going to teach you now. And we were pushed into the police van
> with shoves and kicks. And more and more Jews were pushed into the
> van—altogether 31 of us. Some of them had been beaten up until they
> bled. And then we were brought to the Fuhlsbüttel prison. There again,
> we couldn't move fast enough for them. We were pushed out of the van
> with kicks, shoves and scoldings and then lined up facing the wall of the
> corridor, one next to the other. I can tell you, it was torture, especially
> because it was all so new and unaccustomed, in particular the scoldings,
> the unrepeatable expressions, the beatings. . . .

At about four o'clock we were all lying together in one room. Five had come in before us, so it was a mixed bunch of 36 people who found themselves in there. I recognized Clavier, a certain Levy from the corn exchange, Heymann from Christensen, Heymann & Lüthge, Friedmann from the Eppendorfer Landstraße, better situated people such as Dr. Fritz Warburg and Dr. Carl August Cohn, who both, as I found out later, were in a room above us, as well as simple people such as servants, newspaper sellers, craftsmen, people whose ages ranged from 17 to 68. . . . Clavier was elected "spokesman" and I was to be his "vice." We had been chosen out of this community as, according to the advice of one young man, we could make things easier for ourselves. . . .

What shall I tell you about the dreadful insults and the vile, sadistic treatment by these little constables? Later it turned out that all that was nothing in comparison with everything the others had to go through who were arrested in the first two days and transported to Oranienburg. . . .

After 14 days they gave us a little piece of paper so that we could let our relatives know where we were. Once everyone had written with a 1 cm long stump, the constables tore up the letters which had been so lovingly gleaned together: Do you Judenschweine think we can be bothered with censoring this scribble ? You can write again in four weeks' time. . . . We were supposed to get some exercise every day except on Sundays for 20 minutes in the fresh air, weather permitting. But they led us out into the prison yard at the most three times a week for drilling. Just imagine, old people, being shouted at because they couldn't get their knees up properly.[4]

Like most of his Jewish fellow entrepreneurs, Edgar Eichholz had grown up with a bourgeois system of norms and values, according to which the social ranking of an individual depended on his possessions, education, and degree of success. It was the system of values used by the Hanseatic merchants, which attached great importance to individual *Tüchtigkeit* (efficiency) and respected those who had "proved" their worth with their entrepreneurial success. In the trading city of Hamburg in which traditional elite groups such as the nobility, military, and civil servants were underrepresented, this system of values had become well established. On the other hand, in the National Socialist *Volksgemeinschaft* (community of "racial" Germans), which granted top priority to the "racial status" of the individual, this bourgeois code of values had only limited validity and could simply be turned upside down, as became drastically clear to Eichholz in the Fuhlsbüttel prison: notables who had

47

once belonged to the leading stratum of Hamburg and regarded themselves as firmly anchored in German society were being treated like a criminal fringe group, tormented and harassed by adolescent "constables" whom National Socialism had washed up from the social periphery into the center of power. These wardens savored their power and the total reversal of the traditional social hierarchy to the full. Possessions, education, and prosperity as criteria of social position now only counted within the racial *Volksgemeinschaft*, but not for Jews who were not *Volksgenossen* (comrades) and who were unprotected after the November pogrom. But it was not only their treatment by SS constables that Jewish businessmen like Eichholz found degrading. His comment about the "unpleasant . . . junior petty cash clerk" indicates that he felt twice as hurt in his bourgeois pride as a property owner because he was exposed to the same imprisonment conditions as simple Jewish clerks. The fact that he allowed himself to be elected to the position of "vice-spokesman" demonstrates his hidden desire for inner differentiation among the prison community, although he was not accepted at all in this capacity by the constables and was subjected to even more abuse as a result of it.

Those entrepreneurs who were transported to a concentration camp after the November pogrom had similar experiences. Their treatment by the young SS guards was all the more sadistic whenever they emphasized their former social position or seemed to resemble in their physiognomy the anti-Semitic propaganda cliché of the Jewish *Bonzen*.[5] For the Jewish businessmen—provided they had not already emigrated—the November pogrom in 1938 meant the end of their civilian lives in Germany. When they returned from the concentration camps "with their heads shaven"[6] and "because of frostbite could hardly shake hands"[7] with their non-Jewish friends, they found their businesses in the hands of trustees who had meanwhile been engaged and authorized to sell off everything without their consent. With this act of legally enforced "Aryanization," the National Socialist rulers had robbed the Jewish entrepreneurs of both the basis of their existence and the center of their lives. Those who did not emigrate then and wanted to continue living in Germany using their savings had only one chance of escaping subsequent deportation and murder—to live, like Edgar Eichholz, in a "privileged mixed marriage" with a so-called German blooded wife and children baptized as Christians rather than enrolled as members of a Jewish community.

II

The November pogrom of 1938 and the legally enforced "Aryaniza-tion" of Jewish businesses brought about the end of Jewish commercial enterprises in Germany within a very short period. All Jewish business-men were equally affected by the arrests and elimination procedures: sig-nificant tradesmen such as Edgar Eichholz; bankers and industrialists, who belonged to the Jewish-German economic elite;[8] middle-class busi-nessmen; and self-employed craftsmen and retailers. Before the Novem-ber pogrom, however, there were considerable differences in the economic situation and the persecution of Jewish businessmen.[9] Consti-tuting only 1 to 1.5 percent of the population, Jews were strongly over-represented among the ranks of German employers. Werner E. Mosse estimates Jews' share in the German managerial class at 15 to 18 per-cent.[10] In the individual sectors, such as private banking, textiles, and wholesale and retail trade, Jewish entrepreneurs were particularly well represented; in others, such as heavy industry, they were less prominent.

After 1933 retailers and middle-class businesses were subject to the strongest coercive measures. A great number of anti-Jewish boycott ac-tivities and expulsion actions were directed at them, in particular those initiated by the SA and the Nazi Party, but especially by the "Alliance of Middle-Class Businessmen" and its successor, the National Socialist Hago. The boycott enacted on 1 April 1933 and exercised throughout the whole of the Reich was followed in the next few years by numerous, often violent boycotts and individual activities on a local and regional scale. These were often initiated by middle-class businessmen who, after 1933, wanted to take advantage of the political situation in order to de-nounce their Jewish competitors and expand their shares of the market in the wake of the *nationale Erhebung* (national exaltation). For exam-ple, the Beiersdorf Company that produced cosmetic and pharmaceuti-cal items found itself subjected to months of antisemitic propaganda campaigns instigated by its competitors from 1933 to 1934.[11] Compa-nies such as Queisser & Co. (Hamburg), Mouson AG (Frankfurt am Main), Wolo GmbH (Freudenstadt), or Lohmann AG (Fahr am Rhein), who were direct competitors of Beiersdorf in the skin-cream market, dis-tributed tens of thousands of yellow stickers ("Whoever buys Nivea products is automatically supporting a Jewish company!"), used news-paper advertisements for abusive propaganda ("Do not use any more

Jewish skin cream! Lovana Cream is at least just as good, is cheaper, and is purely German"), sent circulars to chemists and druggists requesting them to "recommend products of national instead of Jewish origin," and also took advantage of the national press for their campaigns.

Such anti-Jewish propaganda actions by middle-class industrial firms found their organizational expression in anti-Jewish trade organizations. In the textile industry, for example, in 1933 the *Arbeitsgemeinschaft deutsch-arischer Fabrikanten der Bekleidungsindustrie* (ADEFA, or Association of German-Aryan Manufacturers in the Clothing Industry)[12] compelled its members to break off all economic contact with Jewish companies. In addition, "non-Aryans" were quickly expelled from the established professional organizations of the middle-class economy. Particularly predominant were the *Reichsverband Deutscher Makler* (RDM, or Association of German Real Estate Agents), the *Reichsverband der Handelsvertreter* (Reich Association of Trade Representatives), the *Reichsfachschaft des deutschen Zeitungs- und Zeitschriftenhandels* (Reich Association of the German Newspaper and Magazine Trade), and the *Reichsverband der ambulanten Gewerbetreibenden* (Reich Association of Traveling Tradesmen).[13] Expulsions of this kind were often carried out against the express will of the Reich Ministry of the Economy.[14] For those concerned there were consequences for their livelihood, since access to markets and trade fairs often went hand in hand with membership in the appropriate association. Exclusion from a professional association thus frequently amounted to a professional ban.

Yet even though most of the boycott initiatives originated from middle-class industrial firms, in particular from retailers and workshops, it is still wrong to classify the whole of the middle-class economy as antisemitic. This is demonstrated by a study comparing the middle-class shoe and leather industries in the southwestern part of Germany.[15] Whereas in the shoe industry and in particular in the shoe retail trade, which was often subjected to boycotts, early "Aryanizations" and liquidations of Jewish businesses were the order of the day and many "Aryan" competitors were renowned for their antisemitic attitudes, it was the custom or "consent of the trade" in the leather industry to try to keep *Rassefragen* (racial issues) out of day-to-day business life. In the shoe industry and the shoe retail trade, moreover, strong competition and the orientation toward the domestic market both tended to encourage antisemitism; in the leather industry in contrast, the structure of the division of labor and the trend toward foreign trade discouraged antisemitic measures, so that any actions taken against Jewish suppliers would have had a damaging and dysfunctional effect on this highly specialized sector and also would have reduced the extent of international outlets.

Most Jewish entrepreneurs in the middle-class economy, however, were not able to withstand the pressure imposed on them. In the retail trade, for example, almost 80 percent of all Jewish retailers had dissolved or sold their businesses by July 1938, and in other middle-class sectors the "displacement quota" was 60 to 70 percent.[16] This process moved most quickly in rural areas and small towns where, due to the rigid social control, boycotting measures were more easily carried out and controlled.[17] Exact figures are available only for Heidelberg, Göttingen, and Marburg.[18] In Heidelberg, with its population at the time of 80,000, 47 percent of all Jewish companies were closed or "Aryanized" at the beginning of 1938; in Göttingen, with around 50,000 inhabitants, 56 percent; and in Marburg, with a population of 30,000, 69 percent. The speed of this displacement developed in inverse proportion to the size of the town—that is, the smaller the town or community, the quicker the liquidation or "Aryanization" was carried out. Elsewhere, in the anonymity of big cities such as Hamburg, where at the beginning of 1938 only 20 to 30 percent of all Jewish companies had given up, the possibilities of existence were much more favorable. Here a "Jewish economic sector" could be formed, here also were large Jewish communities and a tradition of support and self-help, from which the middle-class entrepreneur profited most of all.[19]

After 1933 Jewish large-scale entrepreneurs found themselves in an almost privileged situation compared with that of their middle-class colleagues. They were under less competitive pressure, were hardly affected by boycotts, and enjoyed a certain grace period as the National Socialists were trying to avoid the loss of jobs in large Jewish concerns and also feared a boycott of German goods in foreign countries. In 1933 the Jewish department store Hermann Tietz even received a loan from the Reich with the express permission of Hitler himself.[20] Many Jewish entrepreneurs also retained their positions on the supervisory and executive boards of large German companies.[21]

In the early days of the National Socialist rule, large-scale "Aryan" concerns still reacted to National Socialist racial policy with reserve.[22] Well aware of the potential danger of problems in foreign trade, for example, the chairman of the *Reichsverband der deutschen Industrie* (Association of German Industry), Gustav Krupp von Bohlen, Carl Friedrich von Siemens, and the general director of the Allianz Insurance

Company, Kurt Schmitt, participated in the Spring of 1933 in an initiative of Jewish businessmen led by Carl Melchior and Max Warburg aimed at weakening the anti-Jewish policy of the National Socialists toward the economic sector.[23] The "rate of Aryanization" of Jewish large-scale enterprises was also much lower between 1936 and 1937 than in the middle-class sector, obviously due to the paucity of attractive Jewish large-scale businesses.

On the whole, though, large concerns' willingness to intervene in favor of Jewish colleagues was limited to the rejection of individual cases of business encroachment and did not extend to any repudiation of anti-Semitic policy and practice as such.[24] By 1936–37, indeed, there was no longer any trace of this willingness. The increased repression against Jewish large entrepreneurs was accompanied by a "striking decline in human sympathy"[25] on the part of their "Aryan" colleagues.

The overall situation of Jewish entrepreneurs in National Socialist Germany was not determined by anti-Jewish economic measures alone and is also not clear from the balance sheets of their companies alone. Other measures of National Socialist "Jewish policy" often had a much greater influence on the everyday life of the entrepreneurs and their families, for example, educational discrimination, professional and training prohibitions, and exclusion from societies or public amenities such as parks, theaters, swimming pools, and libraries. Jewish large-scale entrepreneurs, who had been active as donors and patrons and had often held numerous honorary offices, were those who suffered most from this enforced withdrawal from public life. The Jewish industrialist Paul Berendsohn, who ran a shipbuilding yard in the village of Altenwerder near Hamburg, noted that one of the most "degrading acts of humiliation" he suffered occurred when he was not allowed to take part in the annual traditional festival procession through Altenwerder, although he had always contributed toward the needs of the village which, among other things, was indebted to him for arranging its connection to the electricity supply.[26] Simone Lässig has described in detail the process of the social isolation of Jewish entrepreneurs, taking the Dresden banking family Arnhold as an example.[27] The exclusion of the Arnholds from numerous societies and trusts was equal to a "cultural ghettoization."[28] This ghettoization had a decisive effect on the attitude and the identity of the banker's family because their "German identity" was based on their affiliation to German culture. The Arnholds were then only able to live their culturally defined German identity within the Jewish community, which was now developing into a residual depository of German culture and German bourgeoisie—at a time when the basic values of bourgeois liberal culture had been more or less banished from German society.[29]

III

With growing pressure from outside and slowly approaching social isolation, many Jewish entrepreneurs tended to withdraw from social life and retreat into their companies. For example, the Jewish banker Max Warburg wrote in his memoirs that after the National Socialist accession to power in 1933, he had decided to "defend his company like a fortress."[30] He shared this intention with many Jewish businessmen who, in view of the external pressure, would have liked to have kept their companies as refuges, untouched by the political events of the time. But by spring 1933 it was obvious that this yearning for an internal "intact world" was merely an illusion. In almost all middle-sized and larger companies, National Socialist branches had been formed, and the first official action these took was very often the dismissal of all Jewish employees.[31] This "underground organization of our employees"—as the owner of a Berlin clothing company remembers[32]—demonstrated drastically to the Jewish entrepreneurs that they could not rely on the loyalty of their employees to ward off antisemitic animosity and reminded them that their staff was a true reflection of German society at that time.

On the one hand, the interest of the staff in maintaining their jobs sometimes motivated "Aryan" employees to exert their influence on state or party authorities to prevent anti-Jewish actions.[33] On the other hand the Jewish company owners were constantly threatened by their "Aryan" staff, who were paradoxically enflamed by the owners' formally strong legal position as *Betriebsführer* (managing director), which meant that the *Gesetz zur Ordnung der nationalen Arbeit* (Law for the Regulation of National Employment), announced in 1934, created a kind of dictatorial position even for the Jewish owners within their companies and reduced to a minimum the rights of the employees in the enforced harmony of the *Betriebsgemeinschaft* (works community). But because "non-Aryans" were not regarded as full-blooded members of the *Volksgemeinschaft*, according to racist logic, one could not expect any real *Betriebsgemeinschaft* within Jewish companies.

Conflicts within Jewish companies were therefore often popular subjects for articles in the National Socialist press[34]—in particular in the newspaper *Der Stürmer*. They provided welcome opportunities for branding Jewish entrepreneurs "typical Jewish exploiters," as opposed to the press's tireless proclamations of the propaganda chimera of harmony between the interests of employers and their staff. Even if the Jewish company owner in his capacity as *Betriebsführer* was unassailable by the members of staff, he could still be pressured as a "Jew" by means of direct denunciation, arranged intervention of the Gestapo, or similar means.[35] Thus the staff members in Jewish concerns were subjected to constant temptation to ventilate suppressed social conflicts in the sublimated form of "racial conflicts." The works councils and works sector spokesmen, who had very little influence in most companies, developed into influential factors of power within Jewish companies. For the Jewish directors it was therefore "vital not to make these their adversaries."[36]

Hans Robinsohn, a former partner in a clothing company in Hamburg, formulated the paradoxical position of the Jewish *Betriebsführer* as follows: "Legally speaking he was almost the absolute ruler in his company. But in practice he was an individual without power and rights within the National Socialist state system."[37] As Robinsohn reported, even a company's minor internal incidents threatened to turn into a basic conflict, with the works council which could lead to uncalculable risks. He compared his own job with that of an animal tamer, who, despite his inner conviction, had to demonstrate "calmness and resoluteness" to those watching him: "Just like in the arena, the slightest sign of fear, of insecurity and instability would be most dangerous."[38] Although "stable and self-confident behavior" was helpful to company owners in many conflict situations, and although the Labor Courts did not always let themselves be misled in their decisions by racist views, many Jewish businessmen had to reckon with continual intervention by the Gestapo or branches of the National Socialist Party. Some reported that their employees had partly set themselves up as *Herrenmenschen* (the masters).[39]

In particular during the prelude to "Aryanization" the employees, who were aspiring to take over the company, often turned out to be the Jewish owners' most serious opponents. They sabotaged selling negotiations by arranging for National Socialist organizations to intervene, took a personal share of the profits of the "Aryanized" companies, and tried to acquire possession of the company at a low price by holding secret negotiations with potential buyers behind the backs of their employers. "It's our turn to hold the trigger now," was what an employee told his Jewish boss after he had arranged the termination of his boss's rental contract and acquired a new rental contract for himself.[40] When conflict occurred, employees sometimes demonstrated disloyal behavior toward their bosses. Robinsohn reported that the company's own drivers, when delivering goods to customers, often reproached them for having ordered goods from a Jewish firm.[41] One former employee wrote his senior boss a blackmail letter and demanded a payment of 600 RM. If he refused, the man threatened to report him to the Gestapo on the grounds of alleged *Rassenschande* (racial defilement).[42] In other Jewish businesses there were cases where employees conveyed to the National Socialist press the names of "Aryan" customers who then found themselves denounced as *Judenknechte* (slaves to the Jews).

A similar fate awaited those employees who were suspected of being too "close" to a Jewish company owner. For example, employees of the Berlin linen company Grünfeld were denounced, complete with names and addresses, in the *Stürmer* as being Judengenossen (comrades of the Jews). The owner, Fritz V. Grünfeld, remembers in this connection: "The intimidation, the fear of being publicly branded a *Judenknecht* discouraged all those who had followed their natural instinct of loyalty toward the company and encouraged those who were inclined toward sabotage, spying, and betrayal, even including listening in on our telephone calls, 'controlling' our mail and searching through our wastepaper baskets."[43] For this reason, the number of loyal members of staff could be "counted on one hand."

Often an invisible apartheid line was drawn between Jewish and "Aryan" employees so that even an event such as an internal office party threatened to be publicized as a political scandal.[44] One Jewish woman from Berlin remembered that most of the "Aryans" in fact behaved quite "decently and orderly" toward their Jewish colleagues. But they tended more and more "to avoid being seen on the street with them or keeping up any private relationships with them."[45]

Under these circumstances most Jewish companies did not provide a "fortress" in the sense of an untouched stronghold. The external pressure tended, rather, to be accompanied by an internal segmentation which contributed toward the economic exclusion and isolation of Jewish concerns.

IV

Often Jewish entrepreneurs fought the growing acts of repression against their companies with remarkable self-assertion. Many of them reacted to the adverse conditions with flexibility and imaginativeness so that some companies were even able to achieve an increase in sales through direct advertising and special offers on the one hand and rationalization and cost reduction on the other. This self-assertion was not primarily the result of a lack of insight into the political circumstances. On the contrary, the National Socialist state, with its taxation and contribution policy, made the only basic alternative, emigration, so financially unattractive that for many Jewish entrepreneurs emigration meant virtually the compulsory confiscation of their possessions. This was due to both the *Reichsfluchtsteuer* (Reich flight tax) and the required contributions to the *Deutsche Golddiskontbank* (Dego) that had to be paid for currency transfers abroad. In August 1934 the necessary payment already amounted to 65 percent of the whole transfer amount, then increased until June 1938 to 90 percent and in September 1939 reached its peak of 96 percent.[46]

But if a Jewish company owner decided to sell his business, he was only able to obtain a price which corresponded to its actual value until 1935–36. After that, such contracts of sale had to be submitted to the Nazi Party Gauwirtschaftsberater for authorization. This procedure meant the end of freedom of contract for Jewish owners and led to drastic losses when selling their businesses. Under the new rules, the actual value of the company (the goodwill), which was made up of its market position, its range of products, its regular clientele, its business connections, its distribution outlets, and its standing in the community, could not be taken into consideration in setting the value of the company because Jews did not enjoy such "goodwill," according to the National Socialist attitude. The *Gauwirtschaftsberater* generally acted according to the motto "a Jew should not receive an immeasurably high price" and therefore often reduced the agreed selling price to the disadvantage of the Jewish owner.[47]

The "Aryanizations" legally enforced since 1938 continued to limit the scope of action of Jewish entrepreneurs, but extended the circle of people involved in the selling transactions by new groups of professionals and other persons. Now official surveyors were appointed who were engaged by the Chambers of Industry and Commerce to estimate the inventory and stock of Jewish companies. In evaluating warehouse stock, often only the bankruptcy value counted, which constituted only half of the buying price.[48] Jewish property owners were only able to obtain the so-called moderate market value, but often not even the estimated value.[49] In fact, in the case of any of these "Aryanizations" from 1938–39, no genuine market price was paid for inventory, stock, and property. The official surveyors took part in this scandalous price depression and often used their authority to the disadvantage of the Jewish owners. In extreme cases the surveyor offered an "Aryan" buyer the opportunity to buy a business for 10 to 15 percent of the value of the stock of goods and demanded that he should "not be stupid and [should] take advantage of the present situation."[50]

The proceeds for the Jewish owners were even less if the "Aryanization" contract submitted was rejected on the grounds of an alleged "overrepresentation" of the commercial sector and arrangements were made for the liquidation of the company. So-called Aryanization commissions were formed to adjudicate such issues. The commissions comprised, among others, entrepreneurs and representatives of the economic sector in question, for example, representatives of the Guild of Craftsmen, the Chamber of Industry and Commerce and their different trade groups.[51] In this way individual entrepreneurs as representatives of a professional group had an immediate influence on the economic fate of their Jewish competitors. For example, in the case of a liquidation order, a Jewish retailer was not allowed to hold a closing sale, but had to offer his stock to the corresponding group of trade representatives—his competitors—at the liquidation value.

After the November pogrom of 1938 the "Aryanization" constituted a "race for enrichment" on the part of the "Aryan" potential buyers. The participation rights of the Jewish company owners were limited to signing contracts of sale. "The Nazi authorities and *Gauwirtschaftstellen* [regional economic bureaus] declared the sale—and the Jewish company owner was only allowed to stand there and watch how he was being driven to ruin" was the description given by the Hamburg entrepreneur Paul Schiff.[52] Schiff, who had served as a volunteer and front-line officer in the German army during the First World War, was the owner of the wholesale company Gebr. Frank and was arrested on 15 November 1938. An appointed trustee sold the business for about 29,000 RM to a buyer who was a member of both the Nazi Party and the SS. In October 1938 the value of the stock alone had been estimated at around 80,000 RM but was set much lower in order to "facilitate approval by the surveyor of the *Gauwirtschaftsberater*."[53] Schiff, from his prison cell, had no opportunity to intervene and was finally brought forward only to sign the contract in his prison clothes. The conditions of sale for Jewish companies and the taxes and compulsory levies which were extended in November 1938 by a *Judenvermögensabgabe* (Jewish capital tax) resulted in the complete financial exploitation of the Jewish owner.

This exploitation is obvious in the example of Albert Aronson, who in July 1938 was still one of the most wealthy businessmen in Hamburg.[54] He was the sole proprietor of the chocolate factory Reese & Wichmann GmbH, the cigarette import company Havana-Import-Compagnie, and of thirty-six real estate properties, some in the best locations in the city. The total value of his possessions was more than 4 million RM. When Aronson emigrated to London six weeks later, he was only able to salvage 1.7 percent of his fortune. In order to obtain money for his emigration, he had taken out a loan from his bank, M. M. Warburg & Co., amounting to 800,000 RM, of which only 66,000 RM (= 5,413 pounds sterling) was transferred whereas 734,000 RM went as a fee to the *Deutsche Golddiskontbank*. To pay off his loan, Aronson had to sell a fairly large proportion of his properties at a ridiculously low price, while his two companies were "Aryanized." The proceeds from the sale of the two companies, amounting to 800,000 RM, which by no means corresponded to their actual value, were transferred to a security account to which Aronson had no free access. The *Oberfinanzdirektion* (revenue authorities) in Hamburg had in fact blocked his accounts on 12 July 1938. Aronson had to pay 613,713 RM in Reich flight tax, 245,410 RM in Jewish capital tax, and 100,000 RM to a secret fund of the Hamburg Nazi Party regional leader in order to secure the release of his passport. His remaining capital and properties were confiscated in favor of the German Reich on the grounds of the 11th Implementing Order of the Civil Law of the Reich dated 25 November 1941. Within three years Aronson had thus lost 98.3 percent of his fortune.

V

Let us return to Edgar Eichholz. After he was released from prison in November 1938, the *Gauwirtschaftsberater* placed his business under the enforced administration of a trustee, who transferred the company in June 1939 to a former executive of Messrs. Eichholz & Loeser without any compensation for Eichholz.[55] During the period that followed he lived mainly on rental income and his savings. He dismissed any emigration plans on the grounds of his age. Because Eichholz had had the foresight to transfer his house and property to "Aryan" relatives, he was able to remain with his wife in a flat in his grandparents' house until the end of the war. Living in a "privileged mixed marriage," he neither had to move into a "*Judenhaus*" nor wear the yellow star. Furthermore, he was excepted from deportation while many of his Jewish friends were—according to the official terminology—"evacuated" to the East between 1941 and 1942. Eichholz had no illusions as to the fate of those deported, as his memoirs later revealed: "And none of these people, it is said, are still alive. . . . Among the 'Aryans' there are the most dreadful horror stories going around about the transport to Minsk[56] and about the way in which the poor folk are said to have been murdered. In any case, this 6th December 1941[57] will remain unforgotten in my mind. I have never experienced anything so heart-breaking to this very day."[58] In 1943 Eichholz performed forced labor in the factory of a former friend because the age limit for such labor by Jews had been increased from fifty-five to sixty-five years. He was sixty-three at the time. Eichholz, who had once run a big company, now had to knead rat poison with his bare hands and put it into packets. Otherwise he would have been set to sweeping the streets.

In Hamburg Eichholz felt like a "pariah of mankind, with no homeland and no rights, an outcast from society." Although the relatives of his "Aryan" wife and some non-Jewish friends still stood by him, he was often avoided in public "in the most unpleasant manner." In July–August 1943, however, he became aware for the first time of obvious changes in the behavior of those around him and sensed the beginning of his social reintegration. British and American bombing squads had left large parts of the city in ruins in a series of heavy air raids that were part of Operation Gomorrha. More than 45,000 Hamburg citizens lost their lives during the raids, almost 1 million people fled from the city. On 27 July 1943 the house in which the Eichholz family lived was slightly damaged, and the house next door caught fire. Eichholz reported:

I ran outside immediately. I was the only man in the house anyway. . . . Over the bridge . . . , fetched 10 men to get the people out. At first they didn't want to come out because of the bombing. But finally they came out hesitantly, when I spoke of reporting it the next morning as it was a case of saving human lives. . . . In the Heilwigstraße I found a fully manned fire engine: Lads, why aren't you putting out fires? The houses are burning everywhere?! They replied: We haven't had any orders! Really! Who gives the orders around here? They: The sergeant.—Where is he? They: Over there. . . . I see. I will get orders for you immediately. . . . Herr von Hütz, you are the one to give the orders here. Get those lads down here and have them lay a hose to the Isebek.[59] I can take a rope and

59

climb over through the house next door onto the roof of the burning house. . . . To cut the story short, we saved that house and with it the whole of the five houses in the row, including, of course, our own.[60]

For hours Edgar Eichholz directed the fire-fighting and live-saving activities in his area. Satisfied, he recorded that the disaster had revealed the incapability and weakness of the National Socialist authority and that his own authority, which was based on efficiency and years of experience in management, had been accepted without any resistance. Eichholz received numerous tokens of gratitude from people who, shortly beforehand, had not even greeted him. A local NSDAP leader, who had once wanted to refuse him entrance to his "territory," now approached him, cringing with friendliness, and thanked him for his actions: "In any case, it was with great satisfaction that I experienced this rehabilitation so unexpectedly. Others have received the War Service Cross with swords for doing less. But they would not give me, as a non-Aryan, any such award, even if I did even more. I am simply not worthy of it!!! But this gratitude was more than any such medal for me. And neighbors came with cakes, wine etc. to thank me. On the open street, a car driven by an officer pulled up. A beautiful young lady stepped out. Are you Herr Eichholz? I just wanted to thank you for what you have done."[61]

In view of the threatening defeat, the first cracks in the *Volksgemeinschaft*, which up till then had seemed to be hermetically sealed, became apparent.[62] Now, for the first time, an—opportunistically motivated—will to differentiate was revealed to Eichholz which brought him, who had done so much for others, the recognition he would never have received beforehand. The satisfaction it brought him and the remarks about the War Service Cross emphasize how strongly Eichholz still identified himself with German society, despite all the harassment he had suffered. Attentively he noted the first signs that this society was beginning to prepare itself for a possible end to National Socialist rule. The once omnipotent party officials had become meek and appeared to Eichholz to be "small and ugly." Those who had profited from National Socialist rule were now filled with fear. Eichholz noted that "many who had taken over Jewish homes and Jewish possessions now feared that the Jews could return and claim back their possessions and would make those people answer for their plunder and robbery."[63]

When the Allied forces moved in it seemed to him as if there had never been a National Socialist rule in Germany: "Dissolved into thin air, disappeared like a phantom. Where are those institutions, where are the people? Nothing, there is nothing left. Nobody was ever a party comrade. And if so, then only because they had no choice. Oh yes, these heroes."[64] He himself reacted to the surrender of Hamburg without a fight on 3 May 1945 in an ambivalent manner. He felt on the one hand freed, on the other hand somewhat depressed as a "good German": "Free, free, really free! No Gestapo officer behind the door, when the doorbell rings. No new carefully contrived trick to insult and torment us, no more Heil Hitler by the others to which one was not allowed or did not want to respond, no hesitant sounding-out of others to find out their attitude. . . . And yet: Mutti [Eichholz's wife] cried bitterly that day. So low, so endlessly low, so deeply covered in humiliation and disgrace, did our poor Germany have to sink . . . , so that we, and with us the whole of Germany could be ridden of this Nazi plague, these criminals, about whose complete activities we have only just properly learned from the concentration camps such [as] Auschwitz, Dachau, Buchenwald."[65]

He still identified himself with "poor Germany" and therefore contributed without hesitating toward rebuilding it—at the age of sixty-five. In June 1945 Messrs. Eichholz & Loeser went into business again, under his management.[66] Eichholz then belonged to a small minority of Jewish entrepreneurs who either had survived in Germany or had returned from their emigration in 1945 and taken over their old companies again. In Hamburg almost one-quarter of the Jewish entrepreneurs had been deported and murdered or had committed suicide.[67] Over two-thirds had emigrated, most of them to the United States and Great Britain. Many had founded new companies there and had been integrated into society. In view of the persecution they had experienced, the murders of many relatives and friends, and finally the uncertain aspects of the future in a Germany ravaged by war, most Jewish entrepreneurs after 1945 decided to stay in their new countries. The persecution of the Jews under National Socialist rule had therefore put an abrupt and violent end to the long assimilation process of the German Jews within a very short space of time and, in the economic sector, had destroyed company traditions some of which were two hundred years old. The Allied and German reimbursement laws did nothing to change this. Although many Jewish businessmen were able to regain their businesses, they usually rejected any form of restitution and came to an agreement with the "Aryan" buyer regarding a compensation payment. This meant that the restitution managed to provide financial compensation for the Jewish entrepreneurs, but at the same time confirmed the changes of ownership that had occurred as a result of the National Socialist "Aryanization."[68]

NOTES

1. On Edgar Eichholz, see Frank Bajohr, *"Arisierung" in Hamburg: Die Verdrängung der jüdischen Unternehmer, 1933–1945*, 2d ed. (Hamburg, 1998), 270–72; Beate Meyer, *"Jüdische Mischlinge": Rassenpolitik und Verfolgungserfahrung, 1933–1945* (Hamburg, 1999), 36–43. The following comments are based on personal records by Edgar Eichholz during the years 1939–1945, which are in private possession, and on the restitution file of Messrs. Eichholz & Loeser in the Archives of the Reparation Office of the Landgericht Hamburg (in Archives WgA LGHH), Z 286–3.

2. In Hamburg in the 1920s "mixed marriages" constituted almost half of the marriages by Jews. See Ina Lorenz, *Die Juden in Hamburg zur Zeit der Weimarer Republik: Eine Dokumentation*, 2 vols. (Hamburg, 1987), 1:lviii.

3. Original German expression: *mieser Portokassenjüngling*.

4. Quoted from a letter by Edgar Eichholz to his son dated 14 February 1939 (private possession).

5. A Jewish prisoner in the Sachsenhausen concentration camp reported in this connection: "The SS people, of which there were hardly any over the age of 21 years, had got it in for old, fat, Jewish-looking and socially well-situated Jews, e.g. rabbis, teachers, lawyers, whereas sporty-looking Jews were treated more mildly. For example, a former high-ranking legal official who introduced himself with his title, was treated with particular severity and with him the owner of a large restaurant concern." Quoted in Wolfgang Benz, "Der November-Pogrom 1938," in *Die Juden in Deutschland, 1933–1945*, ed. Benz (Munich, 1988), 499–544, quotation 530.

6. Quotation from the diary of Cornelius Freiherr von Berenberg-Goßler (private possession), entry dated 25 November 1938.

7. Ibid., entry dated 22 December 1938.

8. See Werner E. Mosse, *The German-Jewish Economic Élite, 1820–1935: A Socio-Cultural Profile* (Oxford, 1989).

9. See Avraham Barkai, *Vom Boykott zur "Entjudung": Der wirtschaftliche Existenzkampf der Juden im Dritten Reich* (Frankfurt am Main, 1987); Helmut Genschel, *Die Verdrängung der Juden aus der Wirtschaft im Dritten Reich* (Göttingen, 1966); Bajohr, *"Arisierung."*

10. Compare Werner E. Mosse, "Jewish Entrepreneurship in Germany, 1820–1935," in *Jüdische Unternehmer in Deutschland im 19. und 20. Jahrhundert*, ed. Werner E. Mosse and Hans Pohl (Stuttgart, 1992), 54–66, here 55.

11. On the following, see Frank Bajohr and J. Szodrzynski, " 'Keine jüdische

Die antisemitische Kampagne gegen die Hamburger Firma Beiersdorf 1933/34," in *Die Juden in Hamburg, 1590 bis 1990*, ed. Arno Herzig (Hamburg, 1991), 515–26.

12. See Bundesarchiv Berlin, Reichswirtschaftsministerium, 8646 (Adefa-Stiftung). In 1934 the Adefa changed the adjective "deutsch" to "deutscharisch," but reverted to the original version again in November 1938. In August 1939 the Adefa was dissolved after the last Jewish clothing companies had been "Aryanized" or liquidated.

13. Geheimes Staatsarchiv Berlin Dahlem, Rep. 90P, Lageberichte 6.2, sheet 63, Report of the Staatspolizeistelle Königsberg, 9 October 1934; Genschel, *Verdrängung*, 90.

14. However, corresponding intervention by the Reich Ministry of the Economy had little success. See Albert Fischer, *Hjalmar Schacht und Deutschlands 'Judenfrage': Der 'Wirtschaftsdiktator' und die Vertreibung der Juden aus der deutschen Wirtschaft* (Cologne, 1995).

15. On the following, see Petra Bräutigam, *Mittelständische Unternehmer im Nationalsozialismus: Wirtschaftliche Entwicklungen und soziale Verhaltensweisen in der Schuh- und Lederindustrie Badens und Württembergs* (Munich, 1997), esp. 255ff.

16. Barkai, *Boykott*, 123.

17. Christhard Hoffmann, "Verfolgung und Alltagsleben der Landjuden im nationalsozialistischen Deutschland," in *Jüdisches Leben auf dem Lande*, ed. Monika Richarz and Reinhard Rürup (Tübingen, 1997), 373–98.

18. To compare Heidelberg, Göttingen, and Marburg, see Alex Bruns-Wüstefeld, *Lohnende Geschäfte: Die "Entjudung" der Wirtschaft am Beispiel Göttingens* (Hanover, 1997), 120–25.

19. Compare Bajohr, *"Arisierung,"* 129ff.

20. On the situation of the Jewish department stores, see Simone Ladwig-Winters, *Wertheim—ein Warenhausunternehmen und seine Eigentümer* (Münster, 1997).

21. Peter Hayes, "Big Business and 'Aryanization' in Germany," *Jahrbuch für Antisemitismusforschung* 3 (1994): 254–81.

22. Ibid., esp. 256f.; David Bankier, *The Germans and the Final Solution: Public Opinion under Nazism* (Oxford, 1992), 87–100.

23. Hayes, "Big Business," pp. 258f.; Avraham Barkai, "Max Warburg im Jahre 1933: Mißglückte Versuche zur Mildering der Judenverfolgung," in, *Juden in Deutschland*, ed. Peter Freimark et al. (Hamburg, 1991), 390–405.

24. Hayes, "Big Business," 256.

25. Ibid., 269.

26. Archives WgA LGHH, Z 191–1, Lebensbericht Berendsohn (undated), sheet 11.

27. Simone Lässig, "Nationalsozialistische 'Judenpolitik' und jüdische Selbstbehauptung vor dem Novemberprogrom: Das Beispiel der Dresdner

Bankiersfamilie Arnhold," in *Dresden unterm Hakenkreuz*, ed. Reiner Pommerin (Cologne, 1998), 129–191.

28. Ibid., 143.

29. Ibid., 144.

30. Max Warburg, *Aus meinen Aufzeichnungen* (New York, 1952), 147.

31. Curt Joseph, "NS-Betriebszellen in Aktion," in *Sie durften nicht mehr Deutsche sein: Jüdischer Alltag in Selbstzeugnissen*, ed. Margarethe Limberg and Hubert Rübsaat (Frankfurt, 1990), 95–97.

32. Fritz V. Grünfeld, *Das Leinenhaus Grünfeld*, ed. Stefi Jersch-Wenzel (Berlin, 1967), 104.

33. On individual examples, see Bajohr, *"Arisierung,"* 142; Geheimes Staatsarchiv Berlin-Dahlem, Rep. 90P, Lageberichte, 14.2, sheet 184, Report of the Staatspolizeistelle Bielefeld, 4 September 1935.

34. See Grünfeld, *Leinenhaus*, 121.

35. See Gerhard Kratzsch, *Der Gauwirtschaftsapparat der NSDAP: Menschenführung—"Arisierung"—Wehrwirtschaft im Gau Westfalen-Süd* (Münster, 1989), 287; Grünfeld, *Leinenhaus*, 116; Bajohr, *"Arisierung,"* 234.

36. Hetti Schiller, "Die Warenhäuser werden 'deutsch,' " in Limberg and Rübsaat eds., *Sie durften nicht mehr Deutsche sein*, 85–94, quotation 85.

37. Hans Robinsohn, "Ein Versuch, sich zu behaupten," *Tradition* 3 (1958): 197–206.

38. Ibid., 201.

39. Bajohr, *"Arisierung,"* 235f.

40. Ibid., 236.

41. Statement by Hans Robinsohn, Archives WgA LGHH, Z 3511–1, sheet 416.

42. Archives of the Forschungsstelle für Zeitgeschichte in Hamburg (FZH), 11/R8, F. 294, sheet 21.

43. Grünfeld, *Leinenhaus*, 121.

44. Schiller, "Warenhäuser," 86.

45. Ibid., 85.

46. Bajohr, *"Arisierung,"* 153f.

47. On the role of the NSDAP Gauwirtschaftsberater see ibid., 174–186; Kratzsch, *Gauwirtschaftsapparat*.

48. Bajohr, *"Arisierung,"* 236f.

49. Angela Verse-Herrmann, *Die "Arisierungen" in der Land- und Forstwirtschaft, 1938–1942* (Stuttgart, 1997), 85–88.

50. Quoted in Bajohr, *"Arisierung,"* 237.

51. Ibid., 231.

52. Archives WgA LGHH, Z 1382–1, sheet 133, Statutory Statement by Paul Schiff dated 28 June 1954.

53. Ibid., sheet 5, letter from Paul Schiff dated 16 July 1949.

54. On the case of Aronson and the following details, see Bajohr, *"Arisierung,"* 297f.

55. Archives WgA LGHH, Z 286–3, sheet 7, letter from Edgar Eichholz dd. 6 April 1948. On the life story of Edgar Eichholz between 1939 and 1945 and its interpretation, see Meyer, *"Jüdische Mischlinge,"* 36–43.

56. On 8 and 18 November 1941, 968 and 407 Jews respectively were deported from Hamburg to Minsk. Of these 952 and 403 respectively were murdered. See *Hamburger jüdische Opfer des Nationalsozialismus,* Gedenkbuch, Hamburg, 1995, p. xix.

57. On 6 December 1941, 753 Jews were deported to Riga. Of these, 726 were murdered. See ibid.

58. Quotation from the records of Edgar Eichholz (1944–45), private possession, 11.

59. Small river in Hamburg.

60. Quotation from Eichholz records, private possession, 27.

61. Ibid., 30.

62. See also Frank Bajohr, "Hamburg—der Zerfall der 'Volksgemeinschaft,'" in *Kriegsende in Europa,* ed. Ulrich Herbert and Axel Schildt (Essen, 1998), 318–36.

63. Eichholz records, private possession, 43.

64. Ibid., 45.

65. Ibid., 44.

66. Archives WgA LGHH, Z 286–3, sheet 7, letter from Edgar Eichholz dated 6 April 1948.

67. On the following details, see Bajohr, *"Arisierung,"* 388.

68. See Jan Philipp Spannuth, *Die Rückerstattung jüdischen Eigentums nach dem Zweiten Weltkrieg: Das Beispiel Hamburg (Magisterarbeit)* (Hamburg, 1994).

CHAPTER 4

When the Ordinary Became Extraordinary

GERMAN JEWS REACTING TO

NAZI PERSECUTION, 1933–1939

MARION A. KAPLAN

WITH THE Nazi seizure of power, Germany turned its Jewish community into official pariahs. The Nazi government—through indoctrination, bribery, and coercion—transformed antisemitic prejudices into a mass movement and official state policy. Despite the confusing, momentary lulls in persecution and the shifts in some policies at the top, Jewish daily life gradually became enveloped by lawlessness, ostracism, and a loss of rights. As Jews went about their lives, most grew increasingly aware of the uneven yet steady growth of hostility and danger around them but remained confused about where it was going or whether it would stop. Still, for most Jews daily life consisted of the commonplace—trying to make a living, nurturing their families, and achieving at school—activities that continued at least until November 1938. They tried to lead "normal" lives while experiencing outward oppression and inward disorientation, tension, and frustration. They tried to cope with practical solutions, sometimes burying themselves in the details. And they assessed their situation by how much they had to suffer while doing their daily tasks. The routine nature of these tasks and the apparent ordinariness with which Jews continued their daily existence notwithstanding, their internal equilibrium was shattered.

On the national policy level, the status of Jews deteriorated irregularly and unpredictably, but on a steady decline from 1933 to 1938. On the individual, experiential level, the lives of Jewish women and families were affected unevenly. There were many mixed signals and complicated situations to which individuals responded with hope, fear, or confusion. For example, in 1933, a ten-year-old observed Nazis marching with placards reading "Germans, don't buy from Jews. World Jewry wants to destroy Germany. Germans, defend yourselves." But in 1935, her father

66

was still decorated for active service in the past war, receiving a citation signed by the chief of police of Berlin.[1] Moreover, Jews' experiences differed according to where they lived: Berliners were able to go about their business and schooling with far less interference than Jews in villages and small towns. Experiences also differed according to age and class. Parents might continue in their occupations, but children's present and future in Germany looked bleak. Many young people got out, many of the elderly were trapped. Wealthier Jews could insulate themselves from certain situations, but only for a time. Gender, too, created distinctive experiences and reactions. Women took on traditional as well as novel roles in this process. They remained the ones to calm the family, to keep up the normal rhythms of life. But gender roles also blurred as women and men tried to salvage some peace of mind by accommodating to their new predicament. And gender roles were dramatically reversed when women, rather than men, had to intercede for their families with state officials and when they pushed for their families to flee Germany.

Private Responses to Expulsion from the "Racial Community"

Families and Individuals

Jews generally reacted to Nazi policies as these affected them on an individual basis: that is, most Jews felt not the full weight of Nazi antisemitic policies but rather the weight of particular decrees or humiliations. Thus individuals responded to the increasing frustrations in daily life in a variety of ways, depending on the extent to which particular Nazi policies touched them. In 1940 Harvard University researchers analyzed the ways in which ninety people who had lived in Germany during the early years of Nazi rule had faced the new and mounting hardships. These included flight into the family and into one's self; the increased importance of Jewish friendships; a change in life philosophy; "an endless procession of petty conformities to the harrowing demands of the Nazi persecutors"; the lowering of ambitions; and increased planning and action.[2]

The Harvard study found heightened in-group feelings among those persecuted by the Nazis, noting: "Most dramatic are the many instances of return to the healing intimacy of the family after bitter experiences of persecution on the street, in the office, or in prison."[3] Later memoirs and interviews affirm that "[l]ife centered more around the family then."[4] In the face of daily stress, increasing ostracism by former non-Jewish friends, and the threat of increased fanaticism, many Jews sought the relative safety and comfort of their families, both nuclear and extended. This emphasis on the family had both positive and negative results. Someone who had been a young adult at the time later commented: "If I search for the special element associated with . . . existence as an outcast, then what I think of first is a positive gain . . . the increase in the intensity of family life. . . . Yet there was a loss here too: in that entire period of ten years . . . I only made two new friendships."[5] Children were even more dependent on the family. They were not only aware of the social ostracism directed toward all Jews, but experienced rejection directly from other children. Some were relatively hearty; the young teenager Peter Gay, for example, could associate with his cousins and absorb himself in soccer magazines to "escape to a playful reality . . . even for a few hours each week, away from the harsher reality of Nazi broadcasts, Nazi posters, Nazi teachers, Nazi fellow-students."[6] Other children were so deeply hurt that their wounds lasted a lifetime. Marion Gardner, born in 1931, wrote: "It didn't take long until one got used to not being allowed to be together with other Germans. . . . I was lonely, and until today . . . it is hard for me to make friends."[7] A mother noted that when her daughter's friends no longer came to their home, "Loneliness enveloped us more and more each day."[8]

Jews turned to one another for friendship and comfort. This was usually not difficult, since most Jews, even those who felt genuinely integrated into a non-Jewish social world, maintained a circle of Jewish friends and colleagues. Given the atmosphere outside, Jews often limited their social life to their own homes or organizations, staying away from public theaters, concerts, and museums, but still, occasionally, frequenting movie houses.[9] Many turned with new zest to their remaining friends.[10] Mally Dienemann, the wife of Rabbi Max Dienemann of Offenbach am Main, marveled at the close friendships she witnessed: "Those who remained behind, whose circle got increasingly smaller, closed ranks all the more tightly. Friendship once again became the essence of life."[11]

Yet in the strained circumstances affecting the entire Jewish community, shadows hovered over social evenings with Jewish friends. Such evenings were hardly relaxing: "As the prisoners in Dostoyevsky's *House of the Dead* speak only of the freedom that they might enjoy in perhaps 20 years, perhaps never, so the people in our circle spoke only of freedom beyond Germany, which they one day hoped to reach."[12] The topic of conversation inevitably turned to the worsening situation for Jews, the emigration of friends and children, and details about visas, foreign lands, and foreign climates, "of an existence where they would no longer be frightened to death when the doorbell rang in the morning, because they would be certain: it is only the milkman!"[13] Moreover, when groups of Jews gathered in private homes, they feared that they were being watched by suspicious neighbors or, worse, the Gestapo.

Upper-middle-class Jews had more options. They could act as though a certain normalcy were attainable, even when this was a self-deception. For example, they took vacations outside of Germany. When fewer German hotels accepted Jewish clientele, Ruth Glaser's parents sent her to Switzerland for a vacation.[14] Others enjoyed France, Italy, and eastern Europe.[15] Daily strains could also be alleviated if one had the financial means. Non-Jewish domestic servants could be asked to shop in markets that no longer welcomed Jews, and those willing to absorb the costs could even order food by telephone and pay delivery charges to avoid aggravation.[16]

Religion provided solace to many Jews. Observant Jews continued their adherence to Jewish laws and their celebration of Jewish holy days, even risking attention and possible eviction when they built a sukkah in their backyard.[17] The Bar Mitzvah of a son, or the rare confirmation of a daughter, was cause for celebration, even amid the official hatred and informal nastiness surrounding them. A substantial number of Jews even became more religious.[18] Rather than a dramatic change of heart, this probably was the accentuation of "dominant pre-existing philosophical tendencies."[19] That is, some Jews who had not practiced in the past began to take religious traditions more seriously. Ruth Glaser described her confirmation in 1935 with ten other girls in white dresses—the first time in Düsseldorf that girls had ever been confirmed. She reflected on the way in which identities were shifting: "First one was a German and then a Jew. Now that we were reminded every day that we were Jewish, we became more aware of it. It became a comfort and something to hold onto and fight for."[20] Religion offered some a realm in which they could feel at home, safe from outside enmity. Synagogue attendance increased dramatically as Jews, depicted as evil and inferior by the government and media, sought balm for their raw nerves and affirmation of their identity. Joachim Prinz, a rabbi in Berlin, called his sermon on the night before the boycott of April 1, 1933, an "attempt at collective therapy."[21]

Other Jews turned toward Zionism, which had been a minority position within Jewish circles. In 1933 this changed and "a mass movement emerged out of the elite movement of German Zionism."[22] New subscribers purchased the Zionists' *Jüdischer Rundschau* looking for moral support. In the first few months of 1933, thousands of people streamed into the Palestine Office of the Zionist Organization in search of a new homeland. Between April 1933 and September 1934 the Haluz societies, or the German branch of the worldwide Zionist worker-pioneer organization, grew from 500 to over 15,000 members.[23]

Jews turned not only to Jewish family, friends, religion, or new ideologies to counter deprivations. Many gradually accommodated to hostility, hoping that the Nazis would go no further and grateful for small loopholes or exceptions. Abuse, insidiously and incrementally, became "normal" to some and familiar to all. A German-Jewish refugee to the United States echoed this sentiment: "I don't think one can ever see if something is on a steady acceleration. . . . the terror is steady and you live with it and you go right along with it. And you really crack only if it suddenly increases."[24] A mother of four, whose children had emigrated and urged her to leave, recalled: "we within the borders of Germany had once more adjusted ourselves to the prevailing conditions."[25] Some acclimated to changed circumstances because they had thicker skin and some because they held different interpretations and perceptions of the malicious behavior or dangers confronting them. Others tried to deaden their feelings, a recurrent theme in Victor Klemperer's diaries. He remarked upon the "unbelievable human capacity to endure and get accustomed," to the increasing cruelties of daily life.[26] Although coping with strained situations is an important human response, this adjustment may have exhausted some, distorting their perspective and harming their ability to make sound judgments about the overall situation.

Frequently it was an outsider, someone who had been out of the country for a couple of years, who could detect the increasing danger which those within the country, who had gradually become accustomed to daily restrictions, no longer saw as clearly. Bella Fromm's daughter, returning from the United States for the Olympics in the summer of 1936, told her mother: "I could not breathe here anymore." In 1937 a seventeen-year-old, whose parents had insisted that he flee while they stay, reported on his return for a visit: "It was 1937 and my parents wanted me back home for my summer vacation! This decision shows the supreme trust my parents, together with their fellow Jews, had in their government, despite what they saw happening around them. It showed how they had somehow accepted and adjusted themselves to the new conditions. Evidently they felt little risk in having their child return to a land that was about to explode."[27]

The Household

In the face of progressively worsening living conditions, it was women who were supposed to "make things work" in the family. Jewish housewives tried, where possible, to prepare less expensive meals, to repair their homes and clothing themselves, and to make do with less help around the house. The Nuremberg Laws (which forbade Jews from hiring female "Aryan" household help under the age of forty-five,) left most middle-class Jewish women entirely to their own devices in running a household with greater problems, in shopping for food in increasingly hostile stores, and in carrying out these tasks with ever-shrinking resources. Moreover, many took on paid work for the first time in their lives. Finally, Jewish women attempted to comfort frightened children and encourage family members in the face of harassment and unhappiness.

Women's organizations urged women to preserve the "moral strength to survive" and pointed to biblical heroines for role models.[28] Increasingly it became apparent that biblical role models would not suffice in providing Jewish women with either the spiritual courage or the practical help they needed. Jewish newspapers began to deal more openly (and perhaps more honestly) with the issues plaguing families, particularly women. For example, as families moved into smaller apartments, or as others took in boarders in order to make ends meet, tighter living quarters caused strain. The League of Jewish Women acknowledged this but, characteristically, urged women to absorb it.[29]

Cooking played a prominent role among issues causing stress because of tight budgets, limited household help, and the difficulties for religious Jews of acquiring kosher meat. Jewish newspapers advised housewives to consider vegetarian menus because they were cheaper, healthier, and avoided the kosher meat problem.[30] After the Nuremberg Laws, the *Central Verein Zeitung*, the newspaper of one of the major Jewish organizations, ran articles entitled "Everyone Learns to Cook" and "Even Peter Cooks . . ."[31] These articles emphasized how children, particularly daughters, could help their mothers.[32] "Daughter exchanges," another alternative to help overworked mothers, provided a half year's

71

training without pay to two young women who switched households.[33] In addition, some Jewish families hired young female relatives to help out, usually in exchange for pocket money, room, and board.[34]

Jewish husbands were expected to pitch in—but only minimally. This seems to have been a particularly sensitive point for women and men alike. When Erna Becker-Kohen found grocery shopping more and more difficult due to the hostility of neighbors and government regulations, her non-Jewish husband took over that burden. She was especially grateful to him for this role reversal, because he had hated going shopping before the Nazis came to power, considering it "unmanly."[35] The League of Jewish Women suggested that since women had to do more for their families and were often the sole support of families as well, men should begin to do some housework.[36] But, male—and female—resistance to such role reversals continued.[37] Moreover, some league members had little faith in men's competence even if they showed good will: "Jewish women cannot count on the practical support of husbands (Jewish men are not as handy as Aryan husbands)."[38] Most commonly, husbands were only asked to limit their expectations[39] and restrain their criticisms if the meals were not what they used to be; to try praising their wives once in a while; to close their eyes to some imperfections: "a husband must also adapt."[40] Thus gender privilege persisted, somewhat modulated, within the family, although conditions had changed profoundly, forcing many previously sheltered women to take on the entire burden of the household for the first time—often as they took on their first jobs as well.

To lighten household chores the League of Jewish Women preached "Spartan simplicity," and Jewish newspapers proclaimed the "gospel of scientific management," ceaselessly urging women to rationalize their households by organizing, streamlining, and cutting back on their tasks.[41] As late as 1938 women could also read articles suggesting that they purchase time- or energy-saving kitchen utensils.[42] Furthermore, advice columns counseled women to hire daily or hourly help where possible.[43] In what must have been desperation, they urged hiring young men to help in the household.[44] Yet rationalizing the household or hiring unconventional helpers was, at best, a partial answer to domestic stresses. Articles in Jewish newspapers addressed overworked, overwrought mothers. Written in the tradition of the psychoanalytic discourse of the 1920s and reworked by Jews in the dismal 1930s, these articles showed psychological and pedagogic sensitivity. They focused on deteriorating mother-child relationships. With titles like "Mommy,

Do You Have Time for Me?" and "Mommy Is So Nervous" they pleaded with mothers not to neglect their small children in their over-crowded days and to repress their outward nervousness by "pull[ing themselves] together if at all possible."[45]

These newspaper articles stand in stark contrast to many retrospective accounts. Whereas news articles chronicle stress, memoirs and inter-views often record action, accentuating the coping *behavior* that preoc-cupied Jews more than their feelings. Although feelings are not absent in memoirs, making them painful to read at times, they are the backdrop to a frenzy of activity. Newspapers, in contrast, in offering "solutions" to crises, actually document the enormous stress weighing on Jewish families, particularly housewives. It is hard to imagine that training daughters, streamlining work, taking on extra tasks, and repressing ner-vousness made life any easier. But then again, maybe exertion and re-pression *did* help some, not only to survive but to be able, in later years, to write a memoir of such anguishing times. Letters to a Jewish newspa-per in August 1938 by women who worked both outside and inside the home affirmed the stress and despair women experienced, but focused on action: "'[Y]ou have to do it' is the eleventh commandment for us all now."[46]

The psychological blow of Nazism affected all Jews deeply. In De-cember 1935 Dora Edinger, a leader of the Jewish women's movement, acknowledged in a letter: "[I]t is hard to bear, even though I had long anticipated it rationally. Again and again, it is something entirely differ-ent to know something and to experience it.[47] The League of Jewish Women acknowledged that "increased burdens oppress Jewish women," but urged that all new hardships should be met as "duties . . . with calm and presence of mind." Its leaders called on Jewish women to maintain the home and family and the honor of the Jewish community.[48]

Trying to protect themselves and their families from the gloom around them, women often engaged in denial of their immediate hard-ships. They did this through what psychologists called "adoption of temporary frames of security," for example in practical efforts, some even taking solace in additional housework burdens.[49] Although in a few cases such distraction may have kept the family from realizing just how significant the increasing deprivations were, some denial was neces-sary in order to preserve personal and family stability. Moreover, most people function on several levels at the same time. People could oc-cupy themselves with the details of daily life while still studying a language useful for emigration, pushing a reluctant spouse to consider emigration, or filling out the mountains of forms necessary to apply to emigrate.

Finding safety in the routines of housework was generally a female form of escapism. This usually lasted longer than the male version, escape by submerging in occupational activities, since many men lost their jobs and businesses. Women also joined voluntary organizations, studied foreign languages, or learned new skills in an effort to help the community and to "deaden [their] worries."[50] In retrospect, many women realized what they had been doing. Alice Baerwald made herself so busy setting up a Zionist youth emigration program in Danzig that she "forgot to dismantle my own life."[51] Mally Dienemann's response to the query How did one survive psychologically in Germany was: "[O]ne studied languages intensely and read a great deal, and with this intellectual diversion and preparing for new careers in handicrafts, one tried to deaden one's worries."[52] These were not only distractions or practical necessities, but "set our mind and spirit free."[53]

Gallows humor may have helped Jews as well. Many remarked on the frustrations of language training. If one studied Spanish or Portuguese to go to Latin America, sudden barriers to entry arose and one had to prepare for another country. If one turned to Hebrew, obstacles to acquiring the necessary certificates were certain to develop and one had to change to yet another language. Thus a joke made the rounds of one town: "'[W]hat language are you learning?' 'The wrong one, of course.'"[54] Children, too, turned to humor. A twelve-year-old in a home for "non-Aryan" children where lunch consisted of potatoes and vegetables called to his friends: "Now we're all vegetarians, so, from behind, we're 'Aryans!'"[55] Later this humor expressed more serious defiance. In 1941, Edith Wolff opposed the regime by writing postcards to Nazi headquarters and bureaucrats echoing a joke making the rounds of Berlin: "Germany is now called Braunschweig: one half is brown [Braun = Nazi uniforms] and the other half is silent [schweig = silence]."[56]

Role Reversals among Jewish Women and Men

Their normal lives and expectations overturned, Jewish families embarked on new paths and embraced new strategies that they would never have entertained in ordinary times. For women, this meant new roles as partner, as breadwinner, as family protector, and as defender of their businesses or practices. These were roles that were often strange to them, but ones that they had to assume if they were to save their families and property.

While managing their households entirely on their own or with minimal help, many women also retrained for vocations that would be useful in emigration. Some women prepared for several possible jobs and studied several different languages at once, assuming that they needed to be versatile should they emigrate. One woman studied English and took lessons in sewing furs, making chocolate, and doing industrial ironing. A mother and her daughter took courses in Spanish, English, baking, and fine cookery. Then they asked their laundress to accept them as her apprentices. This was not only a new role for them, but a reversal of their previous class position as well.[57] Many Jewish women who had never worked outside the home before suddenly needed paid employment. While some sought employment with strangers, others began to work for their husbands, who could no longer afford to pay employees. By 1938 there were "relatively few families in which the wife [did] not work in some way to earn a living."[58] Later that year Hannah Karminski, an officer of the League of Jewish Women, remarked: "The picture of a woman who supports her family's basic sustenance is typical."[59] Still the hope was that "work for married women is only and may only be an expedient in an emergency."[60] By proclaiming the crisis nature of women's new position, Jews, both male and female, could dream of better times and ignore the even more unsettling issue of changing gender roles in the midst of turmoil.

Role reversals were most pronounced where women found themselves representing or defending their men, as was increasingly the case. As early as 1933, a non-Jewish colleague suggested to Dr. Ernst Mueller and his wife Liselotte that because Ernst "had such a Jewish nose," she should appeal to a prominent non-Jewish doctor, Dr. Kleine at the Robert Koch Institute, on behalf of her husband. Discouraged by political events, Ernst agreed that his wife should represent him. When Dr. Kleine interviewed Liselotte, he asked why her husband had not come himself and she began to cry, explaining the circumstances. The doctor thereupon invited them both to dinner. "When I told Ernst about the dinner invitation, he felt as if a miracle had happened. How quickly one's outlook changes! A short time before he would not have considered it a miracle to be invited by a non-Jewish doctor."[61]

Many incidents have been recorded of women who saved family members from the arbitrary demands of the state or from the Gestapo.

In these cases, it was always assumed that the Nazis would not break gender norms: they might arrest or torture Jewish men, but would not harm women. Thus women took on a more assertive role in the public sphere than ever before.[62] In one small town, a Jewish family decided to send two of its women to the city hall in order to ask that part of their house not be used as a meeting place for the Nazi Party. They were successful.[63] Other women interceded for family members with German emigration or finance officials. In some cases they broke not only gender barriers but also normal standards of legality. Many memoirs report that Nazi officials had to be bribed and that, despite their original shock at such requirements, women quickly caught on.[64] Some women actually took responsibility for the entire family's safety, a reversal of previous roles with their husbands. Liselotte Mueller traveled to Palestine to assess the situation there. Her husband, who could not leave his medical practice, simply told her: "If you decide you would like to live in Palestine, I will like it too." She chose Greece. Her husband, older and more educated than she, who in other circumstances had been the decision maker, agreed.[65] Ann Lewis's mother went to England to negotiate her family's emigration with British officials and her medical colleagues. This decision was based on her fluency in English, her desire to meet members of her psychoanalytic profession herself, and her husband's profession—as a medical doctor he was not welcome in Britain but she still was. She, who had always been "reserved with strangers," and for whom asking favors "did not come easily," had to ask for letters of recommendation from British psychiatrists and to apply to the Home Office for residence and work permits. Although her husband had been the one to choose England, it was she who decided where the family would reside.[66]

Women had to call upon assertiveness they did not know they possessed. After traveling to the United States to convince reluctant and distant relatives to give her family an affidavit, one woman had to confront the American Embassy in Stuttgart, which insisted that there was no record of her. She showed her receipts but the secretary just shrugged. At closing time she refused to leave, insisting that her husband's, mother's, and children's lives depended on their chance to go to the United States. She would spend as many days and nights in the waiting room as necessary until they found her documents. After much discussion the consul ordered a search of the files and the documents were discovered. Today her daughter refers to her mother as the "first sit in."[67]

Women often faced routine danger and dramatic situations, requiring both bravery and luck. Twenty-year-old Ruth Abraham urged her parents to move to Berlin to escape the hostility in their small town. The Nazis permitted this move only if the father promised to appear at Gestapo headquarters weekly. Ruth always accompanied her father to these perilous interrogations. When her uncle was arrested in Düsseldorf, she hurried from jail to jail until she found out where he was. Then she appealed to a judge who seemed attracted to her. He requested that she come to his home in the evening, where he would give her a release form. Knowing that she risked a sexual demand or worse, she entered his home. The judge treated her politely and signed the release. She commented in her memoir: "I must add, that I look absolutely 'Aryan,' that I have blond hair and blue eyes, a straight nose and am tall." Later these traits would save her life in hiding; now she was able to gain the interest or sympathy of men who did not want to believe that she was Jewish.[68]

The judge's treatment of Abraham notwithstanding, traditional sexual conventions could be quite menacing. Despite increasing propaganda about "racial pollution" or "racial defilement" (*Rassenschande*), Jewish women recorded frightening incidents in which "Aryans," even Nazis, made advances toward them. In one small town, a young single woman became troubled about her safety on the streets at night. "In daylight they reviled me as a Jewish woman and at night they wanted to kiss me. The whole society disgusted me."[69] Another woman wrote of the perils of sexual encounters: "During the Hitler era I had the immense burden of rejecting brazen advances from SS and SA men. They often pestered me and asked for dates. Each time I answered: 'I'm sorry, that I can't accept, I'm married. . . .' If I had said I was Jewish, they would have turned the tables and insisted that I had approached them."[70]

Sometimes overcoming the stereotypes of female passivity or sexual availability meant confronting still other obstacles rooted in gender conventions. A social worker from Breslau attempted to have her new husband released from prison in June of 1938. Convinced of his innocence, she appealed to his friend, a lawyer, for help. This man warned her that "when a woman is married for six weeks only, she does not know anything of the previous life of her husband." She wrote: "All these shocks undermine your self-confidence and . . . confidence in the world and in the goodness of men."[71] She held tenaciously to her opinion that the wrong man had been arrested, proved it, and saved her husband.

Women's new roles may have increased stress in some cases, but in general both women and men appreciated the importance of the new behavior. Edith Bick summed up the situation: "[I]n the Hitler times . . . I had to take over, which I never did before. Never." Her husband "didn't like it." But "he not only accepted it. He was thankful."[72] As conditions worsened, role reversals became ever more common. Women forced themselves to behave in "unwomanly" ways, some putting up a strong front when men despaired. One woman struggled to retain her self-control for the sake of her children as her husband sank into a deep depression. He could no longer sleep: "He stopped eating, as he said no one had the right to eat when he did not work and became . . . so despondent that it resulted in a deep depression . . . . He feared we would all starve . . . and all his self assurance was gone. . . . These were terrible days for me, added to all the other troubles, and forever trying to keep up my chin for the children's sake." They decided to send the children away because it was not good for them to see their father in such a state and because they were also being constantly humiliated at school.[73]

Many women remarked upon the issue of self-control—its loss or its retention. They saw self-control as an attempt to retain the families' dignity and equilibrium in the face of dishonor and persecution. Probably men rarely describe this kind of behavior because they took it for granted, while women, previously allowed and encouraged to be the more "emotional" sex, were particularly conscious of their own efforts at self-control and their husbands' fragility.[74]

THE EMIGRATION QUANDARY

Assessing and Deciding

As emigration became more and more crucial, women usually saw the danger signals first and urged their husbands to flee Germany. I have discussed the reasons for this and the ensuing family tensions elsewhere,[75] but Peter Wyden's summary of the debates within his own and other Jewish families in Berlin can be seen as representative:

It was not a bit unusual in these go-or-no-go family dilemmas for the women to display more energy and enterprise than the men. . . . Almost no women had a business, a law office, or a medical practice to lose. They were less status-conscious, less money-oriented than the men. They seemed to be less rigid, less cautious, more confident of their ability to flourish on new turf and, if necessary (at least this was true in my cocky mother's case), to find another man who would support them or make an effective partner.[76]

The Berlin artist Charlotte Salomon, who painted a stunning exploration of her life during 1941–42 while awaiting her fate in southern France, also summed up this predicament in her typically ironic way. In one painting, she depicted her short grandmother looking up to her tall grandfather, whose head is above the frame of the painting. The caption reads: "Grossmama in 1933: 'Not a minute longer will I stay here. I'm telling you let's leave this country as fast as we can; my judgment says so.' Her husband almost loses his head."[77]

Regardless of gender differences in picking up warning signals, it is crucial to realize that these occurred in stages that could fool both women and men. At first many Jews saw a renewal of legal discrimination as a return to the recent past. The Weimar Republic had abolished the last of Jewish civic disabilities in 1919. Only slowly did they realize that Germany was not moving backward, toward territory they once knew and endured, but was heading in an entirely new direction. Even then Alice Nauen recalled her own behavior which, I would argue, can be generalized to many others.[78] She and her friends "saw it was getting worse. But until 1939 nobody in our circles believed it would lead to an end" for German Jewry.[79] Nazi policies and events could confuse anyone. Moreover, the signals Jews had to decipher were often profoundly mixed, again bewildering both men and women. When Hanna Bernheim's sister who had emigrated to France returned for a visit in the mid 1930s, the sister wanted to know why the Bernheims remained in their south German town rather than flee. Hanna Bernheim replied: "First of all it is so awfully hard for our old, sick father to be left by all his four children. Second there are so many dissatisfied people in all classes, professions and trades. Third there was the Roehm Purge and an army shake up. And that makes me believe that people are right who told us 'Wait for one year longer and the Nazi government will be blown up!'"[80] Random kindnesses, the most obvious "mixed signals," gave some Jews cause for hope. One woman wrote that every Jewish person "knew a decent German" and recalled that many Jews thought "the radical Nazi laws would never be carried out because they did not match the moderate character of the German people."[81]

That men and women often assessed the dangers differently reflected their different contacts and frames of reference. But decisions seem to have been made by husbands—or, later, by circumstances. Despite some important role reversals, both men and women generally held fast to traditional gender roles in actual decision making unless they were overwhelmed by events.

The prejudice that women were "hysterical" in the face of danger or exaggerated fearful situations worked to everyone's disadvantage. Charlotte Stein-Pick had begged her father to flee in March 1933. Only moments before the SS arrived to arrest him, her husband brought him to the train. Not aware of the SS visit, her husband returned home to say: "[A]ctually, it was entirely unnecessary that your parents left, but I supported you because you were worrying yourself so much."[82] Stein-Pick also overheard a private conversation in a train on November 6, 1938, in which the participants discussed what was about to happen to Jewish men in two days. "When I arrived home I implored my husband and a friend who lived with us to leave . . . immediately. . . . But my counsel was in vain. They believed my nerves had given way: how should these people have known anything and one could not have built camps big enough."[83] Another husband believed his wife to be completely overwrought when she suggested—in 1932—that he deposit some money in a Swiss bank. Cabaret artists were already joking about people taking trips to visit their money in Switzerland, but her husband refused. In this case, the belief that women were not supposed to be involved in business matters further complicated the situation, making her suggestions even less likely to be heeded.[84]

Not only were men inclined to trust their own political perceptions more than their wives', but their role and status as breadwinner and head of household both contributed to their hesitancy to emigrate and gave them the authority to say no. Else Gerstel fought "desperately" with her husband of twenty-three years to emigrate. Fearful that he would not find a job abroad, he refused to leave, insisting: "[T]here is as much demand for Roman law over there as the eskimos have for freezers." "I was in constant fury," she wrote, representing their dispute as a great strain on their marriage.[85]

A combination of events usually led to the final—by then, joint—decision to leave and, as conditions worsened, women sometimes took the lead. In early 1938 one daughter reported that her mother "applied to the American authorities for a quota number without my father's knowledge; the hopeless number of 33,243 was allocated. It was a last desperate act and Papa did not even choke with anger anymore." (Her parents and young brother were deported and killed.)[86] Still another woman responded to narrowly escaping battering by a Nazi mob in her small hometown by convincing her husband to "pack their things throughout the night and leave this hell just the next day."[87] After the November 1938 pogrom, there were wives who broke all family conventions by taking over the decision making when it was unequivocally clear to them that their husbands' reluctance to leave Germany would result in even worse horrors. Else Gerstel recalled that although her husband had been arrested on November 9, he did not have to go to a camp and still "had no intention of leaving Germany, but I sent a telegram to my brother Hans in New York . . . 'please send affidavit.' "[88]

Facing Closed Doors and Poverty

One of the chief objectives of Nazi policies toward the Jews between 1935 and September 1939 had been to foster emigration, once called "the territorial final solution." A series of plans with titles such as "Syrian project," "Madagascar Plan," "Ecuador project," and the "Haavara Transfer" were devised to deposit Germany's unwanted Jews around the globe.[89] The government urged individual emigration as well. Jewish agencies, in particular the *Hilfsverein der deutschen Juden*, the *Hauptstelle für Jüdische Wanderfürsorge*, and the *Palästina Amt*, advised Jews on emigration possibilities, obtaining visas, and financial aid, and the Jewish press ran articles detailing emigration possibilities. Jews had to confront a bewildering array of countries, requirements, and details. Peter Wyden remembered that the language around his house changed between 1935 and 1937:

> Our future had come to depend on three new guideposts: "the quota"—the total number of German refugees permitted to enter the United States under the miserly immigration laws; "the affidavit"—the document from an obscure umpteenth cousin . . . guaranteeing that he would support us if we became destitute; and "the visa"—which would be our stamped admission ticket into the promised land. . . . Beyond [these words] everyone learned about the "*Zertifikat*" from the British authorities to enter Palestine; the Reich Flight Tax that had to be paid to the Nazis as an exit fine . . . and the "certificate of harmlessness" required before one could cross the border.[90]

Profound obstacles to emigration existed. During the worldwide depression of the 1930s, foreign countries restricted immigration. In July 1938 the thirty-two nations assembled at the Evian Conference "regretted" that they could not take in more Jews. The *New York Herald Tribune* concluded: "Powers Slam Doors against German Jews."[91] Those few countries with open doors needed farmers, not middle-class professionals and businesspeople. The German-Jewish age distribution also limited emigration, since German Jews were disproportionately old.[92] No country wanted middle-aged and elderly people who often decided not to become burdens on their children or relatives.

The Nazis created another major obstacle by restricting the amount of currency and property Jews could take with them. The plunder of Jewish property was part and parcel of all emigration proceedings. The Nazis "pressured Jews to leave the country, but the privilege of leaving was expensive."[93] The Reich flight tax (*Reichsfluchtsteuer*), a stringent property tax on emigrés, threatened to impoverish prospective emigrants. First passed by the Brüning government in 1931 to prevent capital flight, the Nazis raised it to punitive heights for emigrating Jews.[94] The Reich flight tax provided the German government with 1 million Reichsmarks in 1932–33 and with 342 million Reichsmarks in 1938–39. In all, the German treasury may have gained as much as 900 million Reichsmarks from it alone.[95] Many people had to sell all of their belongings simply to meet this particular tax requirement. Gerdy Stoppleman, for example, sent her husband, recently released from Sachsenhausen concentration camp, ahead to England while she stayed behind to pay the tax. "To be able to pay the . . . tax I sold our furniture, valuable paintings and carpets, etc., dirt cheap. Many a home of true Aryans, S.A. and S.S. became exceedingly well furnished."[96]

Before long the Nazis blocked the bank accounts of Jews (first in 1936 and later more severely) and forbade them to send money abroad (in 1936). This meant that emigrants could not transfer the remainder of their (after-tax) money abroad but had to deposit it in "blocked accounts in marks for prospective emigrants." From these accounts, they could buy foreign currency—at a very unfavorable exchange rate, amounting to a further punitive tax. Until 1935 the exchange rate stood at half the official market rate of the mark; thereafter the government steadily pushed it downward. By 1939 Jews could buy foreign currency worth only 4 percent of the value of their blocked German money. The Nazis forbade all transfers of money when war broke out.[97] Thus emigrating Jews lost 30 to 50 percent of their capital in the years 1933–1937 and 60 to 100 percent between 1937 and 1939.[98] For many, it became harder and harder to leave because new laws every few months robbed them of the means to start a new life elsewhere.[99] Under these conditions individuals and families hesitated to hurry abroad, and yet the more they hesitated, the more conditions deteriorated.

What these laws meant in terms of people's everyday reality can be seen in the memoirs of Ann Lewis, whose parents tried to leave in 1937. By then, "the sum my parents received in sterling was less than a quarter of what it would have been at the official rate. When the transfer to their English bank had been completed their 27,000 marks had become only £450 instead of the £2,160 which they would have obtained if their funds had been exchanged at what was then the normal rate." Due to this poor transfer rate her parents decided to buy everything they could in Germany, because they would barely have the means for subsistence once they arrived in England: "Nothing would be bought in England that could possibly be brought from Germany, and that applied not only to furniture and other household goods but also to items such as soap and other toilet articles . . . stationery, medical supplies, and of course enough clothes to last us for the next few years."[100]

Jews also faced plunder by individual, corrupt bureaucrats. Gestapo agents, civil servants, packers, and even individuals in foreign consulates demanded bribes and tributes of every sort.[101] "We have come to see what you may take with you when you leave," said two Gestapo agents, transparent in their greed. Lola Blonder responded: "Feel free to look around." She added in her memoirs: "They looked and took whatever little objects they liked—from the wall . . . from the tables. . . . I was used to this by now. Whenever a group of Nazis visited, they helped themselves to . . . valuables. Robbing, robbing! Every day robbing me!"[102] The story of how individual Germans enriched themselves from the theft of Jewish property still needs to be told. Many government officials were highly corrupt, seemingly relishing their new roles, hardly the banal bureaucrats who were just "taking orders."

Material booty collected by the government and individuals was still not the worst of it. The government also limited Jewish mobility in 1937 by the issuance of passports for emigration only. The regime forbade information trips intended to assess the possibilities available in another country, and only people who were ill or visiting children studying abroad could leave and return.[103] Perhaps the major barrier to emigration for most was not having relatives or friends abroad who could sponsor admission into a country of refuge. For those with no contacts, applying abroad for positions as domestic servants became an important

83

route of escape—especially, but not only, for women. Mountains of paperwork had to be completed in order to find such refuge, and the committees in charge of these matters sternly demanded "qualifications" (so that their reputations would be enhanced in order to assist others). Besides photos, autobiographies, school transcripts, and health certificates, individuals needed proof that they were experienced at or capable of domestic service.[104] Then, after being accepted by a potential employer, the required emigration paperwork began.

Despite all hindrances, Jewish emigration was far from negligible, although it took an uneven course. About 37,000 Jews left Germany in 1933.[105] More discrimination, however, was not matched by more emigration. In 1934, 23,000 fled. By early 1935, however, about 10,000 had returned due to the increasing difficulties of middle-class Jewish emigrés abroad who were sliding into poverty. Return emigration halted after the Nazis threatened internment in a concentration camp for returnees in early 1935. By the end of that year (after the Nuremberg Laws) about 21,000 had emigrated.[106] Another 25,000 left Germany in 1936, followed by 23,000 in 1937. With increasing persecution in 1938 another 40,000 emigrated. The first wave of refugees fled to neighboring countries, probably hoping to return home at some point or to continue abroad if necessary. The proportion of the total number of emigrants who fled overseas grew dramatically as the conditions in Europe worsened in the later 1930s.[107]

Statistics give the false impression that Jews smoothly managed to leave Germany and enter the country of their choice. They cover up the individual stories which describe complicated emigration attempts, failures, and new attempts. For example, one family in Leipzig first decided to go to Palestine. The father, who had owned a silverware shop, trained to become a painter. By the time he received his diploma from the Leipzig League of Painters there were too many applications to Palestine. The family next considered Chile and the Dominican Republic, but these did not work out either. Finally, the father wrote to a sister in Brooklyn and his family received a U.S. affidavit in 1937.[108] As the already-mentioned joke about language training alerts us, accounts were legion of Jews having to switch languages in the middle of their studies, because emigration to that spot had just become impossible.[109] Still, before 1938 a significant proportion—about one-quarter—of German Jews left, answering the question posed by one husband to his wife, "Could you really leave all this behind you to enter nothingness?"[110] with a resounding affirmative.

Fleeing after the Pogrom

The Harvard psychologists who studied refugee memoirs determined that almost 40 percent of memoir writers did not give up psychologically until 1938 or 1939. The November pogrom decisively tipped the balance toward emigration for those who were still confused or uncertain. For those in camps, the only way out was proof of readiness to emigrate. And for those not in camps, the violence influenced their decisions.[111] It was only after the brutality of the pogrom that Jews were finally convinced that they faced physical danger. After November 1938, "essentially everyone tried to find a possibility of emigrating."[112]

Still, immigration restrictions in foreign countries and Nazi bureaucratic and financial roadblocks stymied Jews. Countries of potential refuge thwarted Jewish entry. Elisabeth Freund described the many attempts she and her husband made to leave Germany:

> It is really enough to drive one to despair. . . . We have filed applications for entry permits to Switzerland, Denmark, and Sweden. . . . in vain, though in all these countries we had good connections. In the spring of 1939 . . . we obtained an entry permit for Mexico for 3,000 marks. But we never received the visa, because the Mexican consulate asked us to present passports that would entitle us to return to Germany, and the German authorities did not issue such passports to Jews. Then, in August 1939 we did actually get the permit for England. But it came . . . only ten days before the outbreak of war, and in this short time we were not able to take care of all the formalities. . . . In the spring of 1940 we received the entry permit for Portugal. We immediately got everything ready and applied for our passports. Then came the invasion of Holland, Belgium and France. . . . A stream of refugees poured into Portugal, and the Portuguese government recalled . . . all of the issued permits. . . . It was also good that in December 1940 we had not . . . paid for our Panamanian visas, for we noticed that the visas offered us did not . . . entitle us to land in Panama.

Freund was frustrated with friends who urged them to leave Germany: "As if that were not our most fervent wish." She agonized: "There are no more visas for the U.S.A. My husband has made one last attempt and asked our relatives in America by wire for the entry visas for Cuba. . . . No other country gives an entry permit to German Jews any longer, or is still reachable in any way."[113]

Once they received permission to enter a foreign country, Jews still had to acquire the papers to exit Germany. "Getting out . . . is at least as difficult as getting into another country and you have absolutely no notion of the desperation here," wrote sixty-six-year-old Gertrud Grossmann to her uncomprehending son abroad. Getting the required papers took months of running a bureaucratic gauntlet which many women, whose husbands remained in camps, faced alone. They met officials who could arbitrarily add to the red tape at whim: "[T]here was no rule and every official felt like a god."[114] Mally Dienemann, whose sixty-three-year-old husband languished in Buchenwald, raced to the Gestapo to prove they were ready to emigrate. Next she rushed to the passport office to retrieve their passports.

> After I had been sent from one office to another. . . . I had to go to . . . the Emigration Office in Frankfurt, the Gestapo, the Police, the Finance Office, [send] a petition to Buchenwald, a petition to the Gestapo in Darmstadt, and still it took until Tuesday of the third week, before my husband returned. . . . Next came running around for the many papers that one needed for emigration. And while the Gestapo was in a rush, the Finance Office had so much time and so many requests, and without certification from the Finance and Tax offices . . . one did not get a passport, and without a passport a tariff official could not inspect the baggage.[115]

Finally arriving in Palestine in March 1939, Rabbi Dienemann died from his ordeal. By that year new arbitrary laws slowed emigration still more. Peter Gay recalled "the energetic efforts my parents made to flee Nazi Germany . . . and the steps my father undertook, bold, illegal and dangerous, to take us to safety in late April 1939, the last refugees allowed to land in Havana."[116] This situation deteriorated to such an extent by 1940 that Gertrud Grossmann wrote her son who had left in 1938: "Your emigration was child's play compared to today's practically insurmountable difficulties."[117]

Who Remained in Germany?

That women wanted to leave Germany well before their men does not mean that more women than men actually left. To the contrary, fewer women than men left Germany. Why was this so? In part, there were still compelling reasons to stay. First, women could still find jobs as teachers in Jewish schools or as social workers, nurses, and administrators in Jewish social service institutions, or as clerical workers for the Jewish community. Hedwig Burgheim, for example, found challenging and important work. In 1933, she was forced to resign as director of a teacher training institute in Giessen. Thereafter she directed the Leipzig Jewish community's School for Kindergarten Teachers and Domestic Services, which trained young people for vocations useful in lands of emigration. After the November pogrom, her own attempts at emigration having failed, she taught at the Jewish school and, by 1942, headed the old-age home in Leipzig. Along with its residents, she was deported in early 1943 and died in Auschwitz. Dr. Martha Wertheimer, a journalist before 1933, also found her skills in demand thereafter. She plunged into Jewish welfare work and escorted many children's transports to England. Ultimately she wrote a friend in New York that, despite efforts to emigrate, she was no longer waiting to escape: "[A] great dark calm has entered me, as the saying of our fathers goes '*Gam zu le'tovah*' ('this, too, is for the best')." She continued: "It is also worthwhile to be an officer on the sinking ship of Jewish life in Germany, to hold out courageously and to fill the life boats, to the extent that we have some."[118]

While the employment situation of Jewish women helped keep them in Germany, that of men helped get them out. Some men had business connections abroad, facilitating their immediate flight, and others emigrated alone in order to establish themselves and then send for their families.[119] A handful of men, some with wives, received visas to leave Europe from groups hoping to save eminent intellectuals and artists. Women's organizations agreed that, if there was no choice, wives should not "hinder" husbands from emigrating alone, but they argued that it was often no cheaper for men to emigrate without their wives.

Before the war, more men than women faced immediate physical danger, another reason to leave rapidly. After the November pogrom, in a strange twist of fortune, the men interned in concentration camps were released only upon showing proof of their ability to leave Germany immediately. Families—mostly wives and mothers—strained every resource to provide the documentation to free these men and send them on their way while some of the women remained behind. Alice Nauen recalled how difficult these emigration decisions were for Jewish leaders: "Should we send the men out first? This had been the dilemma all along. . . . If you have two tickets, do you take one man out of the concentration camp and his wife who is at this moment safe? Or do you take your two men out of the concentration camp? They took two men out . . . because they said we cannot play God, but these are in immediate danger." Even as women feared for their men, they believed that they themselves would be spared serious harm by the Nazis. In retrospect,

Ruth Klüger reflected on this kind of thinking and the resulting preponderance of women caught in the trap: "[O]ne seemed to ignore what was most obvious, namely how imperiled precisely the weaker and the socially disadvantaged are. That the Nazis should stop at women contradicted their racist ideology. Had we, as the result of an absurd, patriarchal short circuit, perhaps counted on their chivalry?"[120]

Parents sent sons into the unknown more readily than daughters. Bourgeois parents worried about a daughter traveling alone, believing boys would be safer. Families also assumed that sons needed to establish economic futures for themselves whereas daughters would marry.[121] As more and more sons left, daughters remained as the sole caretakers for elderly parents. One female commentator noted the presence of many women "who can't think of emigration because they don't know who might care for their elderly mothers . . . before they could start sending them money. In the same families, the sons went their way." Leaving one's aging parent—as statistics indicate, usually the mother—was the most painful act imaginable. Ruth Glaser described her own mother's agony at leaving her mother to join her husband, who had been forbidden reentry into Germany: she "could not sleep at night thinking of leaving her [mother] behind." Men, too, felt such grief, but proportionately more left nonetheless. Charlotte Stein-Pick wrote of her husband's anguish: "This abandonment of his old parents depressed him deeply. . . . He never got over this farewell. . . . To be sure, he saw that we could never have helped them, only shared their fate. I almost believe he would have preferred it."[122]

As early as 1936, the League of Jewish Women noted that far fewer women than men were leaving and worried that Jewish men of marriageable age would intermarry abroad, leaving Jewish women behind in Germany with no chance of marrying.[123] As late as January 1938, one of the main emigration organizations, the *Hilfsverein*, announced that "up to now, Jewish emigration . . . indicates a severe surplus of men." Blaming this on the "nature" of women to feel closer to family and home and on that of men toward greater adventurousness, it promised that women's emigration would become a priority. Yet only two months later, the society announced it would expedite the emigration of only those young women who could prove their household skills and were willing to work as domestics abroad.[124] Jewish organizations also provided less financial support to emigrating women than to men.[125]

The growing disproportion of Jewish women in the German-Jewish population also resulted because there more Jewish women than men in

Germany to start. In 1933, 52.3 percent of Jews were women, resulting from such factors as male casualties during World War I, greater marrying out and conversion among Jewish men, and greater longevity among women. In order to stay even, a greater absolute number of women would have had to emigrate. The slower rate of female than male emigration, however, meant that the female proportion of the Jewish population rose from 52.3 percent in 1933 to 57.5 percent by 1939. In 1939 one woman wrote:

> Mostly we were women who had been left to ourselves. In part, our husbands had died from shock, partly they had been processed from life to death in a concentration camp and partly some wives who, aware of the greater danger to their husbands, had prevailed upon them to leave at once and alone. They were ready to take care of everything and to follow their husbands later on, but because of the war it became impossible for many to realize this intention and quite a few of my friends and acquaintances thus became martyrs of Hitler.[126]

A large proportion of these remaining women were elderly. Age, even more than being female, worked against timely flight. Together they were lethal. Between June 1933 and September 1939, the number of Jews in Germany under age thirty-nine decreased by about 80 percent. In contrast, the number of people over sixty decreased by only 27 percent. By 1939 the proportion of people over sixty had increased to 32 percent of the Jewish population and by 1941, two-thirds of the Jewish population were past middle age. In Berlin alone, the number of Jewish old-age homes increased from three in 1933 to thirteen in 1939 and to twenty-one in 1942. Even in 1933, the elderly had consisted of a large number of widows, the ratio being 1,400 Jewish women over the age of sixty-five to 1,000 men. By 1937–38, 59 percent of the recipients of Jewish Winter Relief aged forty-five and over were female. In 1939, 6,674 widowed men and 28,347 widowed women remained in the expanded Reich.[127] When Elisabeth Freund, one of the last Jews to leave Germany legally in October 1941, went to the Gestapo for her final papers, she observed "all old people, old women" waiting on line.[128]

Historians who study the Nazis tend to argue that their Jewish policy was either part of a methodical plan (the intentionalist approach) or haphazard, contradictory, and the result of internal bureaucratic dynamics (the functionalist approach). Most recently, the debate has focused on the peculiar character of German antisemitism: its wish to "eliminate"

Jews which led to their extermination by "willing executioners."[129] These debates stem from the bias of looking at the killers. When one examines the hapless victims of these policies the debates pale; they are not something the victims lived. What is striking in the victims' accounts is not whether the Nazis intended the destruction of the Jews due to their unmitigated and unparalleled hatred or whether they backed into it, but the speed *and* the ambiguities of the attack against Jewish life and the speed *and* the ambivalence with which Jews adapted in the years before 1938. Jews thought about and prepared for emigration all the while hoping they would not have to leave their homeland. Although there were many deprivations and humiliations, until November 1938 the majority of Jews attempted to adjust to the new circumstances, clinging to mixed signals, hoping that the regime would fall or its anti-semitic policies would ease. Hindsight may make everything seem inevitable but, at the time, even the November pogrom did not provide a clear indicator of the genocide to come.

Still, between 270,000 and 300,000 Jews managed to flee Germany, about three-fifths of German Jewry. These facts notwithstanding, it has been common, from hindsight, to criticize German Jews for not having emigrated quickly enough, for hoping that they could remain in Germany, for loving Germany too much, for not seeing the writing on the wall. This is a profound and cruel distortion. Condemning Jews for not having left in time fails to acknowledge how unimaginable Nazism was to most contemporary observers or how earnestly Jews tried to emigrate after the November pogrom when the danger was apparent. Although many German Jews did love Germany and did not want to leave at first, many more could not leave. Those who could not were trapped by their obligations or their economic and social circumstances. In any case, perceptions by Jews of their predicament—either before or after 1938— were never the crucial factors affecting emigration. A bureaucratic gauntlet and Nazi plunder, creating the specter of abject poverty abroad, discouraged many, but most important, as we know, the lands of refuge heartlessly slammed their doors.

NOTES

This essay, with minor editions, is reprinted from *Enlightenment, Passion, Modernity: Historical Essays in European Thought and Culture*, edited by Mark S.

Micale and Robert L. Dietle, with the permission of the publishers, Stanford University Press. Copyright © 1999 by the Board of Trustees of the Leland Stanford Junior University.

1. Inge Deutschkron, *Outcast: A Jewish Girl in Wartime Berlin* (New York, 1989), 7, 14.

2. G. W. Allport, J. S. Bruner, and E. M. Jandorf, "Personality under Social Catastrophe: Ninety Life-Histories of the Nazi Revolution," *Character and Personality: An International Psychological Quarterly* 10, no. 1 (September 1941): 14–15.

3. Ibid., 14.

4. "Laura Pelz" in Douglas Morris, "The Lives of Some Jewish Germans Who Lived in Nazi Germany and Live in Germany Today: An Oral History" (B.A. Thesis, Wesleyan University, 1976).

5. Rudolf Lennert, "Zugehörigkeit, Selbstbewusstsein, Fremdheit," *Neue Sammlung* (1986), 393, quoted by Frank Stern, *The Whitewashing of the Yellow Badge: Antisemitism and Philosemitism in Postwar Germany,* trans. William Templer (Oxford, 1992), 37.

6. Peter Gay, "The German-Jewish Legacy—and I: Some Personal Reflections," in *The German-Jewish Legacy in America, 1938–1988,* ed. Abraham J. Peck (Detroit, 1989), 19. See also Peter Gay, *My German Question: Growing Up in Nazi Berlin* (New Haven, 1998).

7. Marion Gardner, in *"Vergessen kann man das nicht": Wittener Jüdinnen und Juden unter dem Nationalsozialismus,* ed. Martina Kliner-Lintzen and Siegfried Pape (Bochum, 1991), 299.

8. Verena Hellwig, Harvard ms., p. 30. The Harvard manuscripts come from the Houghton Library, Harvard University. They are found in the collection BMS GER 91, written for the contest "Mein Leben in Deutschland vor und nach dem 30. Januar 1933." Publication of all citations is by permission of the Houghton Library.

9. Lisa Brauer, memoirs, Leo Baeck Institute, New York (hereafter LBI), 38.

10. Allport, Bruner, and Jandorf, "Personality under Social Catastrophe," 14.

11. Mally Dienemann, Harvard ms., 25.

12. Max Reiner, in *Sie durften nicht mehr Deutsche sein: Jüdischer Alltag in Selbstzeugnissen, 1933–1938,* ed. Margarete Limberg and Hubert Rübsaat (Frankfurt and New York, 1990), 156. See also Monika Richarz, ed., *Jewish Life in Germany: Memoirs from Three Centuries,* trans. Stella and Sidney Rosenfeld (Bloomington, 1991), 402.

13. Reiner, in Limberg and Rübsaat, eds., *Sie durften nicht mehr Deutsche sein,* 156.

14. Ruth Glaser, memoirs, LBI, 15–16.

15. Lisa Grubel (vacation in 1937), memoirs, LBI, 15.

16. Mrs. Elly Busse, Berne, Switzerland, told Atina Grossmann that she phoned stores in order to avoid showing the J on her identification card (even though she was an "Aryan" married to a Jew). April 1993.

17. Barbara Händler-Lachmann, Harald Händler, and Ulrich Schütt, *Purim, Purim ihr liebe Leut, wisst ihr was Purim bedeut?* (Marburg, 1995). See photo of the Hahn family eating in their sukkah in 1936, 125.

18. About one-third of the respondents to the Harvard study, for example, turned to religion for comfort. Sixty-eight percent of the respondents considered themselves Jewish, although some of the Christians were converts from Judaism. Allport, Bruner, and Jandorf, "Personality under Social Catastrophe."

19. Ibid., 16.

20. Ruth Glaser, memoirs, LBI, 16–17.

21. Joachim Prinz, "A Rabbi under the Hitler Regime," in *Gegenwart im Rückblick*, ed. Kurt Grossmann and Herbert Strauss (Heidelberg, 1970); Max Nussbaum, "Ministry under Stress, A Rabbi's Recollection of Nazi Berlin, 1935–40," in Grossmann and Strauss, eds., *Gegenwart.*

22. Benno Cohn, "Einige Bemerkungen über den Deutschen Zionismus nach 1933," in *Zwei Welten*, ed. Hans Tramer (Tel Aviv, 1962), 45.

23. Norman Bentwich, *Jewish Youth Comes Home: The Story of the Youth Aliyah, 1933–1943* (London, 1944), 25; Cohn, "Einige Bemerkungen über den Deutschen Zionismus," 48.

24. Alice Nauen, interview, Research Foundation for Jewish Immigration, New York, 10. For many Germans, awareness of the regime's cruel intentions also came "drip by drip, rather like an anesthetic. . . . It was only after it hit you personally that you knew what was going on." Christabel Bielenburg, interview in the film "World at War: A New Germany" (1977).

25. Elizabeth Bamberger in *Women of Exile: German-Jewish Autobiographies since 1933*, ed. Andreas Lixl-Purcell (Westport, Conn., 1988), 92.

26. Victor Klemperer, *Ich will Zeugnis ablegen* (Berlin, 1995), 1:24, 26, 66, 2:104, 191, 654.

27. Bella Fromm, *Blood and Banquets: A Berlin Social Diary* (London, 1942), 197; Charles Marks, memoirs, LBI, 8.

28. *Blätter des Jüdischen Frauenbundes* (hereafter *BJFB*), February 1935, 12.

29. *BJFB*, July 1938, 13.

30. *Israelitisches Familienblatt* (hereafter *IF*), 25 June 1936.

31. *Central Verein Zeitung* (hereafter *CV*), 27 February 1936. See also *IF*, 19 March 1936.

32. "Junge Mädels lernen der Mutter helfen," *CV*, 9 April 1936; "Häusliche Erziehung," *IF*, 21 May 1936.

33. *IF*, 19 March 1936.

34. Ruth Glaser, memoirs, LBI, 16.

35. Erna Becker-Kohen, diary/memoirs, LBI, 31.

36. *BJFB*, October 1938, 4, 14.

37. "Der Ehemann im Haushalt," in *IF*, 19 May 1938, 19, cited in Sibylle Quack, "Changing Gender Roles and Emigration: The Example of German Jewish Women and Their Emigration to the United States, 1933–1945," in *People in Transit: German Migrations in Comparative Perspective, 1829–1930*, ed. Dirk Hoerder and Jörg Nagler (New York and Cambridge, 1995), 394.

38. *BJFB*, December 1935, 8.

39. *IF*, 19 May 1938, 19.

40. Ibid.

41. *BJFB*, June 1935, 9–10. Scientific management is discussed by Mary Nolan in *Vision of Modernity: American Business and the Modernization of Germany* (New York, 1994), 42 and chap. 10. Nolan stresses the importance of household rationalization during Weimar, but for bourgeois Jewish women the ideology—and necessity—probably first arose in the Nazi era. See also *CV*, 27 May 1936.

42. *CV*, 17 March 1938, ll.

43. *IF*, 19 March 1936; *Frankfurter Israelitisches Gemeindeblatt*, November 1935, 73–74.

44. *IF*, 26 March 1936.

45. "Mutti, hast du Zeit für mich?" *CV*, 27 February 1936; "Mutti ist so nervös!" *CV*, 16 September 1936.

46. *CV*, 25 August 1938, 8.

47. Letter in the Ottilie Schönewald collection, LBI, IV, 1.

48. *BJFB*, October 1935, 2.

49. Allport, Bruner, and Jandorf, "Personality under Social Catastrophe," 14.

50. Ibid.; Mally Dienemann, Harvard ms., 25.

51. Alice Baerwald, Harvard ms., 65.

52. Mally Dienemann, Harvard ms., 25.

53. Lisa Brauer, memoirs, LBI, 38: "[B]eing confined to our quarters all the time and not able to go anywhere for entertainment, we had lots of time on our hands. So we studied both English and Spanish. It did not mean just a hobby for us, it set our mind and spirit free."

54. Mally Dienemann, Harvard ms., 25.

55. "Wir werden jetzt alle Vegetarier,—dann sind wir doch von hinter—'Arier.'" Edith Wolff, Yad Vashem, Ball Kaduri Collection, 01/247, 22.

56. Edith Wolff, Yad Vashem, Ball Kaduri Collection, 01/247, 14, 21–22.

57. Ruth Abraham, memoirs, LBI, 2; job training in *Community of Fate: Memoirs of German Jews in Melbourne*, ed. John Foster (Sydney and London, 1986), 28–30; mother and daughter in Brauer, LBI, 53. Peter Gay wrote about how his mother, who had never worked outside the home and struggled with tuberculosis, tried to become a seamstress in 1936 in order to help support the family in emigration. Peter Gay, "Epilogue: The First Sex," *Between Sorrow and Strength: Women Refugees of the Nazi Period* (Cambridge, 1995), 353.

58. Praising women's flexibility and versatility, the writer noted that women were also sole supports in many families. *IF*, 13 January 1938, 13–14. See also *IF*, July 14, 1938, 12.

59. *CV*, 25 August 1938.

60. *IF*, 14 July 1938, 12.

61. Liselotte Kahn, memoirs, LBI, 21.

62. See, for example, Jacob Ball-Kaduri, memoirs, LBI, 30; Lisa Brauer, memoirs, LBI, 43, 57.

63. Jacob Ball-Kaduri, memoirs, LBI, 30.

64. See, for example, Lisa Brauer, memoirs, LBI, 43, 57 for bribes to a shipping company official and to officials at the Finance Department.

65. Liselotte Kahn, memoirs, LBI, 23.

66. Ann Lewis, memoirs, LBI, 264.

67. Lore Steinitz about her mother, Irma Baum. Note to the author entitled "The first 'sit in' " (January 7, 1995), also deposited at the Leo Baeck Institute.

68. Ruth Abraham, memoirs, LBI, 2.

69. Gerta Pfeffer, in Limberg and Rübsaat, *Sie Durften*, 141.

70. Rosy Geiger-Kullmann, memoirs, LBI, 72. Echoing these fears, the League of Jewish Women worried about the prohibition of its railroad station shelters for young women who might be accosted by men who would take advantage of their situation. Bundesarchiv, Coswig: 75C Jud. Frauenbund Verband Berlin, folder 37—"Protokoll der Arbeitskreistagung vom 2 Nov. 1936, Gefährdung der Jugendlichen."

71. Kate Behnsch-Brower, memoirs, LBI, 4–5.

72. Edith Bick interview, Research Foundation for Jewish Immigration, 18.

73. Hilde Honnet-Sichel, Harvard ms., 72–73.

74. An extreme example of this happened during the deportations when a nurse walked into a double suicide. Terribly upset, she wanted to share her feelings with her husband but could not "because of his own depressions." She did confide in her girlfriend. Frieda Cohn, Yad Vashem, Ball Kaduri Collection, 01/291, 5.

75. Marion Kaplan, "Jewish Women in Nazi Germany before Emigration," in *Between Sorrow and Strength: Women Refugees of the Nazi Period*, ed. Sibylle Quack (Cambridge, 1995), 11–50.

76. Peter Wyden, *Stella: One Woman's True Tale of Evil, Betrayal, and Survival in Hitler's Germany* (New York, 1992), 47.

77. Mary Felstiner, *To Paint Her Life: Charlotte Salomon in the Nazi Era* (New York, 1994), 74.

78. Alice Nauen, interview, Research Foundation for Jewish Immigration, 10.

79. Alice Nauen, interview, Research Foundation for Jewish Immigration, 8.

80. Hanna Bernheim, Harvard ms., 53.

81. Charlotte Hamburger, memoirs, LBI, 41, 46. She decided to flee after her husband and children faced public abuse.

82. Charlotte Stein-Pick, memoirs, LBI, 2.
83. Charlotte Stein-Pick, memoirs, LBI, 38.
84. Elizabeth Bamberger, memoirs, LBI, 5.
85. Else Gerstel, memoirs, LBI, 71.
86. Ilse Strauss, memoirs, LBI, VIII, 44.
87. Hanna Bernheim, Harvard ms., 45.
88. Else Gerstel, memoirs, LBI, 76.
89. Karl Schleunes, *The Twisted Road to Auschwitz: Nazi Policy toward German Jews, 1933–39* (Urbana, 1970), 183–84, 197–98.
90. Wyden, *Stella*, 48, 88.
91. Rita Thalmann and Emmanuel Feinermann, *Crystal Night* (New York, 1974), 22.
92. In 1933 over 35 percent of the Jewish population was over fifty, by 1938 more than half were over fifty and about 20 percent were over sixty-five. Schleunes, *The Twisted Road*, 186; Hazel Rosenstrauch, *Aus Nachbarn wurden Juden: Ausgrenzung und Selbstbehauptung, 1933–1942* (Berlin, 1988), 70.
93. Wyden, *Stella*, 48.
94. Avraham Barkai, *From Boycott to Annihilation: The Economic Struggle of German Jews, 1933–1943*, trans. William Templer (Hanover and London, 1989), 99–100.
95. Michael Marrus, *The Unwanted: European Refugees in the Twentieth Century* (New York, 1985), 131.
96. Gerdy Stoppleman, memoirs, LBI, 6. For a description of how ordinary Germans benefited from the sale of the property of deported Jews, see Frank Bajohr, *"Arisierung" in Hamburg: Die Verdrängung der jüdischen Unternehmer, 1933–1945* (Hamburg, 1997).
97. Barkai, *From Boycott to Annihilation*, 99–100.
98. Marrus, *The Unwanted*, 131.
99. Hilde Honnet-Sichel in Limberg and Rübsaat, *Sie Durften*, 184.
100. Ann Lewis, memoirs, LBI, 269–70.
101. Nazi officials in Hamburg, for example, were aware of the bribes paid by Jews to foreign consulates. On the one hand, they wanted to regulate these payments (the unintended result of which would be to hinder Jewish emigration) and, on the other, they wanted to expedite Jewish emigration. Hamburg Staatsarchiv, Oberfinanzpräsident, 314–15, 9UA2: "Auswanderung jüdische Emigranten, 1936–1941."
102. Carole Garbuny Vogel, ed., *We Shall Not Forget! Memories of the Holocaust* (Lexington, Mass., 1994), 12.
103. Joseph Walk, ed., *Das Sonderrecht für die Juden im NS-Staat: Eine Sammlung der gesetzlichen Massnahmen und Richtlinien—Inhalt und Bedeutung* (Heidelberg, 1981). See 16 November 1937.
104. Bundesarchiv Potsdam, Coswig, 75C Hil HICEM Prag 5 *Coordinating Committee for Refugees*: Domestic Bureau (Fragebogen 1939).
105. It is estimated that 60,000 to 65,000 refugees in total left Germany in

1933 and that about 40 percent of these went to France. Rita Thalmann, "L'im-migration Allemande et l'opinion publiques en France de 1933 à 1936," in *La France et l' Allemagne, 1932–1936* (Paris, 1980), 149–50.

106. Herbert Strauss, "Jewish Emigration from Germany: Nazi Policies and Jewish Responses" (I), *Leo Baeck Institute Yearbook* (hereafter *LBIYB*) (1980): 357.

107. Yehuda Bauer, *My Brother's Keeper* (Philadelphia 1974), 138–39. France absorbed much of the first wave of refugees in 1933 (about 21,000, not all of whom were Jewish.) Shortly thereafter Paris began to restrict the flow, fearful of becoming a dumping ground for refugees. Later the government turned toward repatriation, resettlement, and internment. Marrus, *The Un-wanted*, 146–47. Rita Thalmann shows 25,000 German refugees in France in 1933. "L'immigration Allemande et l'opinion publiques en France de 1933 à 1936," 149–72.

108. Shlomo Wahrman, *Lest We Forget: Growing Up in Nazi Leipzig 1933–1939* (New York, 1991), 77–78.

109. See, for example, "L.I. resident recalls how as small girl she and parents hid from Nazi attacks," *Jewish Week* (Long Island, N.Y.) 19 November 1978. Although they had applied for entry to the United States, Evelyn Pike's parents first studied Spanish, hoping to go to Cuba. When this failed, they studied Por-tuguese, hoping to go to Brazil. They wound up in Shanghai.

110. Pressing her husband to leave Germany, Marta Appel recorded his reac-tions: "Like all other men, he . . . couldn't imagine leaving one's beloved home-land and the duties that fill a man's life. 'Could you really leave all this behind you to enter nothingness?' . . . 'I could,' I said, without a moment's hesitation." Appel, in Monika Richarz, ed., *Jüdisches Leben in Deutschland: Selbstzeugnisse zur Sozialgeschichte, 1918–1945* (Stuttgart, 1982), 3:237.

111. Psychologists who studied refugee memoirs observed that almost 40 percent of memoir writers did not give up psychologically until 1938 or 1939. Allport, Bruner, and Jandorf, "Personality under Social Catastrophe," 4.

112. Ibid.; "everyone" in Bernd-Lutz, Lange, ed., *Davidstern und Weih-nachtsbaum: Erinnerungen von Überlebenden* (Leipzig, 1992), 27.

113. Freund, in Richarz, *Life*, 413–15.

114. Letter from Gertrud Grossmann, 17 January 1939. My thanks to Atina Grossmann for sharing these letters; "god" in Bernheim, Harvard ms., 51.

115. Dienemann, Harvard ms., 35. See also Fromm, *Blood*, 238.

116. "On Not Believing the Unbelievable," *New York Times Book Review*, 29 June 1996, 13.

117. Letter from Gertrud Grossmann, 22 February 1940.

118. *Jüdische Wohlfahrtspflege und Sozial Politik* (hereafter *JWS*), 1937, 7–13, 27, 78–81; Avraham Barkai, "Der wirtschaftliche Existenzkampf der Juden im Dritten Reich, 1933–38," in *The Jews in Nazi Germany, 1933–1945*, ed. Ar-nold Paucker (Tübingen, 1986), 163; Burgheim, LBI archives; Hanno Loewy,

ed., *In mich ist die grosse dunkle Ruhe gekommen, Martha Wertheimer Briefe an Siegfried Guggenheim* (1939–1941), (Frankfurter Lern-und Dokumentationszentrum des Holocaust, Frankfurt am Main, 1993), 6, 9, 13, 15, 22, 37.

119. Among eastern European Jews who returned east between 1934 and 1937, for example, the majority were male, even though almost half of them were married. Trude Maurer, "Ausländische Juden in Deutschland, 1933–39," in Paucker, ed., *Nazi Germany*, 204; *BJFB*, December 1936, 5.

120. Men beaten in Ruth Eisner, *Nicht Wir Allein: Aus dem Tagebuch einer Berliner Jüdin* (Berlin, 1971), 8; Nauen (whose father was secretary of the Hilfsverein in Hamburg) interview, Research Foundation for Jewish Immigration, 15; Ruth Klüger, *Weiter leben* (Göttingen, 1992), 83.

121. Morris, "Lives," 43.

122. "The sons" in *BJFB*, April 1937, 5; Glaser, memoirs, LBI, 26, 71. See also Erika Guetermann, LBI; Stein-Pick, LBI, 46.

123. *BJFB*, December 1936, 1. Bundesarchiv, Potsdam, Coswig: 75C Jüdischer Frauenbund, Verband Berlin, folder 37. Protokoll der Arbeitskreistagung vom 2 Nov. 1936.

124. *Hilfsverein* in *CV*, 20 January 1938, 5, and 3 March 1938, 6.

125. For example, in 1937, of the 7,313 emigrés supported by the emigration section of the Central Organization of Jews in Germany, there were approximately 4,161 men and 3,041 women. The *Hilfsverein* supported 3,250 men and 2,512 women. The Palestine Bureau supported 911 men and 529 women. *Informationsblätter*, January/February 1938, 6–7. Overall immigration into the United States showed a higher proportion of men, evening out only in 1938–39. See *American Jewish Year Book 5699* (1938/39) (1938), 552–54; *5701 (1940/41)* (1940), 608–609; *5702 (1941–42)* (1941), 674–75; Quack, "Changing Gender Roles and Emigration," 391; Christine Backhaus-Lautenschläger, ... *Und standen ihre Frau: Das Schicksal deutschsprachiger Emigrantinnen in den USA nach 1933* (Pfaffenweiler, 1991), 30 (who claims more women than men entered between 1933 and 1941, although this encompasses Jews and non-Jews).

Youth Aliyah required 60 percent boys and 40 percent girls because of what its leaders considered the division of labor on the collective farms where the children would work. Until April 1939, Youth Aliyah sent 3,229 children from Germany to Palestine. My thanks to Sara Kadosh of the Joint Distribution Committee Archives for the figures from Germany.

126. "Martyrs" in Lixl-Purcell, *Women*, 92. Women were also a majority of the Jewish populations of German-dominated Europe: Raul Hilberg, *Perpetrators, Victims, and Bystanders* (New York, 1992), 127; *IF*, no. 9, 27 February, 1936; Bruno Blau, "The Jewish Population of Germany, 1939–1946," *Jewish Social Studies* 12, no. 2 (1950):165.

127. On age, see Strauss, "Emigration," I, 318–19, and Blau, "Population," 165; "dismal" in Rothschild, memoirs, LBI, 125–26; old-age homes in Wolf

Gruner, "Die Reichshauptstadt und die Verfolgung der Berliner Juden, 1933–1945," in *Jüdische Geschichte in Berlin: Essays und Studien,* ed. Reinhard Rürup (Berlin, 1995), 242, 251; Winter Relief in Clemens Vollnhals, "Judische Selbsthilfe bis 1938," in *Die Juden in Deutschland, 1933–1945,* ed. Wolfgang Benz (Munich, 1988), 405, and *BJFB,* October 1938, 4.

128. Disproportionate number of elderly women in Richarz, *Leben,* 61; *JWS,* 1937, 96–97; *JWS,* 1937, 161–63; *JWS,* 1937, 200–201; Klemperer, *Zeugnis,* 1:475; *IF,* 16 January 1936; Freund, memoirs, LBI, 146.

129. Daniel J. Goldhagen, *Hitler's Willing Executioners: Ordinary Germans and the Holocaust* (New York, 1996).

CHAPTER 5

The Nazi Purge of German Artistic and Cultural Life

ALAN E. STEINWEIS

WHEN EXAMINING the historical record of a regime that murdered millions of people and ruined the lives of millions more, it might seem somewhat superfluous to devote attention to cultural purges.[1] Whereas the need to explain the historically infrequent phenomenon of genocide is self-evident, it is less obvious why something so historically normal as cultural ostracism should receive treatment in this volume. There are good reasons why it should. First, during its rise to power in the 1920s the Nazi movement adeptly exploited artistic and cultural issues to underscore its own Germanic authenticity, to undermine the legitimacy of the allegedly "degenerate" Weimar Republic, and to stigmatize Jews, Communists, Social Democrats, and others as culturally "alien."[2] Second, after coming to power the National Socialists employed culture and the arts to legitimize their own rule. Posing as the champions of a truly "Germanic" culture, the Nazis used the power of the state to effect changes both in the content of German artistic life and in the composition of the population that engaged in it, yet they still managed to preserve continuity and a sense of "normalcy" in the way that most Germans experienced art and entertainment. Third, and perhaps most important, the cultural policies of the Nazi regime were inextricably intertwined with the policies of persecution and marginalization, driven by racist ideology, that were targeted at Jews, Roma and Sinti, homosexuals, and other groups.

The Nazi movement achieved power in Germany in the midst of what today would be called a "culture war." During the Weimar Republic, political parties and movements across the ideological spectrum used artistic and cultural propaganda to forge and mobilize constituencies.[3] Although Nazi pronouncements and policies toward intellectual life and the arts were contradictory and often more pragmatic than dogmatic, the Nazi movement was animated by a serious and coherent ideology of culture. From the beginning of its existence as an organized movement, National Socialism had emphasized the need for cultural purification in Germany. In its founding document, the 25-point program of 1920, the Nazi Party had called for the "legal prosecution of all those tendencies in art and literature which corrupt our national life, and the suppression of cultural events which violate this demand."[4] German culture, the Nazis contended, had become adulterated by alien elements, particularly Jews. A central task of the National Socialist state would be to expurgate such aliens, and their cultural production, from German art and culture.[5]

This penchant for relying on the state to intervene actively in the arts was linked with an antimodernist aesthetic sensibility, the latter very much a reaction against cultural developments of the Weimar Republic. The 1920s had seen the full emergence of experimental movements in literature, painting and sculpture, architecture, music, and theater. The new art became the focus of intense political and ideological debate. Cultural conservatives denounced artistic modernism, claiming that it was overly intellectual as well as cosmopolitan (hence un-German). For their part, the Nazis emphasized racial decay as the underlying cause of aesthetic degeneration. Addressing cultural production directly would not suffice; only by means of a thoroughgoing program of racial purification could the basic problem be corrected. Cultural purification would thus constitute a key component in the creation of the *Volksgemeinschaft*.

From the Nazi perspective, biology counted for much more than did aesthetics. In the context of Nazi Germany, therefore, a term such as "cultural victims" has the potential to mislead. Most of the cultural victims of the Third Reich were, in fact, targeted primarily because of their ostensible race rather than because of their actual or suspected cultural or artistic tendencies. Elsewhere I have employed the term "cultural eugenics" as a metaphor for illuminating the connections between cultural policies and the drive to establish a racially pure *Volksgemeinschaft*.[6] The regime's approach to cultural policy was essentially a corollary to its efforts to cleanse the "Aryan race" of hereditary impurities through programs of positive and negative eugenics, nourishing the healthy while weeding out the "unhealthy" and the "alien." Starting in 1933 Nazi cultural policy proceeded on two parallel tracks. One was directed at regulating the content of cultural production through censorship and patronage; the other—and the one on which this essay will focus—involved determining what persons would be allowed to participate in the nation's cultural life. Germans who were considered racially acceptable were permitted employment in artistic and cultural occupations, in many cases as the beneficiaries of public subsidies, provided that they respected officially imposed limits on artistic expression. Those who were deemed racially objectionable were systematically and inexorably excluded, their artistic and political sensibilities notwithstanding.

But although race may have been the dominant factor in the Nazi regime's program for reconstituting German cultural life, it was by no means the only one. Racial classification served as the sole determinant for exclusion only in cases involving individuals who were classified under Nazi racial laws as "full Jews" (and, in much smaller numbers, as "Gypsies"). In most other cases, in order to explain why any particular individual in Nazi Germany was or was not purged from the cultural sector, we must examine how Nazi notions of race interacted with several other factors, the most important of which were artistic ability, economic circumstances, perceived political reliability, aesthetic tendencies, sexuality, and personal prominence.

Jews constituted by far the largest segment of those who were purged from German cultural life on racial grounds. Although precise statistics are difficult to assemble, a good estimate of the number of German Jews who were dismissed from professional activity in the cultural sphere during the 1930s is about 8,000.[7] This purge occurred in two main stages, the first in 1933, the second in 1935–36. Such a phased approach was not the result of any preconceived master plan, but rather reflected the gradual nature of the Nazification of German society and institutions after January 1933. As in other spheres of activity, Jews were purged from German cultural life only when the Nazi regime had managed to attain the legal and procedural means for doing so, and felt confident that it could withstand criticism from abroad and the economic consequences that might arise from anti-Jewish measures.

The initial phase of the purge, that of the year 1933, began as a series of improvised, emergency measures implemented in a semirevolutionary environment, but by the end of the year had evolved into a more systematic, institutionalized effort. In the spring of 1933 Nazi officials, citing as their justification the need to maintain public order, relied on special police powers derived from the Reichstag Fire Decree to prohibit performances by several prominent Jewish artists and entertainers. Among the most celebrated of those affected by these actions was the conductor Bruno Walter, who was prevented from performing in Leipzig and Berlin. Walter soon went into exile.[8] He, like other German Jewish artists and intellectuals who chose exile early on, possessed the advantage of an international reputation that virtually guaranteed employment and a comfortable existence outside of Germany. Although the Walter case, demonstrating that an international reputation offered little protection against a regime that was pledged to eradicate Jewish influence from German culture, was, or should have been, instructive to other Jewish artists who remained in Germany, the vast majority initially chose, or were compelled, to remain. Considerable as the psychological and practical barriers in the way of emigration may have been for all German Jews,[9] they may well have been even greater for artists and intellectuals, whose roots ran deep in German cultural soil and for whom employment prospects seemed dismal in a world still mired in the Depression.

Whereas the emergency decrees had accounted for a relatively small number of high-profile purges, the issuance of the Law for the Restoration of a Professional Civil Service of April 1933 laid the foundation for a more orderly and considerably more widespread dismissal of Jews from culture-related positions. The law forced the dismissal of Jews from positions of public employment, which, in the cultural sector, included all positions in radio broadcasting and the vast majority of positions in educational institutions (including academies of the fine and performing arts), orchestras, theater companies, and museums. To Jews who lost their jobs the blow was extremely hard, as employment in the civil service had provided relatively good compensation and unparalleled job security. Measured quantitatively, the impact of the law on Jews in some fields was minimal. For example, in all of Germany there were only two Jewish musicologists employed in higher education (owing not only to the small size of the musicology profession but also to the traditional animus against Jews in that field).[10] But in other fields, particularly music and theater, the impact of the law was felt much more broadly. In the absence of pertinent statistical compilations, a reasonable estimate of the total number of Jews who lost culture-related positions as the result of the Civil Service Law would be about 1,000.

Although those possessing civil service status had been the most privileged among German Jews active in culture, the fact that they worked for the government had, ironically, made them the most vulnerable to Nazi dismissal policies. The majority of German Jewish artists and intellectuals were privately employed, and therefore remained unaffected by the Civil Service Law. The Nazi regime still required a mechanism for extending the cultural purge into the private sector. It put this mechanism in place in the fall of 1933 with the creation of the *Reichskultur-*

kammer (Reich Chamber of Culture) and its subchambers for Music, the Visual Arts, Theater, Literature, Film, Radio, and the Press. This chamber system was placed under the authority of Propaganda Minister Joseph Goebbels, who was among the more fanatical antisemites within the Nazi leadership. The chambers encompassed several hundred thousand Germans who were either professionally or semiprofessionally engaged in artistic and intellectual life. Neither government agencies nor private associations, the chambers were "corporations of public law" in which membership was made compulsory for all Germans wishing to pursue cultural activity. Ostensibly they would serve a purpose similar to that of the guilds of the Middle Ages, permitting the culture professions to regulate and police themselves and to protect their own economic interests, which had eroded calamitously in the Weimar Republic. Although the economic and regulatory functions of the chambers were genuine and significant, we do not have space to explore them.[11] They are of importance to us here only insofar as they helped to legitimize the Nazi regime in the eyes of many people who were active in German cultural life, and thus made ideologically motivated censorship and purges more palatable.

One provision in the law establishing the chamber system was especially important to the regime's ability to expand the cultural purge. Paragraph 10 provided for refusing membership to persons who did "not possess the necessary reliability and aptitude for the practice of his activity."[12] Unlike the so-called Aryan Clauses that were included in many other Nazi-era statutes, including the Civil Service Law, Paragraph 10 did not specifically employ racial definitions. But it was precisely the elasticity of the language that made Paragraph 10 a versatile weapon in the hands of the regime. The key word "reliability" could be flexibly interpreted so as to exclude from membership in the chambers not only persons who were considered racially alien but also those who were deemed to be politically, artistically, or personally objectionable. Because of the compulsory nature of the chamber system, rejection of membership, or expulsion, was tantamount to cultural blacklisting.

With this new purge mechanism in place by the end of 1933 the regime now had at its disposal the technical and procedural means necessary to build on the dismissals that had ensued from the Civil Service Law and to bring the cultural purge of Jews to completion. But this did not happen immediately. Over a year would pass before widespread, systematic use of Paragraph 10 against Jews would commence. The main reason for the delay was technical. Time was needed during which members and potential members of the chambers could gather and submit documentation about their ancestry. Further time was required for the bureaucratic processing of all this data, as well as for the preparation of lists of Jews who would be refused membership or expelled. But the mountains of paperwork were not the only obstacle. There was also some disagreement within the leadership of the chambers about the speed and thoroughness of the purge. Some objections were based on principle, as was that of Richard Strauss, the famous composer who agreed to serve as president of the Chamber of Music, only to be forced out of that position largely as a result of his opposition. Other objections were based more on pragmatic, and specifically economic, concerns. The minister of economics, Hjalmar Schacht, specifically feared that the application of Paragraph 10 to Jewish-owned publishing houses, art dealerships, and similar cultural enterprises might lead to the collapse of those businesses, which would have a negative impact on Germany's unemployment and balance-of-trade situations. After special provisions were made to allow such economically indispensable Jewish business operators to remain active (at least for a while), the mass expulsion of Jews from the chambers was initiated in early 1935. By the end of 1936 about 6,000 Jews had been purged from the chambers.[13]

It has often been argued that many Jews remained in Germany because, prior to the Kristallnacht in November 1938, the gradual deterioration of their situation presented no single crisis so serious as to justify the drastic step of emigration. To the extent that this was indeed the case, the delay of over one year between the creation of the *Reichskulturkammer* and the beginning of the mass expulsions under Paragraph 10 may have had a psychological effect on German Jews active in the cultural fields. Despite the cultural purge of 1933, and despite professional and occupational purges in other sectors of society, several thousand Jews were members of the cultural chambers throughout the year 1934. Although in retrospect it might be easy to criticize the self-delusion of German Jews who convinced themselves that conditions would not deteriorate further, it is important to recognize the tendency of persons living under such duress to embrace evidence that could be reason for optimism.

There is yet another important factor that is important to understanding the psychological accommodation of German Jews to their victimization by Nazi cultural policy. In response to the initial stage of purges in 1933, Jewish community leaders created the *Jüdischer Kulturbund* (Jewish Cultural League).[14] This organization sponsored musical and theatrical events in order to provide employment opportunities for Jewish performers who had been dismissed from their positions. The regime did more than permit the *Kulturbund's* creation—it actually encouraged it. From the Nazi perspective, the *Kulturbund* would promote Jewish cultural dissimilation by means of cultural segregation. Events sponsored by the *Kulturbund* would feature Jewish artists performing Jewish works before Jewish audiences. Until its dissolution in 1941, the *Kulturbund* was exploited by Nazi propagandists, who could claim that Jews had not been prohibited from indulging in Jewish culture even as they had been separated out from German culture. Although few German Jews endorsed this policy of cultural ghettoization, the *Kulturbund* did create jobs for otherwise unemployable Jewish performers, while Jewish audiences, seeking to make the best of a bad situation, took advantage of the *Kulturbund's* extensive programming. Although from the subjective perspective of German Jews the *Kulturbund* might have ameliorated the impact of cultural marginalization, seen objectively and in retrospect its most significant, and most tragic, consequence may well have been to reinforce a false sense of security about the future.[15]

A very small number of Jews, and larger numbers of so-called *Mischlinge* (those of mixed ancestry) were allowed to remain active in mainstream German cultural life beyond the conclusion of the major purge of 1935–36.[16] These individuals were the recipients of what were known as "special dispensations," which in most cases had been issued for economic reasons but in some instances were the result of favoritism or well-placed connections. In his diaries, which have now been published almost in their entirety, Goebbels referred to these *Mischlinge* and special cases repeatedly, always underscoring his desire to eliminate these residual racial contaminants within German cultural life.[17] That Goebbels could be so distracted by a few instances of ideological inconsistency is compelling evidence of his determination to address the "Jewish question" in his own sphere of authority.[18]

The response of the German public to the exclusion of Jews from cultural life is difficult to measure. The public opinion reports compiled by the Reich Security Police (SD), which constitute a basic source for historians of the Third Reich, are virtually silent on this particular aspect of the Nazi anti-Jewish policy, suggesting that the SD perceived little significant dissent on this matter.[19] Similarly, the internal documentation of the Propaganda Ministry and the *Reichskulturkammer*, the two agencies that were instrumental in carrying out the purge, does not suggest that the officials in charge were overly concerned with public opposition

within Germany. In those instances where delays in the purge of Jews
are discussed, almost always the blame is attributed either to procedural
complications or to the recalcitrance of Schacht or other German officials whose concerns tended to be of a practical nature. When criticism
on the basis of principle did arise, it usually came from individuals acting
in isolation. Among the more well known examples of such outspoken-
ness was the resistance mounted by Wilhelm Furtwängler, the celebrated
conductor of the Berlin Philharmonic Orchestra, to the removal of his
Jewish musicians. Even this case, however, was rather complicated, and
it has been suggested that Furtwängler might have acted as much out of
egoism and careerism as out of moral principle.[20] We should not, to be
sure, underestimate the risks faced by any person who had the audacity
publicly to oppose Nazi measures targeted at Jews. But few were so inclined, especially because the cultural purge exemplified the kind of legal, bureaucratic (as opposed to violent) antisemitism that enjoyed
widespread tacit support in German society.[21] It is also important to
note that expressions of support for such policies were quite common
among non-Jews active in culture and the arts. In addition to the obvious motive of antisemitism, many Germans stood personally to profit
from the purge of Jews from cultural life. These included German artists
who believed that the elimination of Jewish competition would brighten
their prospects for promotion, recognition, and in many cases, something so basic as gainful employment.[22]

This element of perceived competition also helps explain why no
other category of the Third Reich's cultural victims confronted so absolute and persistent a commitment to exclusion as did the Jews. Only in
the case of Roma and Sinti, known as "Gypsies," did the regime institute
anything like a systematic purge based entirely on ostensible racial affiliation. This occurred relatively late, in 1940, when Roma and Sinti performers, mainly musicians, were expelled from the *Reichskulturkammer*.
Unlike the Jewish purge, which had been publicized and justified by a
massive propaganda campaign, the expulsion of several dozen "Gypsy"
performers received scant notice.[23] This difference helps place in perspective how Nazi perceptions of Jews and "Gypsies" diverged. To be
sure, both had been designated as alien races to be separated out from
the German nation. But the preoccupying Nazi fear of Jewish parasitical
control of German society, a fear that was especially pronounced in the
realm of culture, had no analog in the case of Roma and Sinti. The regime presented the purge of Jews from German culture as the most significant step toward re-Germanization, a reclamation by the German

race of its birthright, which had, according to the Nazi view, been hi-
jacked by Jews. In contrast the purge of "Gypsies," though mandated by
the iron logic of Nazi racism, lacked the potential for such symbolic and
psychological gratification and seemed to offer no particular propagan-
distic opportunity.

What the Jewish and Roma/Sinti victims of Nazi cultural policy did
have in common, and what distinguished their treatment from that of all
other categories of cultural victims, was that they were marked and excluded on account of what was assumed to be their innate natures,
rather than because of their behavior. To illustrate this point further, it
is useful to examine the Nazi regime's approach to rooting out homosexuality from German cultural life. Many recent studies have demonstrated the centrality of racist thinking to the Nazi persecution of
homosexuality, pointing to Nazi medical research into the hereditary
determinants of sexuality and to the systematic sterilization of gay men
as an element of eugenicist practice. Nevertheless, the tendency to think
about sexuality in racial terms did not translate into a ironclad set of
universal guidelines about how to deal with homosexuality. As a consequence, agencies at various levels of government operated with considerable latitude, even arbitrariness, in their attempts to define, measure,
and address this "problem." Whereas in some cases measures of persecution were targeted at persons because of their ostensible homosexual
nature, in other cases the persecution was conceived as a deterrent to, or
punishment for, a specific act. Although in the realm of cultural policy
we find evidence of both approaches, the emphasis was overwhelmingly
on behavior. Moreover, we can also point to specific examples of gay
men who suffered few, if any, penalties, because of their talent, prominence, and connections.

The culture chambers and other Nazi cultural institutions treated as
criminals Germans who had been convicted under the provisions of the
key antihomosexuality statute, Section 175 of the Reich criminal code.
Artists suspected of homosexual activity were monitored by cultural
functionaries, who duly recorded denunciations or information received
from the police, but who rarely took action in the absence of a Section
175 conviction. The cultural bureaucrats, in effect, deferred to the criminal justice system the determination of whether a particular individual
was homosexual. But at the same time, the cultural bureaucrats retained
a good deal of flexibility in how to deal with the so-called 175ers.
Conviction under Section 175 did not automatically lead to dismissal
from culture-related employment. There is ample documentation of

107

numerous instances in which artists convicted under Section 175 received warnings but were not expelled from the chambers or dismissed from their positions of employment.[24] Generally speaking, in the cultural sphere the punishment of persons for whom homosexual encounters were deemed aberrational was less severe than that of supposed hardcore "libidinal felons." First-time offenders were treated more leniently than were recidivists, and offenses involving adults were treated more leniently than were those involving the seduction of a minor. Reflecting the broader pattern of persecution of homosexuals during the Third Reich, the purge of gays from cultural life intensified during the war years, when considerably less leniency was extended to first-time Section 175 offenders than had been the case in peacetime.

The most famous gay artist in Nazi Germany was Gustaf Gründgens, the actor and director on whose career in the Third Reich the novel *Mephisto* by Heinrich Mann (and later the film, with the same title, by Istvan Szabo) was based. As the star of the Berlin State Theater, Gründgens was one of the most visible figures in German high culture. His homosexuality was widely recognized, including among the political elite of the Nazi regime. Writing in his diary in 1937, Joseph Goebbels referred to the State Theater as a "swamp" of homosexual perversion, noting that Hitler, with whom Goebbels frequently discussed cultural issues and personalities, shared this view.[25] But Gründgens could rely on the protection offered by two factors: his own prominence and the patronage of Hermann Goering, who presided over the Berlin State Theater in his capacity as minister-president of Prussia.[26]

Although hardly typical of the fate of gay performers in Nazi Germany, the toleration extended to Gründgens does raise the question of whether Nazi leaders acknowledged that participation by gays in German artistic life presented a special problem that would have to be addressed delicately. Although this question has, unfortunately, not yet been systematically explored in the expanding scholarship on the Nazi persecution of homosexuals,[27] some evidence indicates that this was indeed the case. For example, in 1937 Heinrich Himmler issued an order requiring German police to secure permission from him before arresting artists or performers for sexual offenses, except instances in which the culprits were caught "in the act."[28] Although Himmler must have been concerned about offending the powerful political patrons of the artists who were arrested, it is also likely that he feared the embarrassment to the regime that could ensue from the disclosure that homosexuality was common among its artistic elite. There is also evidence suggesting that the Propaganda Ministry encouraged a certain leniency when it came to handling Section 175 convictions that were not considered to be particularly egregious. In a move that would have been inconceivable without the endorsement of Goebbels himself, in the 1930s the ministry instructed the cultural chambers *not* to expel members who had received sentences of less than six months under Section 175. This directive remained in force until 1942.[29]

It should be emphasized that none of this is intended to suggest that the Nazi regime's campaign against homosexuality in the arts amounted to anything less than a brutal oppression, but only that it was complex, shaped both by a recognition of gradations in sexual behavior and by a realistic appreciation of the practical limits and political consequences of enforcement. Characterized by a similar complexity and flexibility was the purge from cultural life of yet a further category of persons: those deemed to be politically undesirable.

The attack on politically incorrect artists began early, coinciding with the first wave of improvised purges of Jewish artists in March and April 1933. Armed with emergency powers, German police rounded up and imprisoned, without even the pretense of judicial process, artists who had links with the Communist movement. These arrests were part of a much broader anti-Communist campaign that followed in the wake of the Reichstag Fire on 28 February. The regime pointed to the arrested artists as evidence of the extent to which degeneracy and treachery had spread within the German art world. In one much publicized raid on a residential colony for artists in Berlin in March 1933, which led to the arrest of several Communist writers, German police used fire-fighting equipment to enter apartments through second-story windows. The widely circulated *Illustrierter Beobachter* sensationalized the event in a full-page story replete with photographs showing the writers being hauled away in a truck as the police publicly burned their literature.[30] Such initial acts of open intimidation and coercion set the tone for the following months. Musical ensembles, galleries, and theaters that had had links to the recently abolished leftist political parties were disbanded. As political opposition to the regime became increasingly criminalized, cultural institutions dismissed employees whose political loyalties were suspect. Political denunciations of artists, both sincere and trumped up, inundated Nazi commissars who had been placed in charge of cultural organizations. At the Berlin State Theater, performers with

109

Nazi sympathies or connections kept records of who among their co-workers saluted the swastika flag when it was first raised above the building.[31]

As the revolutionary atmosphere dissipated, *ad hoc* tactics gradually gave way to a more institutionalized system for monitoring and enforcing political attitudes among those active in German cultural life. Once again, the culture chambers provided the necessary mechanism. The "reliability" clause in Paragraph 10 of the chambers' membership regulations, which was used to expel Jews from the chambers in 1935–36, could also be employed to enforce ideological and political conformity. The assessment of an artist's political sympathies allowed for a much wider latitude of interpretation than did the application of racial classification employed with respect to Jews and Roma/Sinti. The political conduct or connections of an artist before 1933 were treated as being far less important than his or her attitude and comportment since the Nazi takeover. Chamber policy was to issue "emphatic warnings" to politically or ideologically wayward artists before issuing a professional ban. The intended chilling effect was achieved, as expulsions on account of political conduct were rare.

Artists with Communist pasts were given the chance to demonstrate their "reliability" under the new conditions. Permission for professional reinstatement was granted even to artists who had been imprisoned for Communist activism during the Nazi regime. Implicit in such practice was the presumption that genuine rehabilitation could occur. Once released from prison or concentration camp, "upstanding conduct" often led to professional reinstatement. In the case of one woman, an illustrator who spent three years in prison as punishment for underground Communist activity, Security Police chief Reinhard Heydrich personally recommended professional reinstatement, asserting that she had undergone a change of heart.[32] This approach was endorsed by a directive from the Nazi Party Chancellery in 1938, which stipulated that "ex-convicts have atoned for their guilt with the serving of their sentences, and that no obstacles should be placed in the way of the further practice of their profession."[33]

The purge of artists for aesthetic deviations from Nazi principles paralleled that for political and ideological reasons. Ability to adjust to the strictures of the Nazi regime was the key factor to professional survival, whereas tendencies or affiliations of the pre-Nazi era were far less important. An especially compelling illustration of this point can be drawn from the field of architecture. Ludwig Mies van der Rohe was among the most prominent exponents of the Bauhaus movement in architecture. One of the chief targets of Nazi cultural propaganda during the 1920s, the Bauhaus supposedly embodied the de-Germanized, international, overly intellectual (and, of course, Jewish-inspired) aesthetic trends of the Weimar era. Nevertheless Mies, like many other lesser-known architects connected to the Bauhaus, was not forced to flee from Germany after the Nazi takeover. He and others were allowed to continue on as professional architects as long as they respected aesthetic and architectural principles approved by the regime. For some the limitations proved too much to take; Mies himself departed the country in 1937. But the majority remained for the duration of the Nazi period, earning a living under a system that was prepared to reward them for their technical skills even as it constricted their creative powers.[34] Their experiences confirm the observation of the historian Detlev J. K. Peukert that many German artists became adept at generating "forms of artistic production and popular entertainment that were technically polished" but which were "non-political, harmless, and lacking in contemporary relevance."[35]

There is, however, a danger of overstating the vacuousness of German culture under the Nazis. For several decades after 1945 the cultural production of Nazi Germany was dismissed as pure philistinism, hardly worthy of serious analysis. According to this once widely accepted view, Nazi culture amounted to little more than a celebration of Wagnerian bombast, bourgeois kitsch, and mindless entertainment, while it ruthlessly suppressed all manifestations of modernism. In recent years, however, a more complex view has emerged, one that acknowledges two significant characteristics of Nazi culture: first, the existence of certain modernist elements in Nazi aesthetics, and, second, the pragmatic readiness of several Nazi leaders to tolerate or co-opt trends that they regarded as ideologically problematic.[36]

In no cultural sector were these characteristics more apparent than in music, as the historian Michael Kater has demonstrated in his two important recent books on that subject.[37] Even though practically no space existed for musical atonality of the sort promoted by Arnold Schoenberg, other varieties of modernism, particularly those associated with Paul Hindemith and Igor Stravinsky, received a fair degree of official encouragement and attracted respectable numbers of younger composers and musicians. While the regime's condemnation of jazz music was less ambiguous, Nazi leaders could not help but recognize its popularity, especially among German youth, a problem that it addressed by promoting a Germanized (less "hot") version of the music.

The pragmatism with which purge policies were implemented in the cultural sphere was also in part the result of economic considerations. Officials in the Ministry of Propaganda and the Chamber of Culture often expressed concern that purged artists or entertainers might not be able to find alternative means of employment, and would therefore become dependent on state assistance. This fear was especially pronounced in the early years of the regime, when overall unemployment remained a serious problem, although instances of such concern continued into the late 1930s. In one case in 1937, the president of the Reich Theater Chamber, Ludwig Körner, regretted that a particular cabaret entertainer had been banned from performing. The ban had prompted the house to cancel the contract with an entire troupe, and as a consequence, "four people are lying on the street."[38]

An important consequence of this combination of ideological flexibility, political realism, and economic pragmatism was that the Nazi regime purged few artists for exclusively aesthetic reasons. Conservatively inclined to begin with, the vast majority of German artists could adjust to Nazi censorship practices with little difficulty. The minority who found the restrictions intolerable fled the country rather early on, if they possessed the means to do so. Artistic dissidents who remained in Germany for economic or personal reasons understandably tended to protect their jobs (and perhaps much more) by maintaining a low profile and keeping their objections to themselves, a mode of behavior that has often been called "internal exile." A compelling example can be drawn from the biography of the artist Hannah Höch. In the 1920s Höch had pioneered in the creation of the photomontage. She had done so as a member of the Dada movement, a major *bête noire* of Nazi antimodernist propaganda. Yet unlike several of her fellow Dadaists, she remained in Germany for the duration of the Third Reich. She did not exhibit any work during the Nazi period, but was granted membership in the Reich Chamber of the Visual Arts, which secured access to rationed art supplies.[39]

Such an alternative was not open to artists and intellectuals whose treatment was determined by Nazi racial laws. Having been driven from their jobs and from their callings for reasons unrelated to their political or aesthetic sensibilities, Jews (and Gypsies) could not modify or restrict their cultural activity as a strategy for economic, professional, and, ultimately, physical survival. For them, cultural victimization proved to be simply an initial step on the road to a much harsher destiny. This observation is not intended to minimize the magnitude of the Nazi regime's repression of artistic and creative liberty, but only to set that repression in the more virulent, and ultimately genocidal, context in which it unfolded.

NOTES

1. Much of this essay is based on arguments and documentation contained in my book *Art, Ideology, and Economics in Nazi Germany: The Reich Chambers of Music, Theater, and the Visual Arts* (Chapel Hill: University of North Carolina Press, 1993). Several other recent studies of cultural life in the Third Reich, from which the present chapter integrates information and insights, are cited below.

2. I have developed this theme further in "Weimar Culture and the Rise of National Socialism: The *Kampfbund für deutsche Kultur*," *Central European History* 24 (Fall 1992): 402–423. Relatively little work has been done on the Nazi manipulation of artistic-cultural issues before 1933. For a recent local case study, see Colin J. Fallon, "Saving *Deutsche Kultur* in Weimar: The Political Struggle for the German National Theater, 1918–1933" (Ph.D. dissertation, University of Delaware, 1999). For a collection of Nazi views on a wide variety of artistic issues in the Weimar Republic, see Gerhard Kohler, *Kunstanschauung und Kunstkritik in der nationalsozialistischen Presse: Die Kritik im Feuilleton des "Völkischen Beobachters," 1920–1932* (Munich: Franz Eher, 1937).

3. See the insightful comments of Detlev J. K. Peukert, *The Weimar Republic: The Crisis of Classical Modernity*, trans. Richard Deveson (New York: Hill and Wang, 1989), esp. 172–74.

4. NSDAP 25-point platform published in Jeremy Noakes and Geoffrey Pridham, eds., *Nazism, 1919–1945: A Documentary Reader* (Exeter: University of Exeter Press, 1983–1988), 1:16.

5. For the nineteenth-century background of these ideas, several classic studies are still useful, the two most important of which are George L. Mosse, *The Crisis of German Ideology: Intellectual Origins of the Third Reich* (New York: Grosset and Dunlap, 1964); and Fritz Stern, *The Politics of Cultural Despair: A Study in the Rise of the Germanic Ideology* (Berkeley: University of California Press, 1961; pbk. ed. 1974).

6. Alan E. Steinweis, "Cultural Eugenics: Social Policy, Economic Reform, and the Purge of Jews from German Cultural Life," in *National Socialist Cultural Policy*, ed. Glenn R. Cuomo (New York: St. Martin's Press, 1995), 23–37.

7. Estimate based on census statistics of Jewish participation in cultural fields

in 1933 and on Reich Chamber of Culture documentation concerning expulsions. For details, see Steinweis, *Art, Ideolgy, and Economics*, 104–113.

8. On the Walter case, see Michael H. Kater, *The Twisted Muse: Musicians and Their Music in the Third Reich* (New York: Oxford University Press, 1997), 114–16, and Pamela M. Potter, "The Nazi 'Seizure' of the Berlin Philharmonic, or the Decline of a Bourgeois Musical Institution," in Cuomo, ed., *National Socialist Cultural Policy*, 47–48.

9. Two key recent studies are Saul Friedländer, *Nazi Germany and the Jews: The Years of Persecution, 1933–1939* (New York: Harper Collins, 1997), and Marion Kaplan, *Between Dignity and Despair: Jewish Life in Nazi Germany* (New York: Oxford University Press, 1998).

10. Pamela M. Potter, *Most German of the Arts: Musicology and Society from the Weimar Republic to the End of Hitler's Reich* (New Haven: Yale University Press, 1998), 103.

11. These issues are explored thoroughly in Steinweis, *Art, Ideology, and Economics*, 73–102.

12. The text of Paragraph 10 can be found in any one of several reference works and legal compendia published during the Nazi regime, two of the most useful of which are Hans Hinkel, *Handbuch der Reichskulturkammer* (Berlin: Deutscher Verlag für Politik und Wirtschaft, 1937), and Karl-Friedrich Schrieber, Alfred Metten, and Herbert Collatz, eds., *Das Recht der Reichskulturkammer: Sammlung der für den Kulturstand geltenden Gesetze und Verordnungen, der amtlichen Anordnungen und Bekanntmachungen der Reichskulturkammer und ihrer Einzelkammern*, 2 vols. (Berlin: de Gruyter, 1943).

13. For background on Schacht's impact on anti-Jewish policy, see Uwe Dietrich Adam, *Judenpolitik im Dritten Reich* (Düsseldorf: Droste 1972; Athenäum, 1979), 88, 122–24. In his diaries Goebbels reacted bitterly against what he (incorrectly) deemed Schacht's protection of Jews. *Die Tagebücher von Joseph Goebbels: Sämtliche Fragmente*, vol. 1: *Aufzeichnungen, 1924–1941*, 4 vols., ed. Elke Fröhlich (Munich: K. G. Saur, 1987), entry for 4 November 1937.

14. The most detailed study of the *Kulturbund* is Volker Dahm, "Kulturelles und geistiges Leben," in *Die Juden in Deutschland, 1933–1945: Leben unter nationalsozialistischer Herrschaft*, ed. Wolfgang Benz (Munich: C. H. Beck, 1988), 75–267. On the Nazi official who supervised the *Kulturbund*, see Alan E. Steinweis, "Hans Hinkel and German Jewry," *Leo Baeck Institute Yearbook* 38 (1993): 209–219.

15. Elizabeth Bab, the wife of Jewish *Kulturbund* official Julius Bab, later observed, with a good deal of hindsight, that the *Kulturbund* encouraged among some Jews the "fantasy that they could do themselves and their companions some good." Kaplan, *Between Dignity and Despair*, 42.

16. "In der Kammer tätige Voll-, Dreiviertel- u. Halbjuden," 1937, file on "Entjüdung der Einzelkammern," files of the Reichskulturkammer Zentrale,

former Berlin Document Center (hereafter BDC) materials, Bundesarchiv (hereafter BA), Berlin.

17. *Die Tagebücher von Joseph Goebbels*, entries for 4 September, 5 October 1935; 2 July, 11 December, 1936; 5 May, 5 June, 21 September, 9 October, 4 November, 24 November, 15 December, 16 December 1937; 13 January, 9 February, 18 May, 27 July 1938; and 26 January 1939.

18. For a detailed discussion, see Glenn R. Cuomo, "The Diaries of Joseph Goebbels as a Source for the Understanding of National Socialist Cultural Politics," in Cuomo, ed., *National Socialist Cultural Politics*, 197–245.

19. *Meldungen aus dem Reich, 1938–1945: Die geheimen Lageberichte des Sicherheitsdienstes der SS*, ed. Heinz Boberach, 17 vols. (Herrsching: Pawlak, 1984). The SD was not reluctant to report on public dissatisfaction about a wide range of other issues. It must, however, be pointed out that these reports begin in 1938, by which time the purge of Jews from the cultural fields had been largely completed.

20. Kater, *Twisted Muse*, 196–98.

21. The distinction between the German public's approval of legal and orderly antisemitism and its discomfort with violence targeted at Jews is a theme developed in the following works: David Bankier, *The Germans and the Final Solution: Public Opinion under Nazism* (Oxford: Oxford University Press, 1992); Ian Kershaw, *Popular Opinion and Political Dissent in the Third Reich: Bavaria, 1933–1945* (Oxford: Oxford University Press, 1983); Robert Gellately, *The Gestapo and German Society: Enforcing Racial Policy, 1933–1945* (Oxford: Oxford University Press, 1990).

22. For an analysis of this dimension of the response, see Ernst Piper, "Nationalsozialistische *Kulturpolitik* und ihre Profiteure: Das Beispiel München," in *"Niemand was dabei und keiner hat gewusst": Die deutsche Öffentlichkeit und die Judenverfolgung, 1933–1945*, ed. Jörg Wollenberg (Munich: Piper, 1989), 129–57.

23. There was a routine listing of the expelled Roma and Sinti musicians in the official Music Chamber newsletter. *Amtliche Mitteilungen der Reichsmusikkammer*, issues for February and March 1940.

24. Details in Steinweis, *Art, Ideology, and Economics*, 129–30.

25. *Die Tagebücher von Joseph Goebbels*, 27 July 1937.

26. Gründgens provided the model for the central character in Klaus Mann's novel about artistic opportunism in the Third Reich, *Mephisto*. A useful discussion of the Gründgens case is provided in Eberhard Spangenberg, *Karriere eines Romans: Mephisto, Klaus Mann, und Gustaf Gründgens* (Munich: Ellermann, 1982).

27. See, for example, Günter Grau, *Gay and Lesbian Persecution in Germany, 1933–45*, trans. Patrick Camiller (New York: Cassel, 1995), and Burkhard Jellonnek, *Homosexuelle unter dem Hakenkreuz: Die Verfolgung von Homosexuellen im Dritten Reich* (Paderborn: Ferdinand Schöningh, 1990).

28. The order is reproduced in Spangenberg, *Karriere eines Romans*, 84.

29. Goebbels to Schrade, August 1944, Reichstheaterkammer file of Rudolf Brunner, former BDC materials, BA-Berlin.

30. A facsimile of the newspaper page is provided in *Topography of Terror: Gestapo, SS, and Reichssicherheitshauptamt on the "Prinz-Albert-Terrain": A Documentation*, ed. Reinhard Rürup (Berlin: Willmuth Arenhövel, 1989), 46.

31. Material in file of Fritz Fuchs, Reichstheaterkammer collection of the former BDC, now at the Bundesarchiv, Berlin.

32. Documentation in Reichskammer der bildenden Künste file of Carola Gärtner, former BDC materials, BA-Berlin.

33. Schrade to Goebbels, August 1944, Reichstheaterkammer file of Rudolf Brunner, former BDC materials, BA-Berlin.

34. Elaine S. Hochman, *Architects of Fortune: Mies van der Rohe and the Third Reich* (New York: Weidenfeld and Nicolson, 1989). For further background on architecture, see Barbara Miller Lane, *Architecture and Politics in Germany, 1919–1945* (Cambridge: Harvard University Press, 1968).

35. Detlev J. K. Peukert, *Inside Nazi Germany: Conformity, Opposition, and Racism in Everyday Life*, trans. Richard Deveson (New Haven: Yale University Press, 1987), 191.

36. For an excellent presentation of the newer, more complex view, see Jonathan Petropoulos, *Art as Politics in the Third Reich* (Chapel Hill: University of North Carolina Press, 1996).

37. In addition to *Twisted Muse*, see also Kater's *Different Drummers: Jazz in the Culture of Nazi Germany* (New York: Oxford University Press, 1992).

38. Bericht Nr. 26 über die Sitzung der Reichstheaterkammer, 5 May 1937, BA-Berlin, R56III/14.

39. Reichskammer der bildenden Künste file of Hannah Höch, former BDC materials, BA-Berlin. On her career, see Peter Boswell, Maria Makela, and Carolyn Lanchner, *The Photomontages of Hannah Höch* (Minneapolis: Walker Art Center, 1996).

CHAPTER 6

The Limits of Policy

SOCIAL PROTECTION OF INTERMARRIED

GERMAN JEWS IN NAZI GERMANY

NATHAN STOLTZFUS

NATIONAL SOCIALISM strove to build a mass movement and a *Volksgemeinschaft*. The goal was a nation of Germans who naturally acted like Nazis, and the dictatorship sought to control the populace through social norms, not just through force.[1] Hitler considered popular support his most fundamental source of power, and up until the final "radicalized" years of the Third Reich, he prided himself on instituting Nazi precepts as law only when they already appeared to be the natural outcome of social developments. Numbers of Germans participated in racial identifications, denunciations, and expropriations, and each incidence of popular participation in persecution gave the government a green light to introduce further, more radical measures. For intermarriage, by contrast, through noncompliance and protest, non-Jewish partners ("Aryans" in Nazi terminology) rescued German Jews. The large majority of intermarried German Jews escaped death in the Final Solution, and at war's end 98 percent of Germany's surviving Jews who had not gone into hiding were intermarried.[2] This suggests that the regime's ideology might never have developed into genocide had the German people not achieved for the regime the social and economic isolation of the Jews, a prerequisite for their deportation and murder.

The relatively high rate of escape for intermarried Jews stands out sharply against the norm for German Jews. This contrast is yet more striking considering that in Nazi logic intermarried Jews should have been the first Jews killed. Unlike their children (so-called *Mischlinge* or part-Jews), intermarried Jews were "full Jews," without the protection of scientific or bureaucratic considerations about whether they should in fact be spared due to the "Aryan" portion of their blood.[3] Intermarried Jews were more offensive to Nazism than other "full Jews" because of their open defiance of basic Nazi laws such as those prohibiting *Rassen-schande* ("racial defilement" or sexual intercourse between "Aryans" and Jews) and "friendly relations" with Jews. Intermarried couples also affronted the pervasive aura under Nazi propaganda of seamless German unity behind Hitler.

The discrepancy between the extremely vulnerable position of inter-married Jews in Nazi "race" ideology and their actual fate poses the cen-tral social-political problem of intermarriage in Nazi Germany. It was ordinary non-Jewish Germans, primarily, who brokered the extraordi-nary rate of survival among intermarried German Jews. They achieved this with consistent noncompliance and protest directed toward the re-gime's efforts to break up their families, beginning in 1933 and continu-ing throughout the Third Reich. The overwhelming majority refused orders to divorce along with other laws intended to socially isolate the Jews, and in 1943 they took to Berlin's Rosenstrasse in protest against the deportation of family members. Noncompliance and protest forced the regime into a conflict between fulfilling its basic "racial" ideology and its basic political principle of maintaining domestic quiescence. The most appropriate context for interpreting the Berlin Rosenstrasse Pro-test and its results lies in the history of the interactions between the re-gime and intermarried couples during the ten years leading up to and culminating in that street protest.

Facing conflict between basic principles, Hitler avoided any general directive on the treatment of German intermarried Jews. Jewish-"Ar-yan" couples connected *Untermenschen* (subhumans) with the "master race" within the powerful tradition of marriage, causing the regime to unite the fates of German Jews and "Aryan" Germans. Waiting for an opportune moment to deport intermarried Jews whose partners refused divorce, high-ranking Nazis made a series of decisions to defer them and their children from the Final Solution "temporarily." In the context of a war that increasingly overextended Germany's resources, this series of temporary deferments lasted until the close of the war. These decisions were tactical maneuvers within the Nazi strategy to murder these Jews as well. While these tactical deferments continued, the regime's policy of immediately deporting any intermarried Jew whose partner died or di-vorced made it dependent in this regard on the death or cooperation of intermarried "Aryans."[4]

In resisting pressures to divorce, intermarried "Aryans" had to with-stand intense, daily social pressures as well as Gestapo terror. Without the preparatory experience of going against the social tide it is doubtful whether so many could have refused to buckle under government terror. The recently published diaries of Victor Klemperer, which record the experiences of an intermarried Jew of Nazi Germany, indicate that he reckoned with a sort of social death, and the terror of being an extreme outsider, as "Aryan" friends and allies fell away.

In contrast to most Germans, intermarried "Aryans" thwarted the advancement of Nazi anti-Jewish policies with regard to their family members. Had Germany won the war, of course, intermarried Jews too would have been murdered; but just the same, had intermarried Germans gone along with the Nazi leadership their partners would not have survived the war. Intermarried Germans' behavior created conflict between the Nazis' principles of racial purification and their desire to maintain social quiescence. This caused the regime to play politics and brought major power centers into disunity regarding how to respond. In the eastern occupied territories, intermarried Jews (and sometimes their non-Jewish partners) were seized and killed. This suggests that the exemption from the Final Solution of intermarried Jews within Germany stemmed from fear among top Nazi leaders that deporting these Jews would cause destabilizing social unrest and draw attention to the genocide they wanted to keep secret.[5]

In contrast to the efforts of these ordinary Germans, the vigorous efforts of both industry and the military on behalf of Jews these important institutions wished to protect from genocide were less effective.[6] The difference, from the dictatorship's perspective, was that these elite institutions were not based in the will of the "racial" community and could be manipulated without alienating a segment of the "racial" Germans. The churches, Protestant and Catholic, neither protested the state's crushing impact on the tradition of marriage at the time of the Nuremberg Laws in 1935 nor protected those the churches themselves (borrowing the Nazi term) called "non-Aryan Christians" (Jews who had converted to Christianity). The use of this term indicates a neglect of the fundamental Christian principle that salvation depends on personal confession. Some church leaders were moved to make written protests on behalf of "non-Aryan Christians" long after intermarried "Aryans" had begun to disobey Nazi laws, when it was becoming clear that these ordinary Germans were influencing Nazi policies regarding intermarried Jews and *Mischlinge*. Yet the condition determining whether an intermarried German Jew was deported to the camps throughout the Holocaust depended on the actions of the "Aryan" partner, regardless of church membership or military service. Walter Adolph, a close confidant of the principled Bishop Konrad Graf von Preysing of Berlin, recalled—as an example of how the church was able to help "non-Aryan" church members—reuniting one "non-Aryan" member with his estranged German wife. "As a way of saving his 'Aryan' wife trouble, he had moved into his own separate apartment. This, however, had cost him his privileged status. And now he was to be deported. Within a few hours the Relief Office was able to persuade both marriage partners to move together again. And with that the threat to his life was inverted."[7] This anecdote fairly represents the churches as adjuncts of ordinary Germans in the rescue of intermarried Jews.

The history of intermarried couples presents unique opportunities for examining the impact of ordinary Germans on the decision making of Hitler and other Nazi leaders, which was unusually decentralized regarding intermarried Jews. Hitler expected regional party leaders to make their territories "free of Jews" and would have been pleased to have intermarried Jews, like all other "full Jews," out of Germany as quickly as possible. Even without a clear decision from Hitler, regional party chieftains (*Gauleiter*) were nonetheless certain that the Führer's idea of racial purity, and the implications of the Nuremberg Laws, entailed the annihilation of intermarried "full Jews" (while under these laws the large majority of "first-degree *Mischlinge*" were not Jewish). But local and regional officials on occasion disregarded the series of Gestapo instructions to temporarily defer intermarried Jews (and *Mischlinge*) from the general deportations of German Jews, and when this did not cause complaints they got away with it.[8] At the same time, however, hundreds of intermarried German Jews were sent, one by one, to their deaths as criminals under so-called protective custody. A postwar German court identified this as an effort to draw intermarried Jews into the Final Solution without stirring up unrest within the *Volksgemeinschaft*.[9] To a large extent Nazi leaders avoided the threat intermarried Jews potentially represented to their base of popular support (as they perceived it) by exempting them from the Final Solution. To a lesser extent they attempted to destroy intermarried German Jews one by one by disguising their deaths as those of common criminals.

To maintain support as they probed for ways of murdering intermarried Jews, Nazi leaders used means of deception beyond those used to obscure the Final Solution. Murdering intermarried Jews whose partners would not leave them was sure to raise repeated questions and rumors among family members on the "Aryan" side. Sending intermarried "Aryans" to their deaths along with Jewish partners would be just as problematic, as fear spread among those who knew about the Final Solution that "Aryans" too were being deported and murdered. The elimination of all traces of Jewish blood from Germany was a clear objective, but the conflicting principles of mass movement politics were more subjective, and dependent on public perceptions. To fulfill his role as the charismatic dictator who united Germans, Hitler needed deniability—ways of disassociating himself with all unpopular measures, let alone those so terrible they were to be kept secret. Deniability depended on public perception and might be achieved by manipulating public opinion.

Mass opinion was the more malleable element of the two principles that genocide, especially genocide of intermarried Jews, brought into conflict, and Goebbels's most important powers were based on his mandate to control popular opinion. Hitler and Goebbels in particular were inclined to concern themselves with what they called the "psychological" problems of the Final Solution, rather than with the technical ones. The two-sided symbiotic relationship between *Volk* and Führer identified by Ian Kershaw may also be seen in the phenomenon of deception in Nazi Germany: the leaders could deceive the masses to the extent the people chose to allow themselves to be deceived, rather than facing up to more difficult truths.[10]

Goebbels and Hitler thought that mass murder would not find broad acceptance among the Germans, and they approached genocide with "psychological" means of controlling mass perceptions, in this case secrecy. Deniability at the top could be maintained through presenting isolated cases of the deportation of intermarried Jews as an irreversible, if regrettable, *fait accompli*, initiated from lower-level officials. As in other aspects of experience Germans could choose to think that things would have been different "if only the Führer had known." Separating "Aryans" and Jews from the same family, or deporting "Aryans" along with Jews from the same family, however, would generally complicate "psychological" manipulation from the top, forcing Germans to confront the fate of deported Jews in ways, and to an extent, they were otherwise able to ignore.

The history of intermarriages is especially suited to revealing what National Socialism called the "psychological" aspects of the dictatorship—efforts to maintain popular support at those points where Nazi policies departed from popular will and social traditions. A traditional emphasis on force and terror to explain Nazi domination has tended to obscure the regime's more subtle methods of control. Yet "psychological" leadership was the essence of highest-level control for National Socialism, for it mastered popular will, the most basic element of political power for Nazi mass movement politics. Psychological leadership, including the use of the new mass media, moderated the state's reliance on instrumental violence. To control populations, Hitler said in 1943, "force is decisive, but it is equally important to have this psychological something which the animal trainer needs to be master of his beast. They must be convinced that we are the victors."[11]

The decentralization of authority and the variety of types of efforts to eliminate intermarried Jews resulted in a range of intermarried experiences in cities across the Reich. Although the history of "Aryan"-Jewish marriage presents complex problems—both in assessing documents from the top and in the variety of experiences from "below"—it is critical to understanding Nazi decision making on the Final Solution, including the role of social ostracism. Major figures and bureaucratic structures were not the sole power brokers and decision makers. In the examination of the agency of ordinary "no-name" persons in the rise to power of the Nazi Party, the people are held responsible for resistance in measure with the extent that their support raised and maintained the government to be resisted.

WEIMAR AND THE EARLY NAZI YEARS

The decentralization of power with regard to the treatment of intermarried German Jews, the variation in experience among these Jews, and the relatively large survival rate among them all stemmed from the compromises the regime made in dealing with the conflict of principles represented by intermarried couples. How did these couples, within the tradition of marriage, manage to force the regime into a perceived conflict between losing important credibility with the German masses and completing the Final Solution? How were their aggregate efforts effective in creating havens for their family members, within the peculiar Nazi concern about popular morale and support, while German military and industries did not succeed so well in protecting Jews they wished to shield?

Once in power, the Nazi Party quickly reversed the process of assimilation between German Jews and "Aryans" as represented by intermarriage. In 1933, against the grain of the new politics, the trend toward intermarriage was still strong, as 44 percent of the German Jews who married chose non-Jews. In 1934, however, with the tide of anti-Jewish propaganda and persecution rising, the rapid social isolation of Jews was recorded in a Jewish intermarriage rate of just 15 percent. Nazi leaders had reason to think that the social, economic, and other liabilities of intermarriage might be sufficient to dissolve existing intermarriages when in 1935 laws banned further Jewish-"Aryan" marriages, though extant intermarriages were not forcibly dissolved. At the time of these so-called Nuremberg Laws, approximately 35,000 of the 500,000 members of German Jewish communities lived in intermarriages.[12]

In July of 1938 a new German law enabled intermarried "Aryans" to obtain a divorce upon request; the Gestapo then launched a campaign that sought through personal interrogation to persuade intermarried "Aryans" to divorce. These major new efforts may have resulted in a brief upturn in the incidence of divorce among intermarried couples, but the vast majority of intermarried "Aryans" still refused to end their marriages. In 1939 there were still about 30,000 intermarried German Jews (almost one in ten of German Jews). By mid-1943 intermarried Jews were virtually the only ones officially registered in Germany, and as of September 1944, 12,987 of the 13,217 Jews officially registered lived in intermarriages (98 percent). The vast majority if not all, of these intermarried Jews survived the war without going underground or being deported.[13]

Even as the trend toward intermarriage reached its peak, only a tiny minority of non-Jewish Germans married Jews. Often these Germans already considered themselves outsiders, or became outsiders with their marriages. Terror, whether from defying mass conformity or arbitrary Gestapo power, caused some family members to part ways entirely with those who intermarried. Intermarried Germans feared their neighbors as well as family members or police. One Jew admitted that neighbors harassed his non-Jewish wife more than they harassed him. Reich Minister Goebbels, noting their resilience, called intermarriages "extremely delicate questions."[14]

Beginning in 1933 many German professional, social, and religious groups adopted the "Aryan Clause," which expelled Jews from the civil service, for themselves, without official instructions, and some also followed the government's lead in excluding or discriminating against intermarried Germans as well. In a society where so much of life centered on marriage, family, and local clubs, local and voluntary decisions as well as government restrictions forced intermarried Germans to become outsiders. The tension between intermarried Germans and their neighbors and colleagues grew extreme during popular jubilation over national conquests, such as Hitler's reintroduction of conscription in 1935, the military occupation of the Rhineland in 1936, the annexation of Austria in 1938, and the Blitzkrieg victories early in the war. Because they profoundly disagreed with Nazism's fundamental racial principle, Germans who remained with Jewish partners were part of that tiny minority of Germans who could not identify positively with any aspect of Nazism.[15]

FROM KRISTALLNACHT TO THE FINAL SOLUTION

With the so-called Kristallnacht pogrom of November 9, 1938, came a new realization for regime leaders that intermarried Jews were not as isolated, socially, as other German Jews, and that some exceptions would have to be made for them in the upcoming physical isolation of Jews. During the pogrom Jews across the Reich, intermarried or not, were brutalized and imprisoned. The only significant German protests came from intermarried Germans, on behalf of their partners. In the aftermath Hitler accepted a proposal from Reich Marshal Hermann Goering, a main recipient of complaints, to "privilege" some intermarried Jews.[16]

Just as the regime had divided "half-Jewish" *Mischlinge* into two categories with the Nuremberg Laws, so it now also divided "full-Jewish" intermarried couples into two parts. If the Jewish partner was a woman (and the household was thus considered "Aryan"), or if the intermarried couple lived with at least one child who had been baptized as a Christian, Jewish intermarriage partners were "privileged" and exempted from much subsequent persecution. Hitler and Goering apparently undertook this division of intermarriages to preempt future objections like those following Kristallnacht. They would exempt the segment of intermarried Germans they considered most influential. Women were "silent sufferers," and the "Aryan" wives of Jewish men were not privileged unless they had children who were baptized Christians. Women, in the Nazi view, were incapable of political leadership and in any case needed to devote themselves full time to having and rearing as many children as possible. German women, however, had the kind of experience in extraparliamentary action and mass protest that Hitler found particularly threatening, as demonstrated by their efforts to gain the vote a generation earlier. Men had stronger economic and political connections and used force to resist, although the noncompliance and protest Ger-

124

man women used proved more effective for rescuing Jewish family members.

Ironically, Nazi policies forced women who had previously avoided politics into life-risking opposition. The story of opposition by intermarried Germans is largely the story of German women married to Jewish men. In Weimar Germany two-thirds to three-quarters of intermarriages were made up of "Aryan" women and Jewish men. The regime was traditional as well as racist in its gender values, and "Aryan" women married to Jewish men were part of what the regime called "Jewish households" (with the Star of David posted outside their doorways), while Jewish women married to "Aryans" were in "Aryan" households.[17]

As the regime put its racial policies into practice, the private lives of intermarried women became politically important. These women also assumed new, powerful roles within their marriages. As the testimony of Viktor Klemperer and other intermarried individuals shows, "Aryan" women learned to take care of official and everyday matters in Nazi Germany on behalf of their Jewish partners as well as themselves. Intermarried "Aryans" went for both partners to get the newspaper, to procure a business license, to find an apartment, to fetch ration cards, to do the shopping. While Jews had to fear starvation, intermarried "Aryans" shared their more ample rations with their partners. Charlotte Israel, an "Aryan" married to a Jew, remembered that "whenever there was anything to do with official business, my husband always said 'it's better if you go, Charlotte—you with your blonde head.'" Klemperer records a similar growing reliance on his wife. On October 13, 1941, for example, his long-time cobbler asked him to "let your wife come from now on" since the cobblers guild had just prohibited him from serving Jews, two weeks in advance of a new national ban on "friendly relations" between "Aryans" and Jews.[18]

In April 1939 the Jewish Rental Relations Law ordered Jews to move together into so-called Jewish Houses. Reinhard Heydrich, the head of the Security Police (SD), rejected a suggestion that German Jews be ghettoized within single city districts because the "watchful eye of the whole population" kept the Jews under control, "forc[ing] the Jew to behave himself."[19] Here again, however, intermarried "Aryans" were the exception to obliging self-policing (in this case the ostracism of outsiders). Under the Rental Relations Law, Jews in nonprivileged intermarriages were to serve as a test group for the eventual inclusion of all intermarried Jews in the Jewish persecution. The law ordered nonprivileged Jews to move into Jewish Houses, while exempting Jews in

125

privileged intermarriages. Jews in nonprivileged intermarriages were a relatively small percentage of intermarried Jews. More important from the perspective of the regime's effort to identify a group who could be used to test the results of including intermarried Jews in the advancing stages of persecution, these Jews had fewer connections to the churches and "Aryans." They either had no children at all, or none who were baptized Christians.

Perhaps Nazi leaders thought that forcing intermarried Jews into the physical separation of Jewish Houses, finally, would force apart at least this smaller number of less-privileged intermarried couples. Now, for the first time, nonprivileged intermarried couples were also outsiders in relation to the clear majority of their most obvious reference group, other intermarried couples. And yet here again, rather than divorcing, most "Aryan" partners in nonprivileged intermarriages moved into the Jewish Houses as well (as did Victor Klemperer's wife, Eva Klemperer).[20] Thus nonprivileged intermarried couples stood the test at this critical juncture; the trial case of the concentration of Jews in Jewish Houses indicated to the regime that fewer, rather than more, intermarried Jews could be drawn into the general persecution without causing unrest. Jews in privileged intermarriages would not be persecuted along with other "full" Jews until those in nonprivileged intermarriages were, and these were standing their ground.

PROBLEMS OF SECRECY AND THE FINAL SOLUTION

The test case of "Aryans" from nonprivileged intermarriages, who refused to divorce even when they were concentrated in Jewish Houses, helps to explain the regime's decision to temporarily defer all intermarried Jews—privileged and nonprivileged—from the Final Solution, once deportations commenced in Germany in October 1941. In September of that year German Jews had been forced to wear the Star of David. This included some *Mischlinge* (the so-called *Geltungsjuden*) and only some intermarried Jews (those in nonprivileged intermarriages). This division of intermarried Jews regarding the Star of David Decree suggests the regime had ideas for testing the deportation of intermarried Jews beginning with those with fewer relations to churches and "Aryans," who wore the Star of David. Yet for the duration of the Final Solution, Germans Jews living with "Aryan" partners were not deported as a group to death camps.

126

Thus the Final Solution, and specifically party declarations by 1943 that certain territories were now "free of Jews," provided a new, *de facto* definition of the term "Jew," a definition considerably narrower than that in the Nuremberg Laws of 1935. In September 1941 the Star of David Decree modified in practice the Nuremberg definition of who was a Jew through the exemption of those in privileged intermarriages. General directives for the mass deportation of German Jews beginning the next month, however, ordered the "temporary" exemption of all German *Mischlinge* and all intermarried Jews, that is, all with "Aryan" family members. Thus it was specifically not the Nuremberg Laws, or Hitler and Goering's decree privileging some intermarriages, that determined which intermarried "full" Jews would live and which would die; rather it was the relationship to "Aryans" that protected intermarried German Jews, as well as the *Mischlinge*. The Final Solution definition of "German Jew" deviated from National Socialist racial ideology even more than did the Nuremberg Laws, which already represented a glaring compromise.

The fact that "cleansing" Germany of Jews, from 1941 to 1945, required a definition more moderate than even that of Nuremberg sheds light on Hitler's earlier refusal to define the term "Jew" in 1935. By identifying the way the Final Solution definition of "Jew" was narrower than the Nuremberg Law definition we can posit the reason Hitler allowed even the earlier definition at Nuremberg to compromise Nazi ideology. It was for political ("psychological") reasons that Hitler refused to align Nazi ideology and practice with specific orders on intermarried Jews.[21]

Nazi leaders concerned with "psychological" leadership had learned from the project of euthanasia, the first Nazi mass murder, that victimizing part of a family under a program they wanted to keep secret led to unrest. Troubled family members of euthanasia's victims had been the source of fear-ridden rumors that spread throughout society and found a strong public voice in Bishop Clemens von Galen in the late summer of 1941. With Germans talking about a program the regime wished to conduct in secret, Hitler chose to curtail euthanasia until it no longer incited rumors and public denunciations from Germans, by limiting it to persons without strong family connections within the German people.[22]

Popular mass protests are associated with democracies, but they are especially powerful within a closed dictatorship against a secret program. They draw attention to what the dictatorship wants to keep secret (and thus for the protesters are also risky to the point of requiring heroism).

127

Paradoxically, the act of publicly protesting a secret Nazi program could create a public awareness that in turn might provide some protection for the protest. In the problem of intermarriage, as in euthanasia, the regime responded not just to the sheer fact that the persecuted population had "Aryan" relatives, but to the complaints and protests intermarried "Aryans" had already rendered. It was a relationship to German "Aryans" that protected intermarried German Jews, but this protection existed in 1941, as mass murder began, partly because the marriage partners of Jews already had a consistent record as potential troublemakers. The noncompliance of these "Aryans" triggered a conflict for the Nazis between genocide and maintaining quiescence and caused them to temporarily but repeatedly defer all intermarried Jews.

The noncompliance of intermarried Germans with all aspects of the Nazi persecution of Jews—to the extent that it threatened their own families—was consequential for the regime as well as for intermarried Jews. In early 1942 the Reich Press Chamber decreed that Jews should no longer receive newspapers, and instructed post offices and newspaper vendors throughout the Reich not to deliver papers to Jews. Intermarried "Aryans," however, bought newspapers for their partners or changed subscriptions to their own names. This rendered the law ineffective, and the regime was forced to abandon it within six months, since as the post office reported, it was impossible to tell whether an "Aryan" was married to a Jew or not, just by looking. The government could have issued special identifications to all intermarried Germans, but this extra work was never done. This specific case also reveals an additional aspect of the impact on the regime of acts of noncompliance: they caused enervating power plays among rivaling agencies. Trouble with the enforcement of this regulation led to a conflict between Himmler and Goebbels, with each titan insisting his own authority in the matter was paramount.[23]

The impact of noncompliance on the regime is further illustrated by another example from intermarried Germans, who by refusing to divorce influenced the regime not to promulgate a national law. Throughout 1943 and into late 1944 high-ranking ministers convened to consider a proposed law to increase the German population by loosening divorce laws so that barren couples could form more fertile unions. This plan, however, was scrapped for two reasons: SD Secret Police Reports showed that popular opinion would strongly oppose looser divorce standards, and the noncompliance precedent of the German-Jewish intermarriages showed that such laws helped very little anyway. Thus although they did not refuse to divorce to save marriages other than their own, intermarried Germans did extend their impact beyond their own cause. Because they could not be overlooked, a mere several thousand intermarried Germans came to stand for the general norm of German behavior, and the regime suspected that the norms on marriage would hold, despite the laws they made.[24]

In contrast, although there was no law requiring this, many "Aryans" contributed to the government persecution of Jews, making this in turn a socially acceptable practice. To advance their careers, Deutsche Bank employees threatened to denounce Jewish sympathizers (the identity for Nazis of every intermarried German). A case at Daimler-Benz illustrates how far some went to stop intermarried "Aryans." In a letter to Himmler dated 20 August 1942, SS Gruppenführer Burger complained indignantly that, following the death of Daimler-Benz general director Dr. Kissel, "in one fell swoop, men whom Kissel himself had turned down because of their Jewish relatives, had again stepped into leadership." These included "in particular Director Hoppe, married to a full Jew, Director Werner, also married to a full Jew, and Director Haspel [chairman], married to a half-Jew." Burger concluded by saying that an ally of his, Reichsamtsleiter Dickwach of the German Labor Front, was going to present the matter to the Führer himself. Dickwach believed that the "Jewish-related" members of the directorate were traitors who, due to their obviously hostile worldview, could not possibly orient their business "according to basic National Socialist principles in the struggle for securing German rights of life. We don't want anything to do with people who don't know what *Rassenschande* means."[25]

Some historians have suggested on the basis of undated file fragments from the Nazi Ministry of Justice that Hitler had decided by 1942 to put off the murder of intermarried Jews until after the war. This so-called Schlegelberger Minute states in part that Reich Minister Hans Heinrich Lammers reported that the Führer had repeatedly told him that he had decided "to have the solution of the Jewish Question deferred until after the war."[26] The contention that Hitler deferred the deportation of inter-married Jews once and for all rests first on interpreting the phrase "Jew-ish Question" as meaning "intermarried-Jewish Question." There is, however, no decisive evidence for this, and if there were, it would indi-cate how painstaking the inquiry into the history of intermarried Jews must be, given the deceptive use of language regarding them.

Even if Hitler made a final decision by early 1942 to put off deporting intermarried German Jews until after the war, the question of what influenced him to do so still points back to the noncompliance of inter-married "Aryans." The "Schlegelberger Minute" explanation of the fate of intermarried Jews, however, does not illustrate Hitler's style. Just as Hitler avoided written orders, so he also avoided final, inflexible orders, preferring instead to leave hard problems open for resolution at the op-portune moment. Of course, even if Hitler had meant to indicate only intermarried Jews in conversations with Acting Justice Minister Franz Schlegelberger, he may have changed his mind later, or simply contra-dicted himself elsewhere. Hitler went against an earlier "unalterable de-cision" even on an urgently important matter of foreign policy, concern-ing Czechoslovakia. And by mid-1943 he had also given Goebbels and Himmler conflicting signals on the question of intermarried Jews. Fur-thermore, some regulations from the Führer's office on the matter went unheeded. Despite Hitler's order of April 1940, there were still *Misch-linge* serving in the military years later, as indicated by further orders to the same effect. And in 1939 hundreds of intermarried "Aryans" contin-ued to work in the civil service, contrary to regulations four years earlier.[27]

The claim that Hitler by early 1942 had made the final decision to defer intermarried Jews until after the war is undermined not just by his general style and the nature of decision making in the Third Reich but by the record as well. Justice Minister Otto-Georg Thierack, the radical Nazi Hitler chose to replace Schlegelberger, indicated in a letter to Himmler of 9 December 1942 that Hitler had not yet made, but would be making, the "basic decision" regarding "racial intermarriages."[28] Thierack's letter anticipated a decision from Hitler on the fate of inter-married Jews almost a year after the Schlegelberger minute. His letter was in reference to a communiqué from Eichmann's office dated 3 No-vember, in anticipation of Himmler's "De-Judaization [Entjudung] of the Reich Decree" of 5 November 1942. At a Final Solution conference of 27 October, Reich Security Main Office (RSHA) officials agreed that intermarried "full Jews were to be separated from their partners and de-ported.[29] Himmler's de-Judaization decree was issued as it was becom-ing clear that Germany was likely to lose the war, and decreed that even the concentration camps on Old Reich soil were now to be made "free of Jews." Half-Jewish *Mischlinge* were to be included as Jews, indicating the regime certainly intended to deport the ideologically more clear cases of "full" Jews in intermarriage.[30]

Himmler's order for a radical conclusion of the Final Solution in Ger-many came as the Nazi regime was entering its final radicalized form.

THE LIMITS OF POLICY

Himmler had come down firmly against any law to forcibly separate intermarried couples several months before his "De-Judaization" decree, since this would succeed "only [in] binding our own hands."[31] The chief of the German Police—like Goebbels and the Führer—preferred taking forceful action at an opportune moment. In contrast to the highly public nature of Hitler's promulgation of the Nuremberg Laws, the Führer chose to approach the persecution of intermarried Jews through a secret decree, which he could change according to opportunity. On the issue of intermarriage too, Hitler preferred to wait for his intuition to inform him of the ideal moment for taking action: "You must understand that I always go as far as I dare and never further," he said.[32]

THE RADICALIZED REGIME

Hitler apparently never made the "basic" decision on "racial intermarriages" Thierack was expecting on 9 December 1942. The Führer granted party *Gauleiter* discretion on exactly when they purged their regions of Jews, and attempts to solve the intermarried Jewish question during the final, radicalized period of Nazism indicate the initiative of individual *Gauleiter* rather than a Führer decision for all regions. The language in deportation directives ordering the temporary deferment of intermarried Jews illustrates the deliberate ambiguity Nazi officials used as a means of maximizing flexibility in the service of their goals, at local levels.

In early 1943 there were two general efforts centered in the two regions of the Old Reich with the largest Jewish populations: Berlin and Frankfurt am Main. Especially in the Frankfurt region under Party Gauleiter Jakob Sprenger, scores of intermarried Jews were sent to their deaths one by one, as criminals, under protective custody orders.

Also in early 1943, and mainly in Berlin, a "Final Roundup of Jews" was planned to remove as many intermarried Jews as possible. Goebbels, who was slowly winning his struggle to impose "total war" against other Nazi power centers, foreshadowed this action in his total war speech of 18 February 1943. One of his central themes was that Jews were demonic makers of war in league with Bolshevism to construct a terrorist military power. For Goebbels completing the Final Solution was related to the radicalization represented in total war. Goebbels, in fact, apparently perceived the regime's radical solution to the "Jewish problem" to

131

be a point of leverage for attaining support for total war. On 2 March, during the massive Final Roundup, Goebbels argued to Goering, one of his most powerful compeers on the issue, that there was no alternative to total war. The regime, he argued, with its radical approach to the "Jewish problem," had burned its bridges behind it, and was in a life-and-death, do-or-die struggle.[33]

With radicalization, Goebbels, who prided himself on mastery of the delicacies of fundamental, "psychological" approaches to leadership, was losing his touch. The regime was so successful in using violence to achieve its ends in part because it recognized the limits of that instrument. Rather than flailing out with instrumental force to achieve goals at all levels, Hitler—still in mid-1943—stated that force, though "decisive," was no more important than "psychological" mastery. Radicalization and increased use of force accompanied the decline of the dictatorship, and its recognition of its decline, at the expense of its longer-term orientation more sensitive to popular morale.

By early 1943 Jews working for the military industry and intermarried Jews were the largest remaining groups of Jews in the Reich. Those in charge of the Final Solution apparently considered friends of intermarried Jews to be more potentially threatening than those of Jews working for industry. At the third Final Solution conference of 27 October 1942 the fate of Jews working for industry was a foregone conclusion and not discussed, while the fate of intermarried Jews and *Mischlinge*, once again, was discussed in painstaking detail.[34] German employers, reluctant to give up their especially profitable Jewish workers (who labored hard in the knowledge that they were protected from deportation as long as they held their jobs), had raised an obstacle for Final Solution executives by designating thousands of Jewish employees as "indispensable." With a massive arrest action the Gestapo was planning under the code name Final Roundup, Goebbels and the RSHA intended to destroy industry's obstacle to completion of the Final Solution in the Old Reich. They also intended to murder as many intermarried Jews as feasible, beginning with intermarried Jews without children, possibly through deportations to labor camps rather than directly to the gas chambers.

Despite the directives from his office ordering intermarried Jews temporarily deferred from deportations, Adolf Eichmann was preparing a series of plans and guises to remove intermarried Jews in layers. Deportations would begin with the intermarried Jews least likely to arouse public unrest by threatening the regime's official story that Jews were being resettled in work camps. Goebbels wanted to begin with "nonprivileged" intermarried Jews without children, according to a contemporary report from Gerhard Lehfeld.[35] On 24 February 1943, Hitler commemorated the founding of the Nazi Party twenty-three years earlier with a speech promising again that war would lead to the annihilation of the Jews. A decree the same day of the Gestapo in Frankfurt am Oder indicates that the Final Roundup was intended to remove all Jews from positions of forced labor in the Old Reich other than Jews in "closed work camps," according to the historian Wolf Gruner.[36] The decree recognized that Jews who had been living in the Old Reich had been "almost without exception resettled, except for Jews living in Jewish-German intermarriages," and that especially the "Jews living in intermarriages" were to be removed at this time from work sites in the Old Reich. In no case were intermarried Jews to be returned to these jobs. The decree instructs the Gestapo to make protective custody arrests of "protected Jews" guilty of "impudent behavior," while avoiding excesses.

These general RSHA regulations left a great deal to the arbitrary authority of local officials, in the course of removing as many intermarried Jews as they could get away with. "Impudent behavior" was an open category that invokes long-standing Nazi charges against the Jews. Goebbels had a habit of turning the truth on its head, including blaming the Jews for any domestic unrest. Hitler in his speech to the Reichstag promulgating the Nuremberg Laws said the laws were necessary, as indicated by vigorous complaints from all corners of the Reich about the "provocative" bearing of the Jewish element. Jews had caused "international unrest," Hitler said, which on occasion had "escalated to the point of demonstrations."[37]

The delicate task of removing intermarried Jews one layer at a time, under whatever guise possible and including the standard charge of "impudent behavior," was to begin in Berlin. As Reich minister in charge of popular morale, as well as *Gauleiter* of Berlin, Joseph Goebbels held the upper hand on matters of timing regarding the deportation of intermarried Jews. Almost one-half of Germany's intermarried couples lived in Berlin. In addition, Nazi protocol required Goebbels and the Reich capital to set precedents for the rest of the Reich. Aligning Nazi ideology with policy in order to complete the Final Solution was of particular importance to the regime in Berlin where, unlike anywhere else, the RSHA from time to time stepped in to directly control the business of the local Gestapo, regardless of what regulations appeared on paper. In Berlin too, the highest-ranking Nazi officials were associated with preparations for the Final Roundup. Hitler's SS division, the SS Leibstandarte

Adolph Hitler, assisted in the first two days of the Final Roundup, and the SS also arrested intermarried Jews and *Mischlinge* during this action. Goering's air force barracks and garage were used for this action, also implicating levels above the RSHA. Goebbels had a plan for deporting intermarried Jews without children. He instructed editors of the Swedish press in Berlin not to publish anything on the coming mass arrest of Jews (earlier in September 1940, Goebbels had already prohibited any press coverage on the "emigration" of German Jews during the war).[38]

The struggle between intermarried Germans and the Gestapo over the fate of intermarried Jews reached a climax on 27 February 1943, with the Final Roundup's arrest of some 10,000 Berlin Jews. "Aryan" family members of arrested Jews began gathering on Rosenstrasse in front of the Jewish Community Center, where intermarried Jews were imprisoned. These "Aryans," who were overwhelmingly women, began to call out together, "give us our husbands back." Repeatedly the police scattered the women with threats to shoot them down in the streets. Day by day the protest grew; as many as 600 or more came together at once, and as many as 6,000 had joined in by the protest's end. One protester recalled that she had begun her protest as an act of desperation but that as the protest continued, and as the Gestapo was unable to dispel it, she began to view the protest as a means of gaining the release of their husbands.

On 6 March, following a week of noisy disturbances on Rosenstrasse, Goebbels relented, and ordered the release of all intermarried Jews and their children. Hitler probably gave his approval. Once again Nazi decision makers at the highest level had decided to "temporarily defer" deporting intermarried Jews—this time, for the first time, after they had actually arrested them.[39]

For the propaganda minister, success, based in mass conformity, lay in making it appear as though dissent did not exist, especially in Berlin. Goebbels reasoned that releasing the intermarried Jews was the best way to dispel the open protest, visible not just to Germans but to foreign diplomats, journalists, and spies in the German capital. His decision to release the 1,700 to 2,000 Jews imprisoned at Rosenstrasse illustrates a central principle of Nazism's "psychological" leadership. The more the regime was winning its battles at war, the more it might resort to the use of brute force at home to achieve its goals. Goebbels notes in directives to his deputies in the Propaganda Ministry as early as May 1940 an inverse relationship between the need for external controls on popular activities (listening to foreign radio) and war victories.[40] War victories themselves bring close popular cooperation, but in early March 1943 morale in Nazi Germany was at a nadir, brought down by the debacle at Stalingrad and Allied carpet bombings of major German cities.

On 2 February, the day of General Friedrich von Paulus's capture at Stalingrad, Goebbels had perhaps mused in his diaries about whether use of the SS Leibstandarte Adolph Hitler provided the "appropriate means" for achieving his goals, given low popular morale.[41] In the cold calculations of the Nazi leadership, it wasn't worth crushing the protest on Rosenstrasse. This conclusion, however, was due in part to the reputations intermarried couples had earned during the preceding ten years. By the time of their street protest, the regime saw them, unlike other Germans, as persons capable of making a big disturbance; they were guaranteed to cause the kind of social unrest the regime feared. These "Aryans" had already divided the Nazi leadership on how to handle intermarried Jews, and the form of their opposition divided rather than united the leadership around the defeat of a conspiracy. It produced a conflict between Nazi ideology and its perceived policy options, exacerbating power struggles among high officials and influencing Hitler and the Gestapo to hesitate and repeatedly decide to "temporarily defer" deporting intermarried Jews, until the war ended.

Wolf Gruner considers this to be an "idealized" interpretation of the role of intermarried "Aryans."[42] He suggests, on the basis of the Frankfurt am Oder Gestapo decree, that the Berlin Gestapo had arrested Jews in mixed marriages by mistake. Such an error, however, was highly unlikely at that stage in the regime's radicalization, when authorities were in the process of clearing out every last Jew from the Old Reich. Without outside pressure at the time, the Gestapo would hardly have released Jews it had arrested in the course of deportations, despite directives. In any case, the Gestapo was so arbitrary and beyond the letter of the law or regulations by this radicalized point of the Third Reich in the late winter of 1943 that a law or regulation could not have prevented it from pursuing its perceived mission. Without the protest the Gestapo would not have released Jews it had already arrested, even if they had been arrested by mistake. For in cases like this which brought separate Nazi principles into conflict, general directives contained deceptions or were deliberately ambiguous to increase the chances, at local levels, of achieving the ideal of deporting all German Jews while maintaining popular quiescence.

Thirty-six intermarried Jews without children who had been deported to Auschwitz Monowitz during the Final Solution were released from

Auschwitz following the protest, on orders from a high Reich authority. These Jews had been accused of treason on trumped-up charges, in the manner of Jews in the Frankfurt am Main area deported during this time as individual criminals under protective custody orders. On or about the day of their release from Auschwitz Himmler recorded in his diary the results of a telephone conversation with Gestapo chief Heinrich Müller: "No deportation of privileged Jews." On 20 March Goebbels reported to Hitler that "Jews have in large part been evacuated from Berlin," and on 19 May 1943 he declared the capital "free of Jews." On 21 May RSHA director Ernst Kaltenbrunner ordered a stop to the further incarceration of Jews on protective custody cases unless they had "committed real offenses." This order, like others from various offices of the Reich, was certainly violated. But Kaltenbrunner's order that intermarried Jews were to be deported "only when they [had] committed real offenses" was followed, as was his order that "insofar as Jewish intermarriage partners have been deported on general grounds they are to be successively released."[43]

In Dresden, where Victor Klemperer lived, there was also an arrest of Jews corresponding with the Final Roundup in Berlin. Klemperer survived that in intermarriage, and two years later he suspected that the Allied bombing of his city in February 1945 saved him from another planned deportation of intermarried Jews. Certainly it is true that without the context of the Allied war on Germany, intermarried Jews too would have been murdered. In view of how especially loathsome intermarried Jews were to National Socialism, however, the riddle of their survival is not resolved by an Allied bombing so late in the war (Auschwitz had already been liberated). Why were intermarried Jews not among the very first German Jews to be killed? In the last months of the Reich there were rumors of other plans in other locations to finally deport intermarried Jews. Ruth Andreas-Friedrich, in her diary, for example, reported that trucks stood ready in Berlin to deport these Jews on 19 January 1945, but were not used. In September 1944 the SS and police leader of the Düsseldorf region ordered former Einsatzgruppe commando leader Gustav Noske to round up and shoot intermarried Jews and *Mischlinge*, but this failed when Noske "refus[ed] categorically to obey the order."[44]

The regime's apprehension of the potential "psychological" problems intermarried "Aryans" could cause stands in stark contrast to its disregard of efforts by the military armaments industry and the military on behalf of Jews important to them. Like his contemporary German-Jewish war veterans, Klemperer could hardly believe that his outstanding service meant nothing to the Nazis. Because of an exception to the "Aryan Clause" of the Law for the Restoration of a Professional Civil Service which President Hindenburg rung from Hitler, Klemperer, along with other veterans of World War I, did not have to leave his civil service position in April 1933, like other Jews. After the old field marshal died in August 1934, however, the most significant relief from persecution which Jewish veterans had relative to other Jews vanished. Klemperer lost his job in 1935, and, he noted, it was because he was Jewish, not due to the need to cut back at the university, since he was replaced by a non-Jew. "I received my dismissal through the mail on [the] basis of paragraph 6 of the Law for Restoration of Professional Civil Service (30 April 1935). "Stepun reports that my chair will be occupied again. So I have not been kicked out to make savings. But as a Jew" (4 May 1935). "I am after all a front-line veteran and was, indeed, dismissed as a Jew" (2 December 1935). Furthermore Klemperer's hopes based on a regulation stating that Jews who had served at the front would be dismissed but at full pension are dashed, as his pay is slashed by one-half. When he realizes that he will not receive any consideration because he served on the front, he despises the false hope he took in it (31 December 1935).

Military service in World War I, at any level in the hierarchy or any degree of decoration for valor, was never in general a sufficient condition to exempt a Jew from deportation. During the very first deportations, in early 1940 and again in early 1941, thousands of Jews were taken from Vienna and the Protectorate (Czechoslovakia) to ghettos in the General Government (East Poland). These deportations included Jews who had fought on the front for Germany or Austria in World War I, some of whom had even been army officers. Jews were included in these deportations without regard to religion (8,000 persons of Jewish ancestry were baptized Christians) and without regard to age (some men and women were over eighty years old and could barely walk), but not without regard to intermarriage.[45] The Germany military in 1942 did prevail upon the RSHA to have Jewish war veterans deported to Theresienstadt rather than Auschwitz. A central motive for the regime in establishing Theresienstadt, however, was to help cover up the death camps, and war veterans were deported from Theresienstadt to Auschwitz. Kaltenbrunner's memo of May 1941 noted Himmler's order that every Jew be removed from the Reich by June 30, and listed the four categories of Jews who had been exempted up to that point. Three categories, including those industry had designated as "indispensable," were now to be deported. The final category, intermarried Jews, was not: "I order expressly that Jewish intermarriage partners are in no case to be sent."[46]

A number of authors have investigated the Catholic Church to illustrate the influence of popular opinion in Nazi Germany; others have pointed out that Hitler was especially apprehensive of possible unrest among workers. Assembling as neither Catholics nor workers, the protesters on Rosenstrasse indicate that even the regime's policies on racial purification could be influenced by a credible threat of unrest. Intermarried Germans showed that *public* protest could still be successful after 1941–42, even during the period when popular trust in final German victory had grown thin and there was an "acceleration of violence and terror."[47]

It is important to recognize the impressive impact of intermarried "Aryans" who refused to divorce, because their history combines crucial aspects of both everyday experience and the practice of high institutional power in Nazi Germany. Victor Klemperer, like thousands of others, survived Hitler because his partner was "Aryan." He was in a position privileged relative to German Jews in general, and his witness should be identified as reflecting a specific category of German-Jewish experience. The diaries of German Jews who were not intermarried terminate with cruel abruptness (Anne Frank); Klemperer could bear witness to the bitter end because he was married to a non-Jew. Like other intermarried Jews, Klemperer's fate depended on whether his wife divorced. When she, the wife of a Jew, was issued Jewish ration cards, she protested, only to be told "get a divorce." Klemperer indicates that his wife's interest in and respect for his memoirs kept him writing. And of course there is a more direct way in which we owe his diaries to his wife: she took them for safe hiding to the house of non-Jews. The loyalty of "Aryan" partners of Jews during Nazism contrasts sharply with the denunciation of one marriage partner by another in this period. Even if it could be deemed normal for one married partner to stand up for another in normal times, these times were not normal. "One cannot live normally in an abnormal time," Klemperer wrote.[48]

A study of the behavior of intermarried couples during the Third Reich is a good corrective for the tendency to overemphasize the role of simple terror to explain both the consensus the Nazis achieved and the lack of resistance they encountered. Klemperer's witness is the kind of individual account sometimes ignored in the past by scholars in favor of sources considered useful for making grander overviews and interpretations. A single personal diary might be picturesque, but seems to add nothing to overall interpretations of Hitler's power, social patterns, latent social forces, or even the social atmosphere. Searching for "important" episodes, scholars have sometimes ignored events and perceptions of paramount importance for individual persons, like Rosenstrasse, certainly a crucial episode in the lives of those involved, whether as rescued victims or as protesters. The tendency to choose "history" or "society" over ordinary individuals in determining the level of significance of any simple event or source may be the outcome of an intellectual tradition that has turned away from individuals, and considers the acts of anyone who does not hold high office in an established institution insignificant. The notion of a "police state"—so popular as a way of talking about the regime until recently invests both the police and the state with an imaginary omnipotence; and as a corollary, it brackets off from our view the role of society and the notable opposition (and collusion) of ordinary persons. For the survival of German Jews married to "Aryans"—including Victor Klemperer—this opposition made all the difference.

NOTES

1. See Detlev Peukert, *Volksgenossen und Gemeindschaftsfremde: Anpassung, Ausmerze, und Aufbegehren unter dem Nationalsozialismus* (Cologne, 1982).

2. Statistics of the Central Organization of Jews in Germany show that as of September 1944 there were 13,217 officially registered Jews in Germany. All but 230 lived in intermarriage. Bundesarchiv, R 8150, 32. Every surviving Jew in Hamburg in May 1945 was intermarried. Beate Meyer, *"Jüdische Mischlinge": Rassenpolitik und Verfolgungserfahrung, 1933-1945* (Hamburg, 1995), 26.

3. State Secretary Wilhelm Stuckart and others of the Interior Ministry are sometimes credited with helping spare German *Mischlinge* from persecution as Jews, but Stuckart proposed drafting a law which would forcibly dissolve intermarriages to facilitate the deportation of Jewish partners. For political reasons, both the acting minister of justice and the propaganda minister rejected Stuckart's proposed law. Nuremberg Document (hereafter ND) NG-2586-H; ND 4055-PS.

4. On deportation directives see Nathan Stoltzfus, *Resistance of the Heart: Intermarriage and the Rosenstrasse Protest in Nazi Germany* (New York, 1996), 151, 328n.6.

5. Victor Klemperer, *Ich will Zeugnis ablegen bis zum letzten* (2 vols.) (Berlin, 1995). U.S. Holocaust Memorial Museum Archives, Washington, D.C., Orders

of the Reichskommissar for the Eastern Occupied Territories concerning the
"treatment of Jewish Mischehe," Riga, 7 October 1941; see H. G. Adler, *Der
Verwaltete Mensch* (Tübingen, 1974), 283, 284.

6. Ursula Büttner estimates that only 7 to 10 percent of intermarried Germans in the "Old Reich" divorced, based on statistics through October 1942
from Hamburg and Baden-Württemberg. Ursula Büttner, *Die Not der Juden
teilen: Christlich-jüdische Familien im Dritten Reich* (Hamburg, 1988), 57. On
Jewish veterans and armaments workers, see Adler, *Der Verwaltete Mensch*, 194.
During the Final Roundup entrepreneurs and factory foremen went to Gestapo
authorities "to show they had authorization to employ individual Jews. . . .
From military industrial factories, private firms, and also from the military itself
came protests, all with the aim of getting their Jewish workers released
again. . . . All the work books and protests . . . didn't do a bit of good." Statement of Max Reschke Berlin, Landgericht Berlin (hereafter LB), Bovensiepen
Trial, Supporting Document 30, 4 May 1959. Else Hannach, interviewed July
1944, said "the heavy industry moved heaven and earth in order to retrieve
those [employees] taken from the factories. But it was no use." LB, Bovensiepen
Trial, Supporting Document 30. Some Jews industrialists had warned not to
come to work during the arrests escaped. Elke Froelich, ed., *Die Tagebücher von
Joseph Goebbels* (Munich: 1993), part II, vol. 4, 528, entry for 11 March 1943.

7. Walter Adolf, *Kardinal Preysing und zwei Diktaturen: Sein Widerstand
gegen dei Totalitäre Macht* (Berlin, 1971), 177. One member of the German
episcopate, Archbishop Adolf Bertram, did specifically request German Justice
and Interior ministries to withdraw proposals for the compulsory divorce of intermarriages but, like Cardinal Michael von Faulhaber, he did so (1) in a private
letter, and (2) only well after Himmler and Goebbels had already decided that
there should be no such law. Guenter Lewy, *The Catholic Church and Nazi Germany* (New York and Toronto, 1964), 289; Theodore Hamerow, "Cardinal
Faulhaber and the Third Reich," in *From the Berlin Museum to the Berlin Wall:
Essays on the Cultural and Political History of Modern Germany*, ed. David Wetzel (Westport, Conn., 1996), 164. See also note 39.

8. On *Mischlinge* see, for example, the order of October 1942 from Gestapo
chief Heinrich Müller, NO 2522. H. G. Adler, citing T11, references Reinhard
Heydrich's anxiety following protests on behalf of certain Jews who had been
deported in violation of Gestapo directives. The Gestapo must strive to avoid
"these kinds of complaints under all circumstances," Heydrich wrote. Adler, *Der
Verwaltete Mensch*, 195.

9. Third Reich authorities used the appearance of legal procedure since these
Jews had "relatives and friends among the German people." Hessisches Hauptstaatsarchiv, Wiesbaden, Judgment against Heinrich Baab (51 Ks 1/50).

10. Ian Kershaw, *The "Hitler Myth": Image and Reality in the Third Reich*
(Oxford, 1987).

11. ND PS-739.

12. Büttner, *Not der Juden teilen*, 14, citing Herbert Strauss, "Jewish Emigration from Germany: Nazi Policies and Jewish Responses," *Leo Baeck Institute Yearbook* 25 (1980): 317.

13. Bruno Blau, "Mischehe im Nazireich," *Judaica* 4 (1948): 46. By the eve of the Third Reich the intermarriage trend was still strong, with over 57 percent of German-Jewish marriages outside the Jewish faith in Hamburg. Meyer, *"Jüdische Mischlinge,"* 24; Strauss, "Jewish Emigration from Germany, 317. Raul Hilberg, *The Destruction of the European Jews* (New York, 1985) vol. 2., 427, 430. Report by SS statistician Richard Korherr, ND NO-5193; Bundesarchiv, R 8150, 32.

14. Berlin, interview with Günter Grodka, 25 August 1985; *Die Tagebücher von Joseph Goebbels*, II, 3, 432, entry for 7 March 1942.

15. Ian Kershaw wrote that by the late 1930s only a very small part of the German population could not identify positively with "Hitler and his 'achievements'." Kershaw, *The Hitler Myth*, 140–41.

16. Germans married to Jewish victims of the Pogrom complained to Hermann Goering and the Hungarian statesman Nikolaus Horthy. Interview with Rudolph Schottländer, Berlin, 17 July 1987. Report of Goering, 28 December 1938, ND PS-69. For statistics on privileged versus nonprivileged couples, see Monika Richarz, ed., *Jüdisches Leben in Deutschland: Selbstzeugnisse zur Sozialgeschichte, 1918–1945* (Stuttgart and New York, 1982), 466.

17. On "Aryan Households" see Stoltzfus, *Resistance*, 9, 104, 301n.14. For additional statistics on intermarried German couples, see Marion Kaplan, *Between Dignity and Despair: Jewish Life in Nazi Germany* (Oxford, 1998), 74ff.

18. Berlin, interviews with Charlotte Freudenthal, February 1985. Klemperer, *Zeugnis*, 680.

19. Bruno Blau, *Ausnahmerecht für die Juden in den europäischen Ländern, 1933–1945* (New York, 1952), 64ff.; Heydrich quote, ND PS-1816.

20. Klemperer moves to a "Jews house" with his wife by diary entry of 26 May 1940, Klemperer, *Zeugnis*, 527.

21. Compare with Hans Mommsen, *From Weimar to Auschwitz: Essays in German History*, trans. Philip O'Connor (Cambridge, 1991), 159, 229–32.

22. Many of the victims of the new cautionary "wild euthanasia" had no German families. They were orphans or forced laborers from the East. Hans-Walter Schmuhl, "Die Selbstverständlichkeit des Tötens: Psychiater im Nationalsozialismus," *Geschichte und Gesellschaft*, 16, no. 4 (1990): 412, 413; Henry Friedlander, *The Origins of Nazi Genocide* (Chapel Hill, 1996), 152–59, 188.

23. Correspondence among German agencies between 13 January and 25 June 1942, YIVO Institute for Jewish Research, Nr. G 57.

24. Bundesarchiv, 30.01, 10118.

25. Bundesarchiv NS 19/776, SS-Gruppenführer G. Burger to Reichsführer

SS Heinrich Himmler, Re: Leadership of Daimler-Benz, A.G., 20 August 1942; Reichsamtsleiter Dickwach, German Labor Front, to Staatsrat Direktor Dr. E. G. von Stauss, 20 August 1942; NSDAP Reichschatzmeister Schwarz to Reichsführer SS Himmler, Re: Daimler-Benz A.G., 1 February 1945.

26. See the "Schlegelberger Minute," Bundesarchiv, "Behandlung der Juden," R 22/52, which indicates that Hitler had decided to put off solving the "Jewish Question" (not specifically the matter of intermarried Jews) until after the war.

27. After Hitler had shown understanding for Goebbels' release of arrested Jews due to unrest (note 39) Himmler said Hitler told him on 19 June 1943: "the evacuation of Jews was to be radically carried out in the next three to four months, despite the still-developing unrest." Washington, D.C., National Archives, T-175/R 94/26 15097. On Czechoslovakia see Michael Marrus, *The Holocaust in History* (Hanover, N.H, 1987), 36. A survey of Justice Ministry employees (all men) showed that in 1939 there were sixteen non-Jews married to Jews, and thirty-one married to *Mischlinge* of the first degree. (Bundesarchiv RJM 8469, 25, 41, 42, 80, 94.)

28. "Sobald die grundsätzliche Entscheidung des Führers herbeigeführt ist beabsichtige ich dem Ministerrat für die Reichsverteidigung den Erlass einer Verordnung vorzuschlagen, durch [den] die Frage der Scheidung von rassischen Mischehen entsprechend dem Ergebnis der Besprechungen geregelt wird." B.A. Potsdam, microfilm, 10531 P, Nr. 371939, Reichsminister der Justiz Dr. Thierack, Berlin, 9 December 1942, An Chef der Sicherheitspolizei und SD, Betr. "Endlösung der Judenfrage" Schreiben 2 November 1942, IV B 4 B, 1456/41 gRs (1344).

29. Himmler decreed all Jews, including *Mischlinge*, would be removed from German soil. Stoltzfus, *Resistance*, 205, 340n.65. Otto Hünsche, Eichmann's deputy who was present at this conference, said in an interview that the intention of the conferees at the time of the conference was to deport Jews married to Germans, including Jews in privileged intermarriages. Interview (telephone) with Otto Hünsche, 11 August 1986.

30. The concerted effort to deport every Jew from the Reich at the turn of 1942–43 is known in the Reich documents of the time as the "Entjudung des Reichsgebietes." Berlin, Kammergericht, trial against Fritz Wöhrn, Dokument Band 7, 18, or Anklageschrift, trial against Fritz Wöhrn, 147. In the previous month of October 1942 Gestapo chief Müller had already ordered that *Mischlinge* of the first degree were now to be counted as Jews. ND NO-2522.

31. Himmler to Berger, 28 July 1942, Bundesarchiv NS 19/1415.

32. Quoted in Jeremy Noakes and Geoffrey Pridham, *Nazism: A History in Documents and Eyewitness Accounts, 1919–1945* (New York, 1983), vol. 1, 550.

33. On Goebbels' speech see Ralf G. Reuth, *Goebbels* (Munich, 1990), 518; *Die Tagebücher von Joseph Goebbels*, II, 7, 454, entry for 2 March 1943. On

the prerogative of the *Gauleiter* see Peter Longerich, *Hitler's Stellvertreter* (Munich, 1992), 218–19. Walter Stock, the former head of the "Jewish Desk" at the Berlin Gestapo, referred exclusively to the massive arrest beginning in February 1943 (which later became popularly known as the "Factory Action") as "Judenschlussaktion," or variations on this including "Abschluss der Juden Aktion" and "Schlussaktion der Juden." LB, Trial of Walter Stock (PkLs 3/52), interrogation of Stock on 13 August 1951.

34. Summary of 27 October 1942 conference proceedings, ND NG-2586-M.

35. "Die Lage der 'Mischlinge' in Deutschland, Mitte März 1943," a four-page unpublished report from Berlin in mid-March 1943 by Dr. Gerhard Lehfeld, from the archives of Robert A. Graham, S.J., La Civilta Cattolica, Rome. Lehfeld's source was Erich Gritzbach, Hermann Goering's personal advisor at the Office of the Four-Year Plan.

36. Wolf Gruner has brought to light an important document in *Der Geschlossene Arbeitseinsatz deutscher Juden: Zur Zwangsarbeit als Element der Verfolgung 1938–1943* (Berlin, 1997), 316. Gruner uses this "Frankfurt/Oder Gestapo Decree of 24 February 1943 in the Circular Decree of the Landrats in Calau of 25 February 1943" to interpret the arrest action beginning 27 February 1943, which the Berlin Gestapo knew as "The Final Roundup of Jews."

37. Hitler's speech before the extraordinary session of the Reichstag, 15 September 1935 in *Die Reden Adolf Hitlers am Parteitag der Freiheit 1935* (Munich, 1935), 66.

38. Lehfeld, "Die Lage der 'Mischlinge' in Deutschland, Mitte März 1943," 4. Statement to the court of Alexander Rothholz, 2 May 1951, Landgericht Berlin, Trial gegen Walter Stock (PkLs 3/52).

39. Interview with protester Elsa Holzer, 10 December 1989; *Die Tagebücher von Joseph Goebbels*, II, 7, 487, 514, entries for 6 and 9 March 1943. Goebbels' State Secretary, who met with him upon Goebbels' return to Berlin on 4 March 1943 and said Goebbels would have released the Jews earlier if he had known of the protest earlier, said, when shown Goebbels' diary for 9 March 1943 that it meant Hitler had agreed with Goebbels' decision to release Jews at Rosenstrasse while reiterating Berlin must be made "free of Jews." Interview with Leopold Gutterer, 19 August 1986. On the courageous intervention of Catholic leaders on behalf of its arrested members (as of the third day of the street protest) see Ludwig Volk, ed., *Atken deutscher Bishöfe über die Lage der Kirche*, VI, 1943–1945 (Mainz, 1985), 19–21, 25. On the Rosenstrasse Protest, see Stoltzfus, *Resistance*.

40. Bundesarchiv, 50.01 1c, 24 May 1940.

41. *Die Tagebücher von Joseph Goebbels*, II, 7, 244–45. Other interpretations of Goebbels' words are possible.

42. Gruner, *Der Geschlossene Arbeitseinsatz*, 316.

143

43. On released Jews, LB, Bovensiepen Trial, Anklageschrift; on Himmler, BA, NS 19/1440; on Goebbels, *Die Tagebücher*, II, 7, 595, entry for 20 March 1943, and Reuth, *Goebbels*, 525. Kaltenbrunner order, 21 May 1943, LB, Bovensiepen Trial, Supporting Doc. 29 or Internationale Suchtdienst (Arolson, Germany), HO 308/242.

44. Ruth Andreas-Friedrich, *Schauplatz Berlin: Ein deutsches Tagebuch* (Munich, 1962), entry for 19 January 1945; see Adler, *Der Verwaltete Mensch*, 202, 203, on the fate of intermarried persons during the last months of the Reich. Case 9 (Einsatzgruppen Case, U.S. v. Ohlendorf et al.), in *Trials of War Criminals before the Nuremberg Military Tribunals under Control Law no. 10* (Washington, D.C., 1949–1954), 4: 558, 59.

45. Jerusalem, Yad Vashem, JM/2248.

46. Adler, *Der Verwaltete Mensch*, 194. The vast majority of Theresienstadt inmates were sent on to Auschwitz, with the explicit exception of intermarried German Jews. In response to the military requests that Jews who fought with high honors in World War I be protected, the RSHA promised to send them to Theresienstadt, but secretly deported them from there to Auschwitz. LB, Bovensiepen Trial, Supporting Document 29 or Internationale Suchtdienst (Arolson, Germany), HO 308/242; Ernst Kaltenbrunner order, 21 May 1943.

47. Martin Broszat, "A Social and Historical Typology of the German Opposition to Hitler," in *Contending with Hitler: Varieties of German Resistance in the Third Reich*, ed. David Clay Large (Cambridge, 1992), 26.

48. Klemperer, *Ich Will Zeugnis*, diary entries for 28 June 1937, 6 July and 14 October 1940, 364, 536, 556.

CHAPTER 7

The Exclusion and Murder of the Disabled

HENRY FRIEDLANDER

THE POLICIES directed against "outsiders" in Nazi Germany were based
on an ideology of human inequality. Since the late nineteenth century,
this ideology had everywhere gathered increasing support among the
educated and professional classes. In Germany, as well as in other Western countries, theories about human heredity, racist doctrines, and assumptions about the connection between human degeneration and
criminality merged to form a political ideology based on race. The Nazis
both absorbed and advanced this ideology and, after their assumption of
power, created the political framework that made it possible to translate
this ideology of inequality into an official German government policy of
exclusion.[1]

Exclusion was applied to many groups of "outsiders," but was directed in the most consistent and severe manner against those considered alien or degenerate. Determined to preserve and enhance the stock
of the German nation, the Nazi regime moved to exclude them from the
gene pool of the German *Volk*.[2] Members of other races were "aliens," a
term indiscriminately applied to both races and ethnic groups. In Germany, this meant primarily Jews and Gypsies, but exclusion was also applied to other "aliens." For example, one small group of non-Caucasians
were children, usually illegitimate, of German mothers and colonial soldiers in the Allied armies that had occupied the Rhineland after World
War I. The Germans rejected these fathers as so-called colored people;
most were black French soldiers from North Africa, especially Morocco,
but a few were Asians and at least one was an African American. During
the 1930s the German government registered and evaluated these "colored" children, known disparagingly as the "Rhineland bastards," and
thereafter illegally sterilized them against their will.[3]

But in central Europe the principal "aliens" were the Jews. Although
they had lived in the German lands for centuries and had become citizens in the nineteenth century, antisemitic prejudices prevented their
full acceptance and they continued to be viewed as "outsiders."[4] The

same applied to the Gypsies. They too had long resided in central Europe and many had become German citizens; still, antigypsyism remained virulent and to most Germans they remained the quintessential "outsiders."[5]

The so-called degenerates, the other group of "outsiders," were human beings with disabilities, that is, the physically malformed, mentally disturbed, and intellectually retarded. At the end of the nineteenth century geneticists, anthropologists, and psychiatrists led a movement designed to transform popular prejudice against the disabled into a science of exclusion known as "eugenics."[6] Eugenics, a term coined in 1881 by the British naturalist and mathematician Francis Galton, was described by the leading American eugenicist, Charles B. Davenport, as "the science of the improvement of the human race by better breeding."[7] Centered in the United States and Great Britain, the movement advocated both positive and negative eugenics. Positive eugenics was the attempt to encourage increased breeding by those who were considered particularly fit; negative eugenics aimed at eliminating the unfit. Eugenicists viewed individuals with disabilities as subnormal, immoral, and criminal as well as a burden to society and a threat to civilization. In the United States the favorite solution proposed by the eugenicists was sterilization, and in 1910 Davenport thus advocated sterilization "to dry up the springs that feed the torrent of defective and degenerate protoplasm."[8] Eventually more than half of the forty-eight states passed laws for the compulsory sterilization of the disabled. Another thrust of negative eugenics in the United States was the attempt to bar the unfit from entering the country. Applying the label of inferior and unfit to entire ethnic groups, eugenicists campaigned to restrict immigration from southern and eastern Europe, and their lobbying assured passage of the 1924 Johnson Immigration Restriction Act, which imposed quotas that severely limited immigration from countries whose inhabitants were identified as unfit.[9]

Prior to World War I the German eugenics movement, led by Alfred Ploetz and Wilhelm Schallmayer, paralleled eugenics in the United States. Like their American colleagues, the German eugenicists studied family genealogies and problems of degeneration, dividing populations into superior (*hochwertig*) and inferior (*minderwertig*) individuals; they hoped to safeguard the nation's "genetic heritage" (*Erbgut*) and viewed degeneration (*Entartung*) as a threat.[10]

The war shifted the movement's focus to negative eugenics. It also divided it into Nordic and anti-Nordic factions. The Nordic wing, centered in Munich and led by Fritz Lenz, Ernst Rüdin, Eugen Fischer, and Hans F. K. Günther, adopted the theory of Aryan supremacy, that is, the belief in the superior qualities of the Nordic or Germanic peoples. The anti-Nordic wing, centered in Berlin and led by Hermann Muckermann, Arthur Ostermann, and Alfred Grotjahn, rejected Aryan supremacy. The Berlin faction retained eugenics (*Eugenik*) as the name of the movement, while the Munich group adopted the name race hygiene (*Rassenhygiene*).[11]

During the Weimar Republic the eugenics movement emphasized sterilization of the disabled as the solution to the perceived problem of degeneration. However, the publication of an influential book took this one step further. In 1920 the legal scholar Karl Binding and the psychiatrist Alfred Hoche published a polemic advocating the "destruction" of institutionalized disabled patients, which they labeled "mercy death." But they did not use the normal definition of euthanasia, which refers to the death of persons suffering from a painful terminal disease, but defined it as the death of persons "unworthy of life" who were neither terminal nor in pain.[12]

Adolf Hitler's assumption of power made possible the enactment of the eugenic and racial policies of the Nazi movement. The race scientists, that is, the scientists committed to race hygiene, welcomed the Nazi revolution. Fritz Lenz, the professor for race hygiene in Munich and later in Berlin, had in 1931 already provided the Führer with the following testimonial: "Hitler is the first politician with truly wide influence who has recognized that the central mission of all politics is race hygiene and who will actively support this mission."[13]

The race scientists fully supported the regime's policy of exclusion, designed to improve the racial stock of the German nation. In the language used by both the Nazis and the scientists, this policy was called *Aufartung durch Ausmerzung*, which can be translated as "improvement through exclusion." But this translation does not fully transmit the perversion and brutality of the phrase. A better translation is "physical regeneration through eradication"; that is, the Nazi regime and its scientists wanted to improve the stock of the German *Volk* through the eradication of its inferior members and of the racial aliens dwelling within it.[14]

Of course the policy of exclusion required precise definitions of groups and individuals, which only race science could provide. However arbitrary, the "criteria for selection" had to be scientific, and the cooperation of the scientists was an important prerequisite for the successful implementation of the policy of exclusion. Scientific exactitude provided *Rechtssicherheit*, that is, legal reassurance for the masses that the law would protect their own security.[15]

Hitler did not disappoint the race scientists. On 14 July 1933 the German cabinet promulgated a sterilization law, modeled on a law proposed in Prussia one year earlier but adding compulsion as a prominent feature. The sterilization law, with the cumbersome name of Law for the Prevention of Offspring with Hereditary Diseases, was designed to deal with hereditary diseases (*Erbkrankheiten*) and persons carrying such diseases (*Erbkranke*).[16] The opening of the law proclaimed its content: "Any person suffering from a hereditary disease can be sterilized if medical knowledge indicates that his offspring will suffer from severe hereditary physical or mental damage." The law defined a person "suffering from a hereditary disease," and thus a candidate for sterilization, as anyone afflicted with one of the following:[17]

1. congenital feeblemindedness (*Schwachsinn*)
2. schizophrenia
3. *folie circulaire* (manic-depressive psychosis)
4. hereditary epilepsy
5. hereditary St. Vitus's dance (Huntington's chorea)
6. hereditary blindness
7. hereditary deafness
8. severe hereditary physical deformity
9. severe alcoholism on a discretionary basis

To implement the sterilization law, the German government erected a large bureaucratic structure.[18] It created a separate court system to adjudicate all cases and usually ruled in favor of compulsory sterilization. It established hereditary health courts (*Erbgesundheitsgerichte*), each staffed with two physicians and one attorney, as well as appellate courts of hereditary health (*Erbgesundheitsobergerichte*), whose decisions could not be appealed. The health-care and social welfare establishment supplied the names of potential candidates for sterilization to the hereditary health courts: first, the public health service and its public health physicians (*Amtsärzte*); second, directors and physicians in state hospital and nursing homes (the so-called *Heil- und Pflegeanstalten*) as well as hospitals, clinics, and old-age homes; third, directors and teachers in special schools; and fourth, the social workers of the welfare system.

The administration of the entire sterilization enterprise was directed by the Reich Ministry of the Interior, and within it by Department IV, responsible for national health (*Volksgesundheit*). The department was headed by Ministerialdirigent Dr. Arthur Gütt, a strong supporter of race hygiene who played a crucial role in the formulation of not only the eugenic legislation but also the Nuremberg racial laws.[19]

The sterilization law took effect on the first day of 1934, and the hereditary health courts were immediately swamped by thousands of denunciations. During the years 1934, 1935, and 1936 the health, education, and welfare establishment applied for the sterilization of 259,051 disabled victims, and the courts managed to rule on 224,338 of these; but while the courts handed down about 90 percent decisions in favor of sterilization, the hospitals were only able to sterilize about 70 percent.[20] Although exact figures on the number of persons sterilized are only available for the first few years, it is generally agreed that more than 300,000 persons were sterilized during the Nazi period.

For the year 1934, a breakdown by diagnosis of victims undergoing mandatory sterilizations is available.[21] The largest number—52.9 percent of all those sterilized—were diagnosed as suffering from feeblemindedness; schizophrenics were the second-largest category with 25.4 percent; and epileptics the third-largest with 14 percent. The percentages of all other diagnoses were much smaller. Although these surviving statistics cover only the early years of the law's application, they indicate a trend. Of course the reservoir of persons most available for sterilization—patients suffering from mental illness (schizophrenics and manic-depressives), St. Vitus's dance, epilepsy, and severe malformations—was not unlimited. Other categories, however, provided a pool of candidates that could be expanded. The numbers involved fluctuated depending on the flexibility of the application of definitions. This was certainly true for blindness and deafness; the category of those diagnosed with malformations could be expanded indefinitely if harelips, clubfeet, and similar defects were—as a matter of course—considered sufficient cause for sterilization. Further, the definitions for the category of feeblemindedness, which from the beginning provided the largest number of persons for sterilization, were largely determined by social criteria and therefore lacked scientific precision; they could be applied to an ever-increasing number of persons. The group deemed alcoholics, providing a small but substantial number for sterilization during 1933–34, had no doubt been selected on the basis of social and economic position and obviously had not been exhausted by the end of the 1930s.[22]

The sterilization law was only the first shot in the eugenic war launched by the Nazi regime against the disabled. It was soon followed

149

by numerous regulations and amendments designed to increase the effectiveness and severity of the law.[23] One example was the amendment designed to close the loophole involving pregnancies that commenced prior to sterilization. Henceforth sterilization and abortion could be combined. The amendment even permitted an abortion if the mother was healthy but the father suffered from a hereditary disease; at the same time, the amendment restated the prohibition against sterilization under heavy penalties for persons judged healthy.[24]

The sterilization law permitted the public health service to collect a great deal of data on the racial health of the German nation. This ability to collect data was vastly increased with the passage of the so-called marriage health law, promulgated in 1935, only one month after the Nuremberg racial laws.[25] It required permission from the public health offices for all marriages, and every person had to obtain prior to marriage a certificate from the public health service stating that offspring would be genetically sound. Marriages deemed detrimental to the hereditary health of the nation were prohibited. The marriage health law excluded from marriage a group even larger than that affected by the sterilization law. The information thus collected by the public health service grew enormously. The long-range objective, however, was a comprehensive system of registration to provide genealogical charts (*Sippentafeln*), which would ensure the registration of the largest possible group of persons subject to the eugenic and racial legislation. The state wanted to establish an inventory on race and heredity (*erbbiologische Bestandsaufnahme*). The war, however, ended before the inventory could be completed.[26]

Registration, institutionalization, compulsory sterilization, and marriage prohibition, as well as government propaganda in favor of racial health, stigmatized and isolated the disabled as excluded outsiders to the national community (*Volksgemeinschaft*).[27] As a group they had become fair game for any kind of discrimination. As war approached, the Nazi regime moved to implement an even more radical form of exclusion. For this purpose it returned to the ideas first advanced by Binding and Hoche in 1920. The advocates of such action described it as the destruction of life unworthy of life, but often the euphemism "euthanasia" was used. In fact it was mass murder, involving the killing of the disabled.[28] After all, the policy of exclusion stood at the center of the Nazi utopia, and killing operations were only the most radical, final stage of exclusion. Radical Nazis had already advocated euthanasia during the 1930s, but in 1935 Adolf Hitler had told Gerhard Wagner, the

150

Reich physician leader, that he would only implement the killing of the disabled once war had started.[29]

The discussions and preparations preceded the outbreak of the war. First came the decision to kill disabled infants and small children. The case of the disabled Knauer baby served as pretext for Hitler's decision to implement children's euthanasia. In 1938 the parents of the Knauer baby had appealed to the Chancellery of the Führer (Kanzlei des Führers, or KdF) for permission to kill the baby, and Hitler thereafter appointed his escorting physician (*Begleitarzt*), Karl Brandt, and the chief of the KdF, Philipp Bouhler, as plenipotentiaries for children's euthanasia. Brandt and Bouhler assigned the job to Viktor Brack, one of the KdF department heads, and he assembled a team of officials and physicians, including Herbert Linden of the Reich Ministry of the Interior, to plan and organize the killing operation during the spring of 1939.[30]

After planning for children's euthanasia had been completed but before it could be implemented, Hitler expanded the killings to include disabled adults.[31] At first he appointed Dr. Leonardo Conti, Wagner's successor as Reich physician leader and also state secretary for health in the Reich Ministry of the Interior, to direct adult euthanasia. But shortly thereafter the Führer changed his mind and transferred the appointment to Brandt and Bouhler.[32] These appointments probably took place during July and August 1939.[33]

With the decision to commit government-sponsored mass murder, the regime crossed a line into uncharted territory. True, the regime picked the victim group with great care. The disabled had been stigmatized, isolated, and marginalized. Compared with the other targeted and excluded groups, especially the Jews, the disabled had no international visibility or foreign supporters. Still, there was a certain amount of risk. To succeed, the regime required the support of the bureaucracy and the acquiescence of the population. To ensure the latter, the entire enterprise had to be absolutely secret. This is undoubtedly the reason Hitler assigned the job to the KdF and not to the Reich Ministry of the Interior. Although Viktor Brack and his KdF associates needed the ministry to serve as enforcer, and thus included Linden within the operation's managing circle, the KdF retained control; it operated from the shadows, thus screening both state and party from public view.

To hide the participation of state and party, the KdF created front organizations with fancy scientific names to manage the euthanasia killing operation. For children's euthanasia the KdF created the Reich Committee for the Scientific Registration of Severe Hereditary Ailments

(*Reichsausschuß zur wissenschaftlichen Erfassung von erb- und anlagebedingten schweren Leiden*), known as the Reich Committee and managed by the KdF officials Hans Hefelmann and Richard von Hegener. For the larger operation against disabled adults, the KdF created a complex structure of front organizations, including the Reich Cooperative for State Hospitals and Nursing Homes (*Reichsarbeitsgemeinschaft Heil- und Pflegeanstalten*), known as the RAG and headed by the physician Werner Heyde and later Paul Nitsche; the Charitable Foundation for Institutional Care (*Gemeinnützige Stiftung für Anstaltspflege*), known as the Foundation and headed by Gerhard Bohne and later Dietrich Allers; the Charitable Foundation for the Transport of Patients, Inc. (*Gemeinnützige Kranken-Transport, G.m.b.H.*), known as Gekrat and headed by the KdF official Reinhold Vorberg; and to keep the accounts, the Central Accounting Office for State Hospitals and Nursing Homes (*Zentralverrechnungsstelle Heil- und Pflegeanstalten*), headed by Hans-Joachim Becker.[34]

The KdF office at the Voss Straße in Berlin was too small to accommodate the personnel recruited to run euthanasia, and for this reason—as well as to hide the involvement of the KdF—the operation was housed at the Columbus House on the Potsdamer Platz, an office complex located at Berlin's busiest intersection. Soon it had to expand, and the central offices moved into a confiscated Jewish villa at number 4 on Tiergarten Straße; because of this address, the euthanasia killing operation was soon known as Operation T4, or simply T4.[35]

The KdF had to solve three problems before it could implement the T4 killing operation: (1) how to select and collect the disabled victims; (2) how to kill the victims; and (3) how to recruit the killers. Surprisingly, the recruitment of killers proved to be easy.[36] The civil service, both in the Reich ministries and in the offices of the states (*Länder*), collaborated without hesitation. The recruitment of the actual killers—physicians, nurses, scientists, police officers, and common workers—also posed no problems. Recruited almost at random, they represented a cross-section of the German and Austrian population. Most but not all were party members and their recruitment was based on connections or recommendations. They all joined without compulsion. Very few refused. Among the professionals, one psychiatrist rejected the invitation to join because he had moral scruples; one SS physician probably declined to participate because he did not want to get his hands dirty.[37]

Still, there were some hesitations among the physicians and civil servants. They demanded the decriminalization of the euthanasia killings, that is, the removal of the threat of prosecution for physicians who killed their patients. But Hitler refused to promulgate a euthanasia law during the war, and this prevented public decriminalization. Although almost everyone accepted the principle that the Führer's word was law, the KdF functionaries had difficulty convincing physicians and civil servants that they would not be criminally liable for murder in the absence of a duly enacted law clearly authorizing the killing of disabled patients. To convince their collaborators, and possibly to cover themselves as well, the KdF officials decided to ask Hitler for written orders.

In October 1939 Hitler signed a document, more an authorization than an order, that had been prepared by the KdF.[38] But to emphasize that war would not only alter the international status of the Reich but also herald "domestic purification," he predated it to 1 September 1939, the day World War II began.[39] Prepared on Hitler's personal stationery, as if mass murder was his "private affair," but never promulgated or published in any legal gazette, this authorization did not actually have the force of law.[40] It was to serve, however, as the legal basis for the killing operation, and it was used to convince physicians and civil servants to collaborate in the killings.[41]

Typed on white stationery, with the German eagle and swastika as well as the name "Adolf Hitler" printed on the top left, the authorization read:

Berlin, 1 Sept. 1939
Reich Leader Bouhler and Dr. med. Brandt are charged with the responsibility of enlarging the competence of certain physicians, designated by name, so that patients who, on the basis of human judgment, are considered incurable, can be granted mercy death after a discerning diagnosis.
(signed) A. Hitler

The original was kept in a safe at the KdF; copies were shown to various prospective collaborators. One copy was later sent to the Reich minister of justice, Franz Gürtner. The original and all but one copy were destroyed when the war ended. The photocopy sent to Gürtner survived, with a handwritten notation:

Transmitted to me by Bouhler on 27.8.40
(signed) Dr. Gürtner.[42]

To select the disabled victims, T4 created a bureaucratic structure. The first step was registration. Physicians at every clinic, hospital, and nursing home completed a questionnaire for each one of their disabled

153

patients. These questionnaires were distributed and collected by the Reich Ministry of the Interior and, once completed, transmitted to T4. After sorting by T4, the questionnaires were submitted to so-called medical experts—physicians serving as *Gutachter* (experts)—for evaluation. Without examining the patients or reading their medical records, the experts made their selection on the basis of the questionaires and were paid by the piece. T4 then compiled lists of those selected, and Gekrat collected them from their institutions.[43]

The development of a killing technique posed the greatest challenge for the KdF. For children's euthanasia, which came chronologically first, the procedure was relatively simple. T4 established special so-called children's wards for expert care (*Kinderfachabteilungen*) at various hospitals and clinics; eventually more than twenty such killing wards were created. The most notorious of these were at the Brandenburg-Görden hospital headed by Dr. Hans Heinze, Eglfing-Haar headed by Dr. Hermann Pfannmüller, Eichberg headed by Dr. Friedrich Mennecke, Kaufbeuren headed by Dr. Valentin Faltlhauser, and Vienna's Am Spiegelgrund headed by Dr. Erwin Jekelius and later Dr. Ernst Illing.[44] In these wards physicians killed the children through the administration of an overdose of common barbiturates, mostly morphine-scopolamine, luminal (a sedative), and veronal (sleeping tablets), but at times also through starvation.[45]

The development of a method to kill disabled adults rapidly, efficiently, and secretly was a major contribution to all Nazi killing operations. For this purpose the T4 technicians invented killing centers where human beings were murdered in gas chambers. To ensure that this method would work, T4 arranged for a gassing demonstration at the old jail in Brandenburg in December 1939 or January 1940. The demonstration was attended by Brand, Bouhler, Conti, Linden, Brack, and several KdF officials, the T4 physicians Werner Heyde, Paul Nitsche, Irmfried Eberl, Horst Schumann, Ernst Baumhard, the T4 chemists Albert Widmann and August Becker, and the Stuttgart police officer Christian Wirth. Eight disabled men were used for the experiment. They entered the newly constructed gas chamber, the chemists injected carbon monoxide via a pipe, and the dignitaries observed the death of the victims through a viewing window.[46]

The experiment was a great success, and the assembled killers decided to use gas to kill the disabled adults. Brandt informed the Führer, and Hitler approved gas as the killing agent. Even after the war Brandt remained enthusiastic about this application of modern technology and viewed the invention of the gas chamber as a great accomplishment; he proudly told his American interrogator: "This is just one case where in medical history major jumps are being made."[47] Of course success meant that this T4 invention would also be applied to victims who were not disabled. Starting in 1941, the T4 killing centers were also used to murder concentration camp prisoners.[48] Later the T4 system was exported to the East. In December 1941 a duplicate installation was erected at Chelmno, and in the spring and summer of 1942 three larger killing centers, modeled on the T4 example and staffed by experienced T4 operatives, opened at Belzec, Sobibor, and Treblinka.[49]

Eventually T4 established six killing centers. The first were Brandenburg, Grafeneck, Hartheim, and Sonnenstein. Late in 1940 Brandenburg and Grafeneck were closed because their operation had become too public. They were replaced by Bernburg and Hadamar. Each killing center was headed by a physician-in-charge—for example, Irmfried Eberl at Brandenburg and Bernburg (and later at Treblinka), Horst Schumann in Grafeneck and Sonnenstein (later active in Auschwitz), and Rudolf Lonauer in Hartheim—assisted by one or two junior physicians. The physicians shared power with nonmedical supervisors, almost always recruited from the police as, for example, Christian Wirth, Franz Reichleitner, and Franz Stangl at Hartheim.

All six killing centers were equipped with a gas chamber and a crematorium, as well as reception rooms and housing for the staff. But there were no facilities for disabled patients, because they were killed soon after arrival. First, the physician and his staff examined the victims to ensure that the paperwork had been correctly completed. Second, the victims were photographed for the permanent record. Third, they were led to the gas chamber. Once they were locked into the chamber, the physician opened the valve of the carbon monoxide container located next to the chamber; the gas entered the chamber through a pipe while the physician observed the victims through a window. Fourth, after one or two hours the chamber was ventilated, the physician pronounced the victims dead, and the so-called stokers (*Brenner*) removed the bodies. Fifth, the stokers cremated the corpses.[50]

The result was mass murder on the assembly line, a killing technique that rapidly and efficiently moved the victims from arrival to cremation. In addition, T4 added the profit motive to this arrangement. After death and before cremation, physicians mutilated the corpses to remove organs for scientific research from a few selected victims.[51] Prior to cremation, the stokers also looted the corpses as they broke out all gold

155

teeth and gold bridgework.[52] This gold, together with that later collected by similar means elsewhere, eventually found its way into the coffers of the German Reich, but T4 no doubt received, as did other agencies involved in this type of pillage, an equivalent credit to its budget.[53] One of the secretaries at the Hadamar killing center testified after the war about the procedure of collecting gold teeth: "Gold teeth? They were handed to us in the office, whenever there was someone who had gold teeth. Many handed to us? No. They were brought to me in a bowl by one of the stokers. He had a book and I had a book, and we thus confirmed accuracy. We had a little carton, and that is where we kept them until we had accumulated a sufficiently large amount, and we then sent them by courier to Berlin."[54] Copied later in the killing centers in the East, this T4 innovation made possible the collection of an amount of gold sufficient to improve Germany's financial position during the war.[55]

The secrecy surrounding the T4 killings did not prevent knowledge from reaching the public. For this reason—public unrest concerning the killings—Hitler ordered a stop to the gassing in August 1941.[56] By that time about 80,000 disabled victims had been murdered in the T4 gas chambers.[57] Of course this did not mean that the killing of the disabled was discontinued. After August 1941 the killings were decentralized in various institutions throughout the German Reich; instead of gas chambers, the killers used deadly medication in hospital killing wards, imitating the method used in children's euthanasia, which also continued throughout the war.[58]

The disabled patients were the first to pierce the secrecy surrounding the killings. As they were collected by Gekrat for transport to the killing centers, the disabled victims knew their fate as they raised their voices to shame and denounce the killers. Getting on a Gekrat bus, one male patient donned his Iron Cross and one female patient, a Catholic nun, told those around her: "All of us, who have been condemned to death, are now getting on the bus."[59] At one hospital, a female patient asked a visiting panel of T4 physicians: "Well, are you again looking for new victims, you mass murderers?"[60] Another female patient shouted from the Gekrat bus that was taking her to the killing center: "Yes, we shall die, but that Hitler will go to hell."[61] Although T4 launched a vast obfuscation operation involving letters of condolence and fraudulent death certificates designed to fool the relatives of the victims, these measures could not hide the truth for very long. The anger of relatives at the murder of their kin sparked protests from the judiciary and the churches.

Although the regime was able to pacify such official protests, public unrest sparked by the relatives forced Hitler to issue his stop order.[62]

The euthanasia killing program was directed primarily against German (and Austrian) nationals, but it was not restricted to Germans or to so-called Aryans. In Poland the Germans killed almost all disabled Poles; the hospitals were either closed or converted for German use. The same applied in the occupied Soviet Union.[63] At Nuremberg the defendants claimed that Jews were not subject to the eugenic laws, and that no Jews were ever killed within the euthanasia program. This false claim was generally believed. Only much later did the truth emerge during various postwar German trials. Still, even today there has been no widespread acknowledgment of the murder of disabled Jews. The murder of disabled Jews is hardly mentioned in histories of the destruction of the European Jews; and their fate is mentioned only in passing in books about the euthanasia killings. In fact, however, Jews fell under the eugenic legislation from the beginning. They were sterilized alongside non-Jewish Germans, and they were killed in the same gas chambers as were non-Jewish Germans.[64]

The defeat of Nazi Germany did not fully liberate the disabled victims. Although no longer murdered by their caregivers, the disabled remained locked in the same institutions, supervised by the same administrators, often under conditions similar to those they had experienced during the war. Their suffering was not acknowledged. They received no compensation. Only slowly have attitudes and treatment changed. The scars left by the experiences of the war years have not yet healed. Only recently have books appeared that recount the wartime fate of the disabled and discuss their postwar experiences.[65]

NOTES

1. For a more detailed discussion, see Henry Friedlander, *The Origins of Nazi Genocide: From Euthanasia to the Final Solution* (Chapel Hill: University of North Carolina Press, 1995), chap. 1. See also *Hundert Jahre deutscher Rassismus: Katalog und Arbeitsbuch* (Cologne: Kölnische Gesellschaft für Christlich-Jüdische Zusammenarbeit, 1988); Robert Proctor, *Racial Hygiene: Medicine under the Nazis* (Cambridge: Harvard University Press, 1988); George L. Mosse, *The Crisis of German Ideology: Intellectual Origins of the Third Reich* (reprint, New York: Grosset and Dunlap, 1964); Christian Pross and Götz Aly, eds., *Der Wert des Menschen: Medizin in Deutschland, 1918–1945* (Berlin:

Edition Hentrich, 1989); and Charles Roland, Henry Friedlander, and Benno Müller-Hill, eds., *Medical Science without Compassion, Past and Present: Fall Meeting, Cologne, September 28–30, 1988*, Arbeitspapiere-Atti-Proceedings, no. 11 (Hamburg: Hamburger Stiftung für Sozialgeschichte des 20. Jahrhunderts, 1992).

2. See Benno Müller-Hill, *Tödliche Wissenschaft: Die Aussonderung von Juden, Zigeunern, und Geisteskranken, 1933–1945* (Reinbek bei Hamburg: Rowohlt Taschenbuch Verlag, 1984).

3. See Reiner Pommerin, *"Sterilisierung der Rheinlandbastarde": Das Schicksal einer farbigen deutschen Minderheit, 1918–1937* (Düsseldorf: Droste Verlag, 1979).

4. See, for example, Paul Massing, *Rehearsal for Destruction: A Study of Political Antisemitism in Imperial Germany* (New York: Harper, 1949); Eva Reichmann, *Hostages of Civilization: The Social Sources of National Socialist Anti-Semitism* (London: Gollancz, 1950); Peter Pulzer, *The Rise of Political Anti-Semitism in Germany and Austria* (New York: Wiley, 1964); and Saul Friedländer, *Nazi Germany and the Jews: The Years of Persecution, 1933–1939* (New York: Harper Collins, 1997).

5. See, for example, Angus Fraser, *The Gypsies* (Oxford: Blackwell, 1992); Kirsten Martins-Heuß, *Zur mythischen Figur des Zigeuners in der deutschen Zigeunerforschung* (Frankfurt: Haag and Herchen, 1983); and Michael Zimmermann, *Verfolgt, Vertrieben, Vernichtet: Die nationalsozialistische Vernichtungspolitik gegen Sinti und Roma* (Essen: Klartext Verlag, 1989). See also Friedlander, *Origins of Nazi Genocide*, chap. 12.

6. See Stephen Jay Gould, *The Mismeasure of Man* (New York: W. W. Norton, 1981), and Daniel J. Kevles, *In the Name of Eugenics: Genetics and the Uses of Human Heredity* (Berkeley and Los Angeles: University of California Press, 1986).

7. Cited in Garland E. Allen, "The Eugenics Record Office at Cold Spring Harbor, 1910–1940: An Essay in Institutional History," *Osiris*, 2d ser., 2 (1986): 225.

8. Cited ibid., 258.

9. Ibid., 247–48.

10. Sheila Faith Weiss, "The Race Hygiene Movement in Germany," *Osiris*, 2d ser., 3 (1987): 210; Loren R. Graham, "Science and Values: The Eugenics Movement in Germany and Russia in the 1920s," *American Historical Review* 82 (1977): 1136; Benno Müller-Hill, "Selektion: Die Wissenschaft von der biologischen Auslese des Menschen durch Menschen," in *Medizin und Gesundheitspolitik in der NS-Zeit*, ed. Norbert Frei (Munich: R. Oldenbourg Verlag, 1991), 139.

11. See Weiss, "Race Hygiene Movement," 194, 201–202, 222, 226–28; Proctor, *Racial Hygiene*, 20–30, 55–56; Graham, "Science and Values," 1138–39.

12. Karl Binding and Alfred Hoche, *Die Freigabe der Vernichtung lebensunwerten Lebens: Ihr Maß und Ihre Form* (Leipzig: Verlag von Felix Meiner, 1920).

13. Cited in Graham, "Science and Values," 1143 n24.

14. On Nazi language, see Victor Klemperer, *LTI: Aus dem Notizbuch eines Philologen* (Berlin: Aufbau Verlag, 1946).

15. See Müller-Hill, "Selektion," 146–47.

16. "Gesetz zur Verhütung erbkranken Nachwuchses," *Reichsgesetzblatt* 1933, 1:529, English translation in Control Commission for Germany (British Element), Legal Division, British Special Legal Research Unit, "Translations of Nazi Health Laws Concerned with Hereditary Diseases, Matrimonial Health, Sterilization, and Castration (8 Nov. 1945)," 1–5 (mimeographed). See also Friedrich Vogel, "Das 'Gesetz zur Verhütung erbkranken Nachwuchses,'" in *Von der Heilkunde zur Massentötung: Medizin im Nationalsozialismus*, ed. Gerrit Hohendorf and Achim Magull-Seltenreich (Heidelberg: Wunderhorn 1990), 37–52.

17. For a discussion of the categories defined as hereditary diseases, see Arthur Gütt, Ernst Rüdin, and Falk Ruttke, *Gesetz zur Verhütung erbkranken Nachwuchses vom 14. Juli 1933 nebst Ausführungsverordnungen, bearbeitet, und erläutert* (Munich: J. F. Lehmanns Verlag, 1934), 119ff.

18. The most detailed study of the sterilization law and its implementation is Gisela Bock, *Zwangssterilisation im Nationalsozialismus: Studien zur Rassenpolitik und Frauenpolitik* (Opladen: Westdeutscher Verlag, 1986).

19. See Michael H. Kater, *Doctors under Hitler* (Chapel Hill: University of North Carolina Press, 1989), 182; Anna Bergmann, Gabriele Czarnowski, and Annegret Ehmann, "Menschen als Objekte humangenetischer Forschung: Zur Geschichte des Kaiser Wilhelm-Instituts für Anthropologie, menschliche Erblehre und Eugenik in Berlin-Dahlem, 1927–1945," in Pross and Aly, eds., *Der Wert des Menschen*, 131.

20. For sterilization statistics collected by the Reichsministerium des Innern (RMdI), see Bundesarchiv Koblenz (BAK), R18/5585: "Übersicht über die Durchführung des Gesetzes zur Verhütung erbkranken Nachwuchses."

21. Ibid.

22. For a more detailed discussion, see Friedlander, *Origins of Nazi Genocide*, chap. 2.

23. A collection of amendments and regulations (prepared after the Anschluß for the information of Austrian health authorities) can be found in Allgemeines Verwaltungsarchiv, Vienna (hereafter AVA), Bürckel Akte, file 2354, and Dokumentationsarchiv des österreichischen Widerstandes, Vienna (hereafter DÖW), file E19198, Reichsgau Wien, Hauptgesundheitsamt.

24. First amendment of 26 June 1935, *Reichsgesetzblatt* 1935, 1:773. See also BAK, R18/5585: circular from NSDAP Amt für Volksgesundheit und NS-Ärztebund (sig. Gerhard Wagner), 13 September 1934.

25. "Gesetz zum Schutze der Erbgesundheit des deutschen Volkes

(Ehegesundheitsgesetz)," *Reichsgesetzblatt* 1935, 1:1246. English translation in Control Commission for Germany (British Element), "Translation of Nazi Health Laws," 33–34.

26. Henry Friedlander, "Registering the Handicapped in Nazi Germany: A Case Study," *Jewish History* 11, no. 2 (1997): 89–98. See also Götz Aly and Karl Heinz Roth, *Die restlose Erfassung: Volkszählen, Identifizieren, Aussondern im Nationalsozialismus* (Berlin: Rotbuch Verlag, 1984), 96ff. Also BAK, R36/ 1373: circular from the RMdI (sig. Arthur Gütt) to Landesregierungen, "Betr. Erbbiologische Bestandsaufnahme in Heil- und Pflegeanstalten," 8 January 1936.

27. For the film propaganda against the disabled, see Karl Heinz Roth, "Filmpropaganda für die Vernichtung der Geisteskranken und Behinderten im 'Dritten Reich,'" *Beiträge zur nationalsozialistischen Gesundheits- und Sozialpolitik* 2 (1985): 125–93; Michael Burleigh, *Death and Deliverance: "Euthanasia" in Germany, c. 1900–1945* (Cambridge: Cambridge University Press, 1994), chap. 6.

28. For the German literature on the euthanasia killing operation, see Friedrich Karl Kaul, *Nazimordaktion T4: Ein Bericht über die erste industriemässig durchgeführte Mordaktion des Naziregimes* (Berlin: VEB Verlag Volk und Gesundheit, 1973); Ernst Klee, *"Euthanasie" im NS-Staat: Die "Vernichtung lebensunwerten Lebens"* (Frankfurt: S. Fischer Verlag, 1983); Kurt Nowak, *"Euthanasie" und Sterilisierung im "Dritten Reich,"* 2d ed. (Weimar: Hermann Böhlaus Nachfolger, 1980); Alice Platen-Hallermund, *Die Tötung Geisteskranker in Deutschland: Aus der deutschen Ärztekommission beim amerikanischen Militärgericht* (Frankfurt: Verlag der Frankfurter Hefte, 1948); Hans-Walter Schmuhl, *Rassenhygiene, Nationalsozialismus, Euthanasie: Von der Verhütung zur Vernichtung "lebensunwerten Lebens," 1890–1945* (Göttingen: Vandenhoeck & Ruprecht, 1987).

29. Generalstaatsanwalt (hereafter GStA) Frankfurt, Anklage Werner Heyde, Gerhard Bohne und Hans Hefelmann, Ks 2/63 (GStA), Js 17/59 (GStA), 22 May 1962, 40; United States Military Tribunal, Official Transcript of the Proceedings in Case 1, United States v. Karl Brandt et al. (Medical Case), 2482 (testimony Karl Brandt).

30. For a more detailed discussion of children's euthanasia, see Friedlander, *Origins of Nazi Genocide*, chap. 3. See also U.S. Military Tribunal, Transcript of the Proceedings in Case 1, 2398–99 (testimony Karl Brandt); GStA Frankfurt, Anklage Heyde, Bohne und Hefelmann, Ks 2/63 (GStA), Js 17/59 (GStA), 22 May 1962, 53–54 (testimony Hans Hefelmann).

31. For a more detailed discussion of adult euthanasia, see Friedlander, *Origins of Nazi Genocide*, chap. 4.

32. U.S. Military Tribunal, Transcript of the Proceedings in Case 1, 2668–69 (testimony Hans Heinrich Lammers), 2396 (testimony Karl Brandt), 7555–

57 (testimony Viktor Brack). See also GStA Frankfurt, Anklage Heyde, Bohne und Hefelmann, Ks 2/63 (GStA), Js 17/59 (GStA), 22 May 1962, 178–85; GStA Frankfurt, Anklage Reinhold Vorberg und Dietrich Allers, Js 20/61 (GStA), 15 February 1966, 21–22.

33. It is impossible to fix the time Hitler made these decisions with absolute certainty. At Nuremberg, both Brandt and Lammers placed Hitler's appointment of Conti in the early period of the war, September or early October 1939, and the change to Brandt and Bouhler several weeks later. U.S. Military Tribunal, Transcript of the Proceedings in Case 1, 2396, 2400- 2401 (testimony Karl Brandt), 2668 (testimony Hans Heinrich Lammers). But Brack at Nuremberg, and other witnesses interrogated by German prosecutors years later, placed these events several months earlier. Ibid., 7555–57 (testimony Viktor Brack); GStA Frankfurt, Anklage Heyde, Bohne und Hefelmann, Ks 2/63 (GStA), Js 17/59 (GStA), 22 May 1962, 182–83. Evidence does support the earlier date; thus it seems likely that the KdF called its first planning session for adult euthanasia before the start of the war. U.S. Military Tribunal, Transcript of the Proceedings in Case 1, 7565 (testimony Viktor Brack).

34. GStA Frankfurt, Anklage Vorberg und Allers, Js 20/61 (GStA), 15 February 1966, 47–51.

35. See Landesarchiv Berlin: Bauakten, Tiergartenstraße 4: Zeichnung T4 zum Neubau eines Wohnhauses sowie eines Bureaugebäudes auf dem Grundstück Tiergartenstraße Nr. 4 Herrn Banquier Weissbach gehörig.

36. For a more detailed discussion, see Friedlander, *Origins of Nazi Genocide*, chaps. 10–11.

37. On the psychiatrist Gottfried Ewald, see GStA Frankfurt, Anklage Heyde, Bohne und Hefelmann, Ks 2/63 (GStA), Js 17/59 (GStA), 22 May 1962, 553–56; on the SS physician Werner Kirchert, see GStA Frankfurt, Anklage Schumann, Js 18/67 (GStA), 12 December 1969, 120.

38. GStA Frankfurt, Anklage Heyde, Bohne und Hefelmann, Ks 2/63 (GStA), Js 17/59 (GStA), 22 May 1962, 201–206. The language of this authorization, which was sufficiently flexible to permit the inclusion of patients suffering from other than mental disabilities, was probably prepared by a committee, including leading psychiatrists such as Max de Crinis. See also Willi Dressen, "Euthanasie," in *Nationalsozialistische Massentötungen durch Giftgas: Eine Dokumentation*, ed. Eugen Kogon, Hermann Langbein, and Adalbert Rückerl (Frankfurt: S. Fischer Verlag, 1983), 31, 304n18.

39. U.S. Military Tribunal, Transcript of the Proceedings in Case 1, 2369, 2402 (testimony Karl Brandt). See also Platen-Hallermund, *Die Tötung Geisteskranker*, 21.

40. U.S. Military Tribunal, Transcript of the Proceedings in Case 1, 2678–90 (testimony Hans Heinrich Lammers). See also Platen-Hallermund, *Die Tötung Geisteskranker*, 18.

41. See, for example, StA Köln, Anklage Alfred Leu, 24 Js 527/50, 10 July 1951, 5.

42. Nuremberg Doc. PS-630.

43. See, for example, StA Hamburg, Anklage Wilhelm Bayer, Werner Catel, 14 Js 265/48, 7 February 1949, 22–23; National Archives and Records Administration (hereafter NARA), RG 238, Microfilm Publication M-1019, roll 46: interrogation Friedrich Mennecke, 11 January 1947, 6–9. On payment to experts, see Zentrale Stelle der Landesjustizverwaltungen, Ludwigsburg (hereafter ZStL), Heidelberg Doc. 128,217: memo from Werner Heyde and Viktor Brack (Jennerwein), n.d. For facsimile examples of a questionnaire, see DÖW, file 18229; StA Hamburg, Akten des Verfahrens Friedrich Lensch und Kurt Struve, 147 Js 58/67, Gesundheitsbehörde Bd. 1; and Henry Friedlander and Sybil Milton, *Bundesarchiv of the Federal Republic of Germany, Koblenz and Freiburg*, vol. 20 of *Archives of the Holocaust* (New York: Garland Publishing, 1993), doc. 57.

44. GStA Frankfurt, Anklage Heyde, Bohne, und Hefelmann, Ks 2/63 (GStA) [Js 17/59 (GStA)], 22 May 1962, 147ff.; StA Hamburg, Anklage Lensch und Struve, 147 Js 58/67, 24 April 1973, 157ff.; Nuremberg Doc. PS-3865.

45. NARA, RG 238, Microfilm Publication M-1019, roll 52: interrogation Hermann Pfannmüller, 21 September 1946, 23–24; Nuremberg Doc. PS-3816: affidavit Dr. Gerhard Schmidt, 28 March 1946; U.S. Military Tribunal, Transcript of the Proceedings in Case 1, 2433 (testimony Karl Brandt), 7305–7306 (testimony Hermann Pfannmüller); DÖW, file 18282: LG Wien, interrogation Marianne Türk, 25 January 1946; StA Hamburg, Anklage Bayer, Catel, 14 Js 265/48, 7 February 1949, 27; Gerhard Schmidt, *Selektion in der Heilanstalt, 1939–1945*, 2d ed. (Frankfurt: Edition Suhrkamp, 1983), 115, 132–49.

46. U.S. Military Tribunal, Transcript of the Proceedings in Case 1, 7645 (testimony Viktor Brack); StA Stuttgart, Akten des Verfahrens Albert Widmann, Ks 19/62 (19 Js 328/60): interrogation August Becker, 4 April 1960; GStA Frankfurt, Anklage Werner Heyde, Gerhard Bohne und Hans Hefelmann, Ks 2/63 (GStA), Js 17/59 (GStA), 22 May 1962, 290–93 (interrogation Werner Heyde), 293–98 (interrogation August Becker); StA Stuttgart, Anklage Albert Widmann und August Becker, (19) 13 Js 328/60, 29 August 1962, 39–41; GStA Frankfurt, Anklage Aquilin Ullrich, Heinrich Bunke, Kurt Borm und Klaus Endruweit, Js 15/61 (GStA), 15 January 1965, 175–77.

47. NARA, RG 238, International Military Tribunal Interrogations: interrogation Karl Brandt, 1 October 1945 p.m., 7.

48. For a more detailed discussion, see Friedlander, *Origins of Nazi Genocide*, chap. 7.

49. Adalbert Rückerl, *NS-Vernichtungslager im Spiegel deutscher Strafprozesse* (Munich: Deutscher Taschenbuch Verlag, 1977). See also Friedlander, *Origins of Nazi Genocide*, chap. 14.

50. For a more detailed discussion, see Friedlander, *Origins of Nazi Genocide*, chap. 5.

51. GStA Frankfurt, Eberl Akten, II/210/1-3, 1:1-3: Irmfried Eberl to Paul Nitsche, 16 April 1942; GStA Frankfurt, Anklage Ullrich, Bunke, Borm und Endruweit, Js 15/61 (GStA), 15 January 1965, 111, 187, 204–205.

52. DÖW, file E18370/3: Kriminalpolizei Linz, interrogation Vinzenz Nohel, 4 September 1945.

53. StA Stuttgart, Akten des Verfahrens Albert Widmann, Ks 19/62 (19 Js 328/60), testimony Klara Mattmüller, 17 February 1966; StA Düsseldorf, Akten des Verfahrens Albert Widmann, 8 Ks 1/61 (8 Js 7212/59), interrogation Albert Widmann, 15 January 1960, 5.

54. Hessisches Hauptstaatsarchiv, Wiesbaden (HHStA), 461/32061/7: Landgericht (LG) Frankfurt, Akten des Verfahrens Adolf Wahlmann, Bodo Gorgaß, Irmgard Huber, 4a KLs 7/47 (4a Js 3/46), Protokoll der öffentlichen Sitzung der 4. Strafkammer, 3 March 1947, 32 (testimony Ingeborg Seidel).

55. Concerning "looted victim gold" from T4 and the SS, see Independent Commission of Experts Switzerland–Second World War, *Switzerland and Gold Transactions in the Second World War: Interim Report* (Bern: EDMZ, 1998), 30–36.

56. U.S. Military Tribunal, Transcript of the Proceedings in Case 1, 2530–31 (testimony Karl Brandt), 7629 (testimony Viktor Brack).

57. NARA, RG 338, Microfilm Publication T-1021, roll 18, "Hartheim Statistics," p. 1; GStA Frankfurt, Anklage Ullrich, Bunke, Borm und Endruweit, Js 15/61 (GStA), 15 January 1965, 133–38; GStA Frankfurt, Anklage Heyde, Bohne und Hefelmann, Ks 2/63 (GStA), Js 17/59 (GStA), 22 May 1962, 695–701.

58. For a discussion of this so-called wild euthanasia, see Friedlander, *Origins of Nazi Genocide*, chap. 8.

59. Cited in Klee, *"Euthanasie" im NS-Staat*, 187.

60. Cited ibid., 245.

61. Cited ibid., 187.

62. For details of protests from relatives, see Friedlander, *Origins of Nazi Genocide*, chap. 9.

63. ZStL, Sammlung UdSSR, Bd. 245 Ad 1: German summary of information concerning the killing of mental patients presented at Nuremberg by the Hauptkommission zur Untersuchung deutscher Verbrechen in Polen. See also ZStL, Sammlung Verschiedenes, Bd. 17, 276- 313; Angelika Ebbinghaus, and

Gerd Preissler, eds. and trans., "Die Ermordung psychisch kranker Menschen in der Sowjetunion: Dokumentation," *Beiträge zur nationalsozialistischen Gesundheits- und Sozialpolitik* 1 (1985): 75–107.

64. See Friedlander, *Origins of Nazi Genocide*, chap. 13, for the only detailed account of the fate of disabled Jews in Nazi Germany.

65. See, for example, Horst Biesold, *Klagende Hände: Betroffenheit und Spätfolgen in bezug auf das Gesetz zur Verhütung erbkranken Nachwuchses, dargestellt am Beispiel der "Taubstummen"* (Solms-Berbiel: Jarick Oberbiel Verlag, 1988).

CHAPTER 8

From Indefinite Confinement to Extermination

"HABITUAL CRIMINALS" IN THE THIRD REICH

NIKOLAUS WACHSMANN

UNTIL THE 1980s the fate of most social outsiders in the Third Reich was of little interest to historians. Since then the literature on "community aliens," those individuals excluded from the Nazi "national community" and persecuted on racial or eugenic grounds, or for their deviant behavior, has grown quickly. However, this body of historical scholarship has largely ignored criminal offenders. Historians have been uncomfortable dealing with victims of Nazi violence who could not be portrayed as completely innocent.[1] As a consequence, descriptions of the behavior of those imprisoned as criminals in Nazi concentration camps are still largely based on accounts written after the war by a select group of former inmates, in particular German political inmates, who for a long time forged the collective memory of the camps.[2] In these accounts, the relationship between the various camp inmates was often reduced to a struggle between the political inmates, who had to wear a red triangle, and those imprisoned as criminals, who wore green triangles, a struggle which was portrayed as a fight between good and evil. The "greens" were described as a close-knit gang of extremely brutal and sadistic murderers, violent thugs, and sex criminals, who made life hell for all other inmates. They were characterized as "the most despicable elements," "fellow criminals of the SS," and "the plague of the camps."[3]

While little academic research has been carried out on the "greens" in the concentration camps, even less is known about offenders in the state prisons and penitentiaries administered by the Ministry of Justice, which, the last years of the Second World War apart, held significantly more inmates than the concentration camps did (excluding the death camps).[4] In many ways, the history of state penal institutions in the Third Reich remains to be written.[5] The local jails, prisons, and penitentiaries run by the judicial apparatus held a vast variety of different

165

criminal offenders, with sentences ranging from just a few days to life. This essay will focus on one specific group of state prisoners, the so-called security confined (*Sicherungsverwahrte*). This category of prisoners derived from the Law against Dangerous Habitual Criminals, introduced on 24 November 1933, which gave courts the option of ordering the indefinite imprisonment in state penal institutions of "habitual" offenders after the end of their original sentence of imprisonment. This provision was kept deliberately vague. It was left to the courts to decide whether the offender had committed a crime due to a "criminal disposition" and could be regarded as dangerous. The only objective requirement was that the accused have committed at least three criminal acts, even if he or she had never previously been convicted. Up to October 1942 a total of 14,351 offenders were sentenced to security confinement in the Third Reich.[6]

This chapter will first examine the background to the Law against Dangerous Habitual Criminals. As with so many other policies introduced against social outsiders and deviants in the Third Reich, it is necessary to trace its origins back to the pre-Nazi period, in this case to criminological discourse in Germany since the late nineteenth century. Then the chapter turns to the reality of security confinement in Nazi Germany until the outbreak of war in 1939 and investigates which individuals were imprisoned as "habitual criminals" in state penal institutions. The third section examines the fate of those few inmates released from security confinement into Nazi society, and the competition between the legal service and the police over control of "habitual criminals." Finally, the chapter considers the massive radicalization of penal policy during the Second World War, which culminated in the transfer of many "habitual criminals" from state penal institutions to concentration camps, where they were systematically exterminated.

I

In the late nineteenth century a fundamental change took place in the conception of crime in various European states. With the growing medicalization of criminology and penal policy, attention shifted from the offense to the offender. Punishment was to fit the criminal, not the crime, and the purpose of punishment was redefined as the protection of society rather than individual retribution. In Germany this new conception of criminal law was advanced most forcefully by the law professor

Franz von Liszt. In his highly influential *Marburger Programm*, first published in 1882 on the occasion of his appointment to the Marburg law faculty, Liszt argued that the judicial system should aim at the reformation of all "corrigible" offenders through discipline, work, and basic education. Simultaneously Liszt called for the incapacitation of all "habitual criminals," a category which he estimated to include at least half of all the prison inmates. Liszt argued that these offenders were the most dangerous element "in this long chain of symptoms of social disease, which we tend to subsume under the general term proletariat. Beggars and vagabonds, prostitutes of both sexes and alcoholics, cheats and general members of the *demi-monde*, mentally and physically degenerates— they all form the army of fundamental opponents of the social order, in which the habitual criminals appear as the general staff."[7] For these offenders, rehabilitation would be useless. To protect society, Liszt suggested confining them permanently to penitentiaries or workhouses, where they would be subjected to a harsh disciplinarian regime, run "as cheaply as possible, even if these creatures perish."[8]

This demand for the introduction of harsh measures against "habitual criminals" became increasingly popular around the turn of the century, not just in Germany but in other Western states as well. By the 1920s security confinement (*Sicherungsverwahrung*) for "habitual criminals" had become a fixed part of all official German drafts for a new criminal code.[9] Despite the widespread support for its introduction among politicians, prison officials, and criminologists, there were sharp differences of opinion about its operational details. The first debate centered on the question of which offenders should be regarded as candidates for security confinement. In his very influential book *The Professional Criminal* (*Der Berufsverbrecher*), first published in 1926, the criminologist Robert Heindl pointed out that most "habitual criminals" in Germany were harmless small-time offenders. Only a few of them were real professionals. It was these individuals, who specialized in certain crimes (such as bank robberies), whom Heindl saw as responsible for most criminal acts and who should be locked up forever.[10] This construction of the "professional criminal" was highly influential in shaping the public discourse about criminality in the last years of the Weimar Republic. Newspapers often carried features about the organized criminal underworld and its most famous figures, such as the Berlin brothers Saß. Heindl's model was also taken over by the criminal police, who increasingly concentrated their resources on arresting the supposed elite of the underworld, the "professional criminal."[11]

167

Other authors, however, included many more criminal offenders in their proposals for security confinement. Following Liszt, they cast their net much wider and argued that it should be directed at most or all "habitual criminals." With the growth of the eugenics movement, public danger was no longer defined in terms of the threat posed to the community by criminal activities alone. "Habitual criminals" were also seen as a biological menace, because of the supposed "degenerate" traits which they might pass on to future generations. Indefinite imprisonment was seen as one possibility for the "eradication of permanently worthless human material from the national community."[12] Thus beggars, small-time thieves, pickpockets, pimps, and con artists were also described as candidates for security confinement.[13] Most prison officials apparently subscribed to this wider interpretation. In 1927 officials in the larger penal institutions of ten German states classified one in every thirteen of their inmates as a candidate for security confinement.[14] These calls by penal officials for the permanent imprisonment of repeat offenders were intensified by the growing rates of recidivism.

Just as there was no general agreement about which individuals were to be taken into security confinement, so too there were debates about what life in security confinement should look like. Several prison reformers insisted that continued efforts should be made to reform the inmates. To some extent, this demand was reflected in the Weimar drafts for a new criminal code, which set the maximum tariff for security confinement at three years. If the judge after this period still believed that the inmate would be a threat to society, he would have to renew his decision.[15] But the majority of prison officials and criminologists argued that all candidates for security confinement were "incorrigible" and should be interned for the rest of their lives.[16] Many believed that the new criminal-biological examinations would eventually enable officials to single out the "incorrigibles." These pseudoscientific tests had been devised by the influential Bavarian prison doctor Theodor Viernstein, who claimed in 1930 that half of all inmates in penal institutions were "incorrigible," confirming the figure put forward by Franz von Liszt.[17] Although these conclusions were hotly contested by other criminologists, a number of penal officials described criminal biology as an important scientific advance.

Much to the disappointment of most observers, security confinement never became a reality in the Weimar Republic, as the entire draft for a new criminal law failed to pass the Reichstag before the virtual breakdown of parliamentary politics in the early 1930s made its completion impossible.[18] This did not mean, however, that the criminological discourse about the "habitual criminal" failed to have any influence on penal practice. In both Bavaria and Prussia inmates classified by the officials as "habitual" were confined under harsher conditions in special wings.[19] By the time the Nazis came to power in January 1933, not only was there widespread agreement that certain "habitual" offenders had to be eliminated from society, but prison officials and criminologists had already taken the first steps in identifying who these offenders were.

II

When security confinement was introduced on 24 November 1933, the reaction of criminologists and prison governors was enthusiastic.[20] Local prison governors played an important role in the implementation of this new measure. In particular, they made ample use of the provision that inmates already imprisoned could be retrospectively sentenced to security confinement. The prison director in Brandenburg-Görden reported more than a third of his 1,480 inmates to the courts for retrospective sentencing. In the majority of these cases, the courts followed his recommendations and sentenced the inmates to indefinite periods of security confinement.[21] The offenders themselves were not heard. In one case, an inmate protested to the authorities, "I deny that I am an 'incorrigible thief.'" The court, of course, followed the views of the prison governor and sentenced him to security confinement.[22] While the law introduced on 24 November 1933 was modeled on the various Weimar drafts, some subtle changes meant that the number of offenders eligible for security confinement was greatly increased, and in the following years the number of inmates in security confinement institutions (former state penal institutions, or special wings in penitentiaries or prisons) continually grew, from 2,018 in June 1935 to 3,950 in June 1938.[23]

Prison and penitentiary inmates were shocked by the law and were reported to be greatly concerned about its possible consequences.[24] Officials noticed that those inmates transferred after the end of their sentence into security confinement, after being retrospectively sentenced, were unsettled and irritable, because they believed that they were now being unjustly detained. Uncertainty as to when, or even if, they would be released again caused a considerable degree of depression and led in some cases to self-mutilation and drastic weight loss.[25] One female

169

inmate in the security confinement wing of the Aichach penal institution, Franziska K., wrote in 1936 to her family, in a letter censored by the prison authorities: "My dear ones, I am totally embittered, sitting here and not knowing *why* and for *how long* a[nd] still be treated as a *convict.* I will lose my mind if this goes on like that . . . alone a[nd] forsaken I have to sit here a[nd] waste away, this is a *slow suicide.*" Franziska K. was never released from security confinement.[26]

The official line was that "because of his particular hostility against order, the dangerous habitual criminal, the chronically antisocial, requires a specially hard discipline."[27] Thus inmates were drilled in military-style discipline and made to work nine hours' hard labor per day, confined under conditions little different from those in penitentiaries. A small number of inmates were also subjected to racial-hygienic measures such as sterilization or castration, which were introduced into state penal institutions in the first year of the Nazi seizure of power. By the late 1930s the state of health of many inmates had declined considerably, as they suffered from a combination of insufficient food and hard labor. It often proved difficult to fulfill the strict production quotas, because the security confined were significantly older than other prison inmates: more than one in four inmates in 1939 was fifty years or older.[28]

Local penal officials tried to get rid of old or ill inmates by transferring them to other penal institutions. In 1939 the Werl security confinement institution near Dortmund obtained permission to transport thirty prisoners to the Gräfentonna institution in Thuringia. According to the prison doctor at Gräfentonna, four of these men were completely unable to work, while one had actually died during the transport. The remaining twenty-five prisoners were "ridden with diseases and illness to such an extent that they can only perform the simplest kinds of work, like shelling peas or sewing buttons." The doctor warned that in the event of any more such transports "we will cease to be a security confinement institution, and instead become a hospice for the sick and frail."[29] Security confinement developed such a fearsome reputation among other inmates that some offenders mutilated themselves in the expectation that this might save them from being sentenced to it. For instance, when Gerhard F., who already had seventeen previous convictions, was arrested in 1940 for the theft of a coat, he put out both his eyes with a pencil until he was blind. The court found that F. was "fully criminally responsible and did not cause his eye injury because of diminished responsibility but only because of fear of security confinement."[30]

170

Who were the inmates sentenced to security confinement, invariably described in the Third Reich by penal officials and criminologists as "human ruins" and "the scum of the criminal class"?[31] According to official statistics, less than 8 percent of the offenders already in security confinement by 1 January 1937 had been sentenced for crimes of violence or for sex offenses (mainly indecent assault on children, but also exhibitionism and homosexual acts). By contrast, 86 percent of all offenders had been convicted of property offenses. On the whole these offenses were very petty, often involving the theft of bicycles, coats, or small amounts of food and money.[32] This focus on property-related offenses was already evident in Weimar criminological discourse. Theodor Viernstein, for instance, had claimed that his research proved that most property offenders were biologically "incorrigible," while the same could be said for only one in every four violent or sex offenders.[33]

Many of the security confined had been born around the turn of the century, and had spent practically all of their adult life under conditions of severe economic instability. With welfare payments barely above subsistence level, many Germans in the early 1920s were driven to commit property crimes. Criminal convictions more than doubled from 348,247 in 1919 to 823,902 in 1923, at the height of the inflation. The 1920s also saw unprecedented levels of unemployment, highest among the disillusioned "lost generation" aged between twenty and thirty years. In the world economic crisis following the Wall Street crash of October 1929, unemployment soared to new heights, and property-related criminal offenses increased once more.[34] Those individuals later sentenced in the Third Reich to security confinement were poorly equipped to sustain themselves in the perpetual economic crisis of the Weimar Republic. Most of them had been brought up in large families in the most deprived urban social milieu, experiencing great poverty and social insecurity. Many security confined had received no adequate school education or vocational training. If they worked at all, they were engaged in poorly paid casual labour and were thus particularly vulnerable to fluctuations in the market. The vast majority of them had never enjoyed a steady job or income.[35]

For instance, Karl K., born in 1899, had left school after only one year and took casual jobs, working at one time as a coachman. During the 1920s he was frequently imprisoned for minor property offenses, including an eighteen-month prison sentence in 1928 for the theft of three bikes. By this stage he had already been convicted thirteen times and had spent seven years of his life behind bars. In most penal institutions, no efforts were made to prepare the inmates for life on the outside. Prison labor consisted largely of mindless and repetitive manual tasks, and inmates were generally not trained on modern machines or allowed to learn a trade. Thus when Karl K. was released again in January 1930, with a mere 20 Reichsmarks in his pocket as payment for his prison labor, he was still without any job prospects.

Within a few months of his release, Karl K. re-offended, again stealing a bicycle. Even though the court acknowledged his economic hardship, he was still sentenced to eleven months' imprisonment. This time he was classified by prison doctors as a "habitual criminal" and transferred to a special wing for "incorrigibles" in the Plötzensee prison. Released in April 1931, he was back in prison by February of the following year, arrested for the theft of a coat. After seven months' imprisonment, K. was released, only to be sentenced again, in June 1933, after he had stolen a bell and some glue, among other items, while drunk. He was never to leave prison again. Once security confinement had become law, he was retrospectively sentenced, and after the end of his prison term he was transferred to the Brandenburg-Görden penal institution. The governor there described K. as possessing many typical characteristics of the security confined: "poor educational circumstances, breaking off an apprenticeship, irregular labor, early criminality, many convictions, especially quick recidivism; plus his penchant for alcohol."[36] Similar reasons were given by judges when passing sentences of security confinement.[37]

The vast majority of offenders sentenced to security confinement were men. By 1 January 1937, there were 3,121 men in security confinement, compared with only 137 women. In general, these women did not differ in social background or type of offenses committed from their male counterparts. More than 90 percent had been sentenced to security confinement for property offenses. Apparently a number of the women had worked as prostitutes and had previous convictions for stealing from men they had slept with.[38] A typical case was that of Rosa S., who was arrested in August 1934, after she had stolen 40 Reichsmarks from the pocket of an unskilled laborer with whom she had had sex. S. was tried as a "dangerous habitual criminal," following a long tradition in Germany of classifying prostitutes as part of the criminal underworld. The prosecutor cited a previous court sentence which had described S. already in 1927 as a "debased and dangerous street-whore." Only security confinement, he argued, could protect the public from her. The court agreed, and S. was sentenced to sixteen months' imprisonment and subsequent security confinement. Asked in 1936 about her plans for the future, she wrote: "Most of all, I do not want to come back here. . . . I buy myself a sewing-machine a[nd] 1 bed . . . I want to patch a[nd] sew a[nd] embroider." But Rosa S. was never released again.[39]

On average, each inmate had fourteen previous convictions at the time of being sentenced to security confinement in the Third Reich, accumulated over a long period since the 1920s or even earlier. In most cases they had been sentenced for their first offense at the age of twenty-one or younger. With each new conviction, the inmates later sentenced to security confinement became more likely to offend again. Partly this was due to widespread resentment against recidivists among the general German public. One prisoner wrote in 1925 that most people treated former inmates "as if they were dealing with wild animals."[40] Another obstacle to the reintegration of offenders into society was created by the supervision of former inmates. First experiments with police control of released inmates had been made in Berlin at the end of the eighteenth century and supervision later became part of the Prussian criminal code and the German criminal code of 1870–71.[41] Continual visits by police officials often resulted in the dismissal of former inmates from their jobs. It also made it difficult for them to find accommodation, as most landlords were reluctant to rent to former inmates. These police practices contributed to the inability of released inmates to stay on the straight and narrow and played an important role in the creation of the "incorrigible criminal."

The sheer number of convictions meant that many of the security-confined inmates had spent large parts of their adult lives in prison. In a sample of 135 inmates with an average age of forty-three years, each inmate had already spent, on average, twenty-one years behind bars.[42] Such lengthy spells in prison made it difficult to sustain relations with relatives or partners. Most of the inmates in security confinement had little or no social contacts on the outside.[43] And those inmates who still had close relatives or partners could not always count on their support. Some were thrilled by the prospect of lifelong imprisonment for the "black sheep" in their family. Others wrote to the prison administration to stop their imprisoned relatives from sending letters, fearing that association with them could harm their own careers in the Third Reich.[44]

In conclusion, the offenders sentenced to security confinement in the Third Reich did not correspond to the picture of the highly skilled and dangerous "professional criminal" constructed by criminologists like Robert Heindl in the 1920s; the sheer fact that they were caught so frequently is proof enough that they were anything but professionals. Most had been socialized in a milieu which frequently collided with respectable society's legal and moral norms. Essentially they were persecuted not so much as a criminal menace but as social (and racial) deviants, unwilling or unable to conform. This is illustrated also by the case of Maria B., who had received numerous sentences for theft and picking pockets, accumulated in part during the 1920s when her husband was serving a five-year penitentiary sentence for raping one of her children. In 1936 she was convicted for the fifteenth time, this time for the theft of one purse and the attempted theft of another. At that time she earned less than 10 Marks per week washing laundry, while her husband, released from the penitentiary, was unemployed and in debt. From the beginning of the Third Reich, the welfare authorities had cut back on payments for many social outsiders, and in B.'s case, they had cut off all support. Despite the trivial nature of her previous offenses, B. was sentenced to security confinement as a "dangerous habitual criminal" and was never released again.[45]

III

Until the outbreak of the Second World War, release from security confinement was still a remote possibility. A number of inmates initially expected to be released after three years, when their sentences were automatically reviewed by the courts. According to the letter of the law, the inmates could be set free if the courts no longer considered them a danger to society. This decision was based in part on the views of the prison governor. But governors only rarely supported the release of an inmate, because they feared that they would be held responsible if the inmate re-offended. Most prison governors, and by extension most judges, were unwilling to take such risks. By 30 April 1938 only 701 former inmates had been released, while 3,886 were still held in security confinement.[46] Most prisoners were hit extremely hard by the court's rejection of their release. One inmate wrote to her sister in 1937: "I won't do another 3 years here . . . I have stolen, but I will rather do myself in, my dear sister, than be buried alive for that in here."[47] Officials in the Ministry of Justice in Berlin coldly noted that the cases of self-mutilation and suicide attempts among inmates refused release were consequences which had to be accepted.[48]

What happened to the small minority of inmates who were set free?

How did these individuals, classified as "dangerous habitual criminals," fare on the outside? In most cases the courts made the release conditional on the inmates' obeying very strict regulations. In one typical case, an ex-inmate who had been sentenced to security confinement for picking pockets was not allowed to leave her hometown without prior police approval, had to stay at home at night, had to hand over keys to her apartment to the police, and was not permitted to enter larger shops, where it was feared she might steal goods.[49] Every aspect of the former inmate's life was strictly regulated by the court and police. One ex-prisoner was released on the condition that he move in with his brother and accept any job offered by the job center. Others were forced to move to special institutions set up for released inmates, without being allowed to visit their friends or children. In one case, the local prisoner aid organization even examined the prospective bride of a former security-confined offender, who made "not a bad impression" on the officials. Often it was the governors themselves who kept up the pressure on their former inmates to lead exemplary lives.[50]

In view of the strict regulations and controls to which they were subjected, it is hardly surprising that many former inmates were soon committed again to security confinement. Of the 701 inmates released by 30 April 1938, at least 79 were almost immediately arrested again.[51] Overall it seems likely that at least half ended up in security confinement once more.[52] Many former inmates simply re-offended. Willy L., for example, was caught in November 1937, only a few months after his release, stealing in the Kaufhaus des Westens, Berlin's largest department store. L., who was drunk, pleaded in vain with the store detective to let him go. The courts saw L.'s offense as final proof of his "considerable danger to the national community," and sentenced him to three years in the penitentiary with subsequent security confinement.[53] In a number of other cases, former inmates were readmitted not because they had committed further offenses, but because they failed to conform to the norms set by the officials for their work life and private conduct. Numerous former inmates were accused of being "work-shy." Despite the fact that police surveillance made it difficult to find steady employment, the failure to do so was seen by the authorities as a further proof of the offenders' nature as "habitual criminals." Others were recommitted after they had criticized the brutal treatment and harsh conditions in security confinement in public.[54]

In 1938 the Reich Ministry of Justice urged its officials to tighten up still further the conditions for releasing the security confined. In an official publication entitled "Urgent Questions of Security Confinement," State Secretary Roland Freisler repeated views which he had stated two years earlier, when he had explained that "in general, I cannot accept the release of inmates." The only exceptions to this rule were if an inmate became physically so weak that he or she could not offend again, or if a sex offender had lost his sexual drive either through old age or through castration.[55] Freisler was also concerned because the number of sentences to security confinement had fallen from 3,723 in 1934 to only 765 in 1937. Some judges explicitly limited the use of security confinement because they saw custody in concentration camps as the more effective punishment of "habitual criminals."[56]

From the moment the Nazis came to power, the police had begun to develop a parallel system of punishment to that of the existing legal system. Influenced by the criminological research of the 1920s, police made one of their first targets the "professional criminal": in Berlin alone, several hundred suspects were arrested by the police between May and October 1933. On 13 November 1933 the Prussian minister of the interior announced the introduction of preventive police custody (*polizeiliche Vorbeugungshaft*) in concentration camps against individuals suspected of being "professional criminals" or "sex criminals." This provision was initially accepted by the Reich Ministry of Justice as no direct competition to security confinement, because it was directed only at individuals who had not committed a new offense. In addition, the number of individuals held in preventive police custody was initially rather small, with 491 individuals in concentration camps in Prussia at the end of 1935.[57]

Initially the criminal police aimed at the deterrence of most offenders by putting a small number of suspected criminals into concentration camps. But with the appointment of SS leader Heinrich Himmler as the head of the German police in 1936, and the realization among police officials that their policies had failed to realize the utopian goal of the total eradication of criminality, police measures increasingly radicalized. In March 1937, on Himmler's orders, the Prussian criminal police arrested about 2,000 unemployed "professional criminals" and "habitual criminals" and put them into concentration camps. On 14 December 1937, preventive police custody was extended to the whole of Germany, with a dramatically enlarged scope. The police had changed its tactic from the deterrence of most offenders by arresting a few suspects to the eradication of all persons exhibiting non-normative behavior who were seen as threats to the "national community." By the end of 1938 nearly

13,000 people were being held in protective police custody in concentration camps, as compared with 4,264 in state security confinement.[58] In this period the SS leadership attempted to tighten its grip on all "habitual criminals" by demanding their transfer from state penal institutions to the SS. After an investigation by the head of the Chancellery of the Führer, Philipp Bouhler, in summer 1939 revealed that the security confined in one institution were occupied with the painting of toy soldiers, contrary to claims by the judicial officials that such inmates were engaged in essential work projects for Goering's Four-Year Plan, Hitler decided that all expendable prisoners in security confinement should be handed over to the SS.[59] When the SS was informed, it demanded in late August 1939 the transfer of all inmates, not just those judged expendable, from security confinement to concentration camps. The Ministry of Justice opted not to respond to the letter. It must be doubted whether this tactic of silence would have succeeded in the long run. But the outbreak of war on 1 September 1939 saved the ministry, at least temporarily, by bringing other, more urgent issues onto the agenda.

IV

The Second World War led to a general radicalization of Nazi policy against all "community aliens." Increasingly extermination replaced the discriminatory policies of the prewar years. This escalation is also evident in penal policy. Hitler regarded the extermination of certain criminals as an important necessity: "During the war, penitentiaries do not have the function to preserve the criminals for a possible rebellion."[60] The number of death sentences passed by German courts increased from 139 in 1939 to 1,292 in 1941. By 1942 this figure had risen to 4,457. Before 1933 there were only three offenses which were punishable by death. In the last years of the war, there were no less than forty-six. In 1941 the death penalty was made applicable to crimes committed by serious "habitual criminals" and "sex criminals." Instead of sentencing them to security confinement, judges could decide on their execution.[61] This was the main reason for the decline of sentences of security confinement after 1940. Execution, not indefinite confinement, was increasingly seen by the legal establishment as the appropriate treatment for these offenders. Such radical measures, however, could only be applied to "habitual criminals" who came up for sentencing. Those who had already been sentenced continued to be held in security confinement. Their numbers continued to slowly rise in the first years of the war, not least because in May 1940 State Secretary Freisler instructed the courts to reject all future requests for release from security confinement.[62] By October 1942 there were 7,600 inmates in security confinement as well as approximately 5,800 inmates in prisons or penitentiaries with sentences of subsequent security confinement.[63]

With the start of the war, the state of health of inmates in security confinement declined rapidly. The officials in Berlin increased the working day to twelve hours and almost simultaneously reduced food rations to the same level as in concentration camps.[64] The effect of this policy was an increase in tuberculosis, weight loss, and death rates.[65] Some local prison officials started to treat the security confined with murderous neglect, clearly influenced by the harder line taken by the courts against "habitual criminals." For example, the inmate Frieda S. suffered great pains after having swallowed a knife. In early 1942 her weight had fallen to around forty kilos, as it was often impossible for her to eat at all. When she asked the prison doctor for help, he suggested that she should lose another fifty pounds and die. In late May 1942, in a censored letter to her husband, she wrote: "If it goes on like this for long, I will lose my mind, because I am still a human being and no animal."[66]

In the security confinement institution of Gräfentonna, one out of every three inmates in 1940 was judged not fully fit for work. According to the prison governor, such prisoners were a great "burden" for the work process. In particular during the war, economic output increasingly became the sole yardstick by which a governor's performance was measured. Many security confined were clearly in the way: they could only be occupied with easy and unproductive jobs and their presence kept other prisoners from work, since they had to help the more frail inmates clean their cells and carry their food. The solution, according to some officials, was to get rid of them by opening a special institution for frail prisoners.[67] Eventually, the Ministry of Justice responded to these calls and designated the security confinement institution in Tapiau (East Prussia) for old and weak inmates.[68] However, with room for 155 inmates at maximum, Tapiau did little to diminish the governors' desire to get rid of "ballast" in their institutions.[69]

During 1942 the health of inmates declined further. The average weight of the male inmates in security confinement in the Gräfentonna institution in 1942 had fallen to only fifty-seven kilograms, even lower than comparable figures for penitentiary inmates. According to the prison doctor, many of the security-confined inmates suffered from symptoms of malnourishment, such as swollen feet and legs.[70] The desperate conditions are also evident in prisoner letters from this period. Karl K., the thief imprisoned in Brandenburg-Görden whom we encountered above, wrote in a censored letter in September 1942 to his brother and sister-in-law: "My normal weight is supposed to be 67 kilos, and now you will definitely be shocked; for at the moment I weigh exactly 43,3 kilos, that's 87 pounds. You can imagine, what I look like. The only wish I have, is to once eat my fill; for I am always hungry. . . . Hopefully, the war will be over soon, otherwise one will come to grief after all. Two more letters, and Christmas will be there."[71] Two months after he wrote this letter, Karl K. was handed over by the prison officials to the police for "annihilation through labor." Just two days earlier, Willy L., the released inmate who had been caught stealing in the Kaufhaus des Westens, had also been handed over to the police. By Christmas 1942 both men were probably no longer alive.

On 20 August 1942 the former president of the People's Court, Otto-Georg Thierack, had been appointed as the new minister of justice. On the day of Thierack's appointment, Hitler explained to him that it was wrong to "conserve" certain "vermin" in penal institutions. Hitler argued that the war led to a "negative selection," with the "bravest" dying on the battlefield and the criminals surviving in the prisons, which could eventually result in revolution as in 1918. To prevent this, certain criminals had to be exterminated. Only one month later, on 18 September 1942, Thierack agreed in a meeting with SS leader Heinrich Himmler to transfer all "asocial" inmates from the prison service to the police for "annihilation through labor."[72] For Thierack, the transfer was a way of demonstrating to the Nazi leadership the willingness of the judiciary to take brutal measures against "community aliens," as well as to bring the penal system in line with the other Nazi extermination programs such as the Final Solution. The transfer included, among others, all Jews, Gypsies, Russians, and Ukrainians in state penal institutions, Poles with sentences of more than three years, and most of the security confined. The only exception was made for those security confined who were given a positive report by their prison governor. They were to be examined by a commission of the Ministry of Justice as to their "asociality." This provision had little impact, however, as the prison governors classified only approximately 5 percent of all inmates sentenced to security confinement as potentially "reformable."[73]

The transports to the concentration camps soon got under way. By spring 1943 around two-thirds (8,813) of all inmates sentenced to

179

security confinement had been taken to the camps.[74] The transfer was supported by most prison officials, who were radicalized by the war and the growing number of executions carried out in state penal institutions, and believed that brutal measures against "habitual criminals" were justified. They also saw the transfer as a chance to be relieved of unproductive inmates. The Ministry of Justice had made it clear that an offender's illness or weakness was no reason for exemption from the transfer. At the same time, it exempted those security-confined inmates who were occupied in key industries.[75] As a consequence, 2,711 inmates who had received sentences of security confinement were still alive in German penal institutions at the end of 1944.[76] The great majority of the security confined, however, were handed over to the police and killed in concentration camps.

Some women were taken to the Ravensbrück camp; others, including Rosa S., Frieda S. and Maria B., whom we encountered above, were transported by the police to Auschwitz. Most of the male security confined were taken to Mauthausen in Upper Austria. For several months, the security confined were much more likely than any group of inmates in Mauthausen, apart from Jews, to be killed. By 16 February 1944, 7,736 of the 10,231 former state prisoners (mostly security confined) transported to Mauthausen were dead. Death rates were somewhat lower in other camps, but here too the security confined were systematically exterminated. In the Neuengamme camp, not a day went by in the spring of 1943 without at least one former security-confined inmate's being brutally killed. In the Buchenwald camp, one out of seven former security confined inmates died each month in 1943.[77]

Remarkably, this mass extermination coincided with attempts by the SS leadership to reduce the death rate in the camps. From 1942 on, camp inmates were increasingly employed in armaments production and some efforts were made to improve the general conditions. As a consequence a temporary, but marked, fall in the mortality rate of inmates occurred.[78] In early 1943 the monthly mortality rate of inmates in Mauthausen in preventive police custody, those individuals classified in the camp as "professional criminals" (with a green triangle) or as "asocials" (with a black triangle), was less than 1 percent. By contrast, more than one in every four of the security-confined inmates perished each month in Mauthausen.[79] It is not quite clear why the security confined in this period were systematically killed while other camp inmates also classified as criminals were not. Presumably the increasing focus of the SS on productive labor condemned a great number of security confined to death, as they often arrived from state penal institutions barely able to work on account of old age, illness, and malnourishment. Yet even those who could work were killed, often by being worked to death with entirely unproductive labor in the camp's quarry. Clearly ideological factors also played an important role. After all, most security confined had been classified as biologically "incorrigible" and Hitler had repeatedly demanded that all such potential threats to the "national community" be ruthlessly eliminated.

V

The history of "habitual criminals" in state penal institutions in the Third Reich can be broken down into two distinct periods. In the first, until the outbreak of the war, more and more offenders were committed to security confinement in state penal institutions after it had become law on 1 January 1934. This law was firmly rooted in the criminological discourse of the pre-Nazi period. To be sure, the silencing of former critics of security confinement, such as liberal criminologists and prison reformers, made its introduction easier and allowed for the addition of more radical features to the drafts of the 1920s. Still, the Law against Dangerous Habitual Criminals was in many ways the realization of a measure which had been demanded by criminologists, prison officials, and politicians long before the Nazis came to power, and also appears to have had significant backing from the wider population. Since the late nineteenth century, many criminologists in Germany had been gripped by the widespread "blind faith in the omnipotence of social engineering."[80] They optimistically expected that, just as medicine had succeeded in combating epidemic illnesses, social problems like criminality, too, could be eradicated with the help of the emerging human sciences. In a typical expression of the "Janus-faced" nature of modern social policy, many officials and commentators demanded that penal policy should aim to reintegrate into society all offenders who could be reformed and to permanently exclude all "incorrigibles."[81]

It was the pseudoscience criminal biology which offered supposedly objective tools for the division of inmates into these two groups. Already in the Weimar Republic, criminological research had often judged repeated small-time property offenders as "incorrigible." Their recidivism was taken as proof that their "incorrigibility" was caused by biological factors. The fact that they had often grown up in extreme poverty, were unskilled, and were frequently prevented by respectable society from finding employment or accommodation after their imprisonment was often ignored by judges and criminologists both in Weimar and in the Third Reich. Essentially, these offenders were sentenced to indefinite confinement in Nazi Germany not because of the criminal danger they posed to society, but because of their non-normative behavior and their supposed "degenerative" hereditary traits.

Yet there was no straight line from the demand for the exclusion from society of "habitual criminals" to their eventual extermination, just as support for the sterilization of the handicapped and disabled did not inevitably lead to the Nazis' "euthanasia" program. There were no serious advocates in the Weimar Republic for the mass killing of "habitual criminals," and while these offenders, once put into security confinement in the Third Reich, were treated very harshly, there were no proposals to kill them before the outbreak of war in 1939. The crucial shift from indefinite confinement to extermination could occur only within the wider context of the extreme radicalization of Nazi policy against all "community aliens" during the Second World War. Still, the extermination of small-time offenders from 1942 on is a potent reminder of how concepts originally aimed at social exclusion can take on murderous forms if the social and political context in which they were first put forward is radicalized.[82]

The relationship between the police and the legal system in the Third Reich regarding "habitual criminals" was a complex one, characterized by both conflict and cooperation. On one level there was open friction, as the Ministry of Justice in the late 1930s resisted attempts to transfer the security-confined inmates to the police. This was only resolved in 1942, by which time the police had massively increased their influence and the standing of the legal system had reached a new low. Yet this conflict was caused by competition over which agency would ultimately be in control of the "habitual criminals," and not by serious differences of opinion as to their treatment. Both police and legal system were in agreement that these offenders had to be dealt with very harshly. Both systems could also look back on a long history of cooperation in the control of released offenders. And during the war, many prison officials and judges came to share Hitler's view that some "habitual criminals" should be exterminated and eventually supported the transfer of the security confined from state penal institutions to the concentration camps.

Many accounts still portray concentration camp life as a battle between the "red" political inmates and the violent "green" criminals. However, the criminal inmates did not form a homogeneous group. Many individuals imprisoned as criminals were held not for violent crimes, but for their non-normative behavior or for petty property offenses.[83] While a number of "greens" in concentration camps did act as *Kapos* and brutally mistreated their fellow inmates, this was emphatically not true for many others. Far from being "fellow criminals of the SS," as some former political camp inmates claimed, most of the security confined found themselves, after their transfer from state penal institutions, at the bottom of the concentration camp hierarchy and became the victims of excessive, brutal, and unrelenting violence. Witness accounts by former political camp inmates have to be treated with some caution. First, some political prisoners demonized the "greens" in order to retrospectively justify their own actions, which in some cases had not stopped short of murdering "greens." Second, political camp inmates often shared the social and racial prejudice against such deviants which was so widespread in German society.[84] One former political camp inmate noted after the war that he was still convinced "that the security confinement pronounced by the Nazis is based on a sensible idea."[85]

Those security confined who survived the war in state penal institutions were often not immediately released in 1945. In a sample of 250 inmates sentenced to security confinement in the Third Reich, no less than 37 were still imprisoned in 1947. After their eventual release, many were soon recommitted to security confinement. Only in 1970 was the legal framework for security confinement introduced by the Nazis in 1933 finally reformed. Five years earlier, there had still been 1,430 offenders in security confinement in West Germany, many of whom could not be judged as particularly dangerous to society.[86]

In the collective memory of life in the Third Reich, the fate of individuals classified as "habitual criminals" has been widely overlooked. They have not been accepted as victims of the Nazi regime. Even those who were transferred from state penal institutions to concentration camps received no compensation from the German state.[87] Not surprisingly, none of the judicial officials involved in the "annihilation through labor" process were ever convicted, not least because the postwar judicial system put little value on the testimonies of former security confined. Either they were not heard at all, or their testimony was treated as inherently untrustworthy. As a Bavarian court stated in 1949, the former security confined must be treated "from the outset with a certain suspicion because of their criminal past."[88]

NOTES

1. For this argument, see also Richard J. Evans, *Rituals of Retribution* (London: Penguin Books, 1997), 684. For instance, criminal offenders are practically absent from Michael Berenbaum, ed., *A Mosaic of Victims: Non-Jews Persecuted and Murdered by the Nazis* (London: Tauris, 1990).

2. Ulrich Herbert, Karin Orth, and Christoph Dieckmann, "Die national-sozialistischen Konzentrationslager: Geschichte, Erinnerung, Forschung," in *Die nationalsozialistischen Konzentrationslager*, ed. Ulrich Herbert, Karin Orth, and Christoph Dieckmann (Göttingen: Wallenstein Verlag, 1998), 1:17–42; Lutz Niethammer, "Häftlinge und Häftlingsgruppen im Lager," in Herbert, Orth, and Dieckmann, eds., *Die nationalsozialistischen Konzentrationslager*, 2:1046–62.

3. See, for example, Hans Eiden, "Das war Buchenwald: Tatsachenbericht," in *Eh' die Sonne lacht: Hans Eiden—Kommunist und Lagerältester im KZ Buchenwald*, ed. Horst Gobrecht (Bonn: Pahl-Rugenstein, 1995), 207–264; Benedikt Kautsky, *Teufel und Verdammte* (Zurich: Büchergilde Gutenberg, 1946); Eugen Kogon, *Der SS-Staat* (Munich: Wilhelm Heyne Verlag, 1995).

4. In the second half of 1942 the average number of concentration camp inmates was around 95,000. By contrast, on 31 October 1942, there were almost 200,000 inmates in the state penal institutions; Martin Broszat, "Nationalsozialistische Konzentrationslager, 1933–1945," in *Anatomie des SS-Staates*, ed. Hans Buchheim et al. (Munich: Deutscher Taschenbuch Verlag, 1994), 323–448, here 437; Bundesarchiv Berlin (= BA Berlin), R 22/897, Bl. 88: Gesamtbelegung am 31 October 1942.

5. For the first full-length investigation of the Nazi state prison system, see Heike Jung and Heinz Müller-Dietz, eds., *Strafvollzug im "Dritten Reich": Am Beispiel des Saarlandes* (Baden-Baden: Nomos Verlagsgesellschaft, 1996); for a critical evaluation, see my review in *German History* 16 (1998): 121–22.

6. "Auszug aus dem Gesetz gegen gefährliche Gewohnheitsverbrecher und über Maßregeln der Sicherung und Besserung," in *Gesetz zur Verhütung erbkranken Nachwuchses vom 14. Juli 1933*, ed. Arthur Gütt, Ernst Rüdin, and Falk Ruttke (Munich: J. F. Lehmanns Verlag, 1934), 179–214; Lothar Gruchmann, *Justiz im Dritten Reich: Anpassung und Unterwerfung in der Ära Gürtner* (Munich: Oldenbourg, 1990), 838–43; Franz Exner, "Wie erkennt man den gefährlichen Gewohnheitsverbrecher?" *Deutsche Justiz* 11(1943): 377–79. The actual figures are somewhat higher than the one given by Exner, as they did not include the sentences of security confinement passed during the war by special courts (*Sondergerichte*); see Christian Müller, *Das Gewohnheitsverbrechergesetz vom 24 November 1933* (Baden-Baden: Nomos Verlagsgesellschaft, 1997), 54–55.

7. Franz von Liszt, "Der Zweckgedanke im Strafrecht," in his *Strafrechtliche Aufsätze und Vorträge* (Berlin, 1905), 1:126–79, here 167; see also Richard F. Wetzell, "Criminal Law Reform in Imperial Germany" (Ph.D. diss., Standford, 1991), 61, 76.

8. Cited in Michael Baurmann, "Kriminalpolitik ohne Mass—Zum Marburger Programm Franz von Liszts", *Kriminalsoziologische Bibliografie* 11 (1984): 54–79, here 63–64.

9. Robert Gaupp, "Über den heutigen Stand der Lehre vom 'geborenen Verbrecher,'" *Monatsschrift für Kriminalpsychologie und Strafrechtsreform* (= *MSchriftKrim*) 1 (1904): 25–42, here 42; Heinz Müller-Dietz, *Strafvollzugsgesetzgebung und Strafvollzugsreform* (Cologne: Heymann, 1970); Ewald Mezger, "Die Behandlung der gefährlichen Gewohnheitsverbrecher," *MSchriftKrim* 14 (1923): 135–75; Gustav Aschaffenburg, "Die Stellung des Psychiaters zur Strafrechtsreform," *MSchriftKrim* 16 (1925): 145–66. Security confinement was first included in the so-called *Gegenenwurf* of 1911, which had been drawn up by Liszt, Wilhelm Kahl, and Karl von Lilienthal.

10. Robert Heindl, *Der Berufsverbrecher* (Berlin: Pan Verlag, 1926), 192–94.

11. Patrick Wagner, *Volksgemeinschaft ohne Verbrecher: Konzeptionen und Praxis der Kriminalpolizei in der Zeit der Weimarer Republik und des Nationalsozialismus* (Hamburg: Christians, 1996), 17–190.

12. Theodor Viernstein, "Referat auf der Augsburger Tagung vom 3. Juni 1927 des Vereins der höheren Strafvollzugsbeamten," special print, copy in the possession of the author, 17. See also Fritz Lenz, *Menschliche Auslese und Rassenhygiene* (Munich: Lehmanns, 1921), 130. For a more general discussion, see Hans-Walter Schmuhl, *Rassenhygiene, Nationalsozialismus, Euthanasie: Von der Verhütung zur Vernichtung "lebensunwerten Lebens," 1890–1945* (Göttingen: Vandenhoeck & Ruprecht, 1987), 45–46.

13. Grüllich, "Der Gewohnheitsverbrecher nach dem Entwurfe des neuen Strafgesetzbuches," *MSchriftKrim* 18 (1927): 671–78, here 672; Aschaffenburg, "Die Stellung des Psychiaters," 157; Theodor Viernstein, "Über Typen des verbesserlichen und unverbesserlichen Verbrechers," *Mitteilungen der kriminalbiologischen Gesellschaft*, vol. 2 (1929): 26–54, here 44–45; Joachim Schurich, *Lebensläufe vielfach Rückfälliger Verbrecher: Ein Beitrag zur Frage der Sicherungsverwahrung gemeingefährlicher Gewohnheitsverbrecher* (Leipzig, 1930), 158–59.

14. "Statistik des Gefängniswesens im Deutschen Reich," *Stenographische Berichte der Verhandlungen des Deutschen Reichstages*, IV, Wahlperiode (1928), vol. 434, Anlage zu den Stenographischen Berichten, Nr. 814, table 6.

15. Lothar Frede, "Zur Einführung," in *Gefängnisse in Thüringen: Berichte über die Reform des Strafvollzugs* (Weimar, 1930), 1–8; Berthold Freudenthal, "Maßregeln der Sicherung und Besserung," in *Reform des Strafrechts: Kritische*

Besprechung des Amtlichen Entwurfs eines Allgemeinen Deutschen Strafge-setzbuchs, ed. Paul Felix Aschrott and Eduard Kohlrausch (Berlin and Leipzig: de Gruyter, 1926), 153–172; Der Reichsminister der Justiz, Entwurf eines Strafvollzugsgesetztes, dem Reichstag vorgelegt am 9.9.1927, § 309.

16. Grüllich, "Der Gewohnheitsverbrecher"; Aschaffenburg, "Die Stellung des Psychiaters," 161; Schurich, *Lebensläufe vielfach Rückfälliger Verbrecher,* 157–58; Heindl, *Berufsverbrecher,* 386.

17. Theodor Viernstein, "Die kriminalbiologischen Untersuchungen der Strafgefangenen in Bayern," *Mitteilungen der kriminalbiologischen Gesellschaft,* vol. 3 (Graz, 1931): 30–38.

18. Evans, *Rituals of Retribution,* 572–75.

19. Bayrisches Staatsministerium der Justiz, ed., *Der Stufenstrafvollzug und die kriminalbiologischen Untersuchungen der Gefangenen in den bayrischen Strafanstalten,* vol.1 (Munich, 1926); Rudolf Sieverts, "Die preußische Verord-nung über den Strafvollzug in Stufen vom 7. Juni 1929," *MSchriftKrim,* Beiheft 3 (Heidelberg, 1930): 129–51.

20. See Rainer Möhler, "Strafvollzug im 'Dritten Reich': Nationale Politik und regionale Ausprägung am Beispiel des Saarlandes," in *Strafvollzug im "Dritten Reich,"* ed. Jung and Müller-Dietz, 9–301, here 62–65.

21. W. Schwerdtfeger, "Gedanken über die Sicherungsverwahrung," *Monatsblätter für Gerichtshilfe, Gefangenen- und Entlassenenfürsorge* 10 (1934/1935): 81–86.

22. Cited in Müller, *Das Gewohnheitsverbrechergesetz,* 75.

23. Müller, *Das Gewohnheitsverbrechergesetz,* 43–44; Jörg Kinzig, *Die Sicherungsverwahrung auf dem Prüfstand* (Freiburg im Breisgau, 1996), 17–18. For the figures, see BA Berlin, R 3001/9920/2, Bl.1.

24. Bayrisches Hauptstaatsarchiv (= BayHStA), MJu 22510, Direktion des Zuchthauses Kaisheim to Generalstaatsanwalt beim Oberlandesgericht München, 15 June 1934.

25. BA Berlin, R 3001/9852, Bl. 196–7: Vorstand der Frauenstraf- und Sicherungsanstalt Lübeck-Lauerhof to Generalstaatsanwalt in Kiel, 25 May 1938; ibid., Bl. 196–7: Vorstand der Frauenstraf- und Sicherungsanstalt Lübeck-Lauerhof to Generalstaatsanwalt in Kiel, 25 May 1938; Franz Weber, "Erfahrungen in der Sicherungsanstalt," *Blätter für Gefängniskunde* (= *BlGefK*) 68 (1938): 429–48.

26. Staatsarchiv München (= StAMü), Justizvollzugsanstalten Nr. 5470, Franziska K. to her father, mother and siblings, 6 December 1936; emphasis in the original. For reasons of data protection, all the surnames of prisoners in this paper have been abbreviated.

27. Johannes Eichler, "Der Vollzug der Sicherungsverwahrung," in *Dringende Fragen der Sicherungsverwahrung,* ed. Roland Freisler and Franz Schlegelberger (Berlin: v. Decker, 1938), 98–104, here 99.

28. BA Berlin, R 22/1429, Bl. 106–121: Niederschrift über die Bespre-

chung mit den Vorständen der Sicherungsanstalten der Reichsjustizverwaltung am 14.8.1939.

29. Thüringisches Hauptstaatsarchiv Weimar (= ThHStAW), Generalstaatsanwalt beim Oberlandesgericht Jena, Nr. 812, Bl. 148: Vorstand der Sicherungsanstalt Gräfentonna to Generalstaatsanwalt beim Oberlandesgericht Jena, 28 December 1939.

30. Brandenburgisches Landeshauptarchiv (= BLHA), Pr. Br. Rep. 29, Zuchthaus Brandenburg Nr. 4014, Urteil des Landgericht Potsdam vom 9.10.1940. As this injury was seen by the court as reducing F.'s likelihood of re-offending, it decided not to sentence him to security confinement but instead to a lengthy prison sentence. Upon his release in September 1943, F. was transferred to the Berlin police and probably taken to a concentration camp.

31. BA Berlin, R 22/1277, Bl. 131–2: E. Eggensperger to Dr. Eichler, 15 October 1940; Heinz Möller, *Die Entwicklung und Lebensverhältnisse von 135 Gewohnheitsverbrechern* (Leipzig, 1939), 74.

32. Edgar Schmidt, "Sicherungsverwahrung in Zahlen," in Freisler and Schlegelberger, eds., *Dringende Fragen der Sicherungsverwahrung*, 105–113, here 112. Joachim Hellmer, *Der Gewohnheitsverbrecher und die Sicherungsverwahrung, 1934–1945* (Berlin: Duncker & Humblot, 1961), here 41–53, 59–61; Hellmer examined the files of 250 security confined male prisoners from different German regions. Möller, *Entwicklung und Lebensverhältnisse*, 43; Möller examined the files of 135 inmates in the Hamburg area, who had been sentenced retrospectively to security confinement.

33. BayHStA, MJu 22507, Dr. Viernstein, Dr. Trunk, Gutachten vom 4.2.1930.

34. Richard Bessel, *Germany after the First World War* (Oxford: Clarendon Press, 1995), 242; Merith Niehuss, "From Welfare Provision to Social Insurance: The Unemployed in Augsburg, 1918–1927," in *The German Unemployed*, ed. Richard J. Evans and Dick Geary (London: Croom Helm, 1987), 44–72; Detlev J. K. Peukert, *Grenzen der Sozialdisziplinierung* (Cologne: Bund-Verlag, 1986), 166–67; Volker Berghahn, *Modern Germany: Society, Economy, and Politics in the Twentieth Century*, 2d ed. (Cambridge: Cambridge University Press, 1987), 284; Wagner, *Volksgemeinschaft ohne Verbrecher*, 215.

35. Hellmer, *Gewohnheitsverbrecher*, 209–247, 261–66; Ludwig Lotz, *Der gefährliche Gewohnheitsverbrecher* (Leipzig, 1939), 66–88. Lotz's sample consisted of two hundred male and female prisoners from the Bavarian institutions of Straubing and Aichach.

36. BLHA, Pr. Br. Rep. 29, Zuchthaus Brandenburg Nr. 6425.

37. Müller, *Das Gewohnheitsverbrechergesetz*, 68–72.

38. Schmidt, "Sicherungsverwahrung," 105, 112; Lotz, *Gewohnheitsverbrecher*, 62–64.

39. StAMü, Justizvollzugsanstalten Nr. 13693; ibid., Nr. 12340, Krankenakte Rosa S.; for some background, see Lynn Abrams, "Prostitutes in Imperial

Germany, 1870–1918: Working Girls or Social Outcasts?" in *The German Underworld: Deviants and Outcasts in German History*, ed. Richard J. Evans (London: Routledge, 1988), 189–209.

40. Cited in Walter Luz, *Ursachen und Bekämpfung des Verbrechens im Urteil des Verbrechers: Ein Beitrag zur Psychologie des Verbrechers und Verbrechens und zur Reform der Verbrechensbekämpfung* (Heidelberg: Winter, 1928), 194.

41. Alf Lüdtke, *"Gemeinwohl," Polizei, und "Festungspraxis": Staatliche Gewaltsamkeit und innere Verwaltung in Preußen, 1815–1850* (Göttingen: Vandenhoeck & Ruprecht, 1982), 233–37; Walter Obenaus, *Die Entwicklung der preussischen Sicherheitspolizei bis zum Ende der Reaktionszeit* (Berlin, 1940), 58–61; T. Berger, *Die konstante Repression: Zur Geschichte des Strafvollzugs in Preussen nach 1850* (Frankfurt: Verlag Roter Stern, 1974), 115–21.

42. Möller, *Entwicklung und Lebensverhältnisse*, 53, 56.

43. For instance, only 17 percent of the inmates in the Brandenburg-Görden security confinement wing in 1937 were married; Weber, "Erfahrungen in der Sicherungsanstalt," 434.

44. See for example, StAMü, Justizvollzugsanstalten Nr. 12019, Brief im Auftrag der Mutter der W. to Verwaltung der Frauenverwahrungsanstalt Aichach, 2 January 1941; Hellmer, *Gewohnheitsverbrecher*, 285.

45. StAMü, Justizvollzugsanstalten Nr. 1820. See also Rundschreiben des Deutschen Gemeindetags an die Gemeinden und Gemeindeverbände, 15. Januar 1934, reprinted in Wolfgang Ayaß, ed., *"Gemeinschaftsfremde": Quellen zur Verfolgung von "Asozialen," 1933–1945* (Koblenz: Bundesarchiv, 1998), doc. 25.

46. Adolf Wingler, "1. Tagung der Gesellschaft für Deutsches Strafrecht, München 27./29. Oktober 1938," *BlGefK* 69 (1938): 310.

47. StAMü, Justizvollzugsanstalten Nr. 461, Hedwig J. to her sister, 7 March 1937, 14 March 1937.

48. BA Berlin, R 3001/9852, Bl. 294–320: Die Entlassung aus der Sicherungsverwahrung (manuscript, no date).

49. StAMü, Justizvollzugsanstalten Nr. 461, Beschluss des Amtsgerichts Berlin, 19 January 1940.

50. For these examples, see ThHStAW, Generalstaatsanwalt bei dem Oberlandesgericht Jena, Nr. 701, Oberstaatsanwalt in Meiningen to Reichsminister der Justiz, 10 July 1939; ibid., Der Oberstaatsanwalt in Weimar to Reichsminister der Justiz, 25 March 1938; ibid., NSDAP Gau Thüringen, Amt für Volkswohlfahrt to Generalstaatsanwalt bei dem Oberlandesgericht Jena, 17 June 1939; BLHA, Pr. Br. Rep. 29, Zuchthaus Brandenburg Nr. 5117.

51. Wingler, "1. Tagung der Gesellschaft," 310.

52. In Hellmer's sample of 250 security confinement inmates, 15 of the 25 released inmates were readmitted even before the outbreak of the war in 1939; Hellmer, *Gewohnheitsverbrecher*, 366–70.

53. BLHA, Pr. Br. Rep. 29, Zuchthaus Brandenburg Nr.8152.

54. Lotz, *Gewohnheitsverbrecher*, 92; StAMü, Justizvollzugsanstalten Nr. 9000.

55. BA Berlin, R 22/1263, Bl. 36–53: Niederschrift über die Erörterung von Strafvollzugsfragen in der Arbeitstagung der Generalstaatsanwälte im Reichsjustizministerium, 14 November 1936; Roland Freisler, "Ein Querschnitt durch die Fragen der Sicherungsverwahrung," in Freisler and Schlegelberger, eds., *Dringende Fragen der Sicherungsverwahrung*, 7–14. See also Werner Johe, *Die gleichgeschaltete Justiz* (Frankfurt am Main: Europäische Verlagsanstalt, 1967), 142–43.

56. Freisler, "Fragen der Sicherungsverwahrung," 7–8; Karl Leo Terhorst, *Polizeiliche planmäßige Überwachung und polizeiliche Vorbeugungshaft im Dritten Reich* (Heidelberg: C. F. Müller, 1985), 166–67; Ralph Angermund, *Deutsche Richterschaft, 1919–1945* (Frankfurt am Main: Fischer Taschenbuch Verlag, 1990), 166.

57. Patrick Wagner, "'Vernichtung der Berufsverbrecher': Die vorbeugende Verbrechensbekämpfung der Kriminalpolizei bis 1937," in Herbert, Orth, and Dieckmann, eds., *Die nationalsozialistischen Konzentrationslager*, 1:87–110, here 92–93; Terhorst, *Polizeiliche planmäßige Überwachung*, 74–80, 100.

58. Wagner, "'Vernichtung der Berufsverbrecher,'" 93–101; Terhorst, *Polizeiliche planmäßige Überwachung*, 115–53.

59. BA Berlin, R 22/1429, Bl. 123–5: Chef der Kanzlei des Führers to Chef der Reichskanzlei, 26 July 1939; ibid., Bl. 122: Chef der Reichskanzlei to Reichsminister der Justiz, 8 August 1939; ibid., Bl. 133: Reichsführer SS to Reichsminister der Justiz, 26 August 1939; ibid., Vermerk, signed Dr. Nörr, 7 September 1939.

60. Cited in Elke Fröhlich, ed., *Die Tagebücher von Joseph Goebbels* (Munich: K.G. Saur, 1996), part II, vol. 4, p. 405, diary entry for 30 May 1942.

61. Evans, *Rituals of Retribution*, 690, 916, table 1; Martin Broszat, *Der Staat Hitlers* (Munich: Deutscher Taschenbuch Verlag, 1992), 419.

62. BA Berlin, R 22/1337, Bl. 416: Reichsminister der Justiz to Generalstaatsanwälte, 4 May 1940.

63. For these figures, see Nikolaus Wachsmann, "'Annihilation through Labour': The Killing of State Prisoners in the Third Reich," *Journal of Modern History* (September 1999).

64. BA Berlin, R 22/1261, Reichsminister der Justiz to Generalstaatsanwälte, 28 October 1939; ibid., R 22/1442, Bl. 125: Verordnung des Reichsministers für Ernährung und Landwirtschaft, 16 January 1940.

65. BA Berlin, R 22/1443, Bl. 269-276: Reichsministerium der Justiz, Niederschrift über die Besprechung über Fragen der Ernährung und Arbeitszeit der Gefangenen am 9.5.1940.

66. StAMü, Justizvollzugsanstalten Nr. 10463.

67. ThHStAW, Generalstaatsanwalt beim Oberlandesgericht Jena, Nr. 812, Bl. 156: Der Vorstand der Sicherungsanstalt Gräfentonna to General-

staatsanwalt beim Oberlandesgericht Jena, 4 May 1940; ibid., Bl. 153: Der Anstaltsarzt der Sicherungsanstalt Gräfentonna to Generalstaatsanwalt beim Oberlandesgericht Jena, 25 April 1940.

68. ThHStAW, Generalstaatsanwalt beim Oberlandesgericht Jena, Nr. 812, Bl. 217: Der Reichsminister der Justiz to Generalstaatsanwalt beim Oberlandesgericht Jena, 24 October 1941.

69. "Die selbstständigen Vollzugsanstalten der Reichsjustizverwaltung, Stand vom 1. Februar 1941," *BlGefK* 71 (1940/1941): 348.

70. ThHStAW, Generalstaatsanwalt bei dem Oberlandesgericht Jena, Nr. 1069, Bl. 123: Arzt des Zuchthauses Gräfentonna, Jahresbericht über die Gesundheitsführung, 8 January 1943; ibid., Bl. 156: Arzt des Zuchthauses Gräfentonna, Jahresbericht über die Gesundheitsführung, 13 February 1945.

71. BLHA, Pr. Br. Rep. 29, Zuchthaus Brandenburg Nr. 6425, letter from Karl. K to his brother and sister-in-law, 26 September 1942.

72. BA Berlin, R 22/4062, Bl. 35a-37: Besprechung mit Reichsführer SS Himmler am 18.9.1942 in seinem Feldquartier.

73. For further details on the transfer of state inmates to the police, see Wachsmann, "'Annihilation through Labour.'"

74. The figure consists of 4,296 inmates in security confinement (including 223 women), and 4,517 inmates in penitentiaries with subsequent security confinement (including 267 women); BA Berlin, R 22/1417, Bl. 141.

75. BA Berlin, 99 US 2 FC 588, Mikrofilm 22941, Bl. 56–61: Reichsminister der Justiz to Generalstaatsanwälte, 22 October 1942, Nuremberg trial document 648-PS; Zentrale Stelle der Landesjustizverwaltungen zur Aufklärung von NS-Gewaltverbrechen, Ludwigsburg (= ZSLL), VI 416 AR-Nr 1127/66, Bl. 259: Reichsminister der Justiz to Generalstaatsanwälte, 2 November 1942.

76. IfZ, MA 624, Bl. 3664567: Gesamtbelegung der deutschen Justizvollzugsanstalten, 30 December 1944. A number of those inmates were offenders sentenced by the courts after October 1942. Hellmer estimates that another 1,650 inmates were sentenced to security confinement after October 1942; Hellmer, *Gewohnheitsverbrecher*, 16–17.

77. ZSLL, VI 415 AR-Nr 1310/63, Staatsanwaltschaft beim Kammergericht Berlin, Einleitungsvermerk vom 30.4.1965; Hans Marsálek, *Die Geschichte des Konzentrationslagers Mauthausen* (Vienna: Österreichische Lagergemeinschaft Mauthausen, 1974), 97n5; Hermann Kaienburg, *"Vernichtung durch Arbeit": Der Fall Neuengamme* (Bonn: Dietz Nachf., 1990), 429; Falk Pingel, *Häftlinge unter SS-Herrschaft* (Hamburg: Hoffmann & Campe, 1978), 185–86.

78. Ulrich Herbert, "Arbeit und Vernichtung," in *Ist der Nationalsozialismus Geschichte?* ed. Dan Diner (Frankfurt am Main: Fischer Taschenbuch Verlag, 1987), 198–236; Pingel, *Häftlinge unter SS-Herrschaft*, 182–83; Michel Fabréguet, "Entwicklung und Veränderung der Funktionen des Konzentra-

tionslagers Mauthausen, 1938–1945," in Herbert, Orth, and Dieckmann, eds., *Die nationalsozialistischen Konzentrationslager*, 1:193–214.

79. Pingel, *Häftlinge unter SS-Herrschaft*, 186. Figures for January and February 1942.

80. Detlev J. K. Peukert, *The Weimar Republic* (London: Penguin Books, 1993), 134.

81. For the general background, see Peukert, *Sozialdisziplinierung*, 305–309; Detlev J. K. Peukert, "The Genesis of the 'Final Solution' from the Spirit of Science," in *Nazism and German Society, 1933–1945*, ed. David F. Crew (London: Routledge, 1994), 274–99.

82. See Peukert, *Sozialdisziplinierung*, 263–64, 299–301.

83. This point was first made in Toni Siegert, "Das Konzentrationslager Flossenbürg," in *Bayern in der NS-Zeit*, ed. Martin Broszat and Elke Fröhlich (Munich and Vienna: Oldenbourg, 1979), 2:429–92, here 440–41.

84. Wagner, "'Vernichtung der Berufsverbrecher,'" 104–106.

85. Kautsky, *Teufel und Verdammte*, 144.

86. Hellmer, *Gewohnheitsverbrecher*, 342, 378; Kinzig, *Die Sicherungsverwahrung*, 3, 21–23, 569–573.

87. For the general background, see W. Ayaß, *"Asoziale" im Nationalsozialismus* (Stuttgart: Klett-Cotta, 1995), 210–16.

88. BayHStA, StK 113944, Urteil der I. Strafkammer des Landgerichts Regensburg vom 28.2.1949; see also IfZ, MB-1, Amtsgerichtsrat Kunz, Vernehmung von Anna K., 15.7.1948.

CHAPTER 9

The Ambivalent Outsider

PROSTITUTION, PROMISCUITY, AND

VD CONTROL IN NAZI BERLIN

ANNETTE F. TIMM

PERHAPS no other category of social outsider occupied such an ambivalent position in the Third Reich as prostitutes. They were both radically criminalized and officially sanctioned, and their activities were subject to increasingly structured intervention and categorization on the part of police, welfare, and health authorities. Prostitutes were soon categorized as "asocials"; they were placed under increasingly strict surveillance and prevented from plying their trade in public places; and they were thought to be the primary carriers of fertility-threatening diseases likely to damage the future strength of the nation. Despite this outsider status, prostitution was first tolerated and later actively promoted to boost military morale and provide productivity incentives for workers in industry. The wartime construction of state-run brothels then became part of the social mobilization for war and can be understood as a deployment and regulation of sexual energies to help achieve military ends.

A comprehensive account of the treatment of prostitution in the Third Reich would necessarily entail an extensive comparison with policies in the Weimar Republic and a comparative analysis of social practices in various regions. My goal here is more limited. On the basis of evidence drawn primarily from a case study of Berlin, I will describe the transformation of categories first used in VD control during the Weimar Republic into the insider/outsider divisions of the Third Reich. The regime moved through three distinct phases of policy: (1) the rhetorical and legal marginalization of prostitutes; (2) the growing acceptance of prostitution in practice; and (3) the subordination of prostitution policy to the war effort. These policy shifts took place in spite of vociferous opposition from confessional and medical circles and continued concerns about the spread of venereal disease. During the course of the war

Nazi policy toward prostitution decisively turned its back on decades of officially sanctioned social hygienic theory and practice. Indeed, from the fall of 1939, venereal disease control in Germany became almost entirely an effort to regulate and control prostitution in the interests of providing soldiers and war workers with a "safe" outlet for their sexual energies. Government officials explicitly rejected arguments from VD and welfare experts, who argued that confining prostitutes to locked brothels increased the risk of spreading VD.[1]

At the beginning of the Third Reich, welfare policies that had originally aimed at educating the public about the dangers of VD were modified to emphasize harsh punishments for deviations from accepted sexual norms. Venereal disease control increasingly became a matter for the police, a process which helped to harden categories of acceptable and unacceptable sexual behavior. As Jeremy Noakes has written, the Nazis segregated outsiders—those who did not conform to the social and racial norms of the "national community"—into three main categories: ideological enemies; asocials; and biological outsiders (including both racially and genetically "unfit" individuals).[2] Of course these categories overlapped; prostitutes, for instance, were often considered genetically diseased simply by virtue of their profession. But the category "asocial" was the broadest and most subjective, and the one most commonly applied to prostitutes and to victims of venereal disease.[3] This categorization of social misfits, Noakes argues, also allowed the police to usurp control over new areas of social policy. Laws that categorized individuals as "asocial" and punished them with protective custody often removed them from the care of medical and welfare authorities. This necessitated a shift in power away from the local health offices and toward the criminal police, a process which continued to progress throughout the Nazi period.[4]

In the early years of National Socialism, experts in the fields of public health and welfare who supported the regime reacted positively toward this tightening of control and expressed confidence that the "National Socialist spiritual direction," with its emphasis on family and its very strict definition of healthy sexuality, would be much more successful at combating prostitution than previous strategies.[5] Articles in medical journals, newspapers, and educational literature stressed the positive benefits of eugenic controls (which, it was said, would eventually weed out "inferior" social elements like prostitutes) and organized youth activities, sponsored by organizations like the Hitler Youth, the League of German Girls (Bund Deutscher Mädel), and the labor organization

193

Strength through Joy (*Kraft durch Freude*). Channeling youthful energies into sports and outdoor activities, it was argued, would prevent exposure to deviant sexual behavior.[6] Males in particular, the author of an article in *Die Ärztin* wrote, could benefit from an education that stressed physical health and de-eroticized women. Femininity would then be appreciated for its relationship to motherhood rather than to sex.[7] This, at least, was the ideal. The classic image of the dutiful German *Hausfrau*, so common in Nazi propaganda, depicted a guardian of home and hearth—an attentive mother devoid of all erotic characteristics. Yet not all women in National Socialist Germany were so desexualized. Beneath the stated ideal of confining sexuality to "proper" channels and to marriage, there lurked the presence of the prostitute.

Early pronouncements against the scourge of prostitution, emanating from Adolf Hitler himself, misled antiprostitution activists into assuming that the new regime would not tolerate such forms of extramarital sexual activity.[8] Indeed, in the first two years of the Nazi regime, campaigns against prostitution appeared to be aimed at its eradication. We might call this first phase of prostitution policy the phase of legal marginalization. According to Gisela Bock, in 1933, tens of thousands of prostitutes were rounded up and sent to workhouses and concentration camps.[9] These measures occurred under the authority of the Presidential Decree for the Protection of the People and State (issued on 28 February 1933) and May 1933 revisions to the VD law and Section 361 of the criminal code. These modifications included provisions for punishing anyone "who publicly and conspicuously or in a manner likely to annoy the public incites immoral acts or offers immoral services."[10] In September 1935 the Nuremberg Laws further delineated categories of acceptable sexual behavior by banning marriages between Jews and gentiles. This created the legal category of "race defilement"—sexual contact that might lead to miscegenation. Within two years of coming to power, then, the Nazis used the authority of law to label prostitution, promiscuity, and interracial sexual activities as "asocial." "Asocial" behavior for women (though not for men) might even include becoming too easily sexually aroused or creating a "strongly erotic impression."[11] These "over-sexed" women, along with those who infected soldiers with venereal disease, were immediately placed in one or more of three categories: promiscuous individual; prostitute; or sterilization candidate.[12] Their marginalization then justified state control over prostitution to a degree unprecedented in German history.

Increased control over prostitution did not, however, mean that women were to be forbidden from offering sexual services for sale. Although changes to the VD law greatly expanded the number of women who might find themselves taken into custody for "immoral" activities, they did not preclude the existence of locked brothels and red-light districts. In fact by 1936, the Military Supreme Command declared the construction of military brothels "an urgent necessity" and insisted that health authorities should cooperate.[13] Heinrich Himmler made similar promises to SS commanders in 1937.[14] Thus the first phase of the official marginalization of prostitutes was quickly followed by a phase of limited acceptance. Himmler seemed particularly concerned that removing prostitution as an outlet for excess male sexual drives would be injurious to soldiers and might lead to an increased incidence of homosexuality.[15]

Religious organizations and VD experts voiced strong objections to the second phase of Nazi prostitution policy. Drawing on decades of experience in the field of VD control, and alluding to the concerns of confessional welfare organizations involved in the rehabilitation of prostitutes, Bodo Spiethoff, head of the German Society for Combating Venereal Diseases, argued that ethical considerations must take precedence over "purely organizational-technical" priorities: "State-licensed brothels and red-light districts are state-politically and state-ethically unbearable, but they are also to be rejected from any other viewpoint, because the number of prostitutes housed in this way is only ever a small fraction of the prostitutes in a city, and this small fraction would not influence the city landscape in any way, so that no advantages can overcome the ethical, health, and economic disadvantages connected to any brothel-related business."[16] Spiethoff's arguments were cited in the internal communication of the Department for the Protection of Endangered Girls (*Gefährdetenfürsorge*), part of the welfare organization of the Protestant church (the Inner Mission), and they were reprinted in the pages of the journal of the Working Group for Promoting the Health of the *Volk* (the *Arbeitsgemeinschaft für Volksgesundung*, a union of close to three hundred social welfare agencies, women's groups, confessional welfare organizations, and prominent social hygienists, active in Berlin since the early years of the Weimar Republic).[17] Both groups heartily approved of Spiethoff's assessment of the dangers of the Nazi policy on prostitution.[18] The Working Group published several articles on the subject in 1934 and 1937. Anonymous authors stressed their rejection of the state's involvement in organized prostitution. Although the Working Group acknowledged the much "cleaner street picture" that

195

the National Socialist crackdown on prostitutes had achieved, it insisted that the conscientious implementation of the 1927 Reich Law for Combating Venereal Diseases, without the reconstruction of brothels, would have achieved the same result.[19] Interestingly, the Working Group supported the existence of discreet brothels, run by madams rather than by police, and situated in the less populated financial districts of the city. A pragmatic willingness to accept this kind of prostitution, it argued, was preferable to having the state sanction extramarital intercourse by becoming involved in the actual administration of prostitution, and it would also achieve the apparent goal of the National Socialist state to remove this activity from public view.[20] However, they argued that officially run brothels and walled-off red-light districts would instead actually encourage and foster deviant sexual behavior: they would be sites of curiosity for the young, who would certainly try to peek past the walls and ape the behavior they spied.[21] Such brothels would encourage deviant sexual acts through their effects on the mass psychology of their visitors;[22] and they would even provide an incentive for the slave trade in women and children.[23] On the basis of these arguments, the Working Group complained bitterly when the Nazi state began to support the notion of state-sanctioned and -run brothels after 1934, and later on the group repeated arguments that registration of prostitutes not only would increase the spread of venereal disease but would give men the false impression that state-run brothels would protect them from VD.[24]

The views expressed by the Working Group for Promoting the Health of the *Volk* were echoed in a report from the Group for the Protection of Endangered Girls in the Association of Female Welfare Workers. It too argued that regulated brothels and the forced registration and confinement of prostitutes worsened rather than improved the conditions for combating VD. Regulating prostitutes would drive them underground, where they would avoid all forms of health control and surveillance and become even more dangerous to the public. Men who visited regulated brothels were likely to assume that the services provided there included an implicit guarantee of medical safety, when in actual fact confinement had no effect on rates of VD infection. But worst of all, the welfare workers argued, was the ethical message that state-run brothels sent to the general population. Here they were quite explicit:

> The National Socialist state, which has given itself the duty to protect and support the family, whose youth should be trained in self-control and ethical responsibility to the next generation, would endanger its own educa-

tional goals through the toleration, even legalization, of particular places for extra-marital sexual intercourse. Where the police themselves confine women to certain streets to perform acts of prostitution, where they regulate, and for instance provide individuals who wish to engage in prostitution with a particular instructional pamphlet or even identification for which they have to pay, they are granting a concession to prostitution.[25]

The welfare workers also believed that existing laws, if properly applied and enforced with the threat of confinement in a workhouse, would be effective in controlling prostitution without resorting to police regulation of brothels. They expressed indignation that the state seemingly intended only to remove prostitution from public view without attacking it at its roots and without putting the Nazi state's "strong impulse toward ethically renewing our *Volk*" into practice.

In some sense, all of these protests were attempts to use the Nazi regime's own rhetoric against it. Each of the organizations described above had long operated under the assumption that prostitutes were thoroughly marginalized and that welfare measures should seek to rehabilitate those women for their own sake and in the interests of protecting society at large. In this view prostitutes, though individually reformable, could not be condoned or accepted as a group because their "vocation" threatened the health of society and exposed it to the peril of fertility-destroying venereal diseases. The protesters did not immediately understand the shift in policy, because they could not grasp the fact that these outsiders—prostitutes—were suddenly being touted as socially necessary, if not exactly social insiders. At the very least, prostitutes began to occupy a more ambivalent position in German society than had ever been the case in the past. Weimar politicians and VD experts had accepted the inevitability of prostitution as an outlet for what they considered to be irrepressible male sexual urges (*Geschlechtstrieb*). But the impulse to protect the population from VD and an understanding of the limitations of medical diagnosis and treatment had combined to defeat any arguments about the relative safety of brothels.[26] Prostitutes, in this logic, had to be provided with incentives to return to "normal" lifestyles. Under the Nazis, this option was increasingly closed off. Despite the rhetoric against the evils of prostitution and the "biological inferiority" of prostitutes, their role as "necessary" outlets for male sexual energies was soon institutionalized. Prostitutes became available to any German man who found his way to a state-run brothel. Given the apparent absence of further protests against brothels after 1937, it seems plausible

197

to assume that a regime discomfited by the internal contradictions and ambiguities of its own policies quietly put a stop to further discussions of the subject.

The older language and concern about VD did not disappear completely, but was adapted from Weimar predecessors and helped local health officials formulate the bureaucratic categories that facilitated the simultaneous criminalization and acceptance of prostitution in the Third Reich. Since the 1920s, VD-control efforts in Germany had focused attention on those it labeled hwGs (people with *häufig wechseldner Geschlechtsverkehr*—frequently changing sexual partners), or habitually promiscuous individuals. During the Third Reich this categorization of unacceptable sexual behavior underwent a transformation that reflected an increasing concern about the danger of deviancy to the "community of the people" (*Volksgemeinschaft*). On 14 December 1937 the definition of "asocial" was more clearly defined in the Preventive Detention Decree, which instituted protective custody for prostitutes and other "asocials." In practice, according to a Berlin Main Health Office official, this measure particularly affected "healthy hwG individuals, who despite being repeatedly brought before the courts interrupt continued [medical] observation."[27] Not only was promiscuity seen as a threat to the national body (*Volkskörper*) by spreading fertility-destroying diseases, but it also provided evidence that not all citizens were willing to subordinate their sexual desires to the population goals and family ideals of the state.

Policies toward prostitution underwent further transformations during the war, and state officials grew increasingly tolerant of those who wanted to have relations with prostitutes, at least if that happened in state-run brothels. The military and the Ministry of the Interior argued that these kinds of brothels were hygienic and even served a military function: they decreased the risk of venereal disease by controlling the otherwise dangerous activities of "asocial" prostitutes; and they provided rewards for hard-fighting soldiers.

How policies directed against prostitution were enforced at the local level was dependent not only on laws, however, but also upon the specific configuration of powers among medical, police, and welfare authorities in each region. The control of prostitution in the Third Reich depended upon a complex relationship between federal laws and local interpretations and implementation procedures. It had always been the case that laws concerning prostitution were interpreted very differently in different parts of the Reich.[28] The diversity of approaches to the prostitution problem was particularly evident in the level of control ceded to individual doctors in determining how sexual behavior should be categorized.[29] Doctors were given considerable discretion in determining the course of treatment and in deciding the extent of surveillance under which an individual might be placed. In 1938, for example, an Interior Ministry directive advised state and municipal health authorities that doctors should be directed to determine how regularly hwG individuals were to be examined on the basis of "personal cleanliness, their outward living conditions (age, degree of prostitution), and the frequency of sexual intercourse."[30]

In the city of Berlin itself, this reliance on experts for subjective interpretations of individual behavior was evident in the increasingly specific categories for sexual deviance that local health-care authorities used to decide on the appropriate degree of surveillance in specific cases. In the early years of the Nazi era, the very definitions of categories of promiscuity were disputed and ambiguously interpreted. Indeed, in 1936, the Main Health Office in Berlin refused to provide its VD experts with an exact definition of the newly coined category of "alternating intercourse" (*wechselnder Geschlechtsverkehr*, or wG) used to describe occasionally promiscuous individuals whose behavior verged on but did not constitute prostitution or hwG. "The determination of an 'alternating intercourse' can only be determined on an individual basis through discussions between the welfare worker and the patient," a policy statement explained. The distinction between wG and hwG was crucial in determining the degree of surveillance to which an individual was subjected. Nevertheless local state authorities left the exact definitions of these terms up to welfare workers, so that the results in any given case could be quite unpredictable. Whether one was treated like an "ordinary citizen" who happened to be in the wrong place at the wrong time, or like a social outsider who both caused an individual illness and represented a threat to the community at large, depended almost entirely on the subjective interpretation of the attending welfare worker. Under the circumstances of Nazi Berlin, appearance, education, gender, job status, and race were all likely to influence these evaluations in important respects. These arbitrary judgments, though not unique to Nazi welfare work, could be particularly weighty for those women who received negative evaluations, since emphasis was increasingly placed on segregating and confining such dangerous people and much less on rehabilitating "fallen" individuals while seeking to reintegrate them into society.

National Socialist policies encouraged authorities in the Berlin Main

Health Office to use a very broad definition of what constituted dangerous sexual behavior on the part of certain women considered to be on
the fringes of society. These officials included "bar women, table
women, and waitresses" in their surveillance efforts, and they interpreted the Ministry of the Interior directive to mean that "women were
also to be monitored when hwG or wG is impossible to determine."
Preventive practices and efforts to find new sources of infection were
directed primarily at patrolling and raiding streets, bars, pubs, and dance
clubs where prostitutes were known to ply their trade. Welfare and police authorities reported that patrols of bars were more successful than
welfare work on the streets; both known prostitutes and new hwGs apparently reacted by lowering their profile.[31] The Berlin Main Health Office in turn directed district health clinics to concentrate their surveillance efforts on a specific list of "bars and luxury pubs" with names like
Pompeji, Atlantis, Orient, Roxi, Dschungel, Jocky, Hungaria, Femina,
Eden, and Oase.[32] The assumption was that one's very presence in a certain bar constituted suspicious behavior. Despite gender-neutral language, the health office reports suggest that surveillance efforts were primarily focused on women.[33] The primary pathology toward which
health authorities directed their VD-prevention efforts was any public
expression of female sexuality outside the realm of the family. "Good
citizens," and particularly children, were to be spared the danger of en-
countering a prostitute on the street or in other public places. The "sanitation of the street scene," as this removal of prostitutes to brothels was
often called, was meant to preserve the public façade of idyllic family life,
to allow men a private release for their more base sexual needs, and to
protect the image of woman as mother from the contradiction of the
public whore.

There thus emerged a contrast between acceptable and unacceptable
sexual behavior for women—a contrast that contained an ambiguous
and contradictory image of female sexuality, but that in some sense also
gave all women a similar role in Nazi society. True mothers of the *Volk*
and members of the "national community," so Nazi propaganda taught,
contained their sexual expression entirely within the private realm. Their
sexuality was inextricably linked to motherhood and their sole public
function was to act as educator and spiritual guide to their families—to
produce, in other words, new citizens and soldiers.[34] The prostitute represented both a contrast and a mirror. She was defined as having abnormal sexual instincts which demanded her exclusion from the society at
large. But like "respectable" women, prostitutes were also prevented

from expressing sexuality in public; they were confined to brothels. And like "respectable" women, their sexual services were also subjected to the demands of the state. Female sexuality was functionalized to serve the needs of the nation, particularly the needs of a military machine. An increasing tendency to segregate, marginalize, and incarcerate prostitutes (and lesser perpetrators of promiscuity) coincided with the escalation of Nazi repression and persecution in the war years.

A third phase in Nazi prostitution policy began on 9 September 1939, a week and a day after the invasion of Poland, when a secret directive from the Reich Ministry of the Interior ordered the "reconstruction of brothels and barrack-like. concentration[s] of prostitutes." This order foreshadowed a new orientation in VD and prostitution control.[35] Originally this directive applied only to the operational area of the German military (in other words, the goal was to provide prostitutes to German soldiers). Women who were considered prostitutes according to previously instituted definitions were registered and incarcerated in brothels. However, any who resisted this regimentation and went so far as to avoid police and/or medical control were arrested and sent to a concentration camp, where, along with other "asocials," they found themselves at the bottom of camp social hierarchies. In March 1942 Himmler ordered the construction of brothels in the concentration camps to provide "productivity" incentives for male inmates. Women incarcerated in the camps as prostitutes were the first to be chosen for employment in the brothels, though others were also forced to work in them. Some women chose the latter option as a way to survive and to prolong their lives.[36]

Brothels were also established for the civilian population during the war. By 1942 the criminal police, working under the authority of the secret directive, had established twenty-eight brothels in Berlin.[37] Any complaints about the effects of state-regulated prostitution on the ethical or physical health of the population were countered with the argument that this system was put in place "to defend members of the Wehrmacht and the civilian population from the threatening dangers of prostitution."[38] Government officials thus argued that men could be better protected from venereal disease if prostitution were confined to state-run brothels.[39] In the war years brothels were also constructed for foreign workers in Germany. The official justification was that providing foreign workers with prostitutes (particularly when these women were themselves foreigners or "Gypsies") would protect German women from sexual danger and defilement.[40]

201

Along with officially sanctioned prostitution, the war brought heightened concerns about the spread of VD. On 18 September 1939 the Reich Ministry of the Interior circulated a directive stressing the impact that the war was likely to have and asked all health authorities to become more vigilant toward VD.[41] They should track down the sources of the infections in every case, and call in the police to forcibly detain anyone resisting VD controls. These measures represented only minor shifts in policy—they simply emphasized strategies already in place. More noteworthy was the directive to be particularly vigilant regarding all "women who frequent bars and similar facilities for the purpose of stimulating, entertaining, etc. (so-called table or entertainment women, dancers, etc.)." These instructions represented a drastic expansion of the category for police surveillance, since they included women who did not sell sex and who did not necessarily show signs of having VD. Additionally, hwG individuals considered likely to spread VD, and who did not comply with orders to appear for examinations, were henceforth placed in "protective custody." This repeated what had previously been a secret policy sanctioned by the law on asocials of 14 December 1937. The regime in fact began to treat all public displays of female sexuality as signs of asocial and health-threatening behavior.[42]

After 1940 even stricter control of promiscuous individuals was instituted through modifications to the 1927 Reich Law for Combating Venereal Diseases. These modifications, in combination with the law on asocials of 1937, allowed the National Socialist state to formulate increasingly harsh punishments for all forms of "sexual deviance." In October 1940 changes to Section 17 of the VD law established a new authority to keep track of prostitutes and effectively legalized civilian brothels, clearing the way for what would become substantial state involvement in the business of prostitution.[43]

The beginning of the war, therefore, had dramatic effects on VD-control and prostitution policies on the local level. Given the social disruption of drafting young men into the army, incidences of extramarital intercourse multiplied and paranoia about its effects escalated dramatically. These developments put new pressure on local welfare officials to harden bureaucratic categories of sexual aberrance and promiscuity. The need to make the distinctions between the occasionally or the habitually promiscuous (wG and hwG) and the prostitute became particularly acute. Not surprisingly, the construction of state-run civilian and military brothels restricted prostitutes' abilities to move in and out of the profession.[44]

At a meeting on 10 January 1941, Berlin health authorities devised exact classifications for degrees of promiscuity and outlined policies directed against unacceptable sexual behavior. Dr. Paulstich, the head of the Main Health Office at the time, told his subordinates to beware a growing problem of promiscuity, particularly among domestic servants, office workers, saleswomen, and female factory workers.[45] These groups were increasingly turning up in military VD reports as the sources of infection, and they favored dancing halls frequented by soldiers. More surveillance, Paulstich argued, was called for, as wGs (the occasionally promiscuous) were actually more dangerous in terms of spreading the disease than hwGs (prostitutes, who by this time would have come under the direct surveillance of health and police authorities). This effort at more precise definition represents a break with previous practice. Asocial, deviant behavior required more specific delineation in a state that so severely punished outsiders for nonconforming social behavior. Perhaps sensitive to this broader context, Paulstich insisted that the distinction between occasional and habitual promiscuity be strictly maintained. Not having descended to the depths of commercial sex, wGs still had some hope of returning to mainstream society. As another official at the meeting put it, the main concern was the protection of society at large. The impact of promiscuous individuals on society was too negative to be ignored.[46]

Beyond simply posing a health danger, then, promiscuous persons were considered a threat to the productivity and social cohesiveness of the nation; their behavior revealed them to be outsiders. Drastic measures, involving the cooperation of health, police, and welfare authorities, were called for to prevent further degeneration. Health officials accepted the danger of inappropriate measures and the possibility of overzealously policing individuals who were not actually engaging in promiscuous behavior. Still, they argued that during a "war like the present one," the possibility of an individual injustice was justified in order "to protect national strength . . . and prevent sexual epidemics from cropping up."[47]

As the war progressed there were attempts to streamline and rationalize the process of finding and monitoring "dangerous" spreaders of VD. Anyone who admitted to frequently changing his or her sexual partners was placed under the surveillance of health-care authorities, was forced to appear for frequent health examinations, and was provided with counseling by welfare workers.[48] In many cases, Paulstich claimed, individuals voluntarily submitted to these measures.[49] In other cases, the health authorities had to resort to more intense methods of social control, including calling in police to place the individual under protective custody.[50] This system, of course, relied on cooperation between the various district clinics, the Main Health Office, and the police, a triangular relationship that became increasingly complex and difficult during the war. Government agencies informed health officials that all efforts must be drastically stepped up to meet wartime demands, but the limited resources of the district health offices led to inconsistencies in implementation. Administrators tried to counter these problems with longer working hours for clinic staff and authoritarian pronouncements about how clients should be treated. "Those individuals requested to appear in *our* offices," Paulstich admonished, "will over time have to become accustomed to the fact that they cannot respond to orders from the authorities according to their own free will."[51] But as the war dragged on, the attempt to create a seamless organizational structure for the administration of VD-control efforts in Berlin faltered. By late 1942 the Main Health Office was receiving constant complaints about unwillingness to cooperate between the various clinics and administrative offices.[52]

The war, and the attendant change of focus in the control of prostitution, forced officials to be even more specific in their categorization of sexual behavior. Given a lack of detailed instructions from above, local health authorities had to develop their own definitions of sexual deviance and degree of promiscuity. Their decisions were now particularly weighty, since they determined which individuals were candidates for confinement in state-run brothels or concentration camps and which could be reformed and reintegrated into "normal" society. The ultimate goal was to maintain very strict control over sexual expression. Only sexual activities safely ensconced within the family and geared toward reproduction were visible and publicly acceptable, while promiscuity of any type was carefully labeled and hidden from view. This was true even for the type of promiscuity—prostitution—that the state sought to utilize for its own ends. Prostitution stands as an example of the extreme ambiguity of the National Socialists' moral purification project: the regime sought to shield German society from sexual deviancy, yet just past the boundaries of this "cleansed" public sphere lurked officially promoted sexual vice.

The internal contradictions of Nazi attitudes toward prostitution were obvious even to contemporary observers. Policy on prostitution in the Third Reich was directed at reducing the visibility of prostitutes rather than reducing their numbers, but soon it even promoted broth-els, long considered a prime source of venereal infection. The rhetoric about "purification" forced health authorities to downplay the statistical realities of VD control. Objective evaluations of the extent of VD in the population are noticeably scarce in local and federal documents. Soon after being appointed *Reichsgesundheitsführer* in October 1944,[53] Le-onardo Conti was forced to conduct his own unscientific survey of the chiefs of the district health offices. Seventy percent of those questioned admitted to having detected a slight increase in VD rates in previous years. But further statistical evaluations were curtailed by the circum-stances of the war.[54] Interestingly, unlike local commentators in Ber-lin,[55] Conti did not blame the increase on the presence of foreign work-ers in Germany, but insisted that foreign workers mostly infected one another, and that soldiers on furlough were a much more serious source of infection of the civilian population. He generally downplayed in-creases in infection rates (not difficult to do since statistics were virtually nonexistent) and stressed that the heightened sense of personal respon-sibility instilled in citizens by National Socialist ideology had kept in-creases in the VD rate to an absolute minimum compared with condi-tions in the First World War.

The lack of statistical material makes a determination of the effect of National Socialist policies on VD rates impossible to determine conclu-sively. What is certain, however, is that the cloak of war dramatically shifted priorities in VD control, allowing health officials to concentrate the vast majority of their preventive efforts on the "control" of prostitu-tion. This represents a radical departure from Weimar attitudes toward VD control and the relative importance of prostitution within it. In the 1920s VD control had been conceived as a crucial component of popu-lation policy, since these afflictions threatened the fertility of future gen-erations and posed a long-term threat to the birth rate. In the Third Reich, however, particularly during the war years, the Nazis came to conclude that state-run prostitution could play an important role both by serving the military and by contributing to social peace on the home front. The Nazis also recognized that prostitution in general and even state-run brothels spread venereal diseases, but they nevertheless argued that the comprehensive control of all prostitutes and brothels minimized or largely eliminated the health risks.

Prostitutes did not fade away during the course of the twelve-year Reich, but they were further stigmatized and ostracized. In the new Germany it became much more difficult for individual women to redeem themselves in the eyes of the "national community" and reintegrate themselves into mainstream society. Within a remarkably short time, the new regime reformulated policies toward prostitution on the basis of a belief that institutionalized prostitution in state-run brothels could minimize the spread of VD and at the same time play an important social role. Nazi policy makers came to accept a kind of lesser-evil theory of prostitution, in which prostitutes in such brothels would serve soldiers, foreign workers, and even "ordinary Germans" who needed an outlet for their "natural" sexual desires, thus contributing to the war effort. Once identified as prostitutes, however, women rarely were given a choice about their participation in this "patriotic" enterprise, caught up as they were in the tangled networks of welfare officialdom and the police.

NOTES

1. Arguments against regulating prostitution dominated the discussion of the issue in the Weimar Republic and, as we shall see below, continued to be common in the first years of the Nazi regime. The most well known expert on prostitution in the Weimar Republic was Alfred Blaschko. His antiregulationist stance is outlined in detail in Alfred Blaschko, *Hygiene der Geschlechtskrankheiten*, 2d ed. (Leipzig, 1920).

2. Jeremy Noakes, "Social Outcasts in the Third Reich," in *Life in the Third Reich*, ed. Richard Bessel (New York, 1987), 84.

3. Ibid., 85.

4. By 1940 a Community Alien Law had been drafted, which, if it had not been permanently delayed by the war, would have provided the police with even more far-reaching powers to control all individuals considered "alien to the community" (*gemeinschaftsfremd*). See Noakes, "Social Outcasts in the Third Reich," p. 92; and "Gesetz über die Behandlung Gemeinschaftsfremder" in Bundesarchiv, Potsdam (hereafter BArch(P)) R43 II/721a, Bl. 64.

5. Asta v. Mallinckrodt-Haupt, "Die Prostitution und ihre Bekämpfung," *Die Ärztin* 14, no. 9 (September 1938): 250. Note that many welfare and social health experts were of a very different opinion. In Berlin, a large percentage of these professionals were either Socialists or Jewish and thus fell victim to Nazi persecution. Nazi administrators argued that 65 percent of Berlin's doctors were "non-Aryan." See Gerhard Baader and Schultz Heinrich, eds., *Medizin und Nationalsozialismus: Tabuisierte Vergangenheit—ungebrochene Tradition?* (Berlin, 1980), 65.

6. See Johannes Breger, *Die Geschlechtskrankheiten und ihre Gefahren für das Volk*, 2d ed. (1926; Berlin, 1937), 99–101.

7. Ibid.

8. For allusions to Hitler's pronouncements on prostitution, see Anon., "Die Prostitutionsfrage," *Arbeitsgemeinschaft für Volksgesundung e.V.—Mitteilungen*, no. 3 (14 February 1934): 6; Anon., "Stellungnahme zur Prostitutionsfrage," *Christliche Arbeitsgemeinschaft für Volksgesundung e.V.—Mitteilungen*, no. 21 (1 September 1937): 1–3. The latter cites an article by Spiethoff, which quoted Hitler's call for a "battle against the spiritual [*seelischen*] preconditions for prostitution."

9. Similar waves of persecution, Bock tells us, accompanied the 1936 Olympics and the beginning of World War II. Gisela Bock, *Zwangssterilisation im Nationalsozialismus: Studien zur Rassenpolitik und Frauenpolitik* (Opladen, 1986), 417.

10. The German text, difficult to translate accurately, reads: "wer öffentlich in auffälliger Weise oder in einer Weise, die geeignet ist, Einzelne oder die Allgemeinheit zu belästigen, zur Unzucht auffordert oder sich dazu anbeitet."

11. Christa Paul, *Zwangsprostitution: Staatlich errichtete Bordelle im Nationalsozialismus* (Berlin, 1995), 18. She cites Bock, *Zwangssterilisation im Nationalsozialismus*, 401ff.

12. The categories of promiscuity and prostitution will be discussed below. For an account of prostitution and sterilization, see Bock, *Zwangssterilisation im Nationalsozialismus*, 417–18.

13. Paul, *Zwangsprostitution*, 12. Cited from "Niederschrift der Sitzung des Wohlfahrtsausschusses des Deutschen Gemeindetages zum Thema 'Bewahrungsgesetz,'" 27 February 1936, in Detlev J. K. Peukert, *Grenzen der Sozialdisziplinierung: Aufstieg und Krise der deutschen Jugendfürsorge von 1878 bis 1932* (Cologne, 1986), 281.

14. Quoted in Paul, *Zwangsprostitution*, 12.

15. Ibid. Himmler's words: "In this area [prostitution] we will be as generous as we can possibly be, since one can't on the one hand want to prevent that the whole male youth wanders off toward homosexuality and on the other hand leave them no way out."

16. Quoted in Anon., "Bekenntnis zur Sittlichkeit als Grundlage des Kampfes gegen die Geschlechtskrankheiten," *Arbeitsgemeinschaft für Volksgesundung e.V.—Mitteilungen*, no. 20 (15 June 1935): 2.

17. The *Arbeitsgemeinschaft für Volksgesundung* was one of the only organizations concerned with issues of eugenics and sexuality to have escaped the process of *Gleichschaltung* (coordination). All other such organizations, many of which had large representations of Socialist and Jewish members, were either disbanded or absorbed into national organs once the Nazis came to power. See, for example, Atina Grossmann's account of the destruction of the sex reform movement in *Reforming Sex: The German Movement for Birth Control and Abortion Reform, 1920–1950* (Oxford, 1995), The close connection of the Arbeitsgemeinschaft to the Protestant Inner Mission, which maintained a close

working relationship with Nazi welfare organs throughout the Third Reich, and the charismatic leadership of Hans Harmsen (himself a member of the Inner Mission) may explain its staying power. On the Inner Mission in the Nazi years, see Sabine Schleiermacher, "Die Innere Mission und ihr bevölkerungs-politisches Programm," in *Der Griff nach der Bevölkerung: Aktualität und Kontinuität nazistischer Bevölkerungspolitik,* ed. Heidrun Kaupen-Haas (Nörd-lingen, 1986), 73–89.

18. See "Aus dem Jahresbericht 1935 über die Arbeit der Evangelischen Konferenz für Gefährdetenfürsorge," 29–31 January 1935, in Archiv des Dia-konischen Werkes (hereafter ADW), CA Gf/St 10; and "Stellungnahme des Central-Ausschusses für die Innere Mission der deutschen evangelischen Kirche zur Prostitutionsfrage," in ADW, BP 1857.

19. This view is also expressed in Anon., "Die Prostitution unter dem Ge-schlechtskrankengesetz," *Deutsches Ärzteblatt* 62 (1933): 100. One article com-pares Germany's port cities with New York, which, even without state-run brothels and even in "black areas," allegedly maintained a much higher level of public decency than Hamburg or even Berlin. See Anon., "Die Prostitutions-frage," esp. 6.

20. Ibid., 7–8.

21. Anon., "Ist die zunehmende Kasernierung der Prostitution eine Mass-nahme der Jugendschutzes?" *Arbeitsgemeinschaft für Volksgesundung e.V.—Mitteilungen,* no. 16 (1934): 4.

22. Anon., "Stellungnahme zur Prostitutionsfrage," 3. "Just as the masses can, through leadership, be made capable of greatness, so too can the conscious-ness of their numbers encourage them to feel justified in the satisfaction of their most base desires and to free themselves of countervailing inhibitions."

23. Anon., "Die Prostitution als internationale Frage," *Arbeitsgemeinschaft für Volksgesundung e.V.—Mitteilungen,* no. 13 (14 June 1934): 1–5.

24. See Anon., "Kasernierung und Bordellierung," *Christliche Arbeitsge-meinschaft für Volksgesundung e.V.—Mitteilungen,* no. 2 (20 January 1937): 1–5; and Anon., "Stellungnahme zur Prostitutionsfrage," 1–3.

25. "Fachgruppe Gefährdetenfürsorge in der Fachschaft der Wohlfahrts-pflegerinnen" (no recipient named), 12 July 1934, in ADW, CA Gf/St 4. In-structional pamphlets given to prostitutes in Hamburg and Cologne included explicit hygiene instructions. Prostitutes were instructed to take ten-minute baths at 32° C, followed by a cold shower and a thorough washing of the geni-tals. See Anon., "Kasernierung und Bordellierung," 3–4.

26. Annette Timm, "Uncontrollable Urges and Diseased Bodies: Prophylac-tics and the Politics of Fertility in Weimar Germany," paper presented at the meeting of the German Studies Association, 27 September 1997, Washington D.C. On the Weimar view of male sexual drives, see Hertha Riese, *Geschlechtsle-ben und Gesundheit, Gesittung und Gesetz* (Berlin, 1932), 4.

27. The quote is from a letter that Dr. O. Schwéers wrote to Berlin health-

care experts on 22 September 1938, referring to the Prussian Decree of 14 December 1937. This decree called for protective custody for anyone who, though not a "career or habitual criminal," was endangering the public good through "asocial" behavior. See LAB East, Rep. Rep. 03-03/3, Nr. 36. See also Paul Werner, "Die vorbeugende Verbrechensbekämpfung durch die Polizei," *Kriminalistik* 12 (1938): 60, cited in Paul, *Zwangsprostitution*, 13.

28. The Hamburg police, for instance, engaged in state regulation of prostitution despite the explicit language forbidding this in the 1927 VD law. See Richard J. Evans, "Prostitution, State, and Society in Imperial Germany," *Past and Present* 70 (February 1976): 106–129; and Lynn Abrams, "Prostitutes in Imperial Germany, 1870–1918: Working Girls or Social Outcasts?" in *The German Underworld*, ed. Richard J. Evans (London and New York, 1988), 189–209.

29. In Berlin, for example, an agreement between the medical profession and city health authorities, which took effect in July 1936, guaranteed that as many VD patients as possible were referred to doctors in private practice. See "Vereinbarungen zwischen der Stadt und der Kassenärztlichen Vereinigung Deutschlands," circa July 1936, in Landesarchiv Berlin, Ost (hereafter LAB East), Rep. 03-03/3, Nr. 36.

30. Reichs und Preus. Ministerium des Innern to Landesregierungen (in Prussia, directly to state and communal health bureaus), 27 January 1938, in LAB East, Rep. 03-03/3, Nr. 36.

31. Main Health Office (hereafter HGA) (Conti) to GSÄ in districts with VD clinics, 3 December 1937, in LAB East, Rep. 03-03/3, Nr. 36.

32. These and other bars are listed in a memo from the HGA to the VD clinics, 21 September 1942, in ibid.

33. This is clear in the occasional mention of an individual case and in an effort in 1937 to add up the actual financial costs that certain "female" practitioners of hwG had brought upon Berlin's health-care service. See Conti to health authorities, 21 April 1937; and similar requests to hospitals, same date, in ibid.

34. On the Nazi glorification of motherhood, see Claudia Koonz, *Mothers in the Fatherland: Woman, the Family, and Nazi Politics* (New York, 1987); and Irmgard Weyrather, *Muttertag und Mutterkreuz: Der Kult um die "deutsche Mutter" im Nationalsozialismus* (Frankfurt am Main, 1993).

35. Paul, *Zwangsprostitution*, 13; and HGA (Braemer) to GSÄ and VD clinics, 21 September 1942, in LAB East, Rep. 03-03/3, Nr. 36.

36. It is important to note, as Paul informs us, that many of them would have welcomed this opportunity, since conditions in the brothels were slightly better than in the camps at large, and since working in the brothels guaranteed at least a temporary reprieve from the gas chambers. Other inmates often expressed jealousy at the prostitutes' privileged position. (Paul, *Zwangsprostitution*, 134.) According to Paul, Himmler first ordered the construction of a brothel in

KZ-Mauthausen in June 1941, but various administrative problems delayed its construction. He then restated his demand for brothels, this time for all concentration camps, in March 1942. By the end of the war, Paul estimates, there were at least nine concentration-camp brothels. See ibid., 23, 131.

37. VD experts in Berlin's Main Health Office had been put in charge of monitoring the women installed in these brothels. HGA (Braemer) to GSÄ and VD clinics, 21 September 1942, in LAB East, Rep. 03-03/3, Nr. 36.

38. See the response from the Reichsministerium für Volksaufklärung und Propaganda to a lawyer from Heidelberg who complained about the increase in prostitution near military barracks, 18 September 1944, in BArch(P) R55/1221, Bl. 122.

39. See, for example, Oberbürgermeister der Reichshauptstadt Berlin, HGA (Schröder) to Oberregierungsrat Dr. Gußmann, Reichsministerium für Volksaufklärung und Propaganda, 6 September 1944, in BArch(P) R55/1221, 123–24.

40. Ibid., 117. See also the concerns expressed about dangerous foreigners by members of the department for *Gefährdetenfürsorge* in the Inner Mission: "Tätigkeitsbericht der Bezirksstelle der Inneren Mission Kreuzberg für das Jahr 1943," circa 1944, in ADW, BP 645.

41. RMI (Conti) to Landesregierungen, etc., 18 September 1939, in LAB East, Rep. Rep. 03-03/3, Nr. 36.

42. The directive was published in *Der öffentliche Gesundheitsdienst* 5, no. 13 (5 October 1939): 342–43.

43. See the copy from Reichsgesetzblatt, I, 190 (5 November 1940): 1459, in BArch(P) R43 II/725, Bl. 57. Two other sections of the VD law were changed: § 2, paragraph 2, which outlined free treatment for the poor, was reworded to be more general and all-inclusive; and § 18, which discussed the administrative responsibility of the individual states for carrying out the law, was supplemented with a statement about the Reich Ministry of the Interior's responsibility for enacting appropriate laws and policies to aid in the fight against VD. The official justification for these changes said only: "The former § 17 (Verbot der Kasernierung der Prostuierten) does not reflect present needs and practical circumstances and will thus no longer be in force, as is already the case in the Reichsgauen Ostmark and the Sudentenland." See "Begründung," n.d., in BArch(P) R43 II/725, 50–51.

44. HGA (Paulstich) to specialists and counseling clinics for VD, 30 April 1941, in LAB East, Rep. 03-03/3, Nr. 36.

45. Ibid.

46. Comment from St. I. Kördel in ibid.

47. The last comment was provided by Stadtdirektor Dr. Breitenfeld. Ibid.

48. On 18 October 1937, the HGA reminded its subordinates not to undertake lengthy and complex investigations of a person's sexual behavior if he/she

already admitted to hwG. See memo signed by Schwéers, in LAB East, Rep. 03-03/3, Nr. 36.

49. HGA (Paulstich) to specialists, 17 January 1940, in ibid.

50. This possibility was provided for in both the new VD decree of 18 September 1939 and the Preventive Detention Directive of 14 December 1937, both of which are discussed above. See note 41.

51. HGA (Paulstich) to specialists, 17 January 1940, in LAB East, Rep. 03-03/3, Nr. 36.

52. HGA (Paulstich) to specialists, 7 October 1942, in ibid.

53. Conti had far-reaching powers over all aspects of civilian health care. On his appointment as Reichsgesundheitsführer, see Führerhauptquartier, Bormann to Goebbels, 3 October 1944 BArch(P) R55/1221, Bl. 288.

54. Reichsgesundheitsführer to Goebbels, 17 February 1944, in BArch(P) R55 1222, 38–39.

55. Oberbürgermeister der Reichshauptstadt Berlin, HGA (Schröder) to Oberregierungsrat Dr. Gußmann, Reichsministerium für Volksaufklärung und Propaganda, 6 September 1944, in BArch(P) R55/1221, 123–24.

"Gypsies" as Social Outsiders in Nazi Germany

SYBIL H. MILTON

THE MASS murder of between one-quarter and one-half million Roma and Sinti, usually referred to as "Gypsies," during the Holocaust has been largely invisible in current historiography about Nazi genocide. Instead suspicion, prejudice, and stereotypes—"antigypsyism"—have continued to dominate the historical literature.[1] The prevailing academic literature has not granted the "forgotten Gypsy Holocaust" an analogous place with the mass murder of European Jews, although substantial new literature warrants this revision.[2] The prevailing stereotypes assume that "Gypsies" are a single transnational ethnic group characterized by certain negative behavioral clichés. Although the ca. 35,000 Roma and Sinti represented only about 0.05 percent of the 1933 German population of approximately 65 million, they were stigmatized by the majority society as socially marginal, economically unproductive, criminally "inclined," and racially inferior. These stereotypes, defining them as social outsiders, facilitated repression by health, welfare, and police bureaucracies and provided the rationale for their exclusion, concentration, and annihilation in Nazi Germany and occupied Europe.[3]

German scientists (anthropologists, geneticists, demographers, statisticians, physicians, and psychiatrists), utilizing biological and cultural stereotypes advanced by ethnologists, eugenicists, and the medical profession early in the twentieth century that allegedly proved the superiority of European Caucasians against "inferior" non-European races, perceived the Roma as an "insoluble problem." Their theories emphasized the dangers of interbreeding or race crossing. After Germany lost its colonies in World War I, German scientists applied these utopian schemes at home against minorities in Germany: Germans of African decent, Roma and Sinti, Jews, and the handicapped.[4] Linking heredity to disease, and also to crime and antisocial behavior, they advocated limitations on reproduction for humans they considered inferior. These practitioners of racial hygiene provided the intellectual infrastructure for genocide and later wrote and defined the Nuremberg racial laws of 1935 that in turn provided the Nazi bureaucracy with an ostensibly "scientific" justification for the exclusion and later mass murder of Roma and Sinti.[5]

Racial anthropology supplemented the new science of criminology and provided the police with more sophisticated tools for surveillance and group control. The development of identification techniques in the nineteenth century included charts registering body measurements; the varieties of eye, ear, nose, mouth, and skull forms appeared alongside color scales for gradations of skin and hair. These charts became standard elements of twentieth-century anthropological fieldwork, criminal identification records, and the determination of paternity through physiognomy. Moreover, the development of photography in the late nineteenth century led to widespread international police use of mug-shot books for the identification and surveillance of criminals and aliens. Simultaneously, fingerprinting became standard in law enforcement technology.[6] Further, developments in modern statistics and early mechanical tabulation computers facilitated census and resident registration, contributing to more sophisticated administrative possibilities for the governmental screening of populations by race and political affiliation.[7] After 1933 the German state aggressively mobilized this technical knowledge to implement its racial agenda and applied this technology to the persecution and "elimination" of the Roma and Sinti using exclusion, sterilization, and mass murder.

It is clear that intermittent persecution of Roma and Sinti preceded the Nazi assumption of power. Under the Second Empire and the Weimar Republic, the states (*Länder*) turned over the implementation of "Gypsy" policy to the police. The Roma and Sinti minority were viewed by the police as a homogeneous group of outsiders, consisting of non-Caucasian vagabonds, asocials, and criminals. In 1899 Bavaria had established an Information Agency about Gypsies that collected genealogical data, photographs, and fingerprints of Gypsies above the age of six. Despite Article 108 of the Weimar constitution, which ostensibly granted full and equal citizenship rights to German Roma and Sinti, they were nevertheless vulnerable to discrimination. The Bavarian Law for Combating Gypsies, Vagabonds, and the Work-Shy of 16 July 1926 mandated the registration of all domiciled and migratory Gypsies with the police, local registry offices, and labor exchanges. A similar Prussian decree from 3 November 1927 resulted in the creation of special Gypsy

213

identity cards with fingerprints and photographs for 8,000 Roma and Sinti above the age of six. During the last years of the Weimar Republic, arbitrary arrests and preventive detention of itinerant Gypsies—ostensibly for crime prevention—became routine. In April 1929 a national police commission adopted the 1926 Bavarian law as the federal norm and established a Center for the Fight against Gypsies in Germany with headquarters in Munich. Socially isolated and politically helpless, members of the Roma and Sinti minority faced a concerted assault on their civil and employment rights.

After Hitler's assumption of power on 30 January 1933, the German civil service moved rapidly to implement the racial legislation already championed by the Nazi leadership in their 1920 party platform. This involved the expansion of laws imposed in several states (*Länder*) during the Second Empire and Weimar Republic that had allowed arbitrary arrest, preventive detention, registration of domiciled and migratory German Roma and Sinti, and the expulsion of foreign and stateless Roma and Sinti as alleged military security risks. On 18 March 1933 the Cooperative Interstate Agreement to Combat the Gypsy Plague incorporated and expanded the 1926 Bavarian Law for Combating Gypsies, Vagabonds, and the Work-Shy and its 1927 Prussian counterpart that had stigmatized Roma and Sinti as habitual criminals, social misfits, and vagabonds. This agreement included provisions that restricted the issuance and renewal of licenses for Roma and Sinti in itinerant trades, thus increasing poverty and unemployment at a time when municipal welfare payments for the indigent were reduced during the Depression. The agreement also mandated the supervision of school-age Gypsy children by municipal welfare authorities, removing truants to special juvenile facilities and children unable to speak German to special schools for the retarded. Further, this agreement limited freedom of travel to routes designated by the police and remanded Gypsies without proof of employment to workhouses and forced labor camps. It also stipulated that any state could issue additional regulations. The states did not hesitate long. For example, on 10 August 1933 the city-state of Bremen promulgated its Law for Protecting the Population from Molestation by Gypsies, Vagrants, and the Work-Shy, and on 7 July 1933 the Düsseldorf district governor published a decree to "Combat the Gypsy Nuisance."

This interim decentralized patchwork of parallel local decrees provided the prototype for the synchronization and radicalization of measures against Roma and Sinti throughout the Reich after 1935. Although states and provinces had lost their original autonomy under

Nazi rule, they were retained as administrative units and could implement policies on their own initiative as long as they did not contravene national policy. Local measures thus cumulatively imposed greater police surveillance and arbitrary intimidation on German Roma and Sinti, intensified restrictions on their freedom of movement, and limited their employment possibilities. Moreover, the Munich Center for the Fight against Gypsies in Germany, established under Bavarian legislation in 1926, served as the prototype for the Reich Central Office to Combat the Gypsy Menace (*Reichszentrale zur Bekämpfung des Zigeunerunwesens*), which was created in 1936 as a national police data bank on Roma and Sinti under the jurisdiction of the Central Office of the Detective Forces (*Reichskriminalpolizeiamt*, or RKPA) and the Reich Ministry of the Interior.

These initial decrees also facilitated the expulsion of stateless and foreign Roma and Sinti, a precursor of subsequent German expulsions and dumping of several racial groups designated as "undesirables." Roma and Sinti were included as "asocials" in the July 1933 Law for the Prevention of Offspring with Hereditary Diseases and in the November 1933 Law against Dangerous Habitual Criminals. The first law resulted in their involuntary sterilization; the second permitted their incarceration in concentration camps. The Denaturalization Law of 14 July 1933 and the Expulsion Law of 23 March 1934, initially implemented against Ostjuden (eastern Jews), was also used to expel foreign and stateless Gypsies from German soil.

By late 1933 Roma and Sinti had already been arrested and detained in local concentration camps. Typical cases included those of two male Sinti, who were incarcerated for six weeks at Osthofen concentration camp near Worms, and one Düsseldorf Sinto arrested without identity papers, thus "endangering public safety," who was detained for five months at Brauweiler concentration camp near Cologne. Precise statistics for Roma and Sinti arrested and confined in correctional or penal institutions and in concentration camps during police sweeps throughout the Reich, such as the week-long SA and SS roundup of "beggars and vagabonds" from 18 to 25 September 1933, are not available, although it is known that Roma and Sinti were among the arrested and that both "asocials" and "Gypsies" were regarded as social pariahs in German society.

In 1936 the German ethnologist Martin Block was employed as senior government councillor (*Oberregierungsrat*) for racial psychology attached to the Military Supreme Command in Berlin and worked simultaneously as an assistant professor at the Balkan Institute in Leipzig. His 1936 study, *Zigeuner: ihr Leben und ihre Seele*, characterized the "Gypsies" as "stone-age people,"[8] "aliens," and "a primitive race . . . found as migrants among all civilized peoples."[9] Similarly semi-official commentaries to the Nuremberg Laws of 1935 classified Gypsies, along with Jews and Blacks, as racially distinctive minorities with "alien blood" (*artfremdes Blut*).[10]

The so-called marriage health law, promulgated only one month (18 October 1935) after the Nuremberg racial laws, had broader ramifications. All marriages required permission from public health offices, and prior to marriage every person had to obtain a certificate from the public health service stating that offspring would be genetically sound. Marriages deemed detrimental to the hereditary health of the nation were prohibited. The law excluded from marriage a group even larger than that affected by the sterilization law. The information thus collected by the public health service grew enormously. The final aim was a comprehensive system of registration to provide eugenic information on all individuals; the state wanted to establish an inventory on race and heredity (*erbbiologische Bestandsaufnahme*). In any event, on 26 November 1935 an advisory circular from the Reich Ministry of the Interior to all local registry offices for vital statistics prohibited racially mixed marriages between those of German blood and "Gypsies, Negroes, or their bastard offspring."[11] Interior Minister Wilhelm Frick reiterated this point in his article in the *Deutsche Juristenzeitung* in December 1935 and in a decree on 3 January 1936 ordering state governments to apply the two Nuremberg laws (the so-called Citizenship Law and the Law for the "Protection of German Blood") to Gypsies as well as Jews. The belief that "only Gypsies and Jews belonged to the alien races in Europe" became a stock phrase in German governmental decrees and directives on the communal, state, and federal level.[12]

In the ever-escalating series of interlocking Nazi regulations implementing the Nuremberg racial laws, both Gypsies and Jews were slowly deprived of their rights as citizens. Thus both Jews and Gypsies lost the right to vote in Reichstag elections on 7 March 1936. Similarly, neither Jews nor Gypsies were permitted to vote in the 10 April 1938 plebiscite on Austria's incorporation into the German Reich; this directive was issued in Vienna on 23 March 1938, ten days after the *Anschluß* (the incorporation of Austria into the German Reich).[13]

In 1934 the Nazi Racial Policy Bureau (*Rassenpolitisches Amt*) began to compile, in collaboration with the Gestapo, an "asocials catalog," that is, a comprehensive list of so-called antisocial elements. The Nazi police and health bureaucracies thus continued and expanded the systematic registration of Roma and Sinti as potential criminals, genetically defined, that had begun during the Weimar Republic. Anthropological and genealogical registration (*rassenbiologische Gutachtung*) identified Gypsies as "racially inferior asocials and criminals of Asiatic ancestry."[14] Anthropologists, psychiatrists, and geneticists, usually financed by the German Research Foundation, covered the nation to study the hereditary health of twins, families, and small communities, focusing on Roma and Sinti and the handicapped. Dr. Robert Ritter, the leading researcher specializing in the study of Gypsies, assembled a team of assistants and, after the spring of 1936, commenced a systematic genealogical and genetic investigation of Roma and Sinti families as part of his assignment at the Racial Hygiene and Demographic Biology Research Unit, also known as Department L3 of the Reich Department of Health. Ritter's unit was assigned to register the approximately 30,000 Gypsies and part-Gypsies in Germany (and Austria) in order to obtain genealogical and racial data required for formulating a new Reich Gypsy law. Ritter's group aimed to show that among Gypsies, criminal and asocial behavior was hereditary.[15]

On 6 June 1936 the Reich and Prussian Ministry of the Interior issued a decree containing new directives for "Fighting the Gypsy Plague." This order also provided retroactive authorization for the chief of the Berlin Police to direct raids throughout Prussia to arrest all Gypsies prior to the Olympic Games.[16] A few families were deported to the so-called *Rastplatz* Marzahn in late May 1936, and 600 Roma and Sinti were subsequently arrested in Berlin around 4 A.M. on 16 July, prompting the daily *Berliner Lokalanzeiger* to carry a story about "Berlin without Gypsies." This eviction of Roma and Sinti from legally rented domiciles was a precursor for the later expulsion of Polish and stateless Jews from Germany at the end of October 1938 and for the later invalidation of legal protection for Jewish tenants in the spring of 1939.

The arrested Roma and Sinti were either marched under police guard in horse-drawn caravans or their wagons were pulled as freight on flatbeds to a sewage dump adjacent to the municipal cemetery in the Berlin suburb of Marzahn. Although the presence of both sewage and graves violated Gypsy cultural taboos, Berlin-Marzahn became the largest Gypsy camp. Patrolled by a detachment of Prussian uniformed police with guard dogs, the camp consisted of 130 caravans condemned as uninhabitable by the Reich Labor Service. The hygienic facilities were

217

totally inadequate; Marzahn had only three water pumps and two toilets. Overcrowding and unsanitary conditions were the norm; for example, in March 1938 city authorities reported 170 cases of communicable diseases.[17]

At first without perimeter fences, Marzahn was subsequently encircled by barbed wire. Women were permitted to leave only to make household purchases, since there was no commissary inside the camp. Although extended families had sometimes traveled together in small groups, the large number of stationary caravans converted this camp into an oppressive ghetto with virtually no prospect of escape. Unlike the earlier arrests of Roma and Sinti as individuals, Marzahn was a "family" compound, where the internees were assembled, concentrated, and imprisoned, and thus served also as a transit depot for later deportations.

The Roma and Sinti at Berlin-Marzahn were assigned to forced labor. Further, the Reich Department of Health forced them to provide detailed data to the police and health bureaucracies for anthropological and genealogical registration. In turn, this data provided the pretext for the denaturalization and involuntary sterilization of the imprisoned Roma and Sinti. The Berlin-Marzahn Gypsy camp provided evidence of a growing interagency cooperation between public health officials and the police, essential for subsequent developments resulting in the deportation and mass murder of German Gypsies. Anthropological measurements of the prisoners in Marzahn were made by Gerhard Stein, a student of the Frankfurt race scientist Otmar von Verschuer.

Gerhard Stein specialized in the study of twins, sterilization, and eugenic suitability for marriage. Born in 1910 in Bad Kreuznach, he joined the Nazi Party and the SA in 1931 as a Tübingen University student. He completed medical training at the universities of Würzburg, Innsbruck, Tübingen, and Frankfurt, and passed his physician's state examination in Frankfurt in 1937. In 1936 and 1937 he worked at Marzahn as a member of Ritter's unit at the Reich Department of Health, and in 1938 he spent six months at Professor Verschuer's Frankfurt Institute for Hereditary Biology and Race Hygiene. Stein incorporated the results of his Marzahn research into his 1938 dissertation, "The Physiology and Anthropology of Gypsies in Germany," submitted to and accepted by Verschuer at Frankfurt University and subsequently published in 1941 with charts and photographs in the *Zeitschrift für Ethnologie*. In Stein's first report to Ritter from Marzahn, written at the beginning of September 1936, he mentioned "the wildness and licentiousness of Gypsies" and commented that "part-Gypsy bastards are generally dangerous heredi-tary criminals."[18] In his dissertation Stein made a distinction between "full Gypsies," whose "nature is primitive and animalistic; their thoughts and actions guided by instinct . . . understanding and logic having only a subordinate role," and Gypsy hybrids (*Zigeunermisch-ling*), who were "archetypical criminals. Only asocial Germans are in-volved with Gypsies and their descendants combine the criminal predis-position of the asocials with the unrestrained instinctual nature of the Gypsy."[19]

Official publications rationalized the transfer to Marzahn by using the deliberately misleading and innocuous term *Rastplatz*, literally a "road-side rest stop," for this internment and concentration camp. The Nazis used the term pejoratively and ironically, transmuting objective usage into caustic terms of contempt to describe the victims and places that their own policies had created. The official justification for the deporta-tion of entire Roma and Sinti families from their legally rented and regis-tered domiciles and caravan parking sites in Berlin was ostensibly the need to control crime and beggars in the capital prior to the 1936 Olympics.

Created for the 1936 Olympics, the Marzahn camp became a perma-nent place of incarceration for Sinti and Roma. During the war the de-tainees were required to work at forced labor in the Sachsenhausen stone quarries and to clear rubble from Berlin streets after Allied air raids. Eventually most of them were deported to Auschwitz in 1943. In the summer and fall of that year, the few Sinti families still not deported from Marzahn were denounced by their German neighbors.[20]

Marzahn was not the only Gypsy camp, although it was probably the largest. After 1935 several municipal governments and local welfare offices pressured the German police to confine a growing number of German Gypsies in newly created municipal Gypsy camps. These camps were in essence *SS-Sonderlager*: special internment camps combining el-ements of protective custody concentration camps and embryonic ghet-tos; they held full families, including women and young children. Usu-ally located on the outskirts of cities, these camps were guarded by the SS, the gendarmerie, or the uniformed city police. They became reserve depots for forced labor, genealogical registration, and compulsory steril-ization. Between 1933 and 1939 Gypsy camps were created in Cologne, Düsseldorf, Essen, Frankfurt, Fulda, Gelsenkirchen, Hamburg, Königsberg, Magdeburg, Pölitz near Stettin, and other German cities.

These camps evolved after 1939 from municipal internment camps into assembly centers for systematic deportation to concentration camps, ghettos, and killing centers.[21]

After the *Anschluß*, several Gypsy camps were established in Austria, the two largest situated at Maxglan near Salzburg and Lackenbach in the Burgenland. In addition, Austrian Roma and Sinti were sent to various concentration camps, including Mauthausen and Ravensbrück. Thus in the summer and fall of 1938 about 3,000 allegedly "work-shy" Austrian Roma and Sinti were deported: 2,000 male Gypsies above the age of sixteen were sent to Dachau and later remanded to Buchenwald, and 1,000 female Gypsies above the age of fifteen were sent to Ravensbrück.[22] Moreover, Tobias Portschy, illegal *Gauleiter* of Burgenland before 1938, published a pamphlet in the summer of 1938 entitled "The Gypsy Question: Memorandum by the Landeshauptmann of Burgenland," in which he argued for the forced labor and sterilization of Gypsies as "hereditarily tainted . . . a people of habitual criminals, parasites causing enormous damage to the national body [*Volkskörper*]."[23]

It should be emphasized that even before the Gestapo began to compile its *Judenkartei*, a parallel effort to catalog the Roma population of Germany had started. Throughout the 1930s, the same process of centralization that characterized the compilation of data on Jews also occurred for Roma and Sinti and for Roma intermarried with Germans. Special provisions for the registration of Roma under the Reich Registration Law were decreed in December 1938.[24]

The sheer number of state and party institutions collecting specialized racial data was staggering. To name but a few examples, the Racial Policy Bureau of the Nazi Party launched a project to compile a comprehensive register of all Jews, Roma, so-called "asocials," and other racial "foreigners" living within German borders; meanwhile, the head of the Reich Office for Genealogical Research (Reichsstelle für Sippenforschung), Dr. Achim Gercke, began laying the groundwork for what he hoped one day would amount to a "Reich Genealogical Catalog" which would contain the racial pedigree of every German.[25] In 1934 the Protestant churches in Berlin had already begun a genealogical card catalog to assist in proving (or disproving) "Aryan" decent.[26] In 1935 and 1936 the Reich Department of Health started compiling a card catalog of genetically defective persons. In 1936 the Criminal police (Kripo) established a Reich Central Office to Combat the Gypsy Menace, and in the same year, the Racial Hygiene and Demographic Biology Research Unit (*Rassenhygienische und Bevölkerungsbiologische Forschungsstelle*) under the direction of Dr. Robert Ritter was created within the Reich Department of Health to accomplish the registration and fingerprinting of all Roma living in Germany.[27]

Present-day Germans are accustomed to reporting their residence and other personal data to local police, but few realize that this obligation is a legacy of the Nazi regime. The Reich Registration Law (Reichsmeldeordnung) of 6 January 1938 required that all residents of Germany (including foreigners) report any changes in their residence to local police; by 1941 its stipulations had been extended to Austria, the Sudetenland, and territories annexed from Poland.[28] In Germany proper, these data on domicile were exchanged among local police forces (and still are). The explicit purpose of resident registration was social control.

Increasingly, the project of locating Gypsies was concentrated in the Kripo's Reich Central Office to Combat the Gypsy Menace and its comprehensive "racial scrutiny" of the Roma population in the Reich. On the basis of Ritter's conclusions that the "Gypsy problem" was best solved with the tools of "racial science," Himmler ordered the cataloging of all Roma and Sinti into categories defined by racial purity: accordingly, the Kripo employed Ritter's system of racial notation, in which "Z" (*Zigeuner*) indicated a "full Gypsy"; "ZM+" (*Zigeunermischling*) meant a "Gypsy hybrid" of predominantly Roma or Sinti blood; "ZM" indicated a "Gypsy hybrid" with equal amounts of German and Roma blood; and "ZM−" indicated a "Gypsy hybrid" of predominantly German blood. This racial classification system was virtually identical to that used for Jews, and ultimately served the same purpose.[29]

International police cooperation through Interpol, created in Vienna in 1923, resulted in a standing committee on "Gypsy matters," including Gypsy registration questionnaires shared by several European police forces. At the 1935 Interpol conference in Copenhagen, Ministerial Councillor (Ministerialrat) Dr. Bader from Karlsruhe submitted a detailed report about "a three-day Gypsy 'action' or 'roundup' in Baden in 1934 for registering all Gypsies, half Gypsies [*Halbzigeuner*], and travelers behaving like Gypsies, irrespective of their age, gender, family status, or citizenship." Bader saw the "Gypsy problem as primarily a police matter" and recommended that "incorrigible Gypsies . . . be included on rosters of those to be sterilized."[30]

In March 1936 a memorandum prepared for State Secretary Hans Pfundtner of the Reich Ministry of the Interior contained the first references to the preparation of a national Gypsy law (*Reichszigeunergesetz*) for the Reich and to the difficulties of achieving a "total solution of the Gypsy problem on either a national or an international level." The interim recommendations in this memorandum included expulsion of stateless and foreign Gypsies, restrictions on freedom of movement and on issuing licenses for Gypsies with itinerant trades (*Wandergewerbe*), increased police surveillance, sterilization of Gypsies of mixed German and Gypsy ancestry (so-called *Mischlinge*), complete registration of all Gypsies in the Reich, and confinement in a special Gypsy reservation.[31] These recommendations also reflected the consensus of European police forces on anti-Gypsy measures discussed at annual Interpol meetings during the mid-1930s.

As with Jews, the process of locating Roma and Sinti was carried beyond the borders of Germany in 1939. The registration of Austrian Roma was begun in late October 1939, expanding an earlier police card index; a similar census of Roma was also implemented in the Protectorate of Bohemia and Moravia in August 1942. The Dutch Ministry of Justice had already created a central register of Roma in 1936, and in early 1941 a central registry of Roma, nomads, aliens, and stateless persons in the occupied Netherlands was opened in order to facilitate the implementation of German measures for the arrest, internment, and deportation of Dutch Roma. In France, the Vichy Commissariat for Jewish Affairs under Xavier Vallat also had jurisdiction over the Roma populace, as part of its responsibility for the administration of "measures for the maintenance of racial purity."[32]

In 1938 and 1939 the Nazi ideological obsession with Gypsies became almost as strident and aggressive as the campaign against the Jews. Apart from regular stories in the local press stressing Gypsy criminality, national police and race hygiene journals (such as *Neues Volk, Volk und Rasse,* and *Die deutsche Polizei*) carried increasingly polemical articles against Gypsies in Greater Germany, including the Ostmark. In August 1938 Roma and Sinti were expelled, ostensibly as military security risks, from border zones on the left bank of the Rhine, and once war had begun, they were prohibited from "wandering" in the western areas of the Reich. In May 1938 Himmler had ordered that the Munich bureau of Gypsy affairs be renamed the Central Office to Combat the Gypsy Menace and that this agency be placed within the RKPA in Berlin. Moreover, on 8 December 1938 Himmler promulgated his decree "Fighting the Gypsy Plague," basing it on Robert Ritter's anthropological and genealogical registration forms.

Himmler's decree recommended "the resolution of the Gypsy question based on its essentially racial nature" (die Regelung der Zigeunerfrage aus dem Wesen dieser Rasse heraus in Angriff zu nehmen) and mandated that all Gypsies in the Reich above the age of six be classified into three racial groups: "Gypsies, Gypsy *Mischlinge*, and nomadic persons behaving as Gypsies." The guidelines for implementation published in early 1939 stipulated that the RKPA assist "the development of a comprehensive Gypsy law prohibiting miscegenation and regulating the life of the Gypsy race in German space."[33] Comprehensive and systematic residential and genealogical registration of Gypsies by local police and public health authorities was required, and photo identity cards were to be issued to all Gypsies and part-Gypsies. The implementation of Himmler's decree was comprehensive, leading also, for example, to the purge of several dozen Gypsy musicians from the Reich Chamber of Music.

The deportation of German Roma and Sinti began shortly after the outbreak of war. On 17 October 1939, Reinhard Heydrich issued his so-called *Festsetzungserlaß*, prohibiting all Gypsies and part-Gypsies not already interned in camps from changing their registered domiciles; this measure was essential for implementing deportations.[34]

In the second half of October, Arthur Nebe, chief of the RKPA (RSHA Department V), tried to expedite the deportation of Berlin Gypsies by requesting that Eichmann "add three or four train cars of Gypsies" to the Nisko Jewish transports departing from Vienna. Eichmann cabled Berlin that the Nisko transport would include "a train car of Gypsies to be added to the first Jewish deportation from Vienna."[35] However, the failure of the Nisko resettlement scheme at the end of 1939 precluded the early expulsion of 30,000 Gypsies from the Greater German Reich to the General Government in German-conquered Poland. The aborted October 1939 deportation belatedly took place in May 1940, when 2,800 German Gypsies were deported from seven assembly centers in the Old Reich to Lublin and Warsaw. In Austria, the deportations to Poland were planned for the second half of August 1940. The rules concerning inclusion and exemption for Gypsies paralleled regulations used nearly sixteen months later for deporting German Jews. Heydrich's guidelines for Gypsy deportations in May 1940 exempted those above the age of seventy, pregnant women in their seventh month or later, and those physically unable to travel. Gypsies married to German non-Gypsies and close Gypsy relatives of soldiers were also given a reprieve from the transports. Gypsies able to prove that they were foreign nationals were also exempted. Each Gypsy deportee was allowed to take only 50 kilograms of luggage and Polish currency worth 10 Reichsmarks. All other money and jewelry (except for wedding rings) were to be left behind. Deportees were also required to turn in all personal and identity papers, for which they would receive a receipt. At the assembly points, the Roma and Sinti were photographed and fingerprinted and consecutive numbers were painted on their forearms. Ritter's team checked the Gypsies slated for deportation to ensure accuracy, a job similar to that of the physicians who checked the medical records of those to be killed in so-called euthanasia centers.

The property and possessions of the deported Gypsies were confiscated and the deportees were compelled to sign release forms acknowledging the transfer of their possessions as *Volks- und staatsfeindlichen Vermögens* (under the Law for the Confiscation of Subversive and Enemy Property initially used for the seizure of assets of proscribed and denaturalized political opponents after July 1933). The same confiscatory procedures were also employed during the earliest deportations of Jews, prior to the passage of the 11th Ordinance to the Reich Citizenship Law requiring Jews leaving the country to lose their nationality and thus their property.

The deportation of Roma and Sinti from Germany and incorporated Austria was again suspended in October 1940 because the General Government had protested the potential dumping of 35,000 Gypsies as well as the impending arrival of large numbers of German Jews. Again in July 1941, the RSHA halted the deportation of East Prussian Roma and Sinti, probably because of the invasion of the Soviet Union, noting that "a general and final solution of the Gypsy question cannot be achieved at this time." Instead the RSHA proposed to construct a new Gypsy camp enclosed with barbed wire in the outskirts of Königsberg.[36] Nothing is known about conditions in this *Zigeunerlager*, the last special municipal camp for Roma and Sinti before the creation of the Gypsy "family camp" at BIIe in Auschwitz-Birkenau.

The Gypsy camps were parallel structures coexisting with the concentration camp system. Roma and Sinti were confined in these municipal camps for indeterminate sentences in dilapidated housing with marginal sanitation and a lack of provisions. The prisoners suffered from verbal abuse by guards and police and physical intimidation by prying anthropologists, physicians, and geneticists researching their genealogy and folklore. The pattern of deporting and holding Roma and Sinti as family

224

units commenced in the municipal *Zigeunerlager* during the 1930s, continued with deportations during the first year of the war, and ended in the Gypsy "family camp" (BIIe) at Auschwitz-Birkenau. A parallel system existed in the main concentration camps, where thousands of German and Austrian Roma and Sinti were incarcerated. Although prisoners could be transferred at any time from municipal Gypsy camps to concentration camps as punishment for noncompliance with regulations or for attempted escapes, most transfers occurred after 1938 to provide forced labor for the concentration camp system. The municipal Gypsy camps were an early, decentralized, and provisional attempt to segregate Roma and Sinti, and, like the later ghettos in eastern Europe, served in the end only as transfer stations to the killing centers.

The patterns of both Gypsy and Jewish deportations reveal the evolving system of killings. Thus, as with the Jewish deportations to Lodz, the deportation of 5,000 Austrian Gypsies from transit camps at Hartburg, Fürstenfeld, Mattersburg, Roten Thurm, Lackenbach, and Oberwart from 5 to 9 November 1941, dovetailed with the establishment of Chelmno (Kulmhof), where these Gypsies were killed in mobile gas vans in December 1941 and January 1942. Similarly, the Gypsies incarcerated in the Warsaw ghetto were deported to Treblinka in the summer of 1942. By that time, the SS Einsatzgruppen operating in the Soviet Union and the Baltic region had already killed several thousand Gypsies alongside Jews in massacres. The RSHA reported in its "Situation Report USSR No. 153" that "the Gypsy problem in Simpferopol [had been] settled" in December 1941.[37] In October 1947 Otto Ohlendorf, who had headed the Einsatzgruppe that operated in southern Russia and the Crimea, testified at Nuremberg that the basis for killing Gypsies and Jews in Russia had been the same. In similar fashion the Reich Commissar for the Ostland in July 1942 informed the Higher SS and Police Leader in Riga that "treatment of Jews and Gypsies are to be placed on equal footing [*gleichgestellt*]."[38]

In Germany and Austria until 1942, Nazi measures were directed primarily against Gypsy *Mischlinge*, since Ritter's racial research estimated that 90 percent of the German Roma and Sinti were of mixed ancestry. In 1942 the regime dropped the distinction between part- and pure Gypsies and subjected all to the same treatment. In 1942 and 1943, when most Gypsy deportations from the Reich occurred, the Nazis also eliminated all distinctions between the treatment of Gypsies and Jews. On 12 March 1942 new regulations placed Gypsies and Jews on equal footing for welfare payments and compulsory labor.[39]

225

There is suggestive evidence that Hitler may have been involved in the formal decision to kill the Gypsies. On 3 December 1942 Martin Bormann wrote a letter to Heinrich Himmler, protesting that the Reich SS leader had exempted certain pure Gypsies from "the measures to combat the Gypsy plague" until additional research into their "language, rituals . . . , and valuable Teutonic customs" could be completed. Bormann complained that neither the public, nor the party, nor the Führer would "understand or approve." Himmler added a handwritten note on the face of the letter about preparing data on Gypsies for Hitler. The marginalia states: "Führer. Aufstellung wer sind Zigeuner" ("Führer. Information who are the Gypsies").[40] Himmler met with Hitler on 10 December 1942, and six days later, responding to Bormann's pressure and probably to Hitler's order, Himmler issued his Auschwitz decree on Gypsies, which led to their deportation to and eventual murder in Auschwitz-Birkenau.

The evidence suggests that Hitler was directly involved and informed of most killing operations, and that simultaneously the administration of policy by German officials stationed outside Germany cumulatively radicalized the implementation of central policy toward German and European Gypsies.

On 26 September 1942, three months before Himmler's Auschwitz decree, 200 Gypsies had already been transferred from Buchenwald to Auschwitz and assigned to build the new Gypsy enclosure (BIIe) at Birkenau. On 26 February 1943, the first transport of German Gypsies arrived at the newly erected Gypsy "family camp" (BIIe) in Birkenau; Gypsies from occupied Europe arrived at Auschwitz-Birkenau after 7 March 1943. The pattern of deporting Gypsies as a family unit was first established during the May 1940 Hohenasperg deportations to Lublin and continued in Auschwitz. The history and fate of the Gypsies in the Auschwitz-Birkenau *Zigeunerlager* paralleled the creation and later destruction of the so-called *Familienlager* for Theresienstadt deportees in Birkenau BIIb. On 2 August 1944, the Gypsy camp at Auschwitz-Birkenau was liquidated. An earlier SS attempt to obliterate the Birkenau Gypsy camp BIIe on 16 May had failed because of armed resistance; the prisoners fought the SS with improvised knives, shovels, wooden sticks, and stones. By the time Birkenau was evacuated, 13,614 Gypsies from the German Reich had died of exposure, malnutrition, disease, and brutal medical experiments, and 6,432 had been gassed; 32 had been shot while trying to escape. Thus about 20,000 of the 23,000 German and Austrian Roma and Sinti deported to Auschwitz were killed there. Most of those killed had been previously registered by Robert Ritter's unit. On 25 April 1943 both Jews and Gypsies had been denaturalized and placed on an equal footing under the provisions of the 12th Ordinance to the Reich Citizenship Law, and on 10 March 1944 a circular letter from Heinrich Himmler directed that the publication of restrictive decrees against Jews and Gypsies be discontinued as their "evacuation and isolation" had already been largely completed.

Holocaust historiography during the past forty years has emphasized antisemitism and the uniqueness of the Jewish fate but provided only cursory mention of the fate of Roma and Sinti. Despite new sources and research during the past decade, older interpretations are still dominant. Although significant progress has been made toward understanding the connection between Nazi ideology, German social policy, and the genocide of Roma and Sinti, it is clear that the "Gypsies" are still considered separate but not equal in most Holocaust historiography. To be sure, there are still areas to be researched, such as the role of ordinary citizens and their attitude toward Roma and Sinti. Nevertheless, the views of German bureaucrats, scientists, and policemen involved in developing and implementing Gypsy policies is parallel to the data about the perpetrators involved in killing the handicapped and the Jews. In the final analysis, these three groups were considered a threat to German racial purity and were condemned for racial reasons. The lacunae of more than fifty years are only in part corrected by the new conceptualization of Gypsies as "social outsiders in Nazi Germany."

NOTES

1. I will try to avoid the term "Gypsy" and its German equivalent, "Zigeuner," because of their pejorative connotations. "Roma" is the broadest term of ethnic self-description and applies to Sinti as well as Roma in this essay. Sinti are a branch of Roma resident in German-language areas of central Europe.

2. The phrase "The forgotten holocaust" is based on the title of Christian Bernadoc, *L'Holocauste oublié* (Paris: Editions France-Empire, 1979), and Angus Fraser, *The Gypsies* (Oxford and Cambridge, Mass.: Blackwell, 1995), 256.

3. For the development of "Gypsy" stereotypes and "Antigypsism," see Jacqueline Giere, ed., *Die gesellschaftliche Konstruktion des Zigeuners: Zur Genese eines Vorurteils* (Frankfurt and New York: Campus, 1996); Michael Jäger, " 'Gemeinschaftsfremd' im Nationalsozialismus: 'Zigeuner' und 'Asoziale,'" in *Feindbilder in der deutschen Geschichte*, ed. Christoph Jahr, Uwe Mai, and Kathrin Roller (Berlin: Metropol, 1994), 173–200; Kirsten Martins-Heuß, *Zur*

mythischen Figur des Zigeuners in der deutschen Zigeunerforschung (Frankfurt: Haag and Herchen, 1983); Katrin Reemtsma, *"Zigeuner" in der ethnographischen Literatur*, Fritz Bauer Institut Materialien no. 16 (Frankfurt: Fritz Bauer Institut, 1996); Wilhelm Solms, "On the Demonising of Jews and Gypsies in Fairy Tales," in *Sinti and Roma: Gypsies in German-Speaking Society and Literature*, ed. Susan Tebbutt (New York and Oxford: Berghahn Books, 1998), 91–106; Wim Willems, *In Search of the True Gypsy: From Enlightenment to the Final Solution*, trans. Don Bloch (London and Portland, Ore.: Frank Cass, 1997); and Wolfgang Wippermann, *Wie die Zigeuner: Antisemitismus und Antiziganismus im Vergleich* (Berlin: Elefanten, 1997). See also Bundeszentrale für politische Bildung, "Protokoll des Symposiums Antiziganismus in Deutschland (kein) Thoma in der Bildungspolitik" (Braunschweig: Georg Eckert Institut, 1997), typescript courtesy Daniel Strauß, Bad Nauheim, Germany.

4. See Anna Bergmann, Gabriele Czarnowski, and Annegret Ehmann, "Menschen als Objekte humangenetischer Forschung: Zur Geschichte des Kaiser Wilhelm Instituts für Anthropologie, menschliche Erblehre und Eugenik in Berlin-Dahlem, 1927–1945," in *Der Wert des Menschen: Medizin in Deutschland, 1918–1945*, ed. Christian Pross and Götz Aly (Berlin: Edition Hentrich, 1989), 123–42; Annegret Ehmann, "From Colonial Racism to Nazi Population Policy: The Role of the So-called Mischlinge," in *The Holocaust and History: The Known, the Unknown, the Disputed, and the Reexamined*, ed. Michael Berenbaum and Abraham J. Peck (Bloomington: Indiana University Press, 1998), 115–33; George Mosse, *Toward the Final Solution: A History of European Racism* (New York: Howard Fertig, 1978); and Benno Müller-Hill, *Murderous Science: Elimination by Scientific Selection of Jews, Gypsies, and Others; Germany, 1933–1945*, trans. George R. Fraser (Oxford: Oxford University Press, 1988).

5. Sybil Milton, "Der Weg zur 'Endlösung der Zigeunerfrage': Von der Ausgrenzung zur Ermordung der Sinti und Roma," in *Kinder und Jugendliche als Opfer des Holocaust*, ed. Edgar Bamberger and Annegret Ehmann (Heidelberg: Dokumentationszentrum Deutscher Sinti und Roma and Gedenkstätte Haus der Wannseekonferenz, 1995), 32–35; and Hansjörg Riechert, *Im Schatten von Auschwitz: Die nationalsozialistische Sterilisationspolitik gegenüber Sinti und Roma* (Münster and New York: Waxmann, 1995).

6. Sandra S. Phillips, Mark Haworth-Booth, and Carol Squiers, *Police Pictures: The Photograph as Evidence* (San Francisco: Chronicle Books, 1997), 11–27; and Susanne Regener, "Ausgegrenzt: Die optische Inventarisierung der Menschen im Polizeiwesen und in der Psychiatrie," *Fotogeschichte* 10, no. 38 (1990): 23–38.

7. Sybil Milton and David Luebke, "Locating the Victim: An Overview of Census-Taking, Tabulation Technology, and Persecution in Nazi Germany," *IEEE Annals of the History of Computing* 16, no. 3 (Fall 1994): 25–39.

8. Martin Block, *Zigeuner: Ihr Leben und ihre Seele* (Leipzig: Bibliographisches Institut, 1936), 53.

9. Ibid., 1–3.

10. Wilhelm Stuckart and Hans Globke, *Kommentare zur deutschen Rassengesetzgebung* (Munich: C. H. Beck'sche Verlagsbuchhandlung, 1936), 55, 153; and Arthur Gütt, Herbert Linden, and Franz Massfeller, *Blutschutz- und Ehegesundheitsgesetz*, 2d ed. (Munich: J. F. Lehmanns Verlag, 1937), 16, 21, 150, 226.

11. Circular decree of 26 November 1935 issued by the Reich and Prussian Ministry of Interior, *Ministerialblatt für die Preußische innere Verwaltung* (hereafter *MbliV*) (1935): 1429ff. See also Rundschreiben No. 1/43 in *Mitteilungsblatt des Gaues Niederdonau der NSDAP*, 5, no. 1 (1 February 1943), re "Ehegenehmigungsanträge von Zigeunermischlingen auf Grund des § 6 der 1. Ausführungsverordnung zum Blutschutzgesetz."

12. [Wilhelm] Frick, "Die Reichsbürgergesetz und das Gesetz zum Schutz des deutschen Blutes und der deutschen Ehre vom 15. September 1935," in *Deutsche Juristen-Zeitung* (Berlin), 40, no. 23 (1 December 1935): cols. 1389–94, esp. 1391; and Reichs- und Preußisches Ministerium des Innern, vertrauliche Ausführungsverordnung des Blutschutzgesetzes betr. Eheschließungen und "artfremden Blutes," 3 January 1936, No. 1 B (1 B 3 429). Documents courtesy Frank Reuter, Archives of the Dokumentations- und Kulturzentrum Deutschen Sinti und Roma, Heidelberg.

13. Romani Rose, Edgar Bamberger, and Frank Reuter, eds., *Der nationalsozialistische Völkermord an den Sinti und Roma* (Heidelberg: Dokumentations- und Kulturzentrum Deutscher Sinti und Roma, 1995), 37–40.

14. Heinrich Wilhelm Kranz, "Zigeuner, wie sie wirklich sind," *Neues Volk* 5, no. 9 (September 1937): 21–27. For Kranz, see Sybil Milton, "Antechamber to Birkenau: The *Zigeunerlager* after 1933," in Berenbaum and Peck, eds., *The Holocaust and History*, 397n19.

15. Robert Ritter, "Die Bestandsaufnahme der Zigeuner und Zigeunermischlinge in Deutschland," *Der öffentliche Gesundheitsdienst* 6, no. 21 (5 February 1941): 477–89; idem, "Primitivität und Kriminalität," *Monatsschrift für Kriminalbiologie und Strafrechtsreform* 31, no. 9 (1940): 197–210.

16. Reich- und Preussisches Ministerium des Innern, Runderlaß betr. "Bekämpfung der Zigeunerplage," 6 June 1936 (III C II 20, Nr. 10/36), published in *MbliV* 1/27 (17 June 1936): 785.

17. For Marzahn, see Wolfgang Wippermann and Ute Brucker-Boroujerdi, "Nationalsozialistische Zwangslager in Berlin III: Das 'Zigeunerlager' Marzahn," *Berlin Forschungen* 2 (1987): 189–201; idem, "Das 'Zigeunerlager' Berlin-Marzahn, 1936–1945: Zur Geschichte und Funktion eines nationalsozialistischen Zwangslagers," *Pogrom* 18/130 (June 1987): 77–80; Reimar Gilsenbach, "Marzahn, Hitlers erstes Lager für 'Fremdrassige': Ein vergessenes Kapitel der Naziverbrechen," *Pogrom* 17/122 (1986): 15–17; and Wolfgang Benz, "Das Lager Marzahn: Zur nationalsozialistischen Verfolgung der Sinti und Roma und ihrer anhaltenden Diskriminierung," in *Die Normalität des*

Verbrechens, ed. Helge Grabitz, Klaus Bästlein, Johannes Tuchel et al. (Berlin: Hentrich, 1994), 260–79.

18. Bundesarchiv Koblenz (hereafter BAK), ZSg 142/23: Report by Gerhard Stein about Marzahn, 1 September 1936, 5 pp.; and Gerhard Stein, "Untersuchungen im Zigeunerlager Marzahn," Frankfurt, 26 October 1936, 8 pp.

19. Gerhard Stein, "Zur Psychologie und Anthropologie der Zigeuner," reprint from *Zeitschrift für Ethnologie* (1941), 76–79, 109. See also Peter Sandner, *Frankfurt–Auschwitz: Die nationalsozialistische Verfolgung der Sinti und Roma in Frankfurt am Main* (Frankfurt: Brandes and Apsel, 1998), 184–94.

20. Reimar Gilsenbach, "Wie Alfred Lora den Wiesengrund überlebte: Aus der Geschichte einer deutschen Sinti-Familie," *Pogrom* 21, no. 151 (January-February 1990): 14–16.

21. For Cologne, see Karola Fings and Frank Sparing, "Das Zigeuner-Lager in Köln-Bickendorf, 1935–1958," *1999: Zeitschrift für Sozialgeschichte des 20. und 21. Jahrhunderts* 6, no. 3 (July 1991): 11–40. For Düsseldorf, see Angela Genger, ed., *Verfolgung und Widerstand in Düsseldorf, 1933–1945* (Düsseldorf: Landeshauptstadt Düsseldorf, 1990), 126–33; and Fings and Sparing, *"z. Zt. Zigeunerlager": Die Verfolgung der Düsseldorfer Sinti und Roma im Nationalsozialismus* (Cologne: Volksblatt Verlag, 1992). For Essen and Gelsenkirchen, see Michael Zimmermann, "Von der Diskriminierung zum 'Familienlager' Auschwitz: Die nationalsozialistische Zigeunerverfolgung," *Dachauer Hefte* 5 (1989): 87–114; and idem, *Verfolgt, vertrieben, vernichtet: Die nationalsozialistische Vernichtungspolitik gegen Sinti und Roma* (Essen: Klartext, 1989), 18–22. For Frankfurt, see Wolfgang Wippermann, *Die nationalsozialistische Zigeunerverfolgung,* vol. 2 of the four-part study *Leben in Frankfurt zur NS-Zeit* (Frankfurt am Main: Stadt Frankfurt am Main—Amt für Volksbildung/Volkshochschule, 1986); Die Grünen im Landtag Hessen, Lothar Bembenek and Frank Schwalba-Hoth, eds., *Hessen hinter Stacheldraht; Verdrängt und Vergessen: KZs, Lager, Außenkommandos* (Frankfurt: Eichborn Verlag, 1984), 153–68; and Eva von Hase-Mihalik and Doris Kreuzkamp, *"Du kriegst auch einen schönen Wohnwagen": Zwangslager für Sinti und Roma während des Nationalsozialismus in Frankfurt am Main* (Frankfurt: Brandes and Apsel, 1990). For Hamburg, see Rudko Kawczynski, "Hamburg soll 'zigeunerfrei' werden," in *Heilen und Vernichten im Mustergau Hamburg: Bevölkerungs- und Gesundheitspolitik im Dritten Reich,* ed. Angelika Ebbinghaus, Heidrun Kaupen-Haas, and Karl Heinz Roth (Hamburg: Konkret Literatur Verlag, 1984), 45–53.

22. See Selma Steinmetz, *Österreichs Zigeuner im NS-Staat* (Vienna: Europa Verlag, 1966); Erika Thurner, *Nationalsozialismus und Zigeuner in Österreich* (Vienna: Geyer Edition, 1983); Andreas Maislinger, "'Zigeuneranhaltelager und Arbeitserziehungslager' Weyer: Ergänzung einer Ortschronik," *Pogrom* 18/137 (1987): 33–36; Erika Weinzierl, "Österreichische Frauen im nationalsozialistischen Konzentrationslagern," *Dachauer Hefte* 3 (1987): 198–202; and Elisabeth Klamper, "Persecution and Annihilation of Roma and Sinti in Austria, 1938–1945," *Journal of the Gypsy Lore Society* 3, no. 2 (August 1993): 55–65.

23. Dokumentationasarchiv des österreichischen Widerstandes [hereafter DÖW], Vienna: Tobias Portschy, *Die Zigeunerfrage: Denkschrift des Landeshauptmannes für das Burgenland* (Eisenstadt, 1938), 39-page mimeographed typescript.

24. "Verordnung über das Meldewesen (Reichsmeldeordnung) vom 6. Januar 1938," *Reichsgesetzblatt* (hereafter *RGBl*) 1938, I:13; and "Runderlaß des Reichs- und Preußischen Ministers des Innern [RMdI] and die Landesregierungen, den Reichskommissar für das Saarland und alle Polizeibehörden vom 24. Januar 1938," *MBliV* 1938: 191; reprinted with commentary in Georg Schulz, *Die Reichsmeldeordnung und die sonstigen Vorschriften über das Meldewesen und über die Volkskartei* (Dresden, 1942).

25. Karl Themel, *Wie verkarte ich Kirchenbücher? Der Aufbau einer alphabetischen Kirchenbuchkartei* (Berlin, 1936), 46–49. See also Götz Aly and Karl Heinz Roth, *Die restlose Erfassung: Volkszählen, Identifizieren, Aussondern im Nationalsozialismus* (Berlin: Rotbuch Verlag, 1984), 71.

26. Geheimes Preußisches Staatsarchiv Berlin-Dahlem, 309:607, Bild A36036–A36039, 16 November 1936; "Wo erhält man amtliche Abstammungs-Gutachten?" *Neues Volk* 7 (1935): 14–17; Themel, *Wie verkarte ich Kirchenbücher?* 3.

27. "Runderlaß des RMdI vom 5. Juni 1936 zur Bekämpfung der Zigeunerplage," *MBliV* 1936: 783. On Ritter, see Joachim S. Hohmann, *Robert Ritter und die Erben der Kriminalbiologie: "Zigeunerforschung" im Nationalsozialismus und in Westdeutschland im Zeichen des Rassismus* (Frankfurt: Peter Lang, 1991).

28. For the Sudetenland: "Verordnung des RMdI vom 24. April 1939," *RGBl* 1939, I:881; for Austria: "Verordnung des RMdI vom 11. Oktober 1940," *RGBl* 1940, I:1345; for annexed Poland: "Verordnung des RMdI vom 4. Dezember 1941," *RGBl* 1941, I:745; see also Aly and Roth, *Restlose Erfassung*, 39–43.

29. See "Runderlaß des RFSS vom 8. Dezember 1938," *Deutsches Kriminalpolizeiblatt* 12 (1939). On the parallels between racial classification of Jews and Roma, see the semiofficial commentary on the Nuremberg racial laws by their original framers, Globke and Stuckart, *Kommentar zur deutschen Rassengesetzgebung*. According to Globke and Stuckart, the Nuremberg Laws applied in full to Roma as well as Jews, a conclusion reflected in a 26 November 1935 ban against intermarriage between "Aryans" and Roma, Blacks, or their respective racial "hybrids" (*Mischlinge*); see "Runderlaß des RMdI über das Verbot von Mischehen vom 26. November 1935," *MBliV* 1935: 1429–34.

30. Schweizerisches Bundesarchiv, Bern [hereafter BAB], BAR E 4326 (A) 1991/157, vol. 1: Report no. 9 by Dr. Bader, Karlsruhe, at the 11th Interpol meeting in Copenhagen, 1935.

31. BAK, R18/5644: 215–27, containing cover letter and six-page memorandum from Oberregierungsrat Zindel to Staatssekretär Pfundtner, "Gedanken über den Aufbau des Reichszigeunergesetzes," 4 March 1936. The document

states: "Auf Grund aller bisherigen Erfahrungen muss jedenfalls vorweg festgestellt werden, daß eine *restlose Lösung* des Zigeunerproblems weder in einem einzelnen Staate noch international in absehbarer Zeit möglich sein wird" (emphasis in the original). Senior Government Councillor Zindel of the Reich and Prussian Interior Ministry was also a member of the German delegation to the 1935 Copenhagen Interpol meeting, presenting a paper entitled "Sicherungsverwahrung und polizeiliche Vorbeugungshaft gegen Berufsverbrecher im nationalsozialistischen Deutschland"; in BAB, BAR E 4326 (A) 1991/157, vol. 1, report no. 20.

32. See Michael R. Marrus and Robert O. Paxton, *Vichy France and the Jews* (New York: Basic Books, 1981), 366–68. The Nazi plan for the identification, concentration, and deportation of Roma had not been fully implemented before the Allied armies liberated France. See also special issue of *Études Tsiganes* 2 (1995): "France, 1939–1946: L'internement des Tsiganes." Even before the Anschluß, the Austrian police already had a card index of 8,000 Gypsy names, known as the *Zigeunerevidenz*, possibly from the early 1930s. Police headquarters in Vienna served as the central offices of the Interpol anti-Gypsy task force; see DÖW, File 12232.

33. See Runderlaß des Reichsführer SS und Chef der Deutschen Polizei im Ministerium des Innern, 8 December 1938, betr. "Bekämpfung der Zigeunerplage," *Ministerialblatt des Reichs- und Preußischen Ministeriums des Innern* 51 (1938): 2105–2110; and "Ausführungsanweisung des Reichskriminalpolizeiamts," 1 March 1939, published in *Deutsches Kriminalpolizeiblatt* 12, special issue (20 March 1939).

34. Staatsanwaltschaft (hereafter StA) Hamburg, Akten des Verfahren gegen Dr. Ruth Kellermann u.A., Verfahren 2200 Js 2/84: RSHA Schnellbrief to Kripo(leit)stellen, 17 October 1939.

35. Zentrale Stelle der Landesjustizverwaltungen, Ludwigsburg, Slg. CSSR, Bd. 148: 55–57, and Bd. 332: 289–300, 306.

36. StA Hamburg, Verfahren 2200 Js 2/84, RSHA an Kripoleitstelle Königsberg, 22 July 1941.

37. Nuremberg doc. NO-3278: "Ereignismeldungen UdSSR 153," 9 January 1942.

38. Yivo Institute, New York: Berlin Collection, Occ E 3-61: Reich Ministry for the Occupied Eastern Territories to Reichskommissar Ostland, 11 June 1942.

39. StA Hamburg, Verfahren 2200 Js 2/84: Anordnung des Reichsarbeitsministers betr: die Beschäftigung von Zigeuner, 13 March 1942. The parallel law for Jews was "die Verordnung über die Beschäftigung von Juden," 3 October 1941, *RGBl* I:675, and "die Verordnung zur Durchführung der Verordnung über die Beschäftigung von Juden," 31 October 1941, ibid. I:681.

40. BAK, R19/180.

CHAPTER 11

The Institutionalization of Homosexual Panic
in the Third Reich

GEOFFREY J. GILES

SIMPLE explanations are often persuasive and plausible. It would be marvelously easy if we could believe the 1998 book by Kimberley Cornish, *The Jew of Linz*, that Hitler's antisemitism may be explained by his encounters with his Jewish schoolmate in Linz, the future philosopher Ludwig Wittgenstein. Since we know that Wittgenstein's homosexual character was emerging at this time and that he had an adolescent crush on another schoolboy, it is tempting to speculate that the vicious and brutal persecution of homosexuals in Nazi Germany had its roots in sexual advances that young Wittgenstein made to young Hitler at school. Unfortunately this tidy thesis does not stand scrutiny. The object of Wittgenstein's affections was a youth called Pepi, not Adolf. And there is no evidence that the future philosopher and chancellor actually knew each other.[1] It is rather more interesting that it was during Hitler's last and Wittgenstein's first year at the Linz *Realschule* that the twenty-three-year-old Otto Weininger, the homosexual Jewish author of *Sex and Character*, committed suicide and immediately became a cult figure among young Austrians and Germans. We know that both Wittgenstein and Hitler read and admired Weininger, whose book presented a convoluted argument to justify his own misogyny and antisemitism. Weininger's stigmatization of Jewishness as "feminine" (that is, not manly) may have contributed to Hitler's negative feelings about homosexuality (not manly, therefore practically Jewish).[2]

HITLER'S INDIFFERENCE AND HIMMLER'S HOMOPHOBIA

While it is of central importance to examine Hitler's attitude toward homosexuality, it is also crucial to recognize that homophobia was not one of his major obsessions. Hitler does not appear to have been consumed

233

by pornographic fantasies about the sexual activities of gay men in the same way that his comments about Jewish men, lying in wait to assault helpless Aryan women, suggest that his thoughts ran wild about another group of "outsiders." His toleration of Ernst Röhm's homosexuality confirms this essential indifference. I would suggest, however, that his active disgust at homosexuals increased after the Röhm purge, as he sought to justify to himself the cold-blooded murder of one of his most loyal lieutenants and closest acquaintances (—I hesitate to use the word "friend" in Hitler's case). Among his own men, it was Ernst Röhm whose unflinching support during the Beer Hall Putsch in November 1923 had touched Hitler most deeply. The picture of Röhm behind the barricades at army headquarters in Munich became an icon throughout the Nazi movement in the years before his death. And the annual "holy day" of the party, the November 9 reenactment of the 1923 march to the Feldherrnhalle, must inevitably have brought back thoughts of Röhm to Hitler.

The date of Hitler's surprise announcement that Nazi student groups at universities should no longer live in dormitories has always struck me as highly significant. Although such a policy had been universally accepted as greatly facilitating the political education of the students, Hitler suddenly ruled against it at the beginning of November 1934, citing privately the dangers of homosexuality if students shared bedrooms.[3] This decision (a verbal, not a written one) came within a few days of the first anniversary of the Beer Hall Putsch since Röhm's murder four months earlier. It seems highly unlikely that Hitler did not have Ernst Röhm on his mind during this particular week. In public that summer he had played up the danger of having had Röhm as a national leader of young men; there is also evidence that he had justified Röhm's removal in such terms in private to other leaders. Now at the beginning of November 1934 he was getting himself worked up to an appropriate state of righteous indignation about the issue of homosexuality before an emotionally difficult occasion. Politically, he had handled the damage control with considerable aplomb through his speech to the SA at the Nuremberg Rally in September. Yet that was a different kind of event, all about the strength and numbers of the Nazi movement. The ninth of November was about the few, the brave old-timers of 1923, one of the bravest of whom he had now betrayed and killed. Not a faceless Jew, but someone who had been willing to go through thick and thin for him. Hitler needed to salve his conscience, and the thought of Röhm's apparently disgusting sexual habits provided the necessary balm. No public

234

reference to homosexuality was made, unlike the ranting statements of that July. The real reason was concealed, which only increased the confusion about the *volte-face* over dormitory housing among university students.

In the Nazi state some men became very powerful by translating Hitler's passing thoughts into policy. Martin Bormann later grew to be the master of this during the Second World War. From 1934 onward, however, it was Heinrich Himmler who strove to be the most loyal lieutenant in this manner. Insofar as Himmler had any ideas of his own that did not derive from his Führer, we can identify a far more deep-seated homophobia in the head of the SS. Himmler's early thoughts on this question are less mysterious than those of Hitler, because we have the young Himmler's diary. As a twenty-year-old, Himmler read *The Priest and the Acolyte* (attributed at the time to the pen of Oscar Wilde), and found the pictures conjured up by this "idealization of a homosexual" to be "disgusting." It put him in a foul mood, as he noted in his diary. He later happened to have a discussion with one of his fraternity brothers about the nature of homosexuality, which prompted him to look at Hans Blüher's famous book *Die Rolle der Erotik in der männlichen Gesellschaft*, in which the author portrayed homoeroticism as the crucial element in male-centered organizations and institutions. He focused especially on the youth movement but also extended his model to cover the army. Himmler didn't know what to make of this. On the one hand it all sounded quite plausible, yet at the same time he felt that there was some intellectual trickery in Blüher's argument that he was not quite sophisticated enough to see through. Although by temperament a loner who was at his happiest when buried in files at the student government office, Himmler found emotional support in the camaraderie of his student fraternity. He felt very comfortable in this homosocial world. Blüher made him think about the emotional implications of it in an unsettling way, as he confided to his diary: "It is clear that society must be a masculine one. Yet I doubt whether one can describe it as eroticism. Be that as it may, pure pederasty is an aberration of degenerated individuality which is contrary to nature."[4] In this last sentence we have the essence of Himmler's homophobia, as reflected in his later policies and pronouncements, formed during his student years in Munich: "real" homosexuality is actually pederasty, with altar boys or members of youth groups as the principal victims. Even if, or perhaps especially if, the younger partner submits willingly, he may then be turned forever into a degenerate personality who will continue the cycle. There is a clear

235

parallel in Himmler's thinking with Hitler's views about the *permanent* defilement of Aryan women who had sex with a Jew.[5] Raising the specter of homosexuals as likely predators on children was also a handy way to bring the general public around to embrace the former's blanket marginalization as outsiders deserving of contempt.

Ernst Röhm was not a pederast. Nor did he abuse his high-ranking position to surround himself with sexual partners from the ranks of the SA. However, he does appear to have had a vigorous sexual appetite, and had a friend, the office clerk Peter Granninger, procure partners for him.[6] The assignations took place discreetly in the apartments of Granninger or another friend, Count Carl Leon du Moulin Eckart. There is no evidence that Röhm roamed the streets at night, picking up young men, as claimed by one memoirist.[7] Yet the image of not only Röhm but other SA men preying on the innocent youths of Germany was the one that was, if not cultivated, then certainly suggested by Hitler's public statements after the Röhm purge. Just a few days after the murders, Hitler stated in the party press: "I would especially like every mother to be able to offer her son to the SA, the Party, or the Hitler Youth without the fear that he might become morally or sexually depraved. I therefore request all SA officers to pay scrupulous attention to the fact that misdemeanors according to §175 [of the German criminal code, that is, homosexual acts] are to result in the immediate dismissal of those guilty from the SA and Party. I want to see men as SA officers and not disgusting apes."[8] The immediate aftermath of this was widespread panic in the homosexual community, which had felt itself to enjoy a certain immunity under Röhm, and a wave of arrests of gay men followed in many German cities.

Was this a clever piece of improvisation on the part of Hitler, and possibly Himmler too, to shift the blame attached to Röhm *ex post facto* away from the real reason, which was that Hitler needed to satisfy the army generals that the SA would not be more powerful than the army itself (which was at the time still limited in size under the terms of the Versailles Treaty)? There is now evidence to suggest that Hitler was talking to the generals even before Röhm's murder about the damage posed by the SA leader's homosexual nature. Heinrich Himmler was called in by Hitler in June 1934 specifically to discuss the problem of homosexuals in the Nazi movement. He recalled this four years later in a letter to the chair of the SS Court of Arbitration (*Großer Schiedhof beim Reichsführer-SS*): "One day in June 1934 the Führer summoned me. There was a lot of talk back then about the homosexual proclivities of

many SA leaders, which indeed led to the terrible events of June 1934."
Note that Himmler stresses here that homosexuality "indeed led to" the
Röhm purge. The particular person whom Hitler wished to discuss with
Himmler on this occasion was the chief of the SS Head Office, Gruppenführer Kurt Wittje. Himmler's letter continues: "The Führer told me
that General von Blomberg [the minister of defense] had pointed out to
him that in the SS, too, there was a man occupying a position of authority, who had been expelled from the army because of his homosexual
nature." Again, let us examine what is being said here. It is clear that the
question of homosexuality in the SA was already under discussion between Hitler and Blomberg before the purge, because Blomberg inter-
jected that "in the SS, *too*" (emphasis added) there was a problem in the
top ranks. Yet if Blomberg was hoping to crush the SS as well as the SA,
he was disappointed. Hitler needed his SS to bring the Stormtroopers to
heel. Himmler himself, already used to the desperate maneuvering for
position of rival agencies in the Third Reich, smelled a plot by the army
here. His initial reaction was to brush off the accusations with the comment that, were they true, the army would not have given Wittje an honorable discharge with a pension and the continued right to wear its uniform. Himmler did not move immediately to purge Wittje, pointing out
to Hitler the folly of lending credence to every denunciation from outside the party. This would be tantamount to handing a convenient
weapon to opponents of National Socialism, who could then easily get
rid of any party or SS leader whom they disliked.[9]

The Dimensions of Homophobia

It is clear, then, that homosexuality *was* discussed as an issue in the removal of Röhm in the weeks leading up to his murder. It was a useful
card for the party to play, because it allowed Hitler to be seen to deal
resolutely with several of the issues that he wished the regime to highlight. A central item on the political agenda at this time was the need to
placate Germany's conservative forces, who were horrified at the crude
brutality of the Stormtroopers' presence in the streets of Germany. A
significant wing of the conservative forces was the "Moral Right," with
whom the Nazi Party had already allied itself during the Weimar Republic over such issues as the fight against "trashy and dirty literature."
There was, then, a *cultural* side to antigay policies. Right-wing forces
had expressed outrage, among other things, over the availability at

newsstands of the (to our eyes, rather tame) magazines of the nudist movement or homosexual organizations. The radical and outrageous nightlife of cities like Berlin also drew their ire. Seeing a marked libertinism in the sexual mores of the Socialists, the Nazis were more than ready by the mid-1920s to jump on the bandwagon that promised to "clean up" Germany.[10] The new sexual freedom of Weimar made it easy to identify the modern, the emancipated, the "other," as "dirty."

Ideological opposition to homosexuality complemented cultural hostility. Manliness was a vital part of the National Socialist identity. Hitler's Third Reich was conceived as a man's world. Women were to have an entirely subordinate place. Rudolf Hess noted in 1937 how delighted Hitler was to have found in Gertrud Scholtz-Klink, his *Reichsfrauenführerin*, someone who knew her place and that of womankind in general.[11] The need for manliness derived from the militaristic character of the Nazi movement and the state. The metaphor of the good Nazi as a "political soldier" abounded. Any discussion of manliness sooner or later comes back to sexuality. Never wishing to face that embarrassing issue, however, Nazi writers from the top down preferred to deal with unspoken assumptions about what constituted "normal" sexuality. As George Mosse has shown so persuasively, the setting of norms and boundaries came about in conjunction with rising nationalism in a number of countries in the nineteenth century, and is not a peculiarly German phenomenon. Yet it was in Germany that the idea of the *Männerbund* (Men's League) grew to especial importance.[12] Although, as the tremendous popularity of Blüher's writings shows, considerable sentiment existed that homoeroticism could actually strengthen the bonds between men, there was but a fine line between this and actual homosexual behavior. That line was frequently crossed, not least by some of the leaders of the youth movement.[13]

No Nazi leader would ever admit to homoeroticism within his ranks. The preferred term was "comradeship" (*Kameradschaft*), which needed to be developed to the same degree of utter life-or-death dependability that comrades-in-arms had relied on in the trenches of the First World War. It was part and parcel of being a soldier, being a man. Those who either failed to live up to the ideal or went too far into the realm of physical expressions of affection were not whole men. And if you were not a whole man, then there was something effeminate about you. The convenient categorization of all homosexuals as effeminate cowards came up against a huge stumbling block in the person of Ernst Röhm. The last thing that could be said about this rough and ready old soldier was that he was in the slightest way effeminate. He was positively brimming with all the soldierly virtues that Hitler and the party admired, far more so than the lisping Baldur von Schirach, the starry-eyed Rudolf Hess, or even the mouselike Heinrich Himmler. Something was not quite right with the definition of "the homosexual," then, just as the perception of "the Jew" was flawed when it was matched against real life. The falsity of the image in both cases caused only a moment's hesitation for many Germans.

The third dimension of homophobia in the Third Reich was a *political* one. The ties of homosexuals to one another, it was argued (notably by Himmler himself), would be stronger than their loyalty to the state. Himmler did not deny that many homosexuals were intelligent and capable citizens, who were for that reason to be found in every state and party office, as his police inquiries were discovering. He came to the conclusion that gay men would show favoritism in the hiring of other gay men when posts became available. If such practices (for which he had no proof whatsoever) were not nipped in the bud, then eventually gay cliques would be running whole areas of government. Clearly this model is based on similar forerunners: the encirclement of Germany before the First World War, Hitler's obsession with being overrun by the "Asiatic hordes," and of course the fear of the all-pervading influence of the Jews, who had purportedly already taken over the government of the Soviet Union and were well on their way to subverting those of the United States, Great Britain, and other countries.[14]

The fourth dimension of policies against homosexuals in Nazi Germany was a *social* one. The German population had suffered a serious bloodletting in the First World War, and from 1918 onward the boosting of that population became a principal target of the political Right. Germany had to become strong enough to fight the next war. This above all was Hitler's view, and the juxtaposition of two target activities in the single police headquarters office set up to combat both homosexuality *and* abortion has been taken by most recent historians to reflect the centrality of population policies in defining Nazi homophobia. This "rational" explanation is plausible, but in my view not sufficient to explain the pathological brutality with which homosexuals (though not abortionists) were pursued. Even senior members of the Nazi Party professed shock on learning that some young men who had been accused of homosexual offenses (often falsely) had been beaten up and tortured in the cells of the Columbia-Haus in Berlin in order to extract "confessions" from them. Nonetheless, a rational-sounding explanation for the persecution of gay men was a necessary device to raise support for this after a climate of greater tolerance in the Weimar years.[15]

DEFINITIONS OF HOMOSEXUALITY

The first problem that the Nazis faced in dealing with homosexuals was the definition of who they were. A preference for relying on physical appearance could only help them identify flamboyantly effeminate gay men, who were but a small minority. Furthermore, it was no use arresting a homosexual if the courts would not convict him. And here the Moral Right had long encountered a stumbling block. German courts interpreted a criminal homosexual act as having necessarily to involve penetration, usually anal (though sometimes oral). It had to be like heterosexual intercourse (*beischlafähnlich*) to be punishable in the view of the Supreme Court, as it ruled in several cases on appeal.[16] To the frustration of the police, this turned out to be very hard to prove in court, because there were usually no witnesses to the sexual activity of the two men. It therefore became a commonplace view among men with homosexual inclinations that you would not get into trouble with the law provided you did not engage in anal sex; mutual masturbation was, from a legal point of view, safe sex.

Was it unusual for German men to masturbate each other in the early part of this century? It was certainly not uncommon, and there are numerous examples of men from all walks of life, from working-class teenager to *Gauleiter*, who did not find this behavior in any way reprehensible. They believed they had a very clear idea of what made you a homosexual, and that was penetrative intercourse with another man. Anything short of that was just harmless amusement. Even the murder of Ernst Röhm and the ensuing public vilification of gay men did not shake that belief.

Then in the summer of 1935, just one year after the murder of Ernst Röhm, the law was subtly changed. Section 175 spoke no longer of "unnatural indecency" (*widernatürliche Unzucht*) but simply of "indecency." This was done with the specific intention of widening the scope of prosecution. The commentary on the amendment to the law deplored the restrictions under which the police had acted hitherto in their efforts to punish "blatant homosexual lovemaking," noting with satisfaction that "this loophole is now closed by the criminalization of *every* indecency between men" (emphasis added).[17] Already on 1 August 1935 the

Supreme Court upheld the new interpretation, and police prosecution of suspected homosexuals shifted into top gear. Since no clear public announcement of the precise nature of the legal amendments was made, most men remained unsuspecting about the danger they now faced. The chief danger was that the law was applied retroactively, without any constitutional justification for doing so. Even supporters of the Nazi Party who had convinced themselves that they were still living in a society protected by the rule of law were about to learn a hard lesson.

An interesting example at the top of Nazi society is that of Gauleiter Helmuth Brückner, the chief party and government official (*Oberpräsident*) of the province of Silesia. In the fall of 1935, soon after the Supreme Court had altered the definition of the offense, he was arrested on grounds of homosexuality. This threatened to be a scandal of the first order, but Hermann Goering (Brückner's immediate superior as head of the Prussian government) told him not to worry: there would be no court case, and the matter could be handled within the party. Himmler, who at this stage was still convinced that if a man were married, then he could not be gay, admitted rather apologetically that he would have handled the case differently if only he had known about the existence of Brückner's wife from the beginning.[18] Frau Brückner obtained a personal interview with Himmler, and also a one-hour meeting with Hitler himself, who claimed not to know that her husband had been arrested, but this did little good. Hitler was famously loyal to his Old Fighters even in the face of their utter incompetence as party or government officials, but suspicion of homosexuality was, after the Röhm purge, grounds enough to drop someone. Hitler evidently ordered the investigation to continue.

Brückner, a self-confident member of the party's top echelon, was not initially intimidated by this, and fought back vigorously. Interestingly, he was quite open in describing himself as bisexual, but adamantly denied that this was either unnatural, or damaging to the interests of the nation. In Brückner's personal view, these bisexual proclivities derived from his experiences of mutual masturbation enjoyed in his youth. He estimated "the number of German men of my by no means pathological makeup to be at least twelve million." Among those were many respected men whom he suggested he would name, and of whom he would tell tales if brought before a court, which would be highly embarrassing to both party and state. For his part, he remained convinced that he had done nothing reprehensible. He had followed closely the signals apparently being issued by the party for many years. They had not seemed to differ from the practice of the courts, so that simply being a homosexual, or engaging in certain kinds of homosexual acts, appeared to be as acceptable in the party as in German society at large, especially during the Weimar Republic. Brückner was probably not alone in thinking that the promotion of Ernst Röhm to the crucial position of chief of staff of the SA was a signal of "unparalleled tolerance" on the part of the Nazi Party toward homosexuals, even though he was mistaken here. Hitler deliberately chose to overlook, rather than endorse, Röhm's homosexuality. The favorable attitude toward homosexuality seemed to Brückner to be confirmed when Hitler stood by Röhm even after the Socialist press published some compromising letters of the latter, thus making his sexual nature clear to the entire German public.[19] The matter was clinched by the New Year's appointment in 1934 of Röhm as *Reichsminister* by President Hindenburg on the recommendation of Hitler. "Any uncertainty was eliminated by this," Brückner insisted, spelling out the perception again: "*National Socialism not only confirmed in an authoritative and visible manner the recurrent opinion of the Supreme Court in the question of mutual masturbation, but expressly endorsed it, and even removed inhibitions by the public recognition* [accorded to Röhm]" (emphasis in original). Of course it was clear even to Brückner that the tide had turned with the murder of Ernst Röhm and the orders Hitler transmitted to the SA about sexual improprieties in its wake. Yet even here Brückner was not as panic-stricken as many German homosexuals, and argued that the change of policy applied only to the disciplinary code of the Nazi Party and not to the law of the land. And there Brückner made a common, but serious, mistake. Most alert Germans knew enough about the legal system to believe that laws were not applied retroactively. That, however, is precisely what the lower courts began to do with the new interpretation of what constituted a homosexual act.

MODES OF PERSECUTION

In the course of his reorganization of the criminal police in 1936, Heinrich Himmler centralized police intervention against alleged homosexuals in a new Berlin office for the "combating of homosexuality and abortion" at police headquarters in the Prinz-Albrecht-Straße. A gigantic card index would keep track of suspects from all over Germany. The conjunction of the two crimes was not fortuitous, and was explained in a 1937 memorandum in very rational terms. Both homosexual sex and abortions reduced Germany's birth rate—*every* good German ought to be boosting the population figures. The problem was a huge one: in 1933 the police had evidence that two million men were actual members of homosexual organizations and clubs. Nevertheless Himmler was confident that it could be solved in a straightforward manner. He believed that scientists had been quite wrong in claiming that homosexuality was in the genes. Perhaps that was true of 2 percent of men exhibiting homosexual tendencies. Otherwise, the behavior of vast majority of the remainder could be explained by their having been seduced. A spell of good, hard work in a concentration camp would soon cure them of such aberrations. The seducers, in contrast, were beyond a cure; they were traitors, and as such were to be "eradicated." Especially those who were attracted to young men were to be permanently incarcerated.

The instructions police were given on how to identify gay men betray the common prejudices of other periods and countries: homosexuals were said to have a feminine appearance and air, and mincing movements; they liked makeup and perfume, and even wore women's clothing. The police officers were warned that many homosexuals had a predilection for men in uniform, and that they could often be found looking for victims in railway stations, parks, public baths, and swimming pools, and especially near public toilets for men. They were told that if a youth was openly displaying his penis for all to see in a public toilet, he could well be a male prostitute—if he winked or stared pointedly, this would virtually clinch the matter. The memo warned police officers that many homosexuals were very discreet and tended to take their partners to their rooms or spend the night in hotels. How could they be identified? They were the sort of people who shunned the company of women and could almost always be seen with other men. For the rest, hotel porters, taxi drivers, hairdressers, and the attendants in public baths and toilets could often provide leads. Himmler wanted his policemen to inspect hotel registers for signs that two men had shared a double room, and to scan the daily newspapers for incriminating small ads. Every last suspect was to be brought in for questioning, and *every* suspect was to be detained, fingerprinted, and photographed, even if charges could not for the moment be brought. His home was to be searched for incriminating letters, and then the homes of the correspondents searched as well.[20] This makes it sound as though the search for homosexuals was virtually a full-time job.

The police did indeed carry out raids on certain bars and public toilets during the Third Reich, but as Burkhard Jellonnek has shown, staff shortages meant that they were much more likely to react to denunciations and tip-offs from the public than to be proactive in this area.[21] Raids had occurred on gay bars since 1933. For example, the SS Leibstandarte Adolf Hitler sent out a squad of twenty men to assist the Gestapo in Berlin one night in March 1935. Starting just before 11 P.M. they covered eight bars between them, shuttling suspects back to Gestapo headquarters. Next morning they delivered the detainees to the notorious Columbia Haus jail, and had some sport even with those released by making them run the gauntlet of the assembled squad as they left police headquarters.[22]

DENUNCIATION

There was no shortage of denunciations in Nazi Germany, as Robert Gellately has shown.[23] Sometimes a jealous woman lost her patience. Antoinette L. had been Theodor S.'s girlfriend for three years, but the relationship seemed to be going nowhere. The situation grew serious with the outbreak of war and the rapid decline in the number of eligible men on the home front. Antoinette became suspicious of her boyfriend's close friendship with a local gynecologist, Dr. Hanns E. and denounced them to the police as lovers.[24] In another case, a founder of the Regensburg Hitler Youth, Fritz Z., was living together with a sixteen-year-old youth, Ludwig. Their open affection for each other, not to mention his imprudent use of the nickname "Lutsch" ("Suck") in public, caused gossip. Their landlady, whose own bedroom was next door to that of Fritz and Lutsch, reported hearing "loud panting and moaning" at night.[25]

When sexual horseplay took place in an all-male group, which was a common enough occurrence in the barracks and camps of such a militaristic society, the denunciation sometimes came from someone who was perhaps not fully accepted by the others (an outsider himself), or was eager to advance in the Nazi hierarchy, or was simply a prude. Those young men who participated in such horseplay rarely gave it a second thought, and certainly did not consider it to be homosexual behavior. The results, however, could be devastating, and end in prison sentences. An example from Baden illustrates the degree to which homosexual panic had set in among the authorities of the Third Reich over the rather unexceptional behavior of teenage boys.

244

Rolf S., who had been born in Strassburg in 1918, was enthusiastic about his family's move across the border to Germany in 1936. "Wieder ein Vaterland!" (A Fatherland once more!) he noted in his diary (which was subsequently confiscated by the police). Since he was now eighteen years old, he was drafted into the Labor Service. His leaders were so satisfied with him that he was soon put in charge of a work squad as its foreman (*Arbeitsdienst-Vormann*). Some of the youths in Troop III were a year or two younger than he, but they all got along famously. Rolf was possibly less inhibited than the others as a result of his French upbringing and was apparently inclined to walk around the barracks hut naked. There was a good deal of sexual horseplay. On one occasion, the youths noticed one of their pals asleep with an erection, and decided to play a trick on him. One of them masturbated him to the point of ejaculation. The hapless youth woke up to the gales of laughter of his companions, one of whom was wiping the bedsheets clean. A foolish prank, no doubt, and the kind of tomfoolery which earned Troop III the nickname of "Troop Queer" (Trupp Schwul) among the other Labor Service men in the camp. It was hardly, however, grounds for court proceedings, yet that is precisely what happened when one of the members of Troop III, the seventeen-year-old Wilhelm M., felt uncomfortable enough to report these incidents to his superiors. The police swooped down and arrested four young men, including both Rolf and Wilhelm.

It should have been clear to any investigator that Rolf himself did not conform to the Nazi stereotype of a homosexual. His diary for 1936 was full of joyful comments about his meetings with girls. On his birthday he remembered the previous one as "*le jour le plus heureux [de ma vie] . . . , jour de mon anniversaire fêté avec Maysie.*" He seems to have been if anything rather precocious in his sexual relations with girls, and told his interrogators that the homosocial world of the Labor Service had left him in a state of sexual tension: "I probably wouldn't have gone so far with M. and E. if I'd had a girlfriend at the time. It happens that I am highly sexed and I had normal sexual intercourse already at the age of fifteen. I have had quite a lot of girls since then. While I was just a simple Labor [Service] Man, I had home leave every three weeks, which enabled me to get things out of my system."[26] His appointment as foreman, however, meant that he often had Sunday duty and therefore little opportunity for weekends away. He was in a state of sexual frustration, a phenomenon hardly unknown to the average teenager. Such was the fear in Nazi Germany that the pleasure of same-sex activity would "turn" a young man into a homosexual, that trivial incidents such as these were indeed blown up into full-scale court cases. Hundreds of youths found themselves languishing in jail during the Third Reich, largely because there was no public definition of what constituted a homosexual offense. The fear was that frank discussion might actually encourage youthful experimentation. The assumption that §175 only covered anal intercourse remained widespread outside legal and actual homosexual circles. Time and again ordinary Germans were in for a nasty shock. Rolf's father, a physician, was bold enough to express his amazement at the stupidity of the new interpretation of the law:

I take note of the fact that not only pederasty and sodomy are included under the concept of "unnatural indecency," but also kissing, touching and mutual masturbation. Since it is well known that such sexual aberrations occur very frequently in boarding schools, it may be described as a real stroke of luck that almost all educators etc. can consider this in a sufficiently reasonable and humane fashion as not to shout immediately for the state prosecutor in such cases, but to try to lead the sinners back to the path of virtue in a different . . . and discreet way. . . .

The acts committed by my son that constitute the basis of the prosecution (three instances of kissing and touching, *two* cases of mutual masturbation)—*parturiunt montes, partitur mus* [the mountains labored and gave birth to a mere mouse]—represent the youthful aberration of a *youth* committed against and with youths in a state of diminished consciousness, and—in the case of E.—under the serious effect of alcoholic beverages. There is simply no other way to explain these misdemeanors." (Emphases in original.)

There is certainly a suspicion that such trials were mounted in order to frighten others from straying in a similar fashion. However, the avoidance of such terms as "mutual masturbation" in press reporting must have left other young people in the dark about the exact nature of the "crimes," which they would often have continued to assume referred to anal intercourse. The expense of lengthy investigative and court proceedings was in any case pure overkill, as Rolf's very sensible father noted:

In my view it would have been entirely adequate to have issued a formal reprimand to my son and the other poor sinners who have been charged along with him, in order to halt this behavior once and for all. Yet it was held to be necessary to expel my son from the Labor Service in disgrace— and it is not as though he is the son of some influential man—, despite the

246

fact that he came from abroad full of enthusiasm for National Socialism and struggling with linguistic difficulties—he speaks and writes French much better than German—, and apart from this has conducted himself in an exemplary fashion, on the basis of which he was promoted. As if that were not enough, he has been thrown behind prison walls for months on end, where he is still languishing today. And finally he now has to expect a punishment and criminal record that will rob him of the possibility of advancing in life in accordance with his abilities.[27]

In this case, only Rolf was sentenced to prison, for six months. This was a rather light sentence for homosexuality, and his foreign birth is more likely to have affected this than the flimsiness of the case. Nonetheless, the criminal record was there, and the intention in all cases of §175 was to stamp people as outsiders for the rest of their life. In another incident involving a Labor Service camp, this time near Erlangen in the spring of 1944, the head foreman surprised a group of men engaging in mutual masturbation. In reporting the incident, he assumed that two hours of punishment drill would be sufficient to knock some sense into them. Instead they too were put on trial and sent to a penitentiary with sentences as long as twenty-eight months.[28] There was to be no second chance for those convicted of homosexual offenses, as countless rejections for reapplication to the Nazi Party show.

WARTIME RADICALIZATION

The mention of alcohol in the case of Rolf S. was not unusual. Hundreds of defendants blamed their sexual activity on the effects of drink. Both Nazi and military leaders never ceased to pour out warnings about the dire results of the excessive consumption of alcohol.[29] Goering, for example, harangued members of the Luftwaffe that the times were past when getting drunk was a sign of manliness. He coupled this in the spring of 1939 with a warning that court records were repeatedly showing that "excessive consumption of alcohol was responsible for many cases of crimes against §175."[30] General Oho von Stülpnagel issued a memo in February 1940 about the increasing number of crimes committed in a state of drunkenness, warning that this would not be accepted as a mitigating circumstance and giving examples of a number of recent cases where prison sentences were imposed. A sergeant, "knowing that he got such urges after the consumption of alcohol," allowed

himself to be seduced by a willing young man into committing a homosexual act. For this he was stripped of his rank and sent to prison for five
months.[31]

During the war the police sought not just to pillory those charged
with homosexuality as outsiders; rather, they were to be removed from
society altogether. Himmler, convinced that all true homosexuals were
by nature pederasts who were driven to seduce every minor coming
within their grasp, issued a decree in July 1940 that all those sent to
prison for homosexual offenses who had "seduced more than one partner" should be transferred indefinitely to a concentration camp as soon
as they had served out their sentence.[32] This completely illegal subter-
fuge effectively turned the prison sentence into a death sentence for
many. Although the Ministry of Justice treated defendants in a less arbitrary, indeed less brutal, manner than Himmler's SS and police, it is apparent that it was in cahoots with Himmler on this question. An internal
memo of the former reveals that the ministry knew perfectly well what
was going on and welcomed it because "the punishments handed down
[by the courts] sometimes seemed to us, too, to be too lenient." The
ministry was also aware that defendants were whisked off for "protective
custody" in a concentration camp in some cases "before, in spite of, and
after an acquittal," if the police thought that they could lodge a successful appeal. This, too, seemed to the Justice Ministry to be a sensible
course of action to take.[33]

Gestapo chief Ernst Kaltenbrunner, one of the most homophobic
Nazi leaders, wanted to go even further than this. In the summer of
1943 interministerial talks took place to draft a new Law on the Treatment of Societal Aliens. This was to include sweeping provisions for the
compulsory castration of those with multiple morals offenses, such as
sexual assault, bestiality, and homosexuality. The draft explicitly stated
that drunkenness could not be used as a mitigating circumstance to prevent the castration. A Justice Ministry memo makes it clear that it was
Kaltenbrunner who had urged that ordinary homosexuals should be
covered by this provision "as soon as possible." In July 1943 Kaltenbrunner was bothering the Ministry of Justice yet again, claiming that
the compulsory castration of homosexuals had "meanwhile become so
urgent" that he could not wait for the passage of a new law, and requested an emergency edict that would allow him to proceed with the
matter. At a hastily summoned meeting for representatives from several
ministries, the police, and the armed forces, it emerged that the cause of
the RSHA's impatience was the apparent sluggishness in the processing

of applications for voluntary castration from prison inmates. Army psychiatrist Otto Wuth pointed out that there was a misunderstanding here. The Interior Ministry had in fact banned voluntary castrations for the duration of the war, thus backing up the applications, but had subsequently revoked its ban. Thereupon Kaltenbrunner withdrew his request for an emergency decree. If voluntary castrations were possible after all, then the police had ways aplenty to pressure inmates to sign the "voluntary" application.[34] At the same time the army shifted homosexuals closer to Kaltenbrunner's grasp by agreeing to review the files of all soldiers charged with such offenses since the beginning of the war and to dismiss from active service all who appeared to be "incorrigible" homosexuals. A marginal note revealed that there had been 5,806 cases of homosexuality in the army brought to trial since September 1939, or roughly 168 cases per month.[35] The prosecution of homosexuals proceeded apace throughout the war. In a 1998 article on the topic, Günter Grau overlooks this trend toward radicalization and pronounces the overall statistics on the persecution of homosexuals to be unremarkable. He mistakenly believes that the police antihomosexual squad, "with a personnel force of only eighteen employees," was simply "not . . . capable" of leading a massive witch hunt, and that Himmler in any case sought only to wipe out the "image" of homosexuality in public life, rather than destroying individuals. A more careful examination of the sources makes such an optimistic assessment impossible.[36]

CONCLUSION

As was the case with other campaigns to create social outsiders, the Nazis were able to build on the prejudices of previous generations. The *gesunde Volksempfinden* (healthy sense of the people) was most outraged by pederasty, so that was built into the stereotype as an integral part of the makeup of a "genuine" homosexual. Himmler reacted to his amazement at the continuing cases of homosexuality in the ranks of the SS and police in two ways. First, he decided that many of these errant members of the racial elite could not after all be real homosexuals, but their aberrations must be a reaction to a teenage seduction, the results of which could be cured. Second, he tried to scare his subordinates by having Hitler proclaim the death sentence for such offenses in the SS and police after November 1941.[37] The ultimate penalty was indeed applied in some cases, but was not used consistently. Hundreds more, who had not received a death sentence, were worked to death in the concentration camps. Thousands of homosexuals suffered grievously at the hands not only of Nazis but of the other camp inmates. Yet there was no concerted campaign of mass murder equivalent to the Holocaust against the Jews.

Policy about the application of §175 was in many ways rather unclear and certainly inconsistent. A conviction often meant financial ruin. For example, the fifty-nine-year-old tavern owner Alfred B. served a brief, two-month prison sentence for a minor homosexual infraction during the war, but lost his license and his livelihood as a result. He asserted that he was actually bisexual and only felt homosexual urges at certain times of the year, which he could generally control. His fellow publicans in Wuppertal lent him their support for his reinstatement, but all in vain: even an appeals court returned a ruling that a homosexual was "fundamentally unsuitable" to run a bar.[38] Yet despite the abuse of law in the Third Reich, proper procedures were indeed followed sometimes, and appeals resulted in the downward adjustment of sentences, even against such social outlaws. Gerhard D., who had bedded several men after getting them drunk, had four months shaved off his prison sentence after the court acknowledged that it had erred in imposing a punishment for one of the incidents, because it had taken place in Belgium and was therefore outside German jurisdiction.[39] Even acts that involved a combination of taboos did not always bring the harshest of penalties. The twenty-five-year-old Alfred P. was having sex with a Jew, Ernst S., at the same time that he was employed in the local Hitler Youth headquarters. Not only that, but he embezzled and stole money from his office to give to Ernst on several occasions. His expulsion from the party in 1941 was a matter of course, but his jail (not penitentiary) sentence of twelve months seems rather light.[40] Some Jewish homosexuals not only survived the war unscathed but, as Gad Beck's memoir reveals, continued to have a very active sex life with non-Jews.[41] It seems certain from Kaltenbrunner's remarks that he and Himmler would have pressed forward after the successful conclusion of the war with a final solution to the homosexual question. As it was, the priorities lay with the completion of the Nazi agenda regarding the Jews, and with shoring up the worsening military situation. In a sense homophobia, because it touched on an individual's sexuality, was more visceral that antisemitism, and could therefore be easily whipped up to a fever pitch at any time after the war with far less effort than the Nazi Party had had to expend on attempting to create eliminationist antisemitism among the German people.

NOTES

1. Kimberley Cornish, *The Jew of Linz* (London, 1998). Even the period of their possible overlapping at the Linz *Realschule* is unclear. Ray Monk claims they overlapped only in 1904–1905, but a contemporary of Hitler's at Linz, Hugo Rabitsch, gives 1903–1904 as Hitler's final year at school. Ian Kershaw confirms that Hitler was sent to another school fifty miles away in Steyr for the 1904–1905 school year, due to his miserable academic performance at Linz. Wittgenstein was born only six days after Hitler, on 26 April 1889, and arrived at the school in 1903. Despite being exactly the same age, Hitler's poor performance put him two classes behind Wittgenstein. The latter does not feature in the lists of classmates that Rabitsch records in his memoir. Ray Monk, *Ludwig Wittgenstein: The Duty of Genius* (New York, 1990), 15–16; Hugo Rabitsch, *Aus Adolf Hitlers Jugendzeit: Jugenderinnerungen eines zeitgenössischen Linzer Realschülers* (Munich, 1938), 94, 100; Ian Kershaw, *Hitler, 1889–1936: Hubris* (London, 1998), 19.

2. Monk notes Hitler's reported comment at a later date: "Dietrich Eckhart [*sic*] told me that in all his life he had known just one good Jew: Otto Weininger who killed himself on the day when he realised that the Jew lives on the decay of peoples." Monk, *Wittgenstein*, 23.

3. Geoffrey J. Giles, *Students and National Socialism in Germany* (Princeton, 1985), 174.

4. Burkhard Jellonnek, *Homosexuelle unter dem Hakenkreuz: Die Verfolgung von Homosexuellen im Dritten Reich* (Paderborn, 1990), 23–24. Cf. also Peter Loewenberg, "The Unsuccessful Adolescence of Heinrich Himmler," *American Historical Review* 76 (1971).

5. Interestingly there is a Supreme Party Court decision to the contrary. It concerned a party member who was the second husband of a woman who turned out to have been previously married to a Jew and had converted to Judaism. The court ruled that, since she came from full Aryan stock herself, and had converted back to Christianity, she was to be seen as a full-fledged member of the German racial community in the sense of the Nuremberg Laws. She was not even to be viewed as having character flaws, based on her poor judgment in marrying a Jew, because she "doubtless did not then recognize the importance of the Jewish question." Cf. Beschluß des Obersten Parteigerichts in Sachen Fritz Bülow, 2 September 1937, quoted in Helmut Heiber, ed., *Der ganz normale Wahnsinn unterm Hakenkreuz: Triviales und Absonderliches aus den Akten des Dritten Reiches* (Munich, 1996), 44–46.

6. Jellonnek asserts that they were usually around twenty years old, and often unemployed; Eleanor Hancock claims that Röhm's partners ranged from sixteen to twenty years old. Jellonnek, *Homosexuelle*, 85–86; Eleanor Hancock, "'Only

the Real, the True, the Masculine Held Its Value': Ernst Röhm, Masculinity, and Male Homosexuality," *Journal of the History of Sexuality* 8, no. 4 (April 1998), 632.

7. The idea of Röhm roaming the dark city streets alone in 1932 in his SA uniform, at a time when a mere handful of Communists anywhere in Germany would have been delighted to make him a target of political assassination there and then, is utterly improbable. I assume the author's description of Röhm's attempted sexual assault on him to be a pornographic fantasy. Likewise the description of his sexual adventures among the Hitler Youth at the 1930 Nuremberg Rally—in fact there was no rally that year. Konstantin Orloff, "Sprachlos war die Liebe nie: Skizzen einer dunklen Zeit," in Joachim S. Hohmann, ed., *Keine Zeit für gute Freunde: Homosexuelle in Deutschland, 1933–1969—Ein Lese- und Bilderbuch* (Berlin, 1982), 43–49.

8. Section 8 of Befehl des Führers an den Chef des Stabes Lutze vom 1. Juli 1934, *Völkischer Beobachter*, 1 July 1934, translation from my chapter introduction to two interviews in John Borneman, ed., *Gay Voices from East Germany: Interviews by Jürgen Lemke* (Bloomington, 1991), 11.

9. Subsequent interviews with both Blomberg and Major General von Reichenau, head of the Wehrmachtsamt, persuaded Himmler that there was some substance to the matter. Himmler to Schiedmann des großen Schiedhofes beim RFSS, 17 June 1938, Bundesarchiv Berlin–Lichterfelde (hereafter BAL) NS19/ 3940.

10. See, for example, Klaus Petersen, "The Harmful Publications (Young Persons) Act of 1926: Literary Censorship and the Politics of Morality in the Weimar Republic," *German Studies Review* 15, no. 3 (October 1992): 505– 523.

11. Always pleased to tell people they were wrong, Martin Bormann wrote to Robert Ley on 20 November 1937: "The Deputy of the Führer [Hess] regards your view that Frau Scholtz-Klink is aiming for the emancipation of women as completely groundless; there can be no question of this at all." Quoted in Heiber, *Wahnsinn*, 56–57.

12. George L. Mosse, *Nationalism and Sexuality: Respectability and Abnormal Sexuality in Modern Europe* (New York, 1985); Klaus Theweleit, *Männerphantasien* (Basel and Frankfurt am Main, 1986).

13. Cf. some of the letters of confession by youth leaders appended to later editions of Hans Blüher, *Die deutsche Wandervogelbewegung als erotisches Phänomen: Ein Beitrag zur Erkenntnis der sexuellen Inversion*, e.g. 3, Auflage (Charlottenburg, 1918), 171–90. It is of course well known that the Nazis prosecuted leaders of rival youth organizations on grounds of homosexuality. Cf. Stefan Krolle, *"Bündische Umtriebe": Die Geschichte des Nerother Wandervogels vor und unter dem NS-Staat—Ein Jugendbund zwischen Konformität und Widerstand*, 2d ed. (Münster, 1986), 80–110. The Hitler Youth also had its own problems, cf. Geoffrey J. Giles, "Straight Talk for Nazi Youth: The Attempt to Transmit

Heterosexual Norms," in *Education and Cultural Transmission: Historical Studies of Continuity and Change in Families, Schooling, and Youth Cultures*, ed. Johan Sturm, Jeroen Dekker, Richard Aldrich, and Frank Simon (Gent, 1996), 305–318.

14. "They are criminal enemies of the state, because as soon as they fill a leading position somewhere and are the superiors of dependent subordinates, they always want to move in their own circles, not only from 'inclination', but also for reasons of expediency. They form a state within the state, a secret organization that goes against the interests of the country, and is therefore treasonable. This is not a question of 'treating poor, sick people,' but of eradicating traitors." Confidential memorandum of Kriminalpolizei Kassel, "Richtlinien zur Bekämpfung der Homosexualität und der Abtreibung," 11 May 1937, Hessisches Staatsarchiv Marburg 180 LA Eschwege 1718. Some extracts from this fourteen-page memo are quoted in Günter Grau, *Homosexualität in der NS-Zeit: Dokumente einer Diskriminierung und Verfolgung* (Frankfurt am Main, 1993), 129–35.

15. Cf. the comments by the head of the Hessen-Nassau Gau Party Court in BAL BDC/OPG Walter K., described in greater detail in Geoffrey J. Giles, "Männerbund mit Homo-Panik: Die Angst der Nazis vor der Rolle der Erotik," in *Die Verfolgung von Homosexuellen im Dritten Reich*, ed. Rüdiger Lautmann and Burkhard Jellonnek (in press).

16. Before the creation of the Reichsgericht in 1879, interpretations of §175 differed from state to state. A crucial ruling of 23 April 1880 set the guidelines for the next fifty-five years: anal, oral, or intracrural sex was *beischlafähnlich*, manual acts were not. Günter Dworek, "'Für Freiheit und Recht': Justiz, Sexualwissenschaft, und schwule Emanzipation, 1871–1896," *Die Geschichte des §175: Strafrecht gegen Homosexuelle* (Berlin, 1991, 42–61).

17. "Die Einzelheiten der Strafrechtsnovelle vom 28. Juni 1935," *Deutsche Justiz*, 35, p. 994, quoted in Hans-Georg Stümke and Rudi Finkler, *Rosa Winkel, Rosa Listen: Homosexuelle und "Gesundes Volksempfinden" von Auschwitz bis heute* (Reinbek, 1981), 214.

18. The following details from a memorandum on the case for Himmler, dated 1 November 1935 (cover letter missing from file), in BAL NS19/1270.

19. W. U. Eissler, *Arbeiterparteien und Homosexuellenfrage: Zur Sexualpolitik von SPD und KPD in der Weimarer Republik* (Berlin, 1980), 106–114.

20. Cf. note 14.

21. Jellonnek, *Homosexuelle*, 328–31.

22. Meldung Marks, 11 March 1935, Bundesarchiv-Militärarchiv Freiburg (BAMA) NS17/LSSAH 57. My thanks to Sybil Milton for sharing this document with me.

23. Robert Gellately, *The Gestapo and German Society: Enforcing Racial Policy, 1933–1945* (Oxford, 1990).

24. Badisches Generallandesarchiv Karlsruhe (hereafter BGLA), Staatsanwaltschaft Karlsruhe 309/2579–80.

25. Although the twenty-three-year-old Fritz was not exactly mistreating his young partner (and he had made a will, leaving a RM 1,000 life insurance policy in Ludwig's name), he received a sentence of eighteen months in a penitentiary. Urteil, 28 October 1937, BDC OPG Fritz Z.

26. Diary of Rolf S. for 1936, and interrogation on 31 July 1937, BGLA 309/2982.

27. Kuno S. to Rechtsanwalt, 10 October 1937, ibid.

28. Franz Seidler, *Prostitution, Homosexualität, Selbstverstümmelung: Probleme der deutschen Sanitätsführung, 1939–1945* (Neckargemünd, 1977), 228.

29. Geoffrey J. Giles, "Die Alkoholfrage im Dritten Reich," *Drogalkohol* 3 (December 1986): 257–65.

30. "Göring gegen Alkohol- und Nikotinmißbrauch," *Landshuter Zeitung*, 20 April 1939, Bayerisches Hauptstaatsarchiv München, Bayerischer Brauer-Bund 158.

31. By contrast, a drunken young, twenty-three-year-old driver who had buggered a heifer received thirteen months in prison. Memo von Stülpnagel, "Straffälle durch Trunkenheit," 17 February 1940, BAMA RH21–2/v. 60.

32. Erlaß RSHA, Vorbeugende Verbrechensbekämpfung, 12 July 1940, quoted in Frank Sparing, *". . . wegen Vergehen nach §175 verhaftet": Die Verfolgung der Düsseldorfer Homosexuellen während des Nationalsozialismus* (Düsseldorf, 1997), 183. In 1943 a request for the revision of a prison sentence on the grounds of the prisoner's poor health was turned down by the Justice Ministry with reference to this edict. No homosexual was to be released in future. Reichsjustizministerium Vollmer to Generalstaatsanwalt Jena, 9 February 1943, Bundesarchiv Koblenz (now Lichterfelde) R22/970.

33. Karl Heinz Roth points to the origin of this policy in Hamburg, and attributes it to the elevation of Hamburg's Justice Senator Curt Rothenberger to the position of *Staatssekretär* in the Reich Justice Ministry. Karl Heinz Roth, "Ein Mustergau gegen die Armen, Leistungsschwachen und 'Gemeinschafts-unfähigen,'" in *Heilen und Vernichten im Mustergau Hamburg: Bevölkerungs- und Gesundheitspolitik im Dritten Reich*, ed. Angelika Ebbinghaus, Heidrun Kaupen-Haas, and Karl Heinz Roth (Hamburg, 1984), 16. Aktenvermerk zur Unterrichtung von Herrn Staatssekretär Dr. Rothenberger, Schutzhaft über gerichtliche Maßnahmen hinaus, 10 September 1942, Zentrale Stelle der Landesjustizverwaltungen Ludwigsburg, Generalstaatsanwaltschaft beim Kammergericht Berlin I Js 12/65 (RSHA-Ermittlungsverfahren). I wish to thank Hans-Georg Stümke for sharing a copy of this document with me.

34. Entwurf Gesetz über die Behandlung Gemeinschaftsfremder (Stand 4.7.1943); Entwurf 2. u. 3. Verordnung zur Durchführung des Gesetzes über die Behandlung Gemeinschaftsfremder (these had already advanced to the stage

of a *printed* draft [printed in the Tegel prison!]); Schnellbrief Reichsminister der Justiz, 7 July 1943; Wuth to Heeres-Sanitätsinpekteur, 21 July 1943, BAMA H20/479.

35. OKH Befehl, Entlassung von Soldaten aus dem aktiven Wehrdienst wegen widernatürlicher Unzucht, 22 July 1943, ibid.

36. His essay fizzles out in the anodyne statement that "in the end, the racist Nazi regime had a negative effect on all homosexuals." One could make a similar argument about the effect of most German governments in the century following 1870. Günter Grau, "Final Solution of the Homosexual Question? The Antihomosexual Policies of the Nazis and the Social Consequences for Homosexual Men," in *The Holocaust and History: The Known, the Unknown, the Disputed, and the Reexamined*, ed. Michael Berenbaum and Abraham J. Peck (Bloomington, 1998), 340, 342–43.

37. Erlaß des Führers zur Reinhaltung von SS und Polizei, 15 November 1941, in Grau, "Final Solution," 244; on the attempts to cure homosexual members of the SS, see Geoffrey Cocks, *Psychotherapy in the Third Reich: The Göring Institute* (New York, 1985), 202–216.

38. Urteil Reichsverwaltungsgericht III Senat, Alfred B., 18 February 1943, Geheimes Staatsarchiv Dahlem I 184, Senat 3719.

39. Nordrhein-Westfälisches Hauptstaatsarchiv/Schloß Kalkum LGStA Kleve Rep 7/881.

40. Gauleiter Breslau to Pohl, 6 February 1941, BAL BDC Alfred P.

41. Apart from his actual boyfriends, Beck, for example, traded sexual favors with his employer in exchange for his complicity in providing a hiding place for Jews. Gad Beck, *Und Gad ging zu David: Die Erinnerungen des Gad Beck* (Munich, 1997), 164–66.

CHAPTER 12

Police Justice, Popular Justice, and Social Outsiders in Nazi Germany

THE EXAMPLE OF POLISH FOREIGN WORKERS

ROBERT GELLATELY

ALMOST immediately after Hitler's appointment in January 1933, the Nazis began to forge the "community of the people." This process involved the promotion of the positive and wildly idealistic self-images found in German folk culture and the simultaneous persecution of a wide variety of "others" who were pressed to the margins of German society. Hitler's dictatorship developed a bond with the German people and became ever more popular the more it attacked those whom many Germans already regarded as negative, unwanted, feared, and hated. Down to 1938–39, the Nazis invented and propagated a new theory and new practice of law; they took into custody many people who did not fit in, or whom they saw as constituting a problem, and arrested a wide range of social outsiders, from "habitual" criminals to homosexuals, asocials, vagabonds, and "Gypsies." At the same time the Nazis took countless measures against the Jews, uprooting them from the "normalcy" they had known in Germany and about which they had been so proud, in order to harass them into leaving the country.

The war revolutionized all aspects of the Nazi revolution, and also brought home a stunning new fact of life for everyone in the country: Germany could not cope with the war without using hundreds of thousands, and then millions, of foreign forced laborers. By August 1944 there were no less than 5,721,883 foreign workers in Germany, of whom 1,659,764 were Poles—about two-thirds of them used in agriculture.[1] These were the new social outsiders. Given the long history of anti-Slavism in Germany, Poles and others from the East were anything but welcomed by many citizens of Germany. Not only that, but Slavic workers were regarded by the regime that so desperately needed them as posing both a racial danger and a potential social threat behind the lines.

256

My emphasis in this essay is on Polish foreign workers, who are taken as "representative" of the foreigners most despised inside Nazi Germany. The regime was determined to do everything possible to keep the Poles from socializing with Germans, lest that lead to "blood mixing" and supposed racial degeneration. The Nazis established nothing less than an apartheid system for the Poles—who were the first major ethnic group forced to work in Germany—and tried to enforce it with an iron fist. The anti-Polish sentiment was not new, but it was now greatly accentuated.[2] When any of these men and women did not follow regulations or the law, police were given wide-ranging new authority to deal with them.

POLICE JUSTICE

Several early cases illustrate the ways in which Nazi policies turned Polish workers into legally defenseless outsiders. One incident whose tragic consequences were fully documented began in Kaiserslautern on 30 September 1941, when twenty-six-year-old Amalie Benkel went to the Kripo to report that in May she had had a sexual encounter "against her will" with Polish worker Stephan Kroll and was now five months pregnant. She was arrested immediately and, especially because of the charge of rape, so was Kroll. Both had worked for Benkel's mother. By 16 October Kroll was interrogated at length by the Gestapo in Neustadt. He denied the charges, but admitted having sexual relations over a period of months. She kept insisting that the sex was a one-time event and that he had used force. The Gestapo did not believe her, and they decided the "justice" of the case on their own. Such cases were not usually tried in a court of law. Because Benkel was pregnant Kroll was given the standard and perfunctory "race test," which was really nothing more than a subjective evaluation based on impressions of the local Gestapo and on his appearance in photographs sent to the race experts for the region (in Metz). The Neustadt Gestapo's evaluation of Kroll was damning, in that he was described in language laced with personal distaste, racial prejudice, and sexual anxieties, and not surprisingly Kroll failed the test. The Reich Security Main Office (RSHA) in Berlin then asked local authorities to check whether Kroll had been told about the death penalty for such "crimes," to which they soon responded that indeed they even had his signature on a document to prove he had been informed. The RSHA then ordered his execution for 20 April, by mischance, Hitler's birthday.

257

To avoid taking up time on such a momentous occasion, the execution was moved up to 17 April, and took place near the scene of the "crime." According to the "execution protocol," three members of the Gestapo and an SS doctor were present as was a translator, who informed Kroll that "by order of the Reichsführer-SS" Himmler, he was "to be executed by hanging because of the crimes he had committed." As per routine, the execution itself was carried out by two Polish workers; another 155 Poles witnessed the execution and were led past the body. Amalie Benkel was initially released from custody in time to have her baby, after which she was arrested and sent to Ravensbrück to a fate unknown. The brief report on local reactions, written by the gendarme from the area, noted only that the population thought the execution was "justified." He concluded that "generally the view is, that the woman ought to have experienced the same thing, because it was a case of a German woman and she had, through her actions, severely damaged the image of the German woman."[3]

This was the kind of case that judges and others at the time often called "lynch justice." The description is not quite apt. In the Nazi form of "lynch justice," unlike the kinds of events we usually associate with the term, the lynching was not the result of a blind rush to judgment by a mob in a moment of inflamed passion. In Nazi Germany, "lynch justice" was calculated and premeditated killing designed for maximum terroristic effect both on the downtrodden Polish workers and on any German who contemplated sleeping with or comforting the enemy.

During the war years, in spite of widespread public knowledge of what could and did happen to Polish offenders, the Gestapo found no difficulty in obtaining information from the population in the three districts I have studied closely: Düsseldorf and the Rhine-Ruhr; Würzburg and Lower Franconia; and Neustadt an der Weinstraße and the Palatinate. Out of a very large sample, I concluded that the Gestapo itself discovered virtually no breaches of the law on its own, but relied on information from ordinary citizens. Not everyone who informed about some (mis)deed of a Polish worker wanted the full measure of terror used, much less that someone lose his life, but the well-known persecution and execution of legally defenseless individuals did not deter those who informed the Gestapo.

Some citizens went to the police simply to have a worker sent away because he had (mis)behaved. Such a simple intention cost Stanislaus Smyl his life. By all accounts, Smyl was small of stature and at least his Gestapo file states that he was "not fully responsible mentally." From early in 1940 he worked for a farmer in Hampenhausen, which was in the Gestapo jurisdiction of Paderborn. In late May he approached a married woman in the street and, while "emitting strange sounds," exposed himself to the shocked woman who was already upset because of the recent death of her husband. She asked her relatives to contact Smyl's employer, and the latter agreed that Smyl should not be allowed to stay in the village any longer. He informed the Labor Office and asked them to send Smyl somewhere else. Once word got out that Smyl might have committed a crime, however, local police were called in, and soon the case was on the desk of the Gestapo in Paderborn. The investigating official, who at least after the war said he disagreed with the order that Poles who committed morals offenses should be executed, might have been relieved when the medical doctor whom he asked to examine Smyl concluded that the man was both unfit to work and "mentally incompetent." The Paderborn Gestapo recommended that Smyl be sent back to Poland. For the RSHA in Berlin, however, such a move was not in keeping with one of Himmler's many guidelines, and they insisted he be arrested. By July 1940 the RSHA concluded that Smyl should be hanged in public in Hampenhausen. In order to deter others, they also ordered that the execution be publicized in the area; that the Poles there be brought to witness it; and that Nazi Party organizations send representatives. On 26 July 1940 Smyl was executed in the presence of between 100 and 150 people, including the Poles. A priest who was allowed to give Smyl comfort recalled that the man did not understand what was about to happen and asked when he saw the gallows, "What are they doing there?"[4]

"People's Justice"

As the killings of Stanislaus Smyl and Stephan Kroll make clear, the most brutal sides of the enforcement process did not always take place behind closed doors and in secret. Beginning in early 1940, or shortly after the Poles began arriving in large numbers, there were reports from across Germany of these kinds of public executions. The cruel realities of what Germans were practicing in the East began to be brought home with police practices that would have been unthinkable before 1939. As Kroll's case and others show, Poles were dealt with directly by "police justice." They rarely went to court and usually the German involved was dealt with in the same way.

259

At times "people's justice" (*Volksjustiz*) itself struck before the police even arrived, and lashed out not only at the foreign worker but at Germans who were implicated as well, as in the case of the German farmworker August Keidel (born 1894) and the Polish farmworker Rosalie Walktor (born 1914). She had arrived in Lower Franconia in March 1940 and by July their employer (later said) he began to notice that the two had become friendly. Whether he was the one who denounced them is uncertain, but action was swift after the Nazi peasant leader became involved in early August 1940. Local Nazis promptly arranged a public demonstration on 12 August 1940 and Keidel was led through the streets with a sign around his neck that read: "This lad defiles the German honor. He slept with a Polish wench." When the Gestapo arrived to make the arrest, they were not unhappy to find what they described as a scene of "popular justice." Keidel was on display at the marketplace where he was surrounded by about five hundred jeering people and humiliated. Later he was sent to Dachau for three months. Neither he nor the Polish woman was tried in court, but she was sent to Ravensbrück for three months. Although he was released, what became of her is not mentioned in the dossier.[5]

This kind of fraternization with Poles led the Würzburg SD in November 1940 to report that German men, especially farmworkers, "did not have the slightest sensitivity" about having sexual relations with Polish workmates. The SD insisted that "all cases in which contraventions have been established must be dealt with by Draconian measures, because only thus will the necessary deterrent be achieved. Often more effective than a sentence [for the German] are the measures of popular justice, with heads shaved and a marching about with placards in the village."[6] That there was something approaching a consensus among Nazis across Germany can be gathered from similar kinds of reports from elsewhere. The Jena Higher Court president noted in March 1940 that the practice in Thuringia, even before a woman was charged, was to parade her with shaved head and placards through the village.[7] Such an exhibition of "people's justice" was a new form of wartime terror in the German countryside.[8]

Another example from Lower Franconia opened on 19 August 1940 with the typed statement of the Würzburg Gestapo that a certain Walter Freitag ("evangelisch," born 1920) and the Pole Josefa Kurasz (born 1922), both employed on a farm in Enheim, had had sexual relations. It is uncertain whether the Gestapo was at the scene of the public demonstration that took place in Enheim over this "scandalous" event. The dossier notes laconically that shortly before the arrest of Freitag and Kurasz on 18 August, Freitag was led through the village of Enheim by about eighty men of the SA and Hitler Youth to the accompaniment of trumpets. During the parade, Freitag was harassed by village youth and vilified by all. The demonstration, led by Nazis who had come from nearby Kitzingen, ended at the Rathausplatz. There, in the presence of the entire village, the deputy Kreisleiter issued words of warning to Freitag and anyone else who might contemplate such "forbidden relations." An indication of the unequal justice meted out was that for all of his harrowing experiences Freitag was promptly released. Josefa Kurasz, on the other hand, was sent to Ravensbrück for three months.[9]

August Keidel and Walter Freitag were two of the very few German men to be paraded in public in this way. It was far more common for German women to be so defamed.[10] The practice went so far that two young women from a village near Würzburg, one of whom (aged sixteen) had been raped and the other (aged seventeen) sexually assaulted by Polish prisoners of war in May 1940, had their heads shaved by the SA and, with the permission of the magistrate and party boss, were then marched through the streets with signs round their necks that stated they were "without honor." The reaction of Catholic townsfolk was "complete rejection" of such measures.[11] The SD noted, however, that because of the deep shock of parents and family, these public defamation practices (unjust or not) showed the greater social impact of "popular justice" over sending cases to court. The SD wrote that the public relations effects lasted "for weeks" afterward as word of the events circulated. "The most salutary effect" was the fear that such a thing could happen again, so that "at least for the indefinite future" women would consider it prudent to avoid relationships with Poles.[12]

When Himmler learned about such examples of "people's justice," he gave his blessing, as long as the event did not get out of hand.[13] But there were many Germans, grateful for help on the farm, who were slower to adopt racist attitudes toward the Poles, and in pronounced Catholic areas in particular there were continuing reports of socialization with them.[14] From the Nazi point of view, this behavior left a great deal to be desired and was one reason Himmler did not oppose "people's justice."[15] By the autumn of 1941, however, the practice began to be used not only when local authorities discovered illicit affairs with Polish workers but when other nationalities were involved, including some with whom Germany was allied. Indeed, in some places, Germans who were accused of making insulting remarks about Hitler were dealt with

261

by "people's justice." When such practices were brought to Hitler's attention on 16 October 1941, he ordered a halt to further defamations involving foreign workers out of concern for the feelings of Germany's allies and friends.[16] Yet Hitler intervened when he heard of instances when courts showed the slightest sign of being soft on Polish workers. For example, he had a judge removed from the bench after he heard that the judge saw mitigating circumstances in a 1941 case where a Polish worker was charged with sexually assaulting a German girl.[17] Poles who dared raise their hand to their employer—as one did in Ebernburg in August 1941—paid with their lives when the matter was reported, not by the employer in the event, but by his family.[18]

The Gestapo continued to carry out public hangings of Polish men, but did so away from spectators, much to the dismay of judicial authorities. The Nuremberg Higher Court president complained in July 1941 to the minister of justice in Berlin that the Gestapo recently had hanged Julian Majlca for having had an affair with a German who became pregnant (she was later given ten months in jail). "The fact that this execution took place without previous judicial hearing was the subject of lively discussion. Even the Kreisleiter apparently was heard to be opposed." The same letter mentioned a case in which the Gestapo in Regensburg went to the court jail, picked up another Pole being held for having forbidden relations, and executed him. In November the same thing happened in the forest near Eschlbach, where the Pole, Jarek, was hanged for having relations with a twenty-year-old woman. As in the previous case, one hundred or so Poles were led past the corpse.[19] Justice authorities were often left in the dark, knowing neither the charges nor even the extent of the executions that took place on their home turf.[20]

The issue of what should become of a "guilty" German woman was much discussed among police authorities and the people. A popular response, as we have already seen, was that she should not be allowed to get off lightly. In a case from the Düsseldorf area (in June-July 1941), the minimum demand was that the woman at least have to witness the execution.[21] A judicial report of 4 September 1942 said that "some Polish civilian workers" had been hanged by the Gestapo, but, the writer added, "one heard nothing about what might have happened to the German girl or the German woman, apart from perhaps a warning being given. Among the people, that is often not understood. It even causes a certain shock, that the dishonorable and worthless behavior of the German girl or the German woman is not sensibly punished."[22]

When German women became pregnant, they presented the racist regime with a dilemma, especially if the Pole appeared "suitable for Germanization." The issue was discussed in a note from Gestapo chief Heinrich Müller to all Gestapo posts on 10 March 1942. If, in an initial judgment, both parties were deemed "racially acceptable" and if the "racially foreign person" wanted to marry the woman, no further measures would be taken against her. The Pole would be arrested and his "potential for Germanization" assessed. If there was a "positive" result, pictures were to be sent to the RSHA in Berlin, both persons were to be set free, and the case dismissed. If the result was negative, the "usual special handling request" was to be made for the Polish worker, that is to say, steps were to be taken to liquidate the Pole or send him for life to a camp.[23] We need to recall that such examinations and proceedings would have been unthinkable if the man involved was Jewish; the Jews were singled out even among those whom the Nazis called the "racially foreign peoples."

How the Poles were treated elsewhere is suggested by correspondence from other areas in Germany. A report from the Higher Court president in Jena on 31 May 1940 noted that two courts were supposed to deal with a Polish man who was accused of having sexual relations with a German woman; she was given seven years by the court, but before he could be tried, "an official of the Secret State Police appeared, took the files, and declared that the RSHA in Berlin had issued orders to hang the Pole."[24] In another case from the same area, on 24 August 1940 the Gestapo took a man from the court prison in Gotha and hanged him in the presence of fifty Poles on the road between Hörselgau and Fröttstadt; the body remained there for twenty-four hours.[25] More complaints came from Jena in the following months, one of which pointed out that, while "popular justice" might have a deterrent effect, it gave rise to uncivilized behavior—such as the shouts of the village youth at the unfortunate woman—and undermined the justice system.[26] The judges did not seem to object in principle to such extralegal executions.

Letters of complaint about police methods continued to flow from those in charge of the administration of justice all over Germany. Illustrative was one from the Hessian Higher Court president in March 1942. He wrote that on 24 January, a Polish woman near Fulda had killed her employer's child with a cleaver and injured another. She was hanged by the Gestapo on its own authority, in the presence of two hundred Poles brought to see the spectacle. The court president had no doubt that the Pole deserved what she got, and that the courts would have delivered the same verdict, but lamented that the Gestapo, with its "lynch justice," was undermining what was left of the justice system. He was particularly disturbed that the Gestapo had permitted five hundred or so Germans to witness the hanging, along with the two hundred Poles brought to see it as a deterrent.[27]

Himmler reacted to this case in a letter of 22 April 1942 to Minister of Justice Thierack, and noted that the woman would likely have been declared deranged by a judge, not responsible for her actions, and therefore not subject to the death penalty. For Himmler, that was totally unacceptable. He continued: "As Reichsführer-SS and Chief of the German police, however, I am responsible to see that such deeds find their just penalty. The community of the people demands the destruction of such parasites, regardless of whether, according to juristic considerations, a subjective guilt exists or not. I cannot accept that a Polish subhuman escapes their punishment through some legal regulation or other."[28]

These remarks provide a good illustration of what was at the heart of Himmler's notion of a "police system of justice," as does the remainder of his letter. He turned to another case in which a Pole attacked and killed his employer in a small town near Rudolstadt. The deed (committed on 24 November 1941) allegedly caused a local uproar. The Pole, who had also wounded himself seriously, was turned over to the justice authorities, but could not be tried before he died from self-inflicted wounds. Himmler decided in this case that the murder of the German could not be atoned for with the death (or execution) of a single Pole, and so opted for a public execution of eleven more, to be carried out near the scene of the crime. He noted to the minister of justice that "the population had accepted the execution I ordered with satisfaction, but was quite rightly irate that absolutely nothing happened to the real culprit." (Indeed, a later report of the court responsible for this area duly noted that the people regretted only that the "culprit" himself—though already dead—had not been hanged alongside the rest.)[29] Himmler continued that "it would have been better also in this case, if a transferral to the justice authorities had been avoided, and my decision had been immediately sought. I regard it as my duty, therefore, now as in the past, to decide myself upon such cases immediately after the deed."[30]

When Georg Thierack took up his appointment on 20 August 1942 as justice minister, he promptly intensified the "guidance" of the courts and systematized it by issuing regular instructions to judges. He demanded in a meeting with higher justice authorities on 29 September

1942 that they work for still harsher verdicts and more death sentences.[31] Ten days earlier, at Bormann's suggestion, Thierack met with Himmler. They agreed that those who were in custody who were "Jews, gypsies, Russians, Ukrainians, Poles sentenced to over three years, Czechs, or Germans sentenced over eight years" were to be handed over to Himmler, as also was the vaguely defined group of "asocial elements."[32] This agreement (with no basis in law whatsoever) routinized the implicit division of labor by which the Gestapo would henceforth have the blessing of the Justice Ministry to deal with all "racial" problems. Thierack accepted Himmler's claim that "the justice system" was simply not in a position to keep so many people under surveillance and control. In a note to Bormann of 13 October 1942, Thierack made clear the basis of his own thinking on the subject:

> With a view to freeing the German body politic of Poles, Russians, Jews, and gypsies, under the concept of freeing up the eastern areas that have accrued to the Reich for the German people, I intend to pass over to the Reichsführer SS, the criminal prosecution of Poles, Russians, Jews, and gypsies. My point of departure here is that the justice system can only contribute in minor ways to the extermination of these peoples. No doubt, the courts are handing down very hard sentences against such people, but that is insufficient to contribute importantly to the implementation of the above-mentioned concept. It makes no sense to conserve such peoples for years on end in German jails and prisons. . . . Instead of that, I believe in handing such people over to the police, which, freed of legal constraints, can take its measures to obtain far better results.[33]

On 5 November 1942 Himmler informed the Gestapo across the country of the agreement with Thierack, and he spelled out its implications. He said that these foreigners were "racially inferior people," and it followed that they should be subject to a different penal code. Whereas until then, judges had evaluated the personality and motives of the accused, henceforth such considerations were to be ignored. One effect of the Himmler-Thierack agreement was thus to put an end to what remained of the flimsy judicial protection of the rule of law for the Poles and the others mentioned above.[34] At another meeting with Himmler on 13 December 1942, Thierack confirmed and reiterated his intentions about this division of labor by even agreeing that henceforth Himmler's decrees would constitute "the basis for the penal proceedings against the racially foreign peoples."

As we have seen, most of these cases were dealt with outside the courts. If French civilians or prisoners of war were involved it was rare that they were executed, but that happened on occasion, as when one was shot near Dilligen in December 1942.[35] Usually the cases of west Europeans were sent either to the regular courts or, if more serious, to the special courts. However, when it came to the Poles or "east" workers, "police justice," not bringing the case to court, was the preferred approach. "Police justice" was the ultimate form of terror inside wartime Germany, easy to overlook by studying court files, because the courts often did not handle these cases. According to the Himmler-Thierack agreements, the justice system was to deal in future with Germans only,[36] but in fact what was left to the courts was decided by the Gestapo. In the Thierack-Himmler accords, Thierack recognized the validity of a "police system of justice."

Execution orders for Poles, usually carried out as soon as possible and beyond appeal, were formulated in such a way as to make clear that the decision had been made by the Gestapo. As one case from late 1942 put it, "the Head of the Security Police and SD has decided" that the person in question "is to be hanged."[37] The RSHA issued orders to the Gestapo on 30 June 1943 about formally removing Polish and Soviet civilian workers from the German penal code and making them subject to the police. The next day, the few remaining Jews in Germany were also removed, so that the "crimes" of all these people in future would be handled by police measures, not through the courts, unless for some reason the police decided on their own to hand over the accused.[38] Removal of the "racially foreign people" from the regular justice system to the sphere of the police was reinforced by a Himmler directive on 10 February 1944. It pertained to "serious crimes and sexual relations of the foreign workers." The instructions end with the chilling comment that "carrying out of special handling [that is, executions] aims above all as a deterrent to the foreign workers inside Germany."[39]

The administration of justice, or in the more evocative German term, *Rechtsprechung* also concerned how to publicize court decisions. According to the Thierack-Himmler agreements, in rural areas and villages with fewer than 20,000 inhabitants, verdicts were to be carried out as quickly as possible and presented to the public to obtain the maximum social effect. In the cities, where the "administration of justice" was more difficult, reports of crimes and punishments of Poles and the other groups named above were to be published in carefully worded articles in newspapers or distributed on posters in the workplace. The city press offered numerous exemplary stories, not only of the "heavy penalties for unruly Poles," but also of what happened to ordinary citizens.[40] Germans were provided with instructive stories of the "false pity" of passing on the letters of Poles to their families.[41] They could read of a young woman's "disgraceful behavior." She had been "observed" speaking with a Pole (for which she was given six weeks in jail). At the top of the newspaper story was the imperative "Keep Your Distance!"[42] Care was taken in presenting verdicts and assessing reactions. The concept used by Thierack was the "administration of justice through the people itself."[43]

PUBLIC OPINION AND POLICE JUSTICE

A good deal more research is needed into how Germans reacted to the institutionalized inequalities that the Nazi regime imposed on the eastern workers, but the evidence to date suggests that the German people supported the Nazi approach. We can get some idea of how citizens took advantage of the Poles in police files and, especially, in memoirs and oral histories of the Poles.[44]

When it came to how Germans reacted to the executions of the Poles, the historian Ulrich Herbert rightly contends that the German public, when they noticed what was happening, did not go beyond expressing some muttered "discomfort."[45] I have dealt in more detail with popular reactions elsewhere.[46] Here I would like to point to several cases discovered recently. For example, in the Palatinate during 1942 and 1943, we have the records of four executions that include a report on local reactions. More than one hundred Poles were forced to witness each of the executions. In the files, Germans said that the executions were "justified," "correct," "supported," or "thoroughly appropriate."[47] As usual, there was a demand that something be done to punish the German woman, and that point was made elsewhere in Bavaria, such as after the execution of Thomas Wolak on 10 March 1942 in the forest near Landshut. The population reportedly favored the execution, wanted the same thing to happen to the German woman, but beyond dampening the spirits of the Poles there, the matter was little discussed and "had no particular influence on the [general public's] mood."[48] In another case, from December 1942, the population allegedly continued to blame the woman (a war widow) even after she committed suicide, because according to the report of the gendarme from Eisenberg, they felt she had seduced the Pole. The gendarme (who may have had second thoughts about the process) recommended that future executions be carried out away from public view "because it is believed in that way a certain disquiet and upset among the people caused by such an execution will be avoided."[49]

Because most documentation on the reactions of the population has been lost, care needs to be taken not to generalize on the basis of the little evidence that has thus far come to light. Opinions may have been more varied and, to judge by another execution in the jurisdiction of the Gestapo in Düsseldorf, Catholics continued to make little secret of their displeasure. According to a report from 1 October 1942 of the mayor of Kempen-Niederrhein, the recent "hanging of a Pole was regarded by the local population with little understanding, because the great majority of them stand on the side of the Roman Catholic Church, which rejects these kinds of measures. Only a few people judge these executions from the standpoint of maintaining the purity of the German blood."[50] A national survey of the SD from early 1943 reported with exasperation that even "particularly heavy punishments have, unfortunately, not achieved an overwhelmingly successful result" in terms of deterring disobedience.[51]

The RSHA's "working group on foreign workers' security questions" recommended in mid-1943, in addition to trying to uphold the apartheid system by enforcing regulations, and tying workers to their place of work more than ever, that less serious (German) offenders be taken aside and given special instruction courses regarding the racial and other dangers involved in socializing with Poles and other foreigners.[52] All kinds of additional steps were recommended to keep workers in their place, but many of these (unspecified) suggestions "quickly were recognized as unenforceable." Ultimately more emphasis was put on publicizing deviations from regulations and what happened to delinquents.[53] The attorney general's office in Munich continued to complain in June 1944 about the "sad chapter," that German women had not ceased having intimate relations with foreigners of all kinds and that in fact the illicit acts had increased in volume.

It hardly needs to be said, but the Gestapo system, thanks to the involvement in it of ordinary citizens as denouncers, managed to nip the slightest forms of disobedience and resistance in the bud. Ulrich Herbert's study of German workers' complicity in the racism aimed at foreigners at the workplace and in the camps indicates that this behavior emerged as Germans were put in positions of authority over the lowly foreigners.[54] The Gestapo case files, however, make clear that social cooperation or collaboration in enforcing the rules about "forbidden contact" extended well beyond the workplace. Among other things, that vigilance made it virtually impossible for the Poles to find secure enclaves where they could meet and discuss what to do. There was one rare occasion when more than one hundred Polish women dared to refuse to work—at Rheinzabern in mid-1943. The protest stopped three hundred more workers and brought production at the brickworks to a halt. The protest over poor clothing and other conditions collapsed within two hours when the translator told them of the threat that many would be sent to a concentration camp. It was not long before a denouncer came forward and the female ringleader was taken into "protective custody." She was sent to Auschwitz in September 1943 and her death was reported on 5 January 1944.[55]

CONCLUSION

The Nazi approach to social outsiders was partly defined by traditional German values. The Nazis built on and popularized older phobias, but above all pushed for more radical "solutions." The new police (the Gestapo and Kripo) were given broad mandates, about which the public was well informed, and powers that they supposedly needed to deal preventively, and finally, with social outsiders. Thanks to Hitler's support, the police were able to fashion what can be called a "police system of justice" (*Polizeijustiz*) that rivaled, and then outdistanced, the regular judicial system (*Justiz*). Although the courts certainly tried to play their part in Hitler's dictatorship, they were constantly challenged by the police and threatened with becoming redundant. The coming of the war accentuated the conflict between the "police system of justice" and the regular judicial system in that it opened new possibilities for the police, and Hitler's dictatorship more generally, to ignore the courts and to cast aside the last vestiges of the rule of law.

Reading the testimonies of Germans and Poles who became entangled in the police and justice system of Nazi Germany should serve to remind us that the circles of vulnerability grew ever wider in the war years, and that attention to these matters has been neglected for too long. We are only now beginning the work needed to assess what happened to the Poles and other eastern workers inside Germany. The terror system was created between 1933 and 1939, and was used against Jews and a wide variety of social outsiders. War revolutionized everything about the terror, including inside Germany, where it was used primarily for the purposes of enforcing an apartheid system to contain the "racially foreign" eastern workers. The full extent of their victimization has not been established by historians. In July 2000, however, at long last, the German government and many German firms, urged on by the United States, finally made an effort to compensate the surviving victims of oppression and exploitation.

NOTES

1. There were, in addition, 28,316 Polish prisoners of war. After a late start, there were 2,126,753 Soviet workers in Germany, the largest group in that year. There were nearly 2 million prisoners of war in the country at that time. See 31 October 1944: "Der Arbeitseinsatz im Großdeutschen Reich," Nr. 10, reprinted in Ulrich Herbert, *Geschichte der Ausländerbeschäftigung in Deutschland 1880 bis 1980* (Berlin, 1986), table 12, 145.

2. The new citizenship law of 1913 tried to exclude Poles (and Jews) permanently from the body politic by defining citizenship in terms of a community of descent or blood (*jus sanguinis*) rather than one of birth or assimilation. See Rogers Brubaker, *Citizenship and Nationhood in France and Germany* (Cambridge, Mass., 1992), 114ff.

3. Landesarchiv Speyer (hereafter LAS): Gestapo 524.

4. The postwar trial of the responsible Gestapo official—he was sentenced to one year, six months—is in *Justiz und NS-Verbrechen*, vol. 18, 716–26.

5. Staatsarchiv Würzburg (hereafter StA W): Gestapo 7292.

6. StA W: SD 9 (22 November 1940).

7. Bundesarchiv (hereafter BA): R22/3369, 12, GSA beim OLG Jena (30 March 1940).

8. See, for example, BA: NS 29/4, 103–104, for a German woman in Oschatz (in Saxony, September 1940).

9. StA W: Gestapo 10570.

10. StA W: Gestapo 7292.

11. StA W: SD (7 September 1940).

12. StA W: SD (7 December 1940).

13. BA R58/1030, 53: Himmler to Hess (8 March 1940).

14. Heinz Boberach, ed., *Meldungen aus dem Reich, 1938–1945: Die geheimen Lageberichte des Sicherheitsdienstes der SS*, 528 (4 December 1939).

15. See Helmut Witetschek et al., eds., *Die Kirchliche Lage in Bayern nach den Regierungspräsidentenberichten, 1933–1943* (Mainz, 1966–1981), 4:163 (report for December 1939), for other acts of Christian charity, also resulting in the intervention of the Gestapo, and 2:345–46 (report for March 1940).

16. BA: R 43 II, 1542(a), 170, Lammers to Schlegelberger.

17. BA: R 43 II, 1542(a), 193, Bormann to Lammers (26 March 1941).

18. LAS: Gestapo 2004. The Pole was sent to Flossenbürg on 8 December 1941 and his death was reported 26 March 1942.

19. BA: R22/3381, 76ff., 88ff.; OLGP Nuremberg.

20. See, for example, BA: R22/3381 (11 August 1942).

21. See Hauptstaatsarchiv Düsseldorf (hereafter HStA D): Gestapo 23027.

22. BA: R22/3381, 119.

23. BA R58/1030, 168ff.

24. BA: R22/3369, 9ff.

25. BA: R22/3369, 28.

26. BA: R22/3369, 38–39 (31 December 1940).

27. BA: R22/3371, 71: OLGP Kassel (5 March 1942).

28. BA: R22/851, 31ff., Himmler to Schlegelberger.

29. BA: R22/3369, 77ff., OLGP Jena (27 February 1942).

30. BA: R22/821, 31–32, Himmler to Schlegelberger.

31. Thierack's remarks are reprinted in Heinz Boberach, ed., *Richterbriefe: Dokumente zur Beeinflussung der deutschen Rechtssprechung, 1942–1944* (Boppard, 1975), 449–54.

32. BA: R22/4062, 35a, Besprechung Thierack-Himmler (18 September 1942).

33. Schreiben Thierack to Bormann (13 October 1942), cited by the Generalstaatsanwalt bei dem Kammergericht Berlin, Abschulßvermerk (15 September 1970) to 1 Js.1. 64 (RSHA), 66.

34. HStA D: RW36/10, 71 "Strafrechtspflege gegen Polen und Angehörige der Ostvölker."

35. StA Neuburg an der Donau: GL Schwaben 2/27. Even party members were reported to be shocked about the event.

36. BA: R22/4062, 28ff., Besprechung Thierack-Himmler.

37. LAS: Gestapo 5595; the Polish worker was executed one hour after his arrival in Natzweiler.

38. HStA D: RW 36/10, RSHA to Stapo (30 June 1943), "Verfolgung der Kriminalität unter den polnischen und sowjetrussischen Zivilarbeitern."

39. HStA D: RW 36/d43, 95ff., Himmler to all HSSPF.

40. See *Rheinische Landeszeitung* (hereafter *RLZ*) (6 May 1941).

41. *RLZ* (5 September 1940).

42. *RLZ* (9 October 1940).

43. See BA: R22/4062, 28ff.; 35a ff., Besprechungen Thierack and Himmler (18 September 1942) and (13 December 1942).

44. See, for example, Annekatrein Mendel, *Zwangsarbeit im Kinderzimmer: "Ostarbeiterinnen" in deutschen Familien von 1939 bis 1945* (Frankfurt, 1994).

45. Ulrich Herbert, *Fremdarbeiter: Politik und Praxis des "Ausländer-Einsatzes" in der Kriegswirtschaft des Dritten Reiches* (Berlin, 1986), 129.

46. Robert Gellately, *The Gestapo and German Society: Enforcing Racial Policy, 1933–1945* (Oxford, 1990), 232–44.

47. LAS: Gestapo 524.

48. StA Landshut: Rep.164/10, Nr. 2331, Gend.-Posten Adlkofen (15 March 1942).

49. LAS: Gestapo 2313. The cases pertain to Stefan Kroll, Wasyl Pawlyk, Franz Crzesiak, and Leon Dudas.

50. HStA D: Gestapo 74302.

51. BA: R22/3379, 115; GSA beim OLG Munich (10 June 1944).

52. BA: R16/162, recommended (18 July 1943), tried out in Halle-Merseburg and Würzburg (14 October 1943).

53. BA: R16/162, Arbeitskreis meeting (1 October 1943).

54. Herbert, *Fremdarbeiter*, 100–101.

55. LAS: Gestapo 1605.

CHAPTER 13

Sex, Blood, and Vulnerability

WOMEN OUTSIDERS IN

GERMAN-OCCUPIED EUROPE

DORIS L. BERGEN

WOMEN cannot be categorized as outsiders in National Socialist Germany in the same way as can, for example, Jews, Roma, people deemed handicapped, or homosexuals. Nazism did not target women for destruction, persecution, or marginalization simply because of their sex, although as Gisela Bock and others have shown, Nazi Germany was undeniably a sexist society.[1] On the contrary, as Claudia Koonz demonstrated more than a decade ago, National Socialism had its women insiders—promoters, enablers, and beneficiaries—as well as its female victims.[2] Not sex but other factors—political allegiances, religion, family background, health, appearance, ethnicity, and above all what the Nazis called "race" and "blood"—marked some women, like some men, for abuse and murder. As was the case for men, gender shaped the specific forms that attacks on women took, but "blood," not sex, was the primary factor by which the decision makers and implementers of Nazi policy categorized their victims. Accordingly any study of women as outsiders in Nazi Germany and German-occupied Europe is necessarily a discussion of race; it is not possible to separate sex from blood in Nazi ideology and practice.

Women in the territories to the east of Germany were particularly vulnerable to Nazi assault. It was Germany's eastern neighbors—first the Poles, Christian and Jewish, but also Ukrainians, Belorussians, Russians, Lithuanians, and others—who bore the brunt of Nazi German warfare; it was those people who became the objects of enormous, deadly experiments in racial engineering. The Germans enslaved, forcibly relocated, and killed millions of women and men whom they deemed somehow subhuman *Untermenschen*. At the same time, they created insiders from those elements of the eastern European population they considered ethnically German, or "Volksdeutsch."[3] That some ethnic Germans co-operated with the German invaders is well known; many Jewish memoirs tell of Volksdeutschen who stole Jewish property, betrayed their neighbors, or served as guards at concentration camps.[4] But many eastern European gentiles were neither purely victims nor the primary perpetrators of genocide; instead they were its witnesses and beneficiaries. As such they spent the war years in the ambiguous moral universe that Primo Levi called the "gray zone."[5] Few scholars venture into that difficult terrain, and studies of women who are not easily categorized as victims, perpetrators, or resistors are almost nonexistent.[6]

This essay explores the particular conjunction of racism and sexism that shaped the experiences of women relegated to the margins in German-occupied eastern Europe. Central to Nazi treatment of such women was a crude instrumentalization that reduced them to their reproductive capabilities. Whether they were classified as desirable—so-called Aryans—or associated with groups targeted for enslavement or destruction—Slavs, Gypsies, Jews—women represented the production of future generations. Nazi policy and practice instrumentalized men in comparable ways by reducing them to potential soldiers who would fight either for or against the Reich. One could learn a great deal about men as insiders and outsiders in the Nazi system if one looked at how they were recruited, deployed, or rejected by the military. In the case of women Nazi authorities focused on matters of sexual relations, marriage, and reproduction. When we examine treatment of women under each of those three headings we see how Nazi sexism and Nazi racism functioned in interlocking ways that established and reinforced a brutal hierarchy.

A note about sources is in order here. I have drawn mostly on research done for a project on the Volksdeutschen—ethnic Germans—of eastern Europe during World War II.[7] It might seem that this focus would narrow the scope considerably. But in fact the opposite is true. Ethnic Germans existed on the edge of the Nazi knife that separated privilege from penalty. As acknowledged "Aryans," carriers of supposedly pure German blood, the Volksdeutschen of eastern Europe were Hitler's chosen people, selected as the beneficiaries of plunder and genocide. But as outsiders to the Fatherland their pedigrees were always suspect. Ethnic Germans in the conquered territories to the east were suspiciously similar to their Slavic neighbors; sometimes they were indistinguishable from them. Over decades and generations, settlers from German-speaking Europe had intermarried with their neighbors. Many had changed religious allegiances, adopted or adapted cultural practices, abandoned or transformed the German language. Ideological claims of purity notwithstanding, it was thus often simply not possible to draw clear lines separating people of "German blood" from Poles, Ukrainians, Czechs, or even Jews.[8]

Indeed agents of National Socialism in charge of policies toward the Volksdeutschen in the East found that their primary task was identifying precisely who belonged in that privileged category. For this reason, issues of sex, marriage, and reproduction—that is, the very areas in which women were of fundamental interest to Nazi authorities—played an immense role. Meanwhile the tenuousness of the category "Volksdeutsch" itself made the process of classification both arbitrary and dynamic. Nazi racial experts constructed a graduated scale, the so-called German people's list (Deutsche Volksliste), with four levels of "Germanness"; they also reserved the right to practice "Germanization" (Eindeutschung) of their subject peoples, with the exception of the Jews. That is, racial specialists could upgrade the classifications of individual Polish gentiles, for example, for small children who looked suitably "Aryan" and were to be raised by Germans or for adults who had proved to be loyal servants of Germany. Given such practices, it is not surprising that the archival record on ethnic Germans holds many sources on women outsiders. Nazi race and settlement experts devoted massive amounts of time and energy to determining which women—and thereby which offspring, present or future—were desirable and which unwanted inhabitants of the greater Reich.

SEXUAL RELATIONS

The combination of sexism and racism that characterized National Socialism engendered brutal intrusions into the most intimate aspect of people's lives: sexual relations. Although men and women alike were subject to scrutiny, a widespread tendency to associate sex with women—together with a titillation factor for some male officials—ensured that details about women's sexual behavior were more likely to enter the archival record than were particulars about men, at least heterosexual men.[9] Even Nazi sources cited sexual information about some women that showed them to have been victims of inappropriate or criminal male behavior. For example, the famous February 1940 memorandum from General Johannes Blaskowitz in occupied Poland describing

275

German atrocities included the following short account of sexual violence against Jews: "On 18 February 1940 in Petrikau, two sentries . . . abducted the Jewess Machmanowic (age eighteen) and the Jewess Santowska (age seventeen) at gunpoint from their parents' homes. The soldiers took the girls to the Polish cemetery; there they raped one of them. The other was having her period at the time. The men told her to come back in a few days and promised her 5 zloty."[10] Blaskowitz used the example of rape as one of the most powerful ways he knew to illustrate just how extreme German behavior had become. Likewise materials collected from ethnic Germans on the last stages of the war make frequent use of graphic accounts of rape to support charges that the Red Army behaved atrociously.[11]

But Nazi sources also reveal tendencies to regard women as anything but helpless victims. Non-German women, a great deal of correspondence suggested, used sexual wiles to entice Aryan men to their ruin. A pointed example comes from the files of the Nazi Party leadership in Upper Silesia. In March 1944 the Nazi regional office in Bielitz requested revocation of the ethnic German status of a woman named Sofie Trojak. Trojak, who was single, had just given birth to her fourth child. The father of the child, a German soldier named Alois Nagly, had deserted and hid out in Trojak's home. Instead of condemning Nagly's act, the Bielitz Landrat blamed Trojak: "Through her immoral way of life and the sexual intercourse she offered she bound him to her and possibly also urged him not to return to his unit." According to local party bosses, she was a "downright whore" who neglected her children and left them covered with "dirt and filth."[12] Who could be more dangerous to German propriety and honor than a sexual predator who was a poor mother as well?

In the context of Nazism's preoccupation with reproduction and sex, every "non-Aryan woman" became a potential destroyer of the race; she had the power to give birth to new generations of enemies and the ability to lure unsuspecting German men to their doom. Nazi authorities responded to this perceived threat in different ways depending on where a particular woman stood on their racial hierarchy. A look at the Reich Ministry of the Interior's memorandum of October 1942 regarding sexually transmitted diseases is instructive. "For the protection of German blood," the circular began, "bordellos shall be established for the alien workers laboring in the territories of the Reich. They are to be staffed by prostitutes from the respective ethnic groups. General planning is in the hands of the Reich Criminal Police Office." All prostitutes, whether

German or alien, were to be examined regularly for sexually transmitted diseases, but foreign prostitutes were to be kept as isolated as possible from everyone else. Doctors were permitted to examine them in the "B Barracks, that is, the Bordello-Barracks."[13] Both explicitly and implicitly the memo indicated that sexual relations between so-called Aryans and aliens could not be prevented altogether.

A circular from the Military Supreme Command dated 27 January 1943 described measures to be taken against venereal diseases in the brothels established for use by German soldiers. It forbade any uncontrolled prostitution and called instead for establishment of brothels under military supervision. Such places were to be unadvertised and restricted to the use of German soldiers. All of the women working there were to receive a number and a control card so that any sexually transmitted diseases could easily be traced back to individual prostitutes. Doctors would examine each woman twice a week. Almost at the end of the instructions one sentence linked this exploitation of women directly back to the Nazi racial hierarchy: "Jewesses are to be excluded."[14]

In significant ways, as the rape of the Jewish teenagers in Petrikau suggests, the experiences of Jewish women paralleled those of their gentile counterparts. But in other ways, what the Nazis labeled "race" proved to be a crucial dividing line. That 1940 rape in the cemetery could not have been repeated two years later when the Supreme Command issued its memorandum. By 1942 Nazi genocide of the Jews had moved from its experimental stages to full implementation. Even Germans who defied their orders and raped Jewish women would immediately have destroyed the evidence by killing their victims. And in any case, once conditions in the ghettos and camps had reduced most Jews to skeletons—desperate, starving, and diseased—the likelihood of Germans' raping Jewish women may have become increasingly small. It seems reasonable to conclude that rape and sexual slavery by Germans were more common among women from those groups targeted for enslavement—above all, Slavs—than from those slated for destruction: Jews, Gypsies, and people deemed handicapped. Racial taboos toward Slavic women were both less absolute and less zealously enforced than toward Jews, and the physical condition of at least some members of the group after the early phases of war would have been more conducive to their being viewed as objects of sexual desire. German rape or sexual enslavement of Slavic women could reflect a quest for pleasure and an assertion of power over subject peoples as well as a form of torture, mockery, and humiliation. In fact, a 1940 memorandum from

277

Reichsstatthalter Arthur Greiser in Wartheland stipulated that "Polish female persons who engage in sexual relations with members of the German *Volk* can be sent to a brothel."[15] Jewish women, like their Roma counterparts, remained vulnerable to sexual abuses too, but of different, often even more deadly, kinds in keeping with the goals of genocide.

Nazi ideology emphasized the barriers between members of the so-called Aryan race and the targets of genocide: people deemed handicapped, Gypsies, and above all, Jews. They were marked for annihilation; that goal in turn shaped the patterns of sexual assault. If the "final solution" was murder, then it became counterproductive to encourage or permit sexual interaction. Instead Nazi leaders and propagandists worked to discourage German killers and their henchmen from considering women from the groups marked for destruction as objects of sexual desire. Nazi ideology and practice constructed taboos around such women, so that the idea of intercourse with them might seem comparable to having sex with animals or corpses.[16] Viewed in this way, the wartime dread that some Jewish women expressed of "girls' battalions" sent east to service the troops may have been a symptom of how much they misunderstood the Nazi genocidal project.[17] By no means were fears of sexual violence groundless, but Jewish women would encounter it in different forms than they might have imagined: forms whose aim was less sexual gratification of the perpetrators than dehumanization and destruction of the victims.

Use of sex to humiliate and denigrate the targets of Nazi aggression was by no means limited to Jews. On the contrary, preoccupations with sexual behavior provided ammunition to reinforce all manner of prejudices. A glaring example of this process comes from the files of the German special court (Sondergericht) in Bromberg (Bydgoszcz). In 1940 the court heard a case of incest involving a fifteen-year-old woman and her father, both of Polish ethnicity. The man, a basketmaker by trade, was unable to support his family, who lived in a poorhouse. According to the judgment, when his wife had died three years earlier, she had instructed her oldest daughter to "take her place" in the father's bed. Three German judges signed the decision "in the name of the German people." It conveyed the extent to which these men shared prejudices central to National Socialism and used their positions to further key aspects of that ideology.

Although the incest had been carried on for several years, the sentences handed out were relatively light: a year for the daughter, two for her father. As the judgment explained, those decisions had nothing to do with clemency: "The accused are . . . morally deformed people who do not show the slightest understanding of the disgusting nature of their action," the judges wrote. Such moral deficiency, they claimed, was typical of Poles. Polish law too had forbidden sexual relations between relatives, they conceded. But, they continued, "it is nevertheless known to the court that in certain areas of the former Polish state's territory, sexual intercourse between father and daughter was completely common and was not viewed as immoral by the Polish population. The German people has an interest in ensuring that among the members of the *Volk* pure relations reign. But we are not interested to the same extent about whether such things occur among the Polish population in ways that are not visible to the outside world." Why not let them ruin their bloodlines, the judgment implied; they were supposedly inferior in any case, and slated for nothing better than enslavement.[18] This document captures the brutal conjunction of racism and sexism that characterized the treatment of women outsiders in German-occupied Europe. Nazi perpetrators targeted women and men each in gender-specific ways that in turn reified and reinforced the hierarchies of blood that constituted Nazism's new world order.

MARRIAGE

Nazi concern about women's reproductive capabilities naturally extended into matters related to marriage. Who could be permitted to marry whom and presumably bear children together? With regard to this question too, files dealing with the definition and treatment of Volksdeutschen from eastern Europe prove a fruitful source because of the unique position ethnic Germans occupied in the Nazi worldview. When the Ministry of Justice proposed a new marriage law, it planned to prohibit German citizens from marrying foreigners. Drafters of the law wanted to make an exception for ethnic Germans, but "the difficulty of delineating ethnic Germans in a clear and unambiguous way" persuaded them not to do so.[19]

With regard to marriage Nazi officials practiced an astounding level of micromanagement. For example, the mobile killing squad Einsatzgruppe D prepared its own reports regarding Germans from the Black Sea area and made lists of informants among the Russian-German resettlers to the Warthegau. Einsatzgruppe staff also assessed ethnic German populations in its zone of operation, for example, in the Rayon

DORIS L. BERGEN

of Cudovo, near Leningrad. In that district, Einsatzgruppe specialists identified sixty-six of the eighty-six households as German. They deemed Protestant mixed marriages—Germans married to Finns, Estonians, or Latvians—racially acceptable but denounced unions between Germans and Orthodox Russians: "Such mixtures represent entry into the blood of elements with mostly the least desirable results." Very small numbers were concerned: a total of nineteen people in the area came from German–Russian Orthodox mixed households.[20]

A look at issues involving women, marriage, and reproduction illustrates the kinds of day-to-day decisions and initiatives that added up to Nazi racial policy. In January 1944, Einsatzgruppe D and German authorities in Lodz were still struggling to finalize resettlement plans for Germans from Russia. Regulations from the SS Settlement Office in Lodz early that year provided detailed instructions about what constituted a Volksdeutsche family: "If an ethnic German lives in a common-law marriage (that is, unregistered), with an alien, then the alien partner can only be recognized as a settler if there is a wish or intention to marry . . . and if the alien partner belongs to categories I or II. . . . Ethnic German women who expect a child from an alien are to be entered on a list and reported to the administrative staff to be referred to the Race and Settlement authorities." The regulations also stipulated how to deal with children born after resettlement who represented "undesirable" accretions to the population. Such children were to be refused German citizenship, although their names were to be included on the settlement identification papers, and they were to be reported to race and settlement authorities. They could remain with their mothers, "for the time being."[21]

Even when there were specific guidelines from above, middle-level bureaucrats often bent the rules for the sake of stability. For example, by Himmler's order, ethnic Germans of the "renegade" category IV could not marry those with higher classifications. Nevertheless, in 1944, the president of the province of Upper Silesia in Kattowitz wrote to the Reich Security Main Office in Berlin to initiate a change. In two 1943 reports, he indicated, he had already drawn attention to the "extraordinarily urgent matter of marriages between members of categories III and IV of the German people's list." But no ruling had followed, nor had his request for a decision on the specific case he now presented been met.[22]

That particular situation was as follows: Paul Tynior, born in 1894 in Königshütte and living there, had been accepted into the German people's list as a category IV. He had shown "strong affinities for Polish-

280

ness" before 1939 and even married a Polish woman. According to race assessors, that earlier behavior made acceptance into category III "out of the question." Meanwhile the Polish wife died, and Tynior planned to marry a widow of category III. He hoped to marry immediately because he had four small children. "No biological threat to the German *Volk* is on hand in this case," the letter indicated, "because the applicant is 49 years old, his fiancée 43." But the threat and indeed the reality of unrest among those concerned existed. General guidelines were all the more urgent, the correspondence pointed out, "because since creation of the German people's list three years have already gone by, but the biological increase of the population in a majority of cases has not let itself be halted by legal restrictions. At most such restrictions result in annoyance among those concerned when questions of this kind, which after all involve members of one and the same people's community, remain unresolved."[23] The head office of the Security Service (SD) replied in April 1944. Permission to marry was granted, under the condition that it follow relocation to the *Altreich* so that there would be no threat to the German upbringing of the children.[24]

When it came to Nazi family policy, women were anything but marginal. Indeed, issues of marriage occupied tremendous amounts of time and energy for officials at every level. Most thorny were those cases involving men in German uniform. General questions and individual appeals climbed up and down the chain of command with decisions being taken at various points, often in quite arbitrary ways. In late 1943 the district government president in Lodz appealed for clarification from the *Reichsstatthalter* in Posen regarding the prohibition on marriages between Germans and "aliens." "The number of cases is increasing," he wrote, "in which members of the Wehrmacht take a leave with the intention of marrying . . . , but then because they do not have certain permissions they have to return to their units without achieving their goal." As an example he pointed to a Latvian member of the police who wanted to marry a German settler. The man's German commander informed him that, according to the Führer's proclamation of 19 May 1943 (RGBl. 3.315), regarding acquisition of German citizenship through membership in the German Wehrmacht, the Waffen-SS, the German police, or the Organization Todt, he was a German. He was therefore permitted to marry a German settler. The policeman, however, did not have papers to prove his German citizenship, even though he clearly fell under the conditions described in the declaration. When he arrived at city hall, the clerk explained that without papers, he could do nothing. The man had no patience for that kind of thing. At the front he was a German, he

281

retorted, "so why not here at home?" He returned to Latvia furious, without settling his situation. A similar case involved an SS-Unter-sturmführer, an ethnic German citizen from Slovakia.[25]

Marriage requests could put Nazi officials in a position of having to choose between ideological purity and stability. By Supreme Command order of 28 January 1943 (O.K.W. AWA: J (Va) Nr. 13850/42), members of the Wehrmacht were not permitted to marry members of category III of the German people's list for the duration of the war. In November 1943, the mayor of Königshütte in Upper Silesia wrote to the office of the German people's list in Kattowitz requesting flexibility. The current situation produced both unnecessary work for bureaucrats and frustration among the population, he claimed. As a result of the prohibition, he explained, soldiers attempted to have their fiancées upgraded to a higher classification so that the marriages could take place. Usually such requests were rejected. Moreover, he indicated, the prohibition stood in direct contradiction to statements by Gauleiter Albert Forster, who had repeatedly stressed that members of category III were to be placed on the same footing as Germans with full citizenship.[26]

The president of the government of Upper Silesia had already addressed the same issue in a July 1943 letter to the Reich Ministry of the Interior. "Almost daily," he complained, "local offices of the German people's list receive requests for permission to marry for members of categories III and IV of the German people's list. Often it is members of the Wehrmacht, who after serving at the front, take a leave to come home to marry. Once at home, they encounter insurmountable barriers because their fiancées, often together with their parents, have been classified as category IV of the German people's list. In many such cases, a soldier has the understandable wish to give the mother of his children his name so that in case of death, she will be properly looked after." Change was crucial, he warned, because the current situation "only serves to further increase the unrest at the front and at home."[27] In matters of marriage for the Wehrmacht, gender-specific treatment of men as potential soldiers and women as reproducers merged.

REPRODUCTION

Any regime that regards its population above all as a weapon against others becomes obsessed with birthrates and maternity. Hitler's Germany was no exception. A 1944 report entitled "The Role of the

Woman in the Polish People's Struggle" expressed the Nazi preoccupation with reproduction and described prevailing attitudes toward female *Untermenschen*: "In the end every ethnic struggle is decided by the number of cradles that members of one or the other groups of people fills." Polish women, the report warned, posed a particular threat. Forbidden by their church to have abortions or use birth control, "the simple Polish woman . . . carries to term every child that she conceives: 'The Lord has sent it.'"[28]

This report was widely circulated among Nazi officials. Its derogation of Polish women focused on their reproductive powers: it argued that women, egged on by nationalist priests, spawned hordes of sneaky, dangerous Poles. It was women, the report accused, who attacked the Volksdeutschen of Poland with pitchforks and seduced German soldiers in order to infect them with syphilis and gonorrhea. Polish women's reproductive threat, according to the report, went beyond their biological powers: Polish mothers preserved Polishness abroad to the detriment of German ambitions everywhere.[29]

Nazi authorities did not merely identify the threat posed by supposedly inferior women and their wombs; they intervened against unwanted reproduction. Such measures and the policies behind them attacked women who were categorized as undesirable. According to a 1943 report by a Dr. Gallmeier, a Nazi expert on Latvia, outside the Reich German population policy meant above all breaking ties between ethnic Germans and members of alien ethnic groups and preventing new bonds that would bring foreign blood into the *Volk*. Gallmeier's central concerns reflected the perpetually expanding worries of Nazi population policy experts. On the one hand he fretted about people who possessed German blood but had become estranged from their roots: without intervention their valuable offspring would be lost to Germany forever. On the other he warned against illegitimate children whose Latvian mothers lied about the fathers' identities. Some women denied German fathers out of fear that their children would be taken away from them; others tried to pass off as German their sons and daughters by "bolshevik prisoners of war, refugees from the fronts, and riffraff of all kinds" in the hope of landing a German husband.[30] Nazi race and settlement adjudicators assumed that their job of locating and handling Volksdeutschen required them to investigate women's sexual pasts and determine the paternity of their offspring.

Programs of sterilization within the Reich have attracted considerable scholarly attention, but less is known about the expansion of such schemes with the conquest of territories to the east. However even the most committed proponents of sterilization as a "solution" to the Third Reich's self-made ethnic problems realized that it was not possible to prevent reproduction among tens of millions of Slavs. Accordingly the middle-level Nazi officials who managed ethnic policy on the ground in the occupied East concentrated on keeping undesirables out of the privileged category of ethnic Germans. In some cases they reclassified or disqualified women who had earlier been granted Volksdeutsche status when their offspring proved below standard; in other instances they separated mothers from their children in order to salvage one or the other for Germanness.

Files of the network of offices in Himmler's jurisdiction as Reich Commissar for the Strengthening of Germanness provide a wealth of information on individual cases. No matter, it seems, was too minor for concerted attention. In 1944 officials in the Reich Security Main Office itself determined that an ethnic German woman from Galicia could not participate in resettlement schemes unless she abandoned her two children from a previous marriage with a Jewish man. In this instance the woman was not judged an unfit mother; rather her children were deemed unworthy. They could only enter Germany as charges of the Reich Security Main Office, and only if they were sterilized.[31]

In 1944 as well, SS race experts in Wiesbaden plotted to reverse an earlier decision classifying a certain Ottilie Schumann from Czechoslovakia as an ethnic German. Schumann, the report claimed, was worthless, "dirty, asocial, and completely lacking in self-discipline." Twice divorced, the mother of four had a police record for immoral behavior and theft. A disgusted SS inspector described her home as a filthy "Gypsy camp." His solution to the problem Frau Schumann posed demonstrated the mutually reinforcing nature of Nazi sexism and racism. Schumann's equally undesirable common-law husband had not yet received classification as a Volksdeutscher. Why not encourage him to apply for permission to marry her? That request could be granted and at the same time the man's petition for Germanness refused. Then Schumann and her children could be stripped of their German citizenship.[32]

Nazi officials showed an often stunning arbitrariness when they categorized women as desirable or undesirable reproducers of German blood. Many files reveal that supposedly scientific distinctions of blood were in fact rather low on the list of criteria for defining Germanness. One such case involved two Polish sisters. One of the women received ethnic German status; the other did not. As of April 1944, Johanna and Danuta Wierzejska lived and worked near Kassel. Although their parents were "pure Polish," they applied for Germanization (*Eindeutschung*).[33] Authorities in Cholm approved Johanna's application, but their Lublin counterparts rejected Danuta. When her son by an SS man received Volksdeutsche status, Danuta, backed by her employer, SS-Standartenführer Richter, requested a review of her case.[34]

Richter called Danuta hardworking and expressed the hope that "German girls" too would possess such properties.[35] That endorsement, along with a note of support from the Race and Settlement Office in Berlin, failed to produce the necessary papers.[36] The only reason given for rejecting Danuta was that "she did not look so good." Her status caused practical problems because the sisters lived together. Under the terms of Nazi racial law, ethnic Germans such as Johanna were to eschew all social contact with Poles like Danuta whose passports were stamped with a "P."[37] Moreover Danuta's own child was not permitted interaction with his mother. By September 1944, despite a hefty correspondence in which conflicting photographs of Danuta changed hands and her boss stressed the value of her "German soul,"[38] nothing had been resolved. Authorities in Lodz requested copies of Johanna's papers,[39] and the Cracow Race and Settlement Office got involved as well. In the shuffle, some of Johanna's documents went missing and Danuta's files fell prey to conditions at the front.[40] Further details are unavailable. What is known, however, is that the practice of removing children assessed as ethnic Germans from mothers who received lower racial classifications was both widespread and enshrined in official policy.[41]

Control over women's reproduction provided a convenient tool for Nazi population policy. Both forced pregnancy and abortion became weapons against women deemed inferior. For example, SS inspectors assessed the racial potential of the fetuses of pregnant slave laborers in Germany. If the fetus was ruled "desirable," the woman was required to carry the pregnancy to term and submit the child for "Germanization"; if it was found "undesirable," she was forced to abort. Files of the SS-Race and Settlement Office's Wiesbaden branch contain the records of one particular inspector for early 1945. He traveled across southwestern Germany to appraise the claims to Germanness of people from Ukraine, Poland, and other parts of Europe. His report for January 1945 evaluated the racial potential of several fetuses.[42]

One particular case dragged on for months in 1943 and 1944. The SS

DORIS L. BERGEN

inspector assessed both a pregnant Polish slave laborer named Hedwig Sikora and her Polish lover, Richard Drapsala, as Germanizable, indeed as exemplary specimens. Sikora, however, wanted an abortion. Her request was denied on the grounds that her child would be a valuable member of the German *Volk*. Officials ordered Sikora to deliver the child and then be separated both from it and from its father. When Drapsala refused to abandon Sikora, Nazi agents reversed their previously glowing reports of him. He was devious and weak, they contended, and under the sway of Sikora, "a fanatical Polish nationalist." A new report recommended that neither one be admitted to the German *Volk*. Accordingly Sikora received permission for an abortion, only to have that decision reversed by a higher-ranking official. She married Drapsala in the late spring of 1944 and both submitted applications for Germanization.[43] The file does not specify further details.

Programs to assess the racial value of women, their fetuses, and their children showed no regard for the well-being of any of the individuals in question. In January 1945 the Arbeitsamt (Labor Office) in Dillenburg informed the SS Race and Settlement Office in Wiesbaden that a Polish woman laborer wished to terminate her pregnancy, now in the fourth month. SS authorities forbade an abortion on the grounds that the mother was "racially desirable"—part German—the father "tolerable." When the couple resisted Germanization, however, the SS official declared them of no interest; he would consider the child valuable only if it were separated from its parents. The pair agreed to apply for Germanization but dragged their feet, arguing that because they came from Kalisch, a German city before 1918, they were already Germans. The SS man was furious. That attitude, he complained, was typical of those "waiting to see what developments in the East will bring."[44] His final word on the case expressed the utter cynicism characteristic of Nazi ethnic policy. "It cannot be in our interest," he wrote, "to leave for the Polish world human material [*Menschenmaterial*] such as this case represents, in particular with respect to the German blood that is on hand here. In situations such as this, in my opinion, there must be only two possibilities: either extermination [*Vernichtung*] or absorption into Germandom [*Deutschtum*]."[45]

In some cases women and men tried to manipulate Nazi obsessions with reproductive issues to their own advantage. An ethnic German man, for example, wrote to the *Einwandererzentralstelle*—the SS office in charge of resettling ethnic Germans from the East—to complain about the farmwork his wife had been assigned. The couple had two small children and the woman was four months pregnant. "I assume," her husband wrote, "that when you number us as among the German race you have an interest in the growth of that race. I ask you gentlemen to release my wife from labor duty."[46]

More often, however, the conjunction of Nazi racism and sexism and the enormous bureaucratic energies backing it left its targets helpless. A well-documented case comes from the files of the Kripo in Bromberg (Bydgoszcz). In 1941 police found a female corpse in the nearby village of Mrotschen. Papers found next to the body identified the woman as an ethnic German cook named Gertrud Redmer. Redmer was three months pregnant. Investigation revealed that her sexual partner was a shoe-maker's apprentice named Emil Anders. Anders, also an ethnic German, was eleven years younger than the thirty-six-year-old Redmer. He had no intention of marrying her and paid a Polish co-worker named Chrabkowski 100 RM to arrange for an abortion.

Chrabkowski brought Redmer to see a local Polish woman named Susanna Wrona and served as an interpreter for the two women. Wrona's first attempt to terminate Redmer's pregnancy failed. On the second visit, 4 May 1941, Wrona injected Redmer with soapy water. In intense pain Redmer fainted, and Wrona panicked. She found Chrabkowski and the two of them dragged Redmer's body out of the flat to a bridge where they left her for dead. Later each testified that the other had killed Redmer as she lay unconscious on a sofa.[47]

Official correspondence on the case reveals a great deal about the vicious convergence of Nazi racism and sexism. Police reports characterized Wrona as a kind of crazed monster wallowing in her own filth and suggested that she may have strangled Redmer with the woman's own undergarments. Wrona, it turned out, had performed many abortions for Polish women. It was only when she dared to end the pregnancy of a certified ethnic German that she faced trouble. A German judge sentenced her to eight years in prison; Chrabkowski got a two-year term, and Anders was released. The judge's statement emphasized what he considered to be the severity of Wrona's crime: "Precisely here, in the incorporated eastern territories, anything that damages the power of the German *Volk* against the Polish population with its high birthrate is particularly dangerous and despicable. I therefore consider performing abortions on German women in this area to deserve an especially heavy punishment."[48] Nowhere did any of the police inspectors or judges involved address the death of Redmer as a human being. Instead her fatality represented simply one less ethnic German womb to bear children for the Reich.

Having intercourse, getting married, becoming pregnant, seeking an abortion, giving birth to a child—in the context of a system based on hierarchies of race and blood, all of these acts assumed enormous political proportions. Small wonder that one finds in the archives hints that some women cracked under the pressure. Might such strain be at least part of the explanation for the teenaged Polish girl who gave birth to her baby on a train and then flushed it down the toilet to its death? The relatively light sentence she received—one year in prison—reflected not leniency but dismissal on the part of German judges who considered both the woman and her baby beneath contempt.[49]

NOTES

I acknowledge with gratitude the generous support of the University of Vermont; the University of Notre Dame; the Max Planck Institute for History in Göttingen; the German Academic Exchange Service (DAAD); the Charles H. Revson Foundation for Research on the Holocaust Using Archival Materials from the Former U.S.S.R., Center for Advanced Holocaust Studies, United States Holocaust Memorial Museum; and the German Marshall Fund of the United States. Thanks also to Julia Douthwaite, Sandra Gustafson, and Glenn Hendler of the University of Notre Dame for comments on a draft.

1. See Gisela Bock, *Zwangssterilisation im Nationalsozialismus* (Opladen: Westdeutscher Verlag, 1986); also Lisa Pine, *Nazi Family Policy, 1933–1945* (Oxford and New York: Berg, 1997).

2. Claudia Koonz, *Mothers in the Fatherland* (New York: St. Martin's Press, 1987). Also influenced by Koonz's analysis is Alison Owings, *Frauen* (New Brunswick, N.J.: Rutgers University Press, 1993). On the debate between Koonz and Bock, see *Geschichte und Gesellschaft* 14, no. 3 (1988): 364 and 15, no. 4 (1989): 563.

3. On the process of defining Volksdeutschen, see Doris L. Bergen, "The Volksdeutschen of Eastern Europe, World War II, and the Holocaust," in *Germany and Eastern Europe, 1870–1996: Cultural Identities and Cultural Differences*, ed. Keith Bullivant, Geoffrey Giles, and Walter Pape (Berlin: Walter de Gruyter, forthcoming); also Götz Aly, *"Endlösung": Völkerverschiebung und der Mord an den europäischen Juden* (Frankfurt am Main: S. Fischer Verlag, 1995); Valdis O. Lumans, *Himmler's Auxiliaries: The Volksdeutsche Mittelstelle and the*

German National Minorities of Europe, 1939–1945 (Chapel Hill: University of North Carolina Press, 1993); and Robert L. Koehl, *RKFDV: German Resettlement and Population Policy, 1939–1945: A History of the Reich Commission for the Strengthening of Germandom* (Cambridge: Harvard University Press, 1957).

4. For example, Volksdeutsche appear as perpetrators in Alexander Donat's *The Holocaust Kingdom: A Memoir* (New York: Holt, Rinehart, and Winston, 1965); and Adina Blady Szwajger's *I Remember Nothing More: The Warsaw Children's Hospital and the Jewish Resistance* (London: Harvill, 1990).

5. Primo Levi, "The Gray Zone," in *The Drowned and the Saved*, trans. Raymond Rosenthal (New York: Vintage International, 1989).

6. In addition to the works of Bock on sterilization, an abundant literature addresses women as victims of National Socialism. Examples are Sigrid Jacobeit, *Kreuzweg Ravensbrück* (Cologne: Verlag für die Frau, 1987); *Ehemaliges Frauenkonzentrationslager Ravensbrück* (Berlin: Freie Universität Berlin, 1997). Less common but nevertheless available are works on women perpetrators, such as *Opfer und Täterinnen* (Nördlingen: F. Greno, 1987). A disproportionate number of works address women resisters: for example, Gerda Zorn, *Frauen gegen Hitler* (Berlin (West): VAS in der Elefantin Press, 1984). More recently there has been an increased interest in the everyday life of women under Nazism, but those works available in English and German focus almost exclusively on either European Jewish women or German gentiles: for example, *Frauenleben im NS Alltag* (Bonn: Frauen Museum, 1991).

7. This research was conducted at the Bundesarchiven in Koblenz, Berlin-Lichterfelde, and Potsdam (hereafter BA Koblenz, BA Berlin-Lichterfelde, BA Potsdam); the Bundesarchiv-Militärarchiv Freiburg (hereafter BA-MA Freiburg); the Institut für Zeitgeschichte in Munich (hereafter IFZ); the Hessisches Hauptstaatsarchiv Wiesbaden (hereafter HHStA Wiesbaden); the Center for the Preservation and Study of Documents of Recent History in Moscow (hereafter Osobyi); the Archiwum Panstwowe in Bydgoszcz, Lodz, and Poznan (hereafter AP Bydgoszcz, AP Lodz, AP Poznan); the Archive of the Main Commission for the Investigation of Crimes against the Polish Nation, the Institute of National Memory (hereafter AGK Warsaw); and the Archive of the United States Holocaust Memorial Museum Archives (hereafter USHMMA). I am grateful to the staffs of all these institutions for their assistance.

8. On the difficulties in identifying ethnic Germans and the implications of that ambiguity, see Bergen, "The Nazi Concept of 'Volksdeutsche' and the Exacerbation of Antisemitism in Eastern Europe, 1939–1945," *Journal of Contemporary History* 29, no. 4 (October 1994).

9. Klaus Theweleit, *Male Fantasies*, 2 vols. (Minneapolis: University of Minnesota Press, 1985), focuses on a different group of men at an earlier time, but offers perhaps at least an idea of the content of Nazi officials' images of women from groups deemed inferior.

10. Attachment to report from the Senior Commander, Eastern Division

(Oberbefehlshaber Ost), Headquarters Castle Spala, 6 February 1940, in BA-
MA Freiburg, RH 53–23/23, p. 28 in file.

11. On the subject of rapes at the end of the war, see Atina Grossmann, "A
Question of Silence," *October 72* (Spring 1995); Gertrud Koch, "Blood, Sperm,
and Tears," *October 72* (Spring 1995); and Marlene Epp, "Soviet and East European Mennonite Refugees and Rape in the Second World War," *Journal of
Women's History 9*, no. 1 (Spring 1997): 58–87.

12. Landrat, Kreisjugendamt, Bielitz (Oberschlesien), signed Buchwald, to
Zweigstelle der Deutschen Volksliste, Bielitz, 24 March 1944, Osobyi 1232/1/
36, 75.

13. Circular, Reichsminister des Innern, to Reichsstatthalter in den Reichsgauen (Landesregierungen), Regierungspräsidenten, Polizeipräsidenten in Berlin, Gesundheitsämter, "Betr.: Bekämpfung der Geschlechtskrankheiten. Ärzt-
liche Betreuung der fremdvölkischen Prostituierten," Berlin, 24 October 1942,
1–2, AP Poznan/299 (Reichsstatthalter)/2161 (Bekämpfung der Geschlechtskrankheiten 1942–43).

14. Oberkommando der Wehrmacht, signed i.A. Dr. Handloser, to various,
including OKH/S In; OKM/AMA/G; Reichsführer SS; Wehrmachtbefehls-
haber, Berlin, 27 January 1943, in various places, 4–5, AP Poznan/299/2161,
pp. 23–24.

15. Reichsstatthalter, signed Greiser, to Höheren SS- und Polizeiführer beim
Reichsstatthalter in Posen, Posen, 25 September 1940, "Betrifft Umgang der
deutschen Bevölkerung des Reichsgaues Wartheland mit Polen," 2, USHMMA
RG-15.029M.

16. Propaganda films comparing Jews to rats, such as the notorious "Der
Ewige Jude," and bus tours through the ghettos sponsored by the Nazi leisure
agency Strength through Joy, during which Germans could see the "subhuman"
existence of the Jews, all served to create an image of Jewish women as beneath
sexual interest. See document 786, report by Polish government in exile regarding Warsaw, May 1942, in Jeremy Noakes and Geoffrey Pridham, *Nazism: A
History in Documents and Eyewitness Accounts, 1919–1945*, 2 vols. (New York:
Schocken, 1988), 2:1069. On the film, see Yizhak Ahren et al., *"Der Ewige
Jude": Wie Goebbels hetzte* (Aachen: Alano Verlag, 1990).

17. See, for example, Judith Magyar Isaacson, *Seed of Sarah: Memories of a
Survivor* (Urbana: University of Illinois Press, 1990), esp. 44 and 61.

18. Judgment, signed Raasch and two others, "Wegen Blutschande," 2–3,
AP Bydgoszcz 80/248, 25–26.

19. Dr. Gurtner, Reich Ministry of Justice: "Verabschiedung des Gesetz-
entwurfs über die Eheschließung Deutscher mit Ausländern durch die Reichsre-
gierung," BA Potsdam 51.01/23544, 3.

20. "Berichte der Kommandos der Einsatzgruppe D über das Schwarzmeer-
deutschtums, Vertrauensmänner der Russlanddeutschen Umsiedler in einzelnen
Kreises des Warthegaues," Appendix 3, "Rayonbericht," no date or signature,

re: Rayon Cudovo, in Gebiet Leningrad, 7–8, in AP Lodz L-3578/10, 8; also in same file, 11: SS-Untersturmführer Dr. W. Gradmann to Leiter der EWZ SS-Oberstumbannführer von Malsen, "Vermerk" re: "Bericht über das im Reichssicherheitshauptamt vorliegender Material über die Deutschen im Schwarzmeergebiet," to which this appendix is attached, Berlin, 12 November 1941, 2.

21. Chef der Sicherheitspolizei und des SD Einwandererzentralstelle, signed SS-Oberstumbannführer v. Malsen, "Anordnung Nr. 219," Litzmannstadt, 27 January 1944, re: "Schleusung volksdeutscher Umsiedler aus Russland," AP Lodz L-3578/10, 22–40.

22. Oberpräsident der Provinz Oberschlesien to Reichssicherheitshauptamt, SS Standartenführer Ehlich, re: "Ehegenehmigung zwischen Angehörigen der Abt. 3 und 4 der DVL. Einzelfall Tynior-Walla," Kattowitz, 25 January 1944, Osobyi 1232/1/28, 41.

23. Ibid.

24. Chef der Sicherheitspolizei und des SD to Oberpräsidenten der Provinz Oberschlesien, 14 April 1944, Osobyi 1232/1/28, 71.

25. Regierungspräsident von Litzmannstadt, "Vermerk" and drafts of correspondence to Reichsstatthalter in Posen, Litzmannstadt, 1 November 1943, 2, AP Lodz, Bestand 176 (Akt Rejencji Lodzkiej/Regierungspräsident von Litzmannstadt, 1940–1945)/363 (Anordnungen betr. Verbot der Eheschliessungen zwischen deutschen und Polen), 75–77.

26. Oberbürgermeister der Stadt Königshütte Oberschlesien to Regierungspräsidenten, Bezirksstellen der DVL, Kattowitz, Königshütte, 8 November 1943, Osobyi 1232/1/28, 85.

27. Oberpräsident der Provinz Oberschlesien to Reich Minister of the Interior, Kattowitz, 29 July 1943, Osobyi 1232/1/28, 86.

28. Undated report [1944], "Die polnische Frau im Volkstumskampf," 4–6, in BA Koblenz R59/65/fiche 2, 60–62. An additional copy is located at the AGK Warsaw, Reichsstatthalter im Warthegau/352. A cover letter from the Sicherheitsdienst of the Reichsführer-SS, SD-Leitabschnitt Posen, to Reichsstatthalter, Posen, 26 July 1944, says: "This report was assembled from material seized from Polish partisan groups since 1939 in addition to information from Polish publications before and after 1918."

29. Ibid., 8–13/fiche 2, 64–69.

30. Regierungsrat Dr. Gallmeier, "Die Aufgaben deutscher Volkstumspolitik in Lettland," Riga, 29 December 1943, 1–2, USHMMA RG 18.002M, reel 2, 262.

31. SS-Oberstumbannführer (signature illegible) to Reichskommissar für die Festigung deutschen Volkstums—Stabshauptamt—Schweiklberg/Post Vilshofen Ndb., 10 February 1944, IFZ NO 5342. For another case of an ethnic German woman who had been married to a Jewish man and had children by him, see Anna Lokczynski to Reichsstatthalter Greiser, Kalisch, 18 November 1941, in AGK Warsaw, Reichsstatthalter im Warthegau/255, 53. In this case

the mother renounced her husband but tried to save the children by claiming they were not his.

32. Höhere SS- und Polizeiführer Rhein-Westmark, Fürsorgekommando/ RuS-Wesen, to Geheime Staatspolizei Staatspolizeistelle Darmstadt, Wiesbaden, 14 October 1944, HHStA, 483/11375. In same file, see also Sicherheitsdienst des Reichsführers SS, SD Abschnitt Frankfurt/M, to Geheime Staatspolizei Staatspolizeistelle Kassel, 26 October 1943, re: Protektoratsangehörigen Arbeiter Karl Patocka.

33. SS-Sturmbannführer Pfefferberg, Höhere SS- und Polizeiführer im Bereich des Wehrkreises IX, to the Rasse und Siedlungshauptamt-SS, Aussenstelle, Litzmannstadt, Kassel, 15 April 1944, USHHMA RG 15.021M, reel 6, folder 38, 77.

34. SS- und Polizeiführer im Distrikt Lublin, Volksdeutsche Mittelstelle, der Kreisbeauftragte, to the Rasse- und Siedlungsamt, Litzmannstadt, Lublin, 17 April 1944, USHMMA RG 15.021M, reel 6, folder 38, 79.

35. Hans-Joachim Richter, Arolsen, 6 June 1944, USHMMA RG 15.021M, reel 6, folder 38, 81.

36. Schwalm, Chef des Rasse- und Siedlungshauptamtes-SS: Der Stabsführer, to Leiter der Außenstelle L'Stdt, des RuS-HA-SS, SS-Stubaf. Dongus, Berlin, 29 June 1944, USHMMA RG 15.021M, reel 6, folder 38, 86.

37. Höhere SS- und Polizeiführer im Bereich des Wehrkreises IX, Der SS-Führer im Rasse- und Siedlungswesen, to Rasse- und Siedlungshauptamt-SS Aussenstelle, Litzmannstadt, Arolsen, 6 July 1944, USHMMA RG 15.021M, reel 6, folder 38, 87.

38. RuS Außenstelle, Litzmannstadt, to SS-Standartenführer Hans-Joachim Richter, Arolsen/Waldeck, Litzmannstadt, 8 July 1944; Richter, Arolsen, 13 July 1944; Richter to the Rasse- und Siedlungshauptamt, Nebenstelle Litzmannstadt, Arolsen, 6 June 1944; Richter to Sturmbannführer Dongus, RuS, Außenstelle, Litzmannstadt, Arolsen, 13 July 1944; SS-Hauptsturmführer, Der Stabsführer der Außenstelle, RuS, to Richter, Litzmannstadt, 19 July 1944; all in USHMMA RG 15.021M, reel 6, folder 38, 88–92.

39. SS-Hauptsturmführer, RuS, to the Höhere-SS- und Polizeiführer "Fulda-Werra," Kassel, 1 September 1944; SS-Führer im RuS, to RuS Aussenstelle, Litzmannstadt; and Richter to RuS, Litzmannstadt, Arolsen, 4 September 1944, USHMMA RG 15.021M, reel 6, folder 38, 94–96.

40. SS-Hauptsturmführer, Chef der Sicherheitspolizei und des S.D., Einwandererzentralstelle, to RuS, Aussenstelle Litzmannstadt, Cracow, 21 November 1944, USHMMA RG 15.021M, reel 6, folder 38, 103.

41. Circular from Reichsführer SS und Chef der Deutschen Polizei, Reichskommissar für die Festigung Deutschen Volkstums, to a whole series of addressees, including die Obersten Reichsbehörden; the Länderregierungen (except for Prussia); Reichsstatthalter; Gauleiter; Oberpräsidenten und Regierungspräsidenten in Preußen; Höheren SS- und Polizeiführer; Staatspo-

lizei(leit)stellen; and others, Berlin, 16 February 1942, 3, BA Koblenz R 18/ 5468/fiche 2, 163.

42. SS-Oberscharführer Reinhold Ratzeburg: "Dienstreisebericht 2/45," Wiesbaden, 28 January 1945, HHStA Wiesbaden 483/7360, 1–2.

43. Höh. SS- und Pol. Führer Rhein/Westmark, Der RuS-Führer, signed SS-Sturmbannführer, [Rödel] to Befehlshaber der Sicherheitspolizei und des SD, Wiesbaden, 5 January 1945, "Betr.: Polnischen Volkszugehörigen Richard Drapsala, geb. 10.7.21, eingesetzt bei Landwirt L. Hillarich in Lorbach, Kr. Büdingen," HHStA Wiesbaden 483/7324. See also in same file: Aktennotiz, signed SS-Sturmbannführer, Wiesbaden, 4 January 1945; and in HHStA Wiesbaden 483/7362, 62–75, including letter from NSDAP, Kreisleitung Büdingen, Gau Hessen-Nassau, dated 19 September 1944, to NSDAP, Gauleitung Hessen-Nassau, Gauamt f. Volkstumsfragen, Frankfurt/Main. More on the case in HHStA Wiesbaden 483/7262, 87–100, under name of Hedwig Sikora.

44. Arbeitsamt Dillenburg, 2 January 1944 [should be 1945]; response from SS-Sturmbannführer Rödel, Höhere SS- und Polizeiführer Rhein/Westmark, SS-Führer im RuS–Wesen, to Reichsärztekammer, Bezirksstelle Gießen/Lahn, Wiesbaden, 15 February 1945; Rödel to Jugendamt des Landkreises Dillenburg, 16 February 1945; Rödel to NSDAP Gauamtsleitung Hessen, Amt für Volkswohlfahrt Frankfurt/Main, 16 February 1945; and orange cards (Hauptuntersuchung) for the Lisiaks, 2 February 1945; all in HHStA Wiesbaden 483/ 11374.

45. Rödel to Gauamt für Volkstumsfragen, 15 February 1945, HHStA Wiesbaden 483/11374.

46. Stanislaw Musialek to Einwandererzentralstelle, Rasse und Siedlungsamt, Aussenstelle Litzmannstadt, Selbach b. Sachsenhausen, n.d., USHMMA RG 15.021 M, reel 3, file 20AII, 289.

47. Staatliche Kriminalpolizei—Kriminalpolizeistelle Bromberg to Oberstaatsanwalt, 6 May 1941, AP Bydgoszcz 80/506, 1.

48. Oberstaatsanwalt Herder als Leiter der Anklagebehörde beim Sondergericht to Reichsminister der Justiz, "Handakten zu der Strafsache gegen Wrona," Bromberg, 28 July 1941, AP Bydgoszcz 80/506.

49. AP Bydgoszcz 1561/38.

Social Outcasts in War and Genocide

A COMPARATIVE PERSPECTIVE

OMER BARTOV

THE LINKS between war, genocide, and the formation and reconstruction of collective and individual identity in the twentieth century are both obvious and extremely complex. A great deal has been written on the connection between modern, industrial, total war, and the phenomenon of mass murder of civilian populations.[1] There is also a rich literature on the relationship between war and national identity[2] as well as on the effects of this century's traumatic events on individual psychology.[3] And yet most commentators have tended to focus on discrete national or thematic perspectives: the German invasion of the Soviet Union as a necessary context for the Holocaust,[4] the impact of Nazism on postwar German or Jewish identity,[5] the so-called Vichy syndrome in France,[6] the psychological and ideological makeup of perpetrators and victims, collaborators and bystanders.[7] What remains missing is a synthesis of the innumerable elements and infinitely complex links that, when looked at as a whole, have made for that uniquely modern phenomenon of both perpetrating unprecedented material and mental destruction and re-creating collective and individual identities from the debris of man-made devastation.

What follows is a brief summary of my attempt elsewhere to grapple with this issue.[8] This is not a synthesis of the twentieth century as a whole; rather, it touches on a few of the main events, protagonists, and questions related to my central theme. It is, however, an argument about the merits of viewing this century as a period in which the actions and perceptions of various groups and individuals reflected one another in what became a vicious circle whose single most crucial characteristic was the link between destruction and construction. What interests me, then, is not a total history of the period but rather an analysis of what I perceive to be a central dynamic of the modern era, namely, its predilection to transform the discourse on identity into an annihilatory process in which one's image of oneself was forged through the distorting mirror image of the other. Finally, I should note that although I have focused primarily on Germany, France, and the Jews, I believe that many of the issues raised in these cases have a more general relevance for our understanding of a central feature of the twentieth century.

I

My first theme concerns the glorification of violence. Much has been said about the enthusiasm with which European nations marched to war in 1914.[9] But of greater significance for the future was the effect of the war's grim realities on a whole generation. For the image of battle as a glorious charge over a field of flowers was replaced by a glorification of the frontline soldiers' suffering as the true expression of the nation's vital qualities and as a model to be emulated by postwar society. And since this image was forged in the midst of slaughter, it contained all the ingredients of violence, aggression, and anxiety characteristic of fighting. Moreover, because World War I was fought by anonymous masses of conscripts, it was ultimately personalized through the figure of the "unknown soldier," who both embodied the nameless fallen and incarnated the nation's perception of past and future conflict. And yet both the view of the past and the expectation of the future were articulated very differently in France and Germany. For the French, the unknown soldier symbolized loss and mourning and the need to avoid any future carnage. Conversely, in Germany, rather than entombing the unknown soldier in a national sepulcher, both the unknown fallen and the survivors came to be perceived as messengers of a future war that would reverse the verdict of the past and bring to the nation the glory it had lost by defeat and betrayal.[10]

These polar readings of the war experience were expressed in the establishment of very different communities of war veterans in France and Germany. French veterans associations saw themselves—and by extension, the whole nation—as a community of suffering. While they glorified individual heroism and martyrdom, they conceived their primary goal as preventing the recurrence of war. For their part, German veterans associations saw themselves as the representatives of the battle community, whose qualities of unity, camaraderie, and sacrifice were to serve as an example for the rest of society as it prepared for the challenge of inevitable future struggles. From the *Kampfgemeinschaft* (battle community) of the front, animated by the intensity and purity of the *Fronterlebnis* (front experience), was to spring the *Volksgemeinschaft* (the national or "racial" community), whose invincible solidarity would be accomplished through ruthless exclusion of all that threatened its purity. Hence, while the French community of suffering strove to banish war, the German battle community was geared to banish the polluting elements that had caused defeat and thereby to establish a "racial community" purged of domestic enemies and capable of overcoming all foreign foes.[11]

This naturally influenced the manner in which the next war was imagined. French fear of war led to the establishment of the Maginot line, which was intended either to dissuade the enemy from attacking or at least to prevent the human and material cost of World War I.[12] German conceptualizations of a battle of annihilation (*Vernichtungsschlacht*) and total war, dating well before 1914, were expanded in the 1920s and 1930s to a concept of a war of extermination (*Vernichtungskrieg*) whereby not only enemy armies but whole populations would need to be wiped out in order to ensure victory.[13] Moreover, the precondition for the successful conduct of such a war was supposed to be a massive purge of German society itself so as to prevent the recurrence of what was believed to have been the "stab in the back" of 1918. Following Hitler's "seizure of power," the newly established Wehrmacht became the embodiment of the mythical battle community and the tool for the practice of annihilatory warfare, inculcating in its troops the notion that Germany's salvation depended on the ruthless extermination of its domestic and foreign, military and civilian, political and "biological" enemies.[14] Even more radically, the SS based its very identity on a concept of honor defined as the ability to commit genocide while—as Himmler put it—remaining "decent." It was at this point that the community of battle was finally transformed into a community of murder, one of whose most powerful adhesives was the consciousness that it was involved in a horrendous crime which could only remain "a glorious page in history" if Germany won the war.[15]

French fear of war was closely linked to the debacle of 1940 and the initial support for Pétain's regime. But it was under Vichy that violence came to be glorified once more, both by the regime, which became complicit in murder and genocide, and by the Resistance, which expanded in the last two years of the war.[16] Precisely because violence was practiced by both sides in the Franco-German wars, and because France went on to conduct a number of murderous colonial wars after the Liberation, it became all the more necessary to erect a myth of universal, heroic resistance to Nazism as a convenient prism through which to view a dubious past.[17] Hence too the strong reaction to this myth in the last two decades by those who have claimed that it merely acted as a cover for ideological and opportunistic collaboration or for cowardly accommodation with the Nazis.[18]

Postwar Germany sought to redefine the relationship between violence and national honor by presenting itself as a bulwark against Communism—both under Hitler and in NATO—and in glorifying the attempted assassination of Hitler on 20 July 1944, by a few generals and civilians, as an act which saved the army's shield of honor and confirmed its postwar claim of having served as a haven from and a domestic bulwark to Nazism.[19] Since the Wehrmacht represented a vast share of Germany's male population, it was impossible to concede that it had conducted a war of destruction and annihilation without thereby leveling accusations of collective guilt against postwar Germany. Indeed, even today such arguments are met with anger or at least skepticism in wide circles in Germany.[20]

II

My second theme concerns the links between violence and illusion. The reigning illusion in 1930s France was that war could somehow be averted. Although this hope was shared across the political spectrum, it brought conflict rather than unity. Widespread pacifist sentiments were accompanied by growing xenophobia and militant domestic politics. Fear of war only enhanced the urge to suppress those perceived as harbingers of international conflict and agents of foreign foes.[21] Following the debacle of 1940, collaboration was encouraged both by the illusion of sharing power with Germany and by the illusion of sparing France from the devastation of war. Both these goals seemed to necessitate purging the nation of its alleged domestic enemies. Yet Vichy's illusion of rejuvenating France by both reversing history and becoming a junior partner of the Reich disintegrated under the pressures of German exploitation and increasing Pétainist authoritarianism and violence. Growing resistance to Vichy and the Germans, and the brutal deportations of political opponents and "racial" undesirables, made a mockery of Pétain's rhetoric of uniting the nation.[22]

The final illusion of the Occupation was that of self-liberation. This was the tenuous basis on which the myth of the Resistance was constructed, and the reason that it lasted until well into the 1970s had more to do with the need to refashion a confident sense of national identity after a period of civil strife that lasted from the riots of 1934 to the end of the Algerian War in 1962 than with ignorance about the true realities of Vichy.[23] But even after the collapse of the myth, France has had great difficulty in coming to terms with the past, since behind the façade of heroism was nothing less than complicity in genocide. Considering France's self-appointed role as the carrier of universal humanistic values, for many this has not been an acceptable mirror in which to see their nation's reflection. Hence the recent tendency to universalize victimhood, and the rejection of the alleged Jewish inclination to over-emphasize the Holocaust at the cost of all other cases of atrocity and genocide.[24]

France thus prefers to see itself mirrored in the heroism and solidarity of World War I rather than in the turmoil and confusion of Vichy. The renewed fascination with 1914–1918 has been manifested in the expansion of scholarly studies as well as in the popularity of some works of fiction.[25] Among the latter, Jean Rouaud's novel *Fields of Glory* stands out as a best-selling rumination on the memory of an event presented as a crucial episode in the creation of a modern French identity, seen through the prism of several generations of the same family.[26] Yet just as World War I leads inevitably to Vichy, so too the loss and trauma of 1914–1918 are intimately linked to shattered identities of the Holocaust. A considerable number of memoirs and works of fiction (or combinations thereof) have tried to grapple with the relationship between individual identity and the historical cataclysms of the century, as illustrated, for example, by such remarkable works as Albert Camus' *The First Man* and George Perec's *W or The Memory of Childhood*.[27] Indeed, one of the most devastating legacies of our century is the loss of parents in war or mass murder, and consequently the loss of childhood memory and identity.[28] The case of Jewish children who were converted and handed over by their parents to Christian institutions during the Holocaust is possibly the most telling instance of lost and regained identity in conditions of war and genocide. As we read in Saul Friedländer's *When Memory Comes* and in Shlomo Breznitz's *Memory Fields*, such children were compelled to construct an identity for themselves with hardly any references to their past.[29] In this, however, they are also an example of the extraordinary recuperative powers of humanity in the aftermath of self-inflicted catastrophe.

III

My third theme concerns the phenomenon of elusive enemies. If total war and genocide destroy identity, they are also about establishing it by means of defining enemies and making victims.[30] This process, which is inherent in the emergence of the nation-state, greatly intensified in the aftermath of World War I, when an initial sense of national solidarity was transformed into a quest for those responsible for the slaughter. Here too, however, we find a marked difference between France and Germany. In interwar France the nation's domestic enemies remained elusive in the sense that no consensus could be reached about their identity. This reflected increasing civil strife which hampered preparation for war, but it also prevented the concerted persecution of any single group, despite the expansion of antisemitism in the 1930s.[31] Conversely, in Germany the defeat was increasingly attributed to the Jews, who came to be seen as exemplary of the nation's pernicious outsiders.[32] Nazism further constructed "the Jew" as the elusive enemy par excellence, in that the obsession with racial purity made everyone suspect of some Jewish heritage, just as the only way to determine "Aryan" identity was by proving the absence of any Jewish ancestry.[33]

While Nazi definitions of "the Jew" owed much to the antisemitic discourse of the turn of the century, the Zionist movement was also greatly influenced by antisemitic characterizations of the Jewish Diaspora as abnormal. Indeed, Zionism aimed at "normalizing" Jewish existence by taking the Jews out of the Diaspora—into a Jewish national state—and by taking the Diaspora out of the Jews—by eradicating their alleged physical and mental deformities attributed to life in the Exile.[34] In this sense, both Nazism and Zionism perceived "the Jew" as the enemy within, with the important distinction that the Nazi solution for the "Jewish question" was to murder the Jews, while the Zionist solution was to establish a Jewish state.

Nazi constructions of "the Jew" were predicated on the notion that Germany was the victim of the Jews even while the regime was murdering them en masse. Indeed, the Nazi notion of German identity required the existence of "the Jew" just as much as the eradication of the Jews was an ideological sine qua non perceived as a moral imperative rather than as a crime. Thus the Jews had to be wiped out and yet were necessary as an ideological adhesive and the ultimate justification for Nazi rule. This dynamic meant that the nihilistic tendencies of Nazism could not come to an end even if all the Jews were murdered. By killing the Jews, Nazism both accomplished its self-appointed world-historical task and undercut its raison d'être; hence it would always have to find more "Jews" to kill.[35]

At the core of modern genocide is a ubiquity of perpetrators and victims and the frequent confusion between them. This confusion of categories is also characteristic of coming to terms with genocide and re-creating identity following the catastrophe. In the immediate aftermath of the war, Germans saw themselves as victims of destruction, perpetrated on them both by Hitler and by his enemies. They thus associated themselves with their own victims while displacing the latter in favor of their own suffering; at the same time, they associated Germany's victims with the agents of its destruction.[36] This process of inversion and continuity enabled Germany to forge a new identity both related to its past and cleansed of responsibility for its crimes.[37] At the center of this re-scripting of the past stood the figure of "the Nazi," who now replaced "the Jew" as the nation's elusive enemy, being both everywhere and no-where, potentially lurking in everyone yet ultimately unrecognizable as anyone; in other words, "the Nazi" as an un-German outsider.[38] This image greatly diminished the sphere of the perpetrators and greatly enhanced the sphere of the victims to include almost everyone.[39]

If Germany constructed a universe of ubiquitous victims, France became a community of martyrs. Pétain's regime had tried to present the nation as the victim of its domestic enemies, among whom the Jews featured most prominently. Hence the swiftness with which Vichy passed the antisemitic Jewish Statutes.[40] Yet Vichy, too, failed to accomplish a national consensus about the identity of the enemy within. Indeed, by the latter part of the Occupation and during the Liberation, it was the collaborators who came to be seen as France's elusive enemies.[41] But as de Gaulle realized, national unity could only be achieved by claiming that, by and large, the nation as a whole had been martyred by a few traitors from within and especially by foreign conquest. This made it impossible to highlight the unique fate of the Jews lest it qualify France's unifying self-presentation as a martyred nation. Hence the transformation of the Jews into the status of elusive victims, whose victimhood could not be dissociated from that of the nation as a whole.[42]

On the face of it, as far as the Jews were concerned, there was nothing elusive about their enemies. But both the scale of the enormity, and the tremendous difficulty of reestablishing individual and collective identity, have led to painful controversies about the distinctions between enemies and the victims. Hence the furor over Hannah Arendt's argument regarding the bureaucratic and nonideological motivation of the perpetrators, and the complicity of the victims in their own genocide.[43] Hence too the rejection by the guardians of the Zionist version of the Holocaust at Yad Vashem of Raul Hilberg's assertions about the bureaucratic nature of the process and the passivity of the victims.[44] Arendt and Hilberg made the Jews into their own elusive enemies—due to their inability to adapt to the new circumstances of modern genocide—and portrayed the perpetrators as an elusive bureaucratic, faceless entity. Conversely, their Zionist opponents described them as "self-hating Jews," that is, the proverbial elusive enemy of modern Jewish existence. Ironically, Zionism was haunted by the same vision of the Jews' having "gone like sheep to the slaughter" and for this reason repeatedly stressed the Jewish resistance at the expense of the multitudes of defenseless victims who had no means of opposing the Nazi onslaught. This was consistent with the Zionist argument that Diaspora Jewry was doomed, whereas the resisters were identified with the new, fighting Israeli. Indeed, Israeli society was in fact preoccupied with alleged Jewish collaborators even before the 1961 Eichmann trial which sparked off the Arendt controversy, as can be seen from the Kasztner affair of the 1950s. Hence the anger with which Arendt's and Hilberg's views were met had more to do with their having publicized them in a wider, that is, gentile, context, rather than remaining within the framework of a domestic Jewish dispute. In this sense, they were the enemy within.[45]

In more general terms, what makes the Holocaust so resistant to human understanding is the elusiveness of both its perpetrators and its victims. The former because of the bureaucratic and detached manner in which they *organized* genocide, the latter because the vast majority of them disappeared without a trace and the few who survived have been torn between the urgent need to recount their experience and the terror of plunging into infinite despair by evoking it again. Moreover, we recognize that there can be no relationship between the crime and the punishment, and that while many perpetrators have walked away from their crimes without paying any price, many of the survivors have been consumed by a sense of guilt for having been "saved" while the vast majority "drowned."[46]

That the victim trope is a central feature of modern genocide can be demonstrated by reference to a variety of mass murders throughout the twentieth century, ranging from the Armenian genocide in World War I to genocide and ethnic cleansing in Rwanda, Bosnia, and Kosovo in the

1990s.[47] It is also, of course, a crucial component of coming, or of avoiding coming, to terms with guilt and responsibility. This can be seen not only in the case of Germany and France but also in that of Japan, which has presented itself as the victim of nuclear attack rather than as the perpetrator of mass crimes in China and elsewhere.[48] The victim trope is, moreover, central to the process of establishing or reestablishing identity after atrocity and catastrophe. But an identity based on victimhood is constantly on the lookout for perpetrators who must be victimized in turn. It is thus part of the same mechanism that produced victims in the first place.

IV

My fourth and last theme concerns the issue of apocalyptic visions. In 1932 the German legal theorist and political philosopher Carl Schmitt articulated what he called a "concept of the political" predicated on a friend-and-enemy relationship between and within states, whose ultimate manifestation was the willingness to die and kill in war against a recognized collective enemy. This, to his mind, gave politics, and therefore the state, the meaning and commitment that ultimately makes for human existence.[49] Not surprisingly, Schmitt ended up providing the legal and philosophical legitimization for the Nazi regime and, by extension, for its genocidal policies.[50] But the roots of his argument and the reasons for its impact must be sought in a wider context of apocalyptic visions that determined the manner in which war, genocide, and identity were conceptualized in the twentieth century.

Apocalyptic visions combine notions of utter desolation with aspirations of a utopian future; they are expressions of the urge to remake humanity by means of unmaking the present and erasing the heritage of the past. Hence utopia sets up boundaries between reality and vision, the familiar and the alien, and perceives transgression as a threat to harmony even as it establishes itself by transgressing conventional norms and practices. Modern utopias strive to control and direct not only social structures but also natural forces and biological evolution. They legitimize themselves by claiming to have discovered the laws of nature and history and by their assertion of channeling them toward their natural destination of ultimate perfection.[51]

Since the modern era is preoccupied with the idea of remaking man and society, nature and the environment, according to precisely laid out plans, it has also manifested a tendency to eradicate resistance to such schemes, perceiving it as regressive, reactionary, degenerate, or abnormal. While asserting compliance with its laws, modern utopianism postulates the need to tamper with nature or change the course of history, and to order the elimination of those who do not fit into nature's plan or the unfolding of history. Hence the view that conventional morality is inherently immoral if it obstructs the higher morality of leading humanity into an idyllic future.[52]

Images of an idyllic future, however, are informed by recollections of a mythical past, just as they require erasing the reality and memory of the present so as to facilitate the emergence of a new world. Thus the construction of utopia requires a radical reorganization of the past and control over historical records, their keepers and interpreters. But along with self-imposed amnesia, utopia legitimizes and sustains itself through vivid but highly selective memories. Such memories are contained not only in historical documents and personal recollections but also in collections of artifacts. And since utopia both aspires to overcome the past and needs to retain a link to it—if only so as to manifest its superiority— it cannot desist from collecting and presenting its relics, even as they indicate its own murderous roots. Thus the Nazis collected items for a museum of Judaica while they were simultaneously exterminating the Jews.[53]

Indeed, utopias offer final solutions to perennial questions of human existence. If nineteenth-century utopian schemes sketched out the path of modern utopia, totalitarian utopia was finally propelled into existence by the event of total, industrial war, which combined modern science and technology, universal mobilization of soldiers and workers, and an elaborate surveillance apparatus geared to control and mold the conduct and mind of the public. Totalitarianism evolved from the crises it claimed to resolve, offering a final solution to humanity's ills predicated on the proven ability to eradicate everything that could not or would not be suppressed, healed, or transformed. Here the goal was not mere control, but making control unnecessary by re-creating humanity in a manner that would ensure its acceptance of and active participation in the new society. Totalitarianism is modern utopia par excellence; obsessed with mobilizing mass society and employing the most sophisticated technological means and administrative practices to establish its rule, it simultaneously strives to put an end to history and to prevent any movement beyond what it perceives as the utopian phase. Once the ideal has been achieved, nothing should be allowed to undermine it; once the

303

undesirable classes have been eliminated, the polluting races exterminated, the old elites smashed, the history and memory of past events
erased or rewritten, time must come to a standstill. From this point on,
change can only spell subversion.[54]

Modern war and totalitarianism therefore necessitate and devise final
solutions in which humanity is perceived as a mass of matter to be
molded, controlled, moved, purged, and annihilated. This conceptualization of the world biologizes society and sociologizes biology; humanity becomes an organism in need of radical surgery, or a social construct
in need of extreme sociological reordering. Hence the vast population
transfers, brutal operations of ethnic cleansing, eradication of whole
social classes, and ultimately outright genocide, the most final solution
of all.[55]

The most drastic attempt to bring redemption to (part of) humanity
by means of a murderous final solution was the Holocaust. And yet, although the genocide of the Jews has been recognized as an event of
apocalyptic dimensions, there is no unanimity as to its lessons.[56] Indeed,
debates on the meanings and implications of the Holocaust reflect a variety of opinions about collective and individual identity, the nature of
man and history, morality and civilization.[57]

Four areas may be marked out as particularly significant in this context. First, in the sphere of *politics and ideology*, it has been assumed that
since the Holocaust was perpetrated by a racist totalitarian regime, its
enemies were committed to eradicating genocide. The democracies,
however, waged war against Germany primarily to protect their own political and strategic interests.[58] Moreover, the "Final Solution" was organized and implemented in a manner consistent with the structures of
contemporary modern states.[59] The notion that the best guarantee
against a recurrence of genocide is a firm belief in progress, science, and
the rule of law can hardly be maintained considering the rhetoric of im-
proving humanity, the rational scientific assertions, and the reasonable
legal arguments that were crucial to legitimizing, organizing, and implementing the Holocaust.[60]

Second, the cataclysmic nature of the Holocaust has prompted profound disagreements over its *theological and moral lessons*. Having occa-
sioned a final break with God by some Jews, the Holocaust has impelled
others to seek religious comfort in the face of man-made atrocity and to
reassert Jewish survival and continuity by adhering to Judaic tradition.[61]
Conversely, the complicity in, or indifference to, Nazi policies of many
established Christian churches has led both to denial and to belated ad-

missions of guilt. It is also true, however, that individual Christians were at times motivated by their faith to resist Nazism and rescue victims, and that some of the Christian clergy attempted to set moral limits to inhumanity.[62]

On the moral plane, the German sociologist Wolfgang Sofsky has argued that the exercise of absolute power in the camps caused the total disintegration of morality among the inmates.[63] To the contrary, the French critic Tzvetan Todorov has defended the existence of moral life in the concentration camps as a guide for posterity.[64] Todorov identifies moral life in the camps by considering the wider context in which the "concentrationary universe" was established; Sofsky rejects the possibility of morality in the camps by viewing them in isolation from the rest of society and denying the importance of ideological factors. Todorov's argument coincides with a similar assertion made twenty years ago by Terrence Des Pres that, while *people* were murdered en masse, *humanity as a moral concept* survived.[65] This view is not shared by camp survivors such as Primo Levi, Tadeusz Borowski, and Jean Améry or by younger observers such as the philosopher Alain Finkielkraut.[66] For camp survivors and others, the Holocaust demonstrated that *humanity as an idea* is mortal, that it is, in fact, possible to assassinate the very concept of moral existence along with millions of individual human beings.

Third, *psychology and sociology* are crucial to our understanding of the Holocaust. Psychological factors played a role in the daily routine of genocide: the death camps were built in part so as to diminish the detrimental effects of face-to-face killing on the perpetrators.[67] Conversely, Jewish resisters felt impelled to transform the perceived predilection of their communities passively to accept their fate, but were also under the terrible strain of having to abandon their families in the ghettos.[68] Outside observers were quick to draw conclusions about the psychological makeup of both victims and perpetrators. Bruno Bettelheim asserted the camp inmates' regression into childhood behavior, while many scholars spoke of a "Diaspora mentality" as the cause for European Jewry having "gone like sheep to the slaughter." Most painfully, survivors not only felt it almost impossible to relate their experiences, they rarely found anyone prepared to listen; this imposed silence greatly added to their mental turmoil.[69]

The psychology of the killers has recently been debated. Christopher Browning argues that the perpetrators were primarily motivated by peer group pressure, whereas Daniel Jonah Goldhagen traces their motivation to a unique brand of long-term German antisemitism.[70] Taking a more sociological approach, Zygmunt Bauman has asserted that the Holocaust was facilitated by modern modes of thinking and organization dating back to the Enlightenment notion of the "gardening society." Thus man's insistence on ordering and controlling his natural environment and his own nature is seen as setting the stage for radical social surgery, made all the more devastating by the advances in science and technology. Progress, in this view, can lead to widespread destruction in the name of human improvement.[71] Influenced no doubt by earlier scholars such as Jacob Talmon and Hannah Arendt,[72] for Bauman the main lesson of the Holocaust is that the values we trust in and the institutions we have created, perceived by us as bulwarks of liberty, justice, and humanism, contain within them seeds of totalitarianism, nihilism, and genocide.[73]

Finally, the *historiography and teaching* of the Holocaust have a great deal to do with national and individual identity and perspective. In the early postwar years, Western historians saw the Holocaust as of secondary importance to the war's military history; Communist historiography integrated it into its story of resistance to Nazism; Zionist historians perceived it as the culmination of centuries-old antisemitic persecution.[74] Later historiographical schools divided into "intentionalists," who underlined the centrality of Hitler's antisemitism and the "peculiarities" of German history, and "functionalists," who argued that the Holocaust was the outcome of structural factors and a unique set of circumstances, whose unanticipated and unintentional byproduct was genocide.[75] Both schools were concerned mainly with the perpetrators, thus maintaining the strict separation between categories initially imposed by the Nazis. Conversely, works on the victims often became entangled in acrimonious debates over Jewish conduct, the reactions of Jewish communities outside the Nazi sphere of influence, the policies of the Zionist leadership in Palestine, and the absorption of survivors into Israeli society.[76]

This raises the question of the intrinsic educational value of teaching the Holocaust. The Israeli historian Yehudah Elkana, himself a child survivor, has argued that the overexposure of Israeli youth to the Holocaust has had a harmful effect on their conduct and mentality. For him, "any lesson or view about life whose origin is the Holocaust is disastrous," since "democracy is about cultivating the present and the future; cultivation of the 'remembered' and addiction to the past undermine the foundations of democracy." He thus called to "eradicate the dominion of the historical 'remembered' over our lives."[77] Whatever the merit of this argument, we may concede that teaching the Holocaust does not necessarily make for better politics, more tolerance, or deeper humanism and compassion; it can also create hatred, frustration, anger, and aggression. Teaching inhumanity, in other words, even with the declared intention of preventing its recurrence, may imbue young minds with images of barbarism that will seek aggressive and violent expression.

The educational value of teaching atrocity was debated by several survivors of the Holocaust, among whom Primo Levi is rightly the most celebrated. But in the Israeli context, the case of a far less well known survivor-chronicler is of greater interest. Hence, by way of conclusion, I would like briefly to discuss the writings of Ka-Tzetnik, whose impact on forging Israeli identity has been as great as his memoirs have been misread and misrepresented. Indeed, Ka-Tzetnik offers a unique window into the relationship between material and moral catastrophe, adherence to and the molding of collective or national identity, and the fragmentation of personality in the face of inhumanity.[78]

Born in Poland in 1917 as Yehiel Feiner, Ka-Tzetnik spent close to two years in Auschwitz. After the war he immigrated to Palestine, where he changed his name to Dinur, or "of fire" in Aramaic. For the next four decades he devoted himself almost exclusively to writing on the Holocaust under the pseudonym Ka-Tzetnik, derived from the German acronym for concentration camp (KZ). Dinur's identity was revealed during the Eichmann trial, where he collapsed shortly after declaring that Auschwitz was "another planet," a universe in which the conventional rules and customs of human civilization did not apply.[79]

Widely read by Israeli youth in the 1950s and 1960s, Ka-Tzetnik both molded the image of the Holocaust for several generations of Israelis and served as the only legitimate source of sadistic and sexually titillating literature in a still very conservative society, due to his explicit prose and his obsession with depravity and violence. Ka-Tzetnik saw himself and was perceived by the educational establishment which disseminated his books as a chronicler of an event that demonstrated the necessity of a Jewish homeland. His immense ideological effect on young Israelis as can be gleaned from a letter written by a soldier shortly before he was killed in the 1967 war: "I have just finished reading Ka-Tzetnik . . . and I feel that from all the horror and helplessness a tremendous ability to be strong is growing . . . in me; . . . [to be] silent and terrible. . . . I want to know that never again will bottomless eyes stare from behind electrified fences! They will not stare this way only if . . . all of us . . . [become] strong and proud Jews! We will never be led again to the slaughter!"[80]

There was, of course, more to reading Ka-Tzetnik than being motivated to fight Arabs as if they were Nazis, but it is difficult to gauge the
effect of his imagery of horror and sexual depravity on the minds of
young readers and on their perceptions of the Holocaust. Ka-Tzetnik's
own desperate efforts to maintain a strict separation between his personality as a victim of Nazi atrocities and his role as their narrator led to his
mental collapse when the court compelled him to admit that Dinur and
Ka-Tzetnik were the same person.[81] Following his long recovery, and
parallel with the decline in his popularity, Dinur's views went through a
profound transformation, reflected in the remarkable final volume of his
memoirs. Yet hardly anyone noticed, since by the 1980s he was largely
forgotten. No longer satisfied with dividing humanity and history into
different planets, Dinur could also not "come to terms" with the past.
Hence his assertion that just as the past is linked to the present, so too
the victim of yesterday may turn out to be today's executioner. In a ter-
rifying apocalyptic vision which reenacts his own selection to go to the
gas chambers, he discovers a truth he had denied himself (and his readers) for forty years. He writes:

> I raise my eyes to see God's face . . . and see before me the face of an SS
> man. . . . His eyes still show the signs of sleep. Before his eyes—a stream
> of skeletons silently flowing from the gate of the barracks to the opening
> of the truck. And then his mouth opens with a long yawn. . . . I look at
> him . . . and . . . ask myself: Does he hate me? After all, he does not even
> know me. . . . Do I hate him? After all, I do not even know his name. . . .
> At that very moment I am struck with . . . horror . . . : If so, then he could
> have been here instead of me, a naked skeleton in the truck, and I, I could
> have been there instead of him . . . making sure that I send him, and mil-
> lions like him, to the crematorium—and just like him I would have
> yawned.[82]

Having set out by dividing humanity into monsters and men, time
into "then" and "now," the world into "there" and "here," Dinur
finally fuses them all together into one continuous apocalyptic vision en-
compassing our own present reality. After hundreds of pages filled with
the most explicit descriptions of that other planet, of sadism and canni-
balism, sexual perversity and torture, he ends his sextet with these
words: "In the past I used to say: Auschwitz is another planet! It can not
be explained and it can not be described. . . . Auschwitz is of hell, of the
night, on the other side of man-in-the-image-of-God. . . . Now Ausch-

OUTCASTS IN WAR AND GENOCIDE

witz threatens all men. Wherever man is, there is Auschwitz, because not Satan created Auschwitz, but I and you."[83]

This is a dark, almost nihilistic vision of our time. But there is a truth in it that we have no right to ignore. For Auschwitz is a mirror in which the history of the twentieth century is reflected. It is by no means the only mirror, and we may well prefer other, more elevating sights. But just as we cannot consign Auschwitz to another planet, so, too, we cannot avoid Ka-Tzetnik's insight, that when we look in the mirror of the Holocaust, we see our own reflection.

NOTES

1. E. Markusen and D. Kopf, *The Holocaust and Strategic Bombing: Genocide and Total War in the Twentieth Century* (Boulder, 1995); O. Bartov, *Murder in Our Midst: The Holocaust, Industrial Killing, and Representation* (New York, 1996).

2. R. G. Moeller, *War Stories: The Search for a Usable Past in the Federal Republic of Germany* (Berkeley, forthcoming); J. Winter and E. Sivan, eds., *War and Remembrance in the Twentieth Century* (Cambridge, 1999).

3. R. Moses, ed., *Persistent Shadows of the Holocaust: The Meaning to Those Not Directly Affected* (Madison, Conn., 1993); J. Bourke, *An Intimate History of Killing: Face-to-Face Killing in Twentieth-Century Warfare* (New York, 1999).

4. A. J. Mayer, *Why Did the Heaven Not Darken? The "Final Solution" in History* (New York, 1988).

5. A. H. Rosenfeld, ed., *Thinking about the Holocaust: After Half a Century* (Bloomington, 1997).

6. H. Rousso, *The Vichy Syndrome: History and Memory in France since 1944*, trans. A. Goldhammer (Cambridge, Mass., 1991).

7. O. Bartov, *Hitler's Army: Soldiers, Nazis, and War in the Third Reich* (New York, 1991); C. R. Browning, *Ordinary Men: Reserve Police Battalion 101 and the Final Solution in Poland* (New York, 1992); D. J. Goldhagen, *Hitler's Willing Executioners: Ordinary Germans and the Holocaust* (New York, 1996); R. Hilberg, *Perpetrators, Victims, Bystanders: The Jewish Catastrophe, 1933–1945* (New York, 1992); I. Trunk, *Judenrat: The Jewish Councils in Eastern Europe under Nazi Occupation* (Lincoln, 1996).

8. O. Bartov, *Mirrors of Destruction: War, Genocide, and Modern Identity* (New York, 2000).

9. P. Fussell, *The Great War and Modern Memory* (Oxford, 1975), 3–35; M. Eksteins, *Rites of Spring: The Great War and the Birth of the Modern Age*

309

(New York, 1990), 55–94; R. Wohl, *The Generation of 1914* (Cambridge, Mass., 1979). More critical assessments in J.-J. Becker, *1914: Comment les français sont entrés dans la guerre* (Paris, 1977); W. Mommsen, *Imperial Germany, 1867–1918: Politics, Culture, and Society in an Authoritarian State*, trans. Richard Deveson (London, 1995), 205–216; N. Ferguson, *The Pity of War* (London, 1998), 174–211.

10. G. L. Mosse, *Fallen Soldiers: Reshaping the Memory of the World Wars* (New York, 1990); J. Winter, *Sites of Memory, Sites of Mourning: The Great War in European Cultural History* (Cambridge, 1995); K. S. Inglis, "Entombing Unknown Soldiers: From London to Paris to Baghdad," and A. Becker, "From Death to Memory: The National Ossuaries in France after the Great War," both in *History & Memory* 5, no. 2 (Fall/Winter 1993): 7–31 and 32–49, respectively; V. Ackermann, "La vision allemande du Soldat inconnu: Débats politiques, réflexion philosophique et artistique," in J.-J. Becker et al., *Guerre et cultures, 1914–1918* (Paris, 1994), 385–96.

11. A. Prost, *In the Wake of War: "Les Anciens Combattants" and French Society, 1914–1939*, trans. Helen McPhail (Providence, 1992); V. R. Berghahn, *Der Stahlhelm, Bund der Frontsoldaten, 1918–1935* (Düsseldorf, 1966); J. M. Diehl, *Paramilitary Politics in Weimar Germany* (Bloomington, 1977); R. Bessel, *Germany after the First World War* (Oxford, 1993), 254–84; N. Ingram, *The Politics of Dissent: Pacifism in France, 1919–1939* (Oxford, 1991).

12. J. M. Hughes, *To the Maginot Line: The Politics of French Military Preparation in the 1920s* (Cambridge, Mass., 1971).

13. P. Paret, ed., *Makers of Modern Strategy: From Machiavelli to the Nuclear Age* (Princeton, 1986), pt. 4; J. L. Wallach, *Das Dogma der Vernichtungsschlacht* (Frankfurt am Main, 1967).

14. M. Messerschmidt, *Die Wehrmacht im NS-Staat: Zeit der Indoktrination* (Hamburg, 1969); O. Bartov, *The Eastern Front, 1941–45: German Troops and the Barbarisation of Warfare* (London, 1985), 68–105; J. Förster, "The German Army and the Ideological War against the Soviet Union," in *The Policies of Genocide: Jews and Soviet Prisoners of War in Nazi Germany*, ed. G. Hirschfeld (London, 1986), 15–29; K.-J. Müller, *The Army, Politics, and Society in Germany, 1933–45: Studies in the Army's Relation to Nazism* (New York, 1987).

15. See Heinrich Himmler's October 1943 Posen speech to SS leaders, and his May 1944 Sonthofen speech to army generals, cited in J. Noakes and G. Pridham, eds., *Nazism, 1919–1945: A Documentary Reader* (Exeter, 1988), 3:1199–1200.

16. T. Todorov, *A French Tragedy: Scenes of Civil War, Summer 1944*, trans. M. B. Kelly (Hanover, N.H., 1996).

17. A. Wieviorka, "Deportation and Memory: Official History and the Rewriting of World War II," in Rosenfeld, ed., *Thinking about the Holocaust*, 273–99; A. Prost, "The Algerian War in French Collective Memory," in Winter and Sivan, eds., *War and Remembrance*, 161–76.

18. A. Wieviorka, "From Survivor to Witness: Voices from the Shoah," in Winter and Sivan, eds., *War and Remembrance*, 125–41; E. Conan and H. Rousso, *Vichy: An Ever-Present Past*, trans. N. Bracher (Hanover, N.H., 1998).

19. A recent balanced assessment is M. Geyer and J. W. Boyer, eds., *Resistance against the Third Reich, 1933–1990* (Chicago, 1994). On the Wehrmacht's successor, see D. Abenheim, *Reforging the Iron Cross: The Search for Tradition in the West German Armed Forces* (Princeton, 1988); D. C. Large, *Germans to the Front: West German Rearmament in the Adenauer Era* (Chapel Hill, 1996). On East and West Germany's competing memories, see J. Herf, *Divided Memory: The Nazi Past in the Two Germanys* (Cambridge, Mass., 1997).

20. K. Naumann, "Wenn ein Tabu bricht: Die Wehrmachts-Ausstellung in der Bundesrepublik," and W. Manoschek, "Die Wehrmachtsausstellung in Österreich: Ein Bericht," both in *Mittelweg 36* 5, no. 1 (1996): 11–24 and 25–32, respectively; Hamburger Institut für Sozialforschung, ed., *Besucher einer Ausstellung: Die Ausstellung "Vernichtungskrieg: Verbrechen der Wehrmacht 1941 bis 1944" in Interview und Gespräch* (Hamburg, 1998); K. Naumann, *Der Krieg als Text: Das Jahr 1945 im Kulturellen Gedächtnis der Presse* (Hamburg, 1998).

21. O. Bartov, "Martyrs' Vengeance: Memory, Trauma, and Fear of War in France, 1918–1940," in *The French Defeat of 1940: Reassessments*, ed. J. Blatt (Providence, 1998), 54–84; E. Weber, *The Hollow Years: France in the 1930s* (New York, 1994); V. Caron, "The Antisemitic Revival in France in the 1930s: The Socioeconomic Dimension Reconsidered," *Journal of Modern History* 70, no.1 (March 1998): 24–73; Z. Sternhell, *Neither Right nor Left: Fascist Ideology in France*, trans. D. Maisel (Princeton, 1996).

22. R. O. Paxton, *Vichy France: Old Guard and New Order, 1940–1944* (New York, 1972); M. R. Marrus and R. O. Paxton, *Vichy France and the Jews* (New York, 1981); S. Zucotti, *The Holocaust, the French, and the Jews* (New York, 1993); P. Burrin, *France under the Germans: Collaboration and Compromise*, trans. L. Lloyd (New York, 1996); O. Bartov, "The Proof of Ignominy: Vichy France's Past and Present," *Contemporary European History* 7, no. 1 (1998): 107–131.

23. P. Novick, *The Resistance versus Vichy: The Purge of Collaborators in Liberated France* (London, 1968); P. Assouline, *L'épuration des intellectuels* (Brussels, 1990); H. R. Kedward and N. Wood, eds., *The Liberation of France: Image and Event* (Oxford, 1995); D. Carroll, *French Literary Fascism: Nationalism, Anti-Semitism, and the Ideology of Culture* (Princeton, 1995); N. Oxenhandler, *Looking for Heroes in Postwar France: Albert Camus, Max Jacob, Simone Weil* (Hanover, N.H., 1996).

24. Conan and Rousso, *Vichy*, 1, 15, deem it necessary "for the future of French identity and the strength of its universalist values" to "get away from the

311

sanctification of the memory of World War II," especially since France's "conscience is obsessed with memories of the Occupation." A. Brossat, *L'Épreuve du désastre: Le xxᵉ siècle et les camps* (Paris, 1996), 20, 23, claims that those who "only stress the singularity" of the Shoah fail to recognize that "the plunder and oppression of the Palestinians appears as compensation for the crime of Auschwitz" and "as the alibi for the . . . uninhibited negation of the Soviet extermination or the colonial atrocities." See also F. Furet, *Le Passé d'une illusion: Essai sur l'idée communiste au xxᵉ siècle* (Paris, 1995); Y. Ternon, *L'État criminel: Les Génocides au xxᵉ siècle* (Paris, 1995); J.-M. Chaumont, *La Concurrence des victimes: Génocide, identité, reconnaissance* (Paris, 1997).

25. See, for instance, the collaborative studies, A. Prost et al., *14–18: Mourir pour la patrie* (Paris, 1992), and Becker et al., *Guerre et cultures.*

26. J. Rouaud, *Fields of Glory*, trans. R. Manheim (New York, 1992). Orig. pub. as *Les Champs d'honneur* (Paris, 1990). See also O. Bartov, "Trauma and Absence (I): France and Germany, 1914–45," in *Time to Kill: The Soldier's Experience of War in the West, 1939–1945*, ed. P. Addison and A. Calder (London, 1997), 347–358.

27. A. Camus, *The First Man*, trans. D. Hapgood (London, 1995). Orig. pub. as *Le Premier homme* (Paris, 1994). G. Perec, *W or The Memory of Childhood*, trans. D. Bellos (London, 1988). Orig. pub. as *W, ou le souvenir d'enfance* (Paris, 1975).

28. N. Tec, *Dry Tears: The Story of a Lost Childhood* (New York, 1984); D. Dwork, *Children with a Star: Jewish Youth in Nazi Europe* (New Haven, 1991); J. Marks, *The Hidden Children: The Secret Survivors of the Holocaust* (New York, 1993); L. Holliday, *Children in the Holocaust and World War II: Their Secret Diaries* (New York, 1995).

29. S. Friedländer, *When Memory Comes*, trans. H. R. Lane (New York, 1978). Orig. pub. as *Quand vient le souvenir . . .* (Paris, 1978). S. Breznitz, *Memory Fields* (New York, 1992). Further in O. Bartov, "Trauma and Absence (II)," in *European Memories of the Second World War*, ed. H. Peitsch et al. (New York, 1999), 258–71.

30. In more detail, O. Bartov, "Defining Enemies, Making Victims: Germans, Jews, and the Holocaust," *American Historical Review* 103, no. 3 (June 1998): 771–816.

31. See note 21. See also, S. Berstein, *La France des années 30* (Paris, 1988); P. Andreu, *Révoltes de l'esprit: Les revues des années 30* (Paris, 1991); J.-F. Sirinelli, *Génération intelectuelle: Khâgneux et Normaliens dans l'entre-deux-guerres* (Paris, 1994).

32. See especially E. Zechlin, *Die Deutsche Politik und die Juden im Ersten Weltkrieg* (Göttingen, 1969); R. Pierson, "Embattled Veterans: The *Reichsbund jüdischer Frontsoldaten*," *Leo Baeck Institute Yearbook* 19 (London, 1974); W. T. Angress, "Das deutsche Militär und die Juden im Ersten Weltkrieg," *Militärgeschichtliche Mitteilungen* 1 (1976): 77–146; U. Dunker, *Der Reichs-*

bund jüdischer Frontsoldaten, 1919–1938: Geschichte eines jüdischen Abwehr-vereins (Düsseldorf, 1977); B. Crim, "War alles nur ein Traum? German Jewish Veterans and the Confrontation with völkisch Nationalism in the Interwar Period" (forthcoming).

33. On the obsession with race, see especially R. N. Proctor, *Racial Hygiene: Medicine under the Nazis* (Cambridge, Mass., 1988); M. Burleigh, *Death and Deliverance: "Euthanasia" in Germany, 1900–1945* (Cambridge, 1994); H. Friedlander, *The Origins of Nazi Genocide: From Euthanasia to the Final Solution* (Chapel Hill, 1995). On antisemitism, see U. Herbert, *Best: Biographische Studien über Radikalismus, Weltanschauung und Venunft, 1903–1989* (Bonn, 1996), pts. 1–2; J. Weiss, *Ideology of Death: Why the Holocaust Happened in Germany* (Chicago, 1996); S. Friedländer, *Nazi Germany and the Jews*, vol. 1: *The Years of Persecution* (New York, 1997).

34. On the Jewish preoccupation with antisemitism and race, see J. Kornberg, *Theodor Herzl: From Assimilation to Zionism* (Bloomington, 1993); J. M. Effron, *Defenders of the Race: Jewish Doctors and Race Science in Fin-de-Siècle Europe* (New Haven, 1994); D. Bechtel et al., eds., *Max Nordau, 1849–1923: Critique de la dégénérescence, médiateur franco-allemand, père fondateur du sionisme* (Paris, 1996).

35. See Hitler's speech on 30 January 1939, in Noakes and Pridham, *Nazism*, 3:1049, and his political testament, in G. Fleming, *Hitler and the Final Solution* (Berkeley, 1984), 92–93, 186–89. See also C. Gerlach, "The Wannsee Conference, the Fate of German Jews, and Hitler's Decision in Principle to Exterminate All European Jews," *Journal of Modern History* 70 (December 1998): 759–812. On Himmler, see note 15. On the murderous dynamic of eugenics, see note 33. See also R. J. Lifton, *The Nazi Doctors: Medical Killing and the Psychology of Genocide* (New York, 1986); G. Aly et al., *Cleansing the Fatherland: Nazi Medicine and Racial Hygiene*, trans. B. Cooper (Baltimore, 1994); J. M. Glass, *"Life Unworthy of Life": Racial Phobia and Mass Murder in Hitler's Germany* (New York, 1997).

36. H. Arendt, "The Aftermath of Nazi Rule," *Commentary* 10 (October 1950): 342–53; S. E. Aschheim, *Culture and Catastrophe: German and Jewish Confrontations with National Socialism and Other Crises* (New York, 1996), 85–114; D. Diner, "Negative Symbiosis: Germans and Jews after Auschwitz," in *Reworking the Past: Hitler, the Holocaust, and the Historians' Debate*, ed. Peter Baldwin (Boston, 1990), 251–61; A. Rabinbach, *In the Shadow of Catastrophe: German Intellectuals between Apocalypse and Enlightenment* (Berkeley, 1997), pt. 2.

37. R. G. Moeller, "War Stories: The Search for a Usable Past in the Federal Republic of Germany," *American Historical Review* 101 (October 1996): 1008–1048; F. Stern, *The Whitewashing of the Yellow Badge: Antisemitism and Philosemitism in Postwar Germany* (Oxford, 1992).

38. O. Bartov, "'. . . seit die Juden weg sind': Germany, History, and

Representations of Absence," in *A User's Guide to German Cultural Studies*, ed.
S. Denham et al. (Ann Arbor, 1987), 209–226; Bartov, "Trauma and Absence
(II)." On contemporary German Jewry, see J. Borneman and J. M. Peck, *So-journers: The Return of German Jews and the Question of Identity* (Lincoln,
1995); S. L. Gilman, *Jews in Today's German Culture* (Bloomington, 1995);
Y. M. Bodemann, *Gedächtnistheater: Die jüdische Gemeinschaft und ihre
deutsche Erfindung* (Hamburg, 1996); M. Brenner, *After the Holocaust: Re-building Jewish Lives in Postwar Germany* (Princeton, 1997).

39. E. Domansky, "'Kristallnacht,' the Holocaust, and German Unity: The
Meaning of November 9 as an Anniversary in Germany," *History & Memory* 4
(Spring/Summer 1992): 60–94; Domansky, "A Lost War: World War II in
Postwar German Memory," in Rosenfeld, ed., *Thinking about the Holocaust*,
233–72.

40. See note 22.

41. See note 23.

42. See notes 17–18. A. Wieviorka, *Déportation et génocide: Entre la
mémoire et l'oubli* (Paris, 1992); S. Farmer, *Martyred Village: Commemorating
the 1944 Massacre at Oradour-sur-Glane* (Berkeley, 1999).

43. H. Arendt, *Eichmann in Jerusalem: A Report on the Banality of Evil*, rev.
ed. (New York, 1977); S. Ettinger, *Modern Anti-Semitism: Studies and Essays*
(Tel-Aviv, 1978 [in Hebrew]), x-xi; S. Almog, ed., *Antisemitism through the
Ages: A Collection of Essays* (Oxford, 1988), essays by Almog, Ettinger, Gutman
and Bauer. Further in T. Segev, *The Seventh Million: The Israelis and the Holo-caust*, trans. H. Watzman (New York, 1993), 357–60, 465; *History & Memory* 8
(Fall/Winter 1996), special issue: *Hannah Arendt and Eichmann in Jerusalem*.

44. R. Hilberg, *The Politics of Memory: The Journey of a Holocaust Historian*
(Chicago, 1996), 110–111.

45. H. Yablonka, *Foreign Brethren: Holocaust Survivors in the State of Israel,
1948–1952* (Jerusalem, 1994 [in Hebrew]); I. Keynan, *Holocaust Survivors and
the Emissaries from Eretz-Israel: Germany, 1945–1948* (Tel Aviv, 1996 [in He-brew]); A. Shapira, "The Holocaust and World War II as Elements of the Yishuv
Psyche until 1948," in Rosenfeld, ed., *Thinking about the Holocaust*, 61–82;
I. Zertal, *From Catastrophe to Power: Holocaust Survivors and the Emergence of
Israel* (Berkeley, 1998).

46. See, for example, Browning, *Ordinary Men*, 143–46, and D. Pohl, *Na-tionalsozialistische Judenverfolgung in Ostgalizien, 1941–1944: Organisation
und Durchführung eines staatlichen Massenverbrechens* (Munich, 1996), 387–96, on the perpetrators; and P. Levi, *The Drowned and the Saved*, trans.
R. Rosenthal (New York, 1988), 82–84, on the survivors.

47. V. N. Dadrian, *The History of the Armenian Genocide: Ethnic Conflict
from the Balkans to Anatolia to the Caucasus* (Providence, 1995); G. Prunier,
The Rwanda Crisis: History of a Genocide (New York, 1995); M. A. Sells, *The*

Bridge Betrayed: Religion and Genocide in Bosnia (Berkeley, 1996); N. Malcolm, *Kosovo: A Short History* (New York, 1998).

48. I. Buruma, *The Wages of Guilt: Memories of War in Germany and Japan* (New York, 1995); I. Chang, *The Rape of Nanking: The Forgotten Holocaust of World War II* (New York, 1997).

49. C. Schmitt, *The Concept of the Political*, trans. G. Schwab (Chicago, 1996), orig. pub. as *Der Begriff des Politischen* (Munich, 1932).

50. For critiques of Schmitt, see, for example, J. Taubes, *Ad Carl Schmitt: Gegenstrebige Fügung* (Berlin, 1987); T. B. Strong, "Foreword: Dimensions of the New Debate around Carl Schmitt," and L. Strauss, "Notes on Carl Schmitt: The Concept of the Political" [orig. pub. as "Anmerkungen zu Carl Schmitt, Der Begriff des Politischen," *Archiv für Sozialwissenschaft und Sozialpolitik*, 67, no. 6 (1932): 732–49], in Schmitt, *Concept of the Political*, ix–xxvii and 81–107, respectively.

51. P. Sahlins, *Boundaries: The Making of France and Spain in the Pyrenees* (Berkeley, 1989); R. Heilbronner, *Visions of the Future: The Distant Past, Yesterday, Today, and Tomorrow* (New York, 1995); P. Loewenberg, *Fantasy and Reality in History* (New York, 1995); S. Kern, *The Culture of Time and Space, 1880–1918* (Cambridge, Mass., 1983); A. Rabinbach, *The Human Motor: Energy, Fatigue, and the Origins of Modernity* (Berkeley, 1990).

52. H. Arendt, *The Origins of Totalitarianism* (New York, 1951); R. Bridenthal et al., *When Biology Became Destiny: Women in Weimar and Nazi Germany* (New York, 1984); M. Burleigh and W. Wippermann, *The Racial State: Germany, 1933–1945* (Cambridge, 1991); R. Conquest, *The Great Terror: A Reassessment* (New York, 1990); S. Kotkin, *Magnetic Mountain: Stalinism as a Civilization* (Berkeley, 1995).

53. J. Petropoulos, *Art as Politics in the Third Reich* (Chapel Hill, 1996); A. E. Steinweis, *Art, Ideology, and Economics in Nazi Germany* (Chapel Hill, 1993); L. H. Nicholas, *The Rape of Europe: The Fate of Europe's Treasures in the Third Reich and the Second World War* (New York, 1994).

54. D. Pick, *War Machine: The Rationalisation of Slaughter in the Modern Age* (New Haven, 1993); J. J. Reid, "Total War, the Annihilation Ethic, and the Armenian Genocide," in *The Armenian Genocide: History, Politics, Ethics*, ed. R. G. Hovannisian (New York, 1992); L. Kuper, *Genocide: Its Political Use in the Twentieth Century* (New Haven, Conn., 1981); R. J. Rummel, *Death by Government* (New Brunswick, N.J., 1994); P. Holquist, "'Information Is the Alpha and Omega of Our Work': Bolshevik Surveillance in Its Pan-European Context," *Journal of Modern History* 69 (September 1997): 415–50.

55. S. Wheatcroft, "The Scale and Nature of German and Soviet Repressions and Mass Killings," *Europe-Asia Studies* 48, no. 8 (1996); N. Naimark, "Ethnic Cleansing between War and Peace in the USSR," P. Holquist, "State Violence as Technique: The Logic of Violence in Soviet Totalitarianism," and A. Weiner,

"Delineating the Soviet Body National in the Age of Socialism: Ukrainians, Jews and the Myth of the Second World War," in a forthcoming volume edited by A. Weiner; A. Bullock, *Hitler and Stalin: Parallel Lives* (New York, 1992); I. Kershaw and M. Lewin, eds., *Stalinism and Nazism: Dictatorships in Comparison* (Cambridge, 1997).

56. For an update on sources for research, see J. Fredj, ed., *Les Archives de la Shoah* (Paris, 1998).

57. See, for example, G. M. Kren and L. Rappoport, *The Holocaust and the Crisis of Human Behavior*, rev. ed. (New York, 1994); G. E. Markle, *Meditations of a Holocaust Traveler* (New York, 1995); J. K. Roth and M. Berenbaum, eds., *Holocaust: Religious and Philosophical Implications* (New York, 1989).

58. On the Western Allies' failure to help the victims, see M. Gilbert, *Auschwitz and the Allies* (New York, 1981); D. S. Wyman, *The Abandonment of the Jews: America and the Holocaust, 1941–1945* (New York, 1984); W. Laqueur and R. Breitman, *Breaking the Silence* (New York, 1986); B. Wasserstein, *Britain and the Jews of Europe, 1939–1945* (Oxford, 1988). W. D. Rubinstein, *The Myth of Rescue: Why the Democracies Could Not Have Saved More Jews from the Nazis* (London, 1997), rejects these arguments.

59. Of course the defeat of Hitler's dictatorship would not have been possible without the massive sacrifice of Stalin's tyranny. See, for example, J. Erickson, *Stalin's War with Germany*, 2 vols., 2d ed. (London, 1985).

60. On the medical profession, see notes 33 and 35. On other professionals, see G. Aly and S. Heim, *Vordenker der Vernichtung: Auschwitz und die deutschen Pläne für eine neue europäische Ordnung* (Frankfurt am Main, 1993); M. Kröger and R. Thimme, *Die Geschichtsbilder des Historikers Karl Dietrich Erdmann: Vom Dritten Reich zur Bundesrepublik* (Munich, 1996); G. Aly, *Macht-Geist-Wahn: Kontinuitäten deutschen Denkens* (Berlin, 1997); I. Müller, *Hitler's Justice: The Courts of the Third Reich* (Cambridge, Mass., 1991); H. Sluga, *Heidegger's Crisis: Philosophy and Politics in Nazi Germany* (Cambridge, Mass., 1993); A. D. Beyerchen, *Scientists under Hitler: Politics and the Physics Community in the Third Reich* (New Haven, 1977).

61. R. L. Rubenstein, *After Auschwitz: History, Theology, and Contemporary Judaism*, 2d ed. (Baltimore, 1992); Z. Braiterman, *(God) After Auschwitz: Tradition and Change in Post-Holocaust Jewish Thought* (Princeton, 1998); G. Greenberg, "Orthodox Jewish Thought in the Wake of the Holocaust: Tamim Pa'alo of 1947," in *In God's Name: Genocide and Religion in the Twentieth Century*, ed. O. Bartov and P. Mack (forthcoming).

62. P. Ericksen and S. Heschel, "The German Churches Face Hitler: Assessment of the Historiography," *Tel Aviver Jahrbuch für deutsche Geschichte* 23 (1994): 433–59; W. G. Jeanrond, "From Resistance to Liberation Theology: German Theologians and the Non/Resistance to the National Socialist Regime," in Geyer and Boyer, eds., *Resistance*, 295–311; and chapters by Ericksen,

Heschel, B. Griech-Polelle, and D. L. Bergen, in Bartov and Mack, *In God's Name*. On France, see W. D. Halls, *Politics, Society, and Christianity in Vichy France* (Oxford, 1995); E. Fouilloux, *Les Chrétiens français entre crise et libération, 1937–1947* (Paris, 1997). For rescue, see P. Hallie, *Lest Innocent Blood Be Shed: The Story of the Village of Le Chambon and How Goodness Happened There*, 2d ed. (New York, 1994); chapter by Jessica A. Sheetz in Bartov and Mack, *In God's Name*.

63. W. Sofsky, *The Order of Terror: The Concentration Camp*, trans. W. Templer (Princeton, 1997).

64. T. Todorov, *Facing the Extreme: Moral Life in the Concentration Camps*, trans. A. Denner and A. Pollak (New York, 1996).

65. T. Des Pres, *The Survivor: An Anatomy of Life in the Death Camps* (New York, 1976).

66. Levi, *The Drowned and the Saved*; T. Borowski, *This Way for the Gas, Ladies and Gentlemen*, trans. B. Vedder (New York, 1967); J. Améry, *At the Mind's Limits: Contemplations by a Survivor on Auschwitz and Its Realities*, trans. S. and S. P. Rosenfeld (New York, 1986); A. Finkielkraut, *Remembering in Vain: The Klaus Barbie Trial and Crimes against Humanity*, trans. R. Lapidus (New York, 1992).

67. Y. Arad, *Belzec, Sobibor, Treblinka: The Operation Reinhard Death Camps* (Bloomington, 1987).

68. See, for example, Y. Arad et al., eds., *Documents on the Holocaust: Selected Sources on the Destruction of the Jews of Germany and Austria, Poland, and the Soviet Union* (Jerusalem, 1981), 301–304, 433–34, 461–71; Y. Gutman, *The Jews of Warsaw, 1939–1943: Ghetto, Underground, Revolt*, trans. I. Friedman (Bloomington, 1989); A. Tory, *Surviving the Holocaust: The Kovno Ghetto Diary*, trans. J. Michalowicz (Cambridge, Mass., 1990); S. Rotem (Kazik), *Memoirs of a Ghetto Fighter: The Past within Me*, trans. B. Harshav (New Haven, 1994).

69. B. Bettelheim, "Individual and Mass Behavior in Extreme Situations," *Journal of Abnormal and Social Psychology* 38, no. 4 (October 1943): 417–52. See notes 3, 28, 43–45, above. See also J. E. Dimsdale, ed., *Survivors, Victims, and Perpetrators: Essays on the Nazi Holocaust* (Washington, D.C., 1980).

70. See note 7. See also O. Bartov, "Ordinary Monsters," *New Republic* (29 April 1996): 32–38.

71. Z. Bauman, *Modernity and the Holocaust* (Ithaca, N.Y., 1991).

72. Arendt, *The Origins of Totalitarianism*; J. L. Talmon, *The Origins of Totalitarian Democracy* (1952; Boulder, 1985). On the concept, see A. Gleason, *Totalitarianism: The Inner Life of the Cold War* (New York, 1995).

73. Such criticism of the Enlightenment, modernity, and modern science can also be found in M. Foucault, *The Order of Things: An Archeology of the Human Sciences* (London, 1970); T. W. Adorno, *Negative Dialectics* (New York, 1973);

D. J. K. Peukert, "The Genesis of the 'Final Solution' from the Spirit of Science," in *Reevaluating the Third Reich*, ed. T. Childers and J. Caplan (New York, 1993); A. Beyerchen, "Rational Means and Irrational Ends: Thoughts on the Technology of Racism in the Third Reich," *Central European History* 30, no. 3 (1997): 386–402.

74. See, for example, D. G. Schilling, "Re-Presenting the Holocaust in the General Histories of World War II" (unpublished paper, 1998); L. S. Dawidowicz, *The Holocaust and the Historians* (Cambridge, Mass., 1981), chaps. 4–5; R. S. Wistrich, *Antisemitism: The Longest Hatred* (New York, 1992).

75. The best surveys of these schools are C. R. Browning, *The Path to Genocide: Essays Launching the Final Solution* (Cambridge, 1992), chap. 5; M. R. Marrus, *The Holocaust in History* (New York, 1987), chap. 3; I. Kershaw, *The Nazi Dictatorship: Problems and Perspectives of Interpretation*, 3d ed. (London, 1993).

76. See especially Trunk, *Judenrat*; Y. Gutman and R. Manbar, eds., *The Nazi Concentration Camps: Structure and Aims. The Image of the Prisoner. The Jews in the Camps* (Jerusalem, 1984 [in Hebrew]); Y. Gutman and R. Manbar, eds., *Patterns of Jewish Leadership in Nazi Europe, 1933–1945* (Jerusalem, 1979 [in Hebrew]); and note 45 above.

77. Y. Elkana, "Bizhut ha-shihehah" (In Praise of Forgetting), *Ha'aretz* (2 March 1988): 3. See also M. Zuckermann, "The Curse of Forgetting: Israel and the Holocaust," *Telos* 78 (Winter 1988–89): 43–54; Zuckermann, *Shoah in the Sealed Room: The "Holocaust" in Israeli Press during the Gulf War* (Tel Aviv, 1993 [in Hebrew]), 17–31.

78. In more detail, see O. Bartov, "Kitsch and Sadism in Ka-Tzetnik's Other Planet: Israeli Youth Imagine the Holocaust," *Jewish Social Studies* (Spring 1997): 42–76. See also D. Meron, "Between Books and Ashes," *Alpayim* 10 (1994 [in Hebrew]): 196–224.

79. See H. Gouri, *The Glass Cage: The Jerusalem Trial* (Tel Aviv, 1962 [in Hebrew]), 123–126, chapter entitled "Star of Ashes."

80. Ka-Tzetnik, *House of Dolls* [*Beit ha-bubot*] (Tel Aviv, 1994 [in Hebrew]), 229. Orig. pub. in *Ba-mahaneh*, 23 April 1987. Now inscribed on a stone tablet on the site of the battle in Jerusalem where this soldier fell.

81. Segev, *The Seventh Million*, 3, cites Dinur's testimony on 7 June 1961. See also Gouri, *The Glass Cage*, 123–26; Ka-Tzetnik, *The Code: The Burden of the Nucleus of Auschwitz* [*Ha-tsofen: Masa ha-garin shel Auschwitz*] (Tel Aviv, 1994 [in Hebrew]), 77; E. Wiesel, "The Accident," in *The Night Trilogy*, 3d ed. (New York, 1988), 246. On the sense of two irreconcilable selves among survivors, see L. L. Langer, *Holocaust Testimonies: The Ruins of Memory* (New Haven, 1991).

82. Ka-Tzetnik, *The Code*, 22–24.

83. Ibid., 113.

Contributors

FRANK BAJOHR is a historian at the Forschungsstelle fuer Zeitgeschichte in Hamburg and lecturer at the Department of History, University of Hamburg.

OMER BARTOV is John P. Birkelund Professor of European History at Brown University.

DORIS L. BERGEN is associate professor of history at Notre Dame University.

RICHARD J. EVANS is professor of history at Cambridge University.

HENRY FRIEDLANDER is professor of history in the Department of Judaic Studies at Brooklyn College of the City University of New York.

ROBERT GELLATELY is Strassler Family Professor for the Study of Holocaust History at Clark University.

GEOFFREY J. GILES is associate professor of history at the University of Florida.

MARION A. KAPLAN is professor of history at Queens College.

SYBIL H. MILTON was an independent historian and former senior historian of the United States Holocaust Memorial Museum.

ALAN E. STEINWEIS is associate professor of history and Judaic studies at the University of Nebraska–Lincoln.

NATHAN STOLTZFUS is associate professor of history at Florida State University.

ANNETTE F. TIMM is a postdoctoral fellow at the Berlin Program for Advanced German and European Studies at the Free University of Berlin.

NIKOLAUS WACHSMANN is a research fellow in history at Downing College, University of Cambridge.

Index

abortion, 239, 242, 285–87; and disabled, 150

Alliance of Middle Class Businessmen, 49

Allies, bombing of Germany, 59, 135–36

Améry, Jean, 305

Andreas-Friedrich, Ruth, 136

anti-Communism, 3–5, 109–10

antiliberalism, 3–4

antisemitism, 3, 5–7, 20–21, 35, 39, 48, 115n.21, 145; boycotts of Jewish businesses and, 49–51, 66; bureaucratic, 106; central importance of, 15, 306; in France, 299–300; German businesses attempting to mitigate, 51–52; harassment and persecution of Jewish entrepreneurs, 45–49, 53–55, 61; Hitler and, 5–6, 233, 306; Nazi culture and, 106; Nazi ideology and, 299; Nuremberg Laws and, 71, 120,124, 127, 131, 133, 194, 216; as official state policy, 66; propaganda and, 49–50, 66, 68, 123, 290n.16

anti-Slavism, 256

apartheid system for Poles in Germany, 14, 257, 268, 270

apocalyptic vision(s), 302, 308

Arendt, Hannah, 301, 306

art, artists: aesthetic deviations and, 110; communist purge of, 109–10; Dadaism, 112; denunciation of, 109; Jewish, removal of, 9, 109; Nazi opinion of modern, 100, 111–12; patronage and, 100; reinstatement and rehabilitation of, 110

"Aryan Clause" of the Law for the Restoration of the Professional Civil Service, 103, 123, 137

"Aryan" households, 124–25

Aryanization of Jewish businesses, 8, 45, 48, 50–52, 57–58, 63n.12

Aschaffenburg, Gustav, 31

asocials, anti-socials, 11, 20; black triangles and, 180; colony of, 12; definition of, 12;

internment of, 33; prostitutes as, 12, 33, 192–94, 198; in the 20th century, 34, 38. *See also* social outsiders

Auschwitz concentration camp, 61, 87, 137, 155, 180, 219, 225–26, 269, 307–9; release of intermarried Jews from, 135

Austria: annexation of, 124, 216; deportation of Jews from, 137

baptism of Jews, 48, 92n.18, 124, 137, 298

Bar Mitzvah during the Third Reich, 69

Bauhaus, 111

Bauman, Zygmunt, 306

Beer Hall Putsch, 234

beggars, 12, 23–24

Berlin: homosexuals in, 29, 35; Jewish population of, 67, 78, 131, 133–36

Bettelheim, Bruno, 305

Binding, Karl, 147, 150

birth rate decline in 20th century Germany, 31, 34

Blitzkrieg, 124

Blüher, Hans, 235, 238

Bock, Gisela, 273

Bohne, Gerhard, 152

Bormann, Martin, 226, 235, 265

Borowski, Tadeusz, 305

boycotts: international, Nazi fear of, 51; of Jewish businesses, 49–51, 66

Brack, Viktor, 151, 154

Breznitz, Shlomo, 298

bribes, bribery, 76, 83

Browning, Christopher, 305

Brückner, Helmuth, 241–42

Buchenwald concentration camp, 61, 86, 180

Burleigh, Michael, 19n.48, 41n.1, 44n.44

castration, 248–49. *See also* sterilization

Catholics: displeasure of at public defamation and executions, 261, 268;

tice" and, 269; prostitution and, 207n.8; public defamation and, 262; racial hygiene and, 3, 147–48; Röhm purge and, 236; Roma and Sinti and, 226; social outsiders and, 5; social unrest, apprehension of, 124, 133

Hitler Youth, 193, 236, 252nn.7,13

Höch, Hannah, 112

Hoche, Alfred, 147, 150

Holocaust: apocalyptic visions and, 302, 308; collective and individual identity of, 294, 300–301, 304, 306; collective guilt and, 297; coping with the past and, 300–302; functionalist interpretation and, 89, 306; historiography and teaching of, 306–9; intentionalist interpretation and, 89, 306; modern genocide and war and, 301–4; perpetrators and victims of, 300–302, 305; perpetrators' motivation in, 305; politics and ideology of, 304; postwar perspective on, 301, 304–9; psychology and sociology of, 305–6; theology and moral lessons concerning, 304–5; victims in, 305. See also Final Solution

homeless, 12; number of, 37. See also vagrancy, vagrants

homophobia: cultural, 237; ideological, 238–39; political, 239; social, 239

homosexuality and homosexuals: in Berlin, 29, 35; Blüher, Hans, and, 235, 238; criminal code of 1871 and, 13; as criminals, 35, 253n.14; defined, 240; denunciation of, 107, 244–47; dismissal from Nazi Party of, 247, 250; effeminacy of, 35; execution of, 249–50; fear of declining birth rate because of, 34, 243; Gestapo and, 13; Goebbels and, 108–9; Goering and, 108; Himmler and, 13, 108, 235–37, 239, 241–43, 248–50; Hitler and, 13, 108, 233–34, 236–37, 241–42, 249; homoeroticism and, 235, 238; imprisonment and internment in concentration camps of, 244, 247–48, 250; Jewish, 250; Kripo and, 13; legalization of during the Empire, campaign for, 36; lesbianism and, 13–14; in the 19th century, 23, 29; organizations and

clubs of, 243; persecution of, 242–44, 249; purge from cultural life of, 107–9; raids on gay bars and, 244; not released from prison, 254n.32; section 175, campaigning for the abolition of, 35; sodomy and, 23, 246; sterilization and castration of, 107, 248–49; university dormitories and, 234–35; in Weimar, 13, 34–35. See also homophobia

Illing, Ernst, 154

Illustrierter Beobachter, 109

incest, 278

industrialization, 21, 25, 27

Intentionalist interpretations, 89, 306

intermarried couples, 9; "Aryan" men married to Jewish women, 124–25; "Aryan" women married to Jewish men, 124–25; baptism of children of, 48, 124; decentralization of power and, 120, 122; in Hamburg, 45, 62n.2; as an influence on Nazi policies, 120, 122, 135; law banning further intermarriages, 123, 194, 231n.29; law proposed for the dissolving of intermarriages, 139n.3, 140n7; as members of Jewish households, 125; murder of, in eastern occupied territories, 119; neighbors of, 46, 123; nonprivileged, 124–26, 132; Nuremberg Laws and, 119–20, 123–24, 127, 131, 133; privileged, 48, 58, 124, 126–27, 136; Rental Relations Law and, 125; social exclusion of the Jews and, 125–26; statistics on, 139n.2, 140n.6, 141nn.13,17; testimony of a Jewish survivor of, 17n.30. See also intermarried Germans; intermarried Jews

intermarried Germans: in the civil service and Justice Ministry, 130, 142n.27; denunciation of, 129; deportation of, 120–21; discrimination against, 123, 129; identification card of, 92n.16; newspaper ban thwarted by, 125, 128; noncompliance and protest of, 117–19, 124–25, 128, 130, 141n.16; Rassenschande and, 118, 129; refusal to divorce, 118, 123, 126, 128–29, 138;

mentally ill and physically handicapped
(*cont.*).
  death certificates, 156; hereditary disease
  and health courts and, 148–49; institutionalization of, 150; Jewish disabled,
  157; Nazi policies against, 147–57; in the
  19th century, 28, 30; opposition to killings of, 156–57; registration of, 150, 153;
  sterilization of, 11, 146, 148–50; in the
  20th century, 37; in the Weimar Republic,
  37. *See also* eugenics; euthanasia; racial hygiene; T4 killing operations
Mezger, Edmund, 39
Mischlinge: definition of, 117; deportation
  and temporary deferral from deportation
  of, 120, 127, 130, 132, 134, 136; as
  "Geltungsjuden," 126; German cultural
  life and, 105; German-Gypsy children,
  221–23, 225; legal certification of, 7;
  married to Germans, 142n.27; military
  service and, 130; number of, 7; Nuremberg Laws and, 120, 124; ordinary Germans influencing Nazi policy towards,
  119; Roma and Sinti, mixed Germans
  and, 221–23, 225; Star of David decree
  and, 126. *See also* intermarried couples;
  mixed marriages
mixed marriages, 280; between Germans
  and Gypsies, 223. *See also* intermarried
  couples; *Mischlinge*
Muckermann, Hermann, 147
Mühsam, Erich, 36
Müller, Heinrich, 136, 140n.8, 142n.30,
  263

Napoleonic Wars, 25
Nazi cultural policies, 99; aesthetic degeneration and deviation and, 100, 110;
  anti-modernism, 100, 111–12; antisemitism and, 106; communist artists, purge
  of, 109–10; contradictions of, 99; cultural eugenics, 100; cultural ghettoization, 52, 105; cultural purification, 100;
  cultural war, 99; Goebbels and, 103; homosexuals, cultural purge of, 107–9;
  Jewish cultural life, removal of, 9, 101–6,
  109–10; *Jüdischer Kulturbund*, early sup-

port and later dissolution of, 105; *Mischlinge* in German cultural life, 105; music
  and Reich Chamber of Music, 104, 111–
  12; Paragraph 10, 103–4, 110; Reich
  Cultural Chamber system, 103–4, 107,
  109–10, 112, 128; *Reichskulturkammer*,
  102–6; Roma and Sinti, purge of, 106–7;
  Volksgemeinschaft and, 100
Nazi ideology: antisemitism, 299; concerning the Final Solution and genocide,
  117, 133; inconsistent and mixed signals
  of, 66, 79, 90, 105, 250; intermarried
  Germans and Jews, 118, 121–22, 127,
  130, 135; German women and, 124,
  194, 200; non-German women and,
  278; against social outsiders, 4
Nazi regime: antisemitism, centrality of,
  15, 66, 306; censorship by, 9, 100, 103,
  112, 178–79; definition of a Jew, 127;
  fear of international boycott on German
  goods, 51; *Kripo* (criminal police), 13,
  257; party goals, 3, 4; "psychological"
  politics of, 121–22, 132, 136; political
  repression, 26, 29, 32; social unrest, fear
  of, 119–20, 132, 135, 138; stance on
  Jews, 5; radicalization during World War
  II, 11, 39, 132, 177, 182, 249, 257–60,
  269–70, 262–64, 268–69. *See also* Gestapo; racial hygiene
Nitsche, Paul, 152, 154
Noakes, Jeremy, 193
nordic supremacy, 32, 147
Noske, Gustav, 136
Nuremberg Laws, 71, 119–20, 123–24,
  127, 131, 133, 149–50, 194, 213, 216

Operation Gomorrah, 59
Ostermann, Arthur, 147

patronage, 100
Paulus, Friedrich von, 135
penal system. *See* prison(s)
"people's justice," 260–63
Pétain, Henri Philippe, 296–97, 300
Peukert, Detlev J.K., 111
Pfannmüller, Hermann, 154
Pfundtner, Hans, 221

physically handicapped. *See* mentally ill and physically handicapped

Ploetz, Alfred, 146

police custody, 176–77, 180. *See also* protective custody

"police justice," 257, 259, 264, 266, 269

Polish workers in Germany: anti-Polish sentiment, 14, 257; apartheid system and, 14, 257, 268, 270; denunciations of, 258, 268–69; execution and lynching of, 257–59, 262–64, 268; fraternization with Germans, 14, 257, 260–63, 267–68; identification of with "P," 14; "people's justice" and, 260–63; "police justice" and, 257, 259, 264, 266, 269; popular opinion and punishment of, 256, 261–62, 267–68; public defamation of, 260–61; race tests given to, 257, 263; statistics on, 270n.1; women as, 14, 269, 283–88

popular opinion: antisemitism and, 6–8; Catholics' displeasure at public defamations and executions, 261, 268; fraternization and, 268; German gratitude towards a Jew, 60; Goebbels and, 121, 132; Hitler and, 121–22, 132; public morale, 117, 122, 132–33, 135; Roma and Sinti and, 227; social exclusion of Jews and, 105–6; sterilization and, 10, 37

Preysing, Bishop Konrad Graf von, 120

prison(s): failure in reforming criminals, 29, 40, 172; Jewish entrepreneurs, internment in, 46–48; medicalization of penal policy, 38, 40, 166; 19th century reform of, 29; penal administrators in the Weimar Republic, 26; 20th century reform of, 32, 36

propaganda, 3, 18n.35, 36, 49–50, 66, 68, 105–6, 118, 123, 194, 200, 290n.16

property: confiscation of, Jews and, 56, 60; Law for the Confiscation of Subversive and Enemy Property, 224; Roma and Sinti and, 224

prostitutes and prostitution: acceptance of, 195, 197; as asocial, 12, 33, 192–94, 198; control of in the Third Reich, 198–99, 201, 204–5, 209n.28; as criminal, 172; deportation to concentration camps of, 194, 201, 204, 209–10n.36; deportation to work camps, 12, 194, 197, 201; "habitually promiscuous persons" and, 199–200, 202–3, 209n.33, 211n.48; Himmler and, 195, 201, 209–10n.36; Hitler and, 207n.8; hygiene and, 208n.25; image of, 200; Law for Combating Venereal Diseases, 196, 202; legal marginalization of, 194–95; "Magdalen homes" and, 29–30; medical examinations of, 276–77; and Nazi-run brothels, opposition to, 195–97, 206n.1; in the 19th century, 28; public decency in Germany and, 208n.19; registration of, 196; rehabilitation of, 199; removal of from the street, 200; in the 16th and 17th centuries, 24; state-run brothels, 12–13, 192, 195–98, 200–202, 204–6, 277; surveillance of, 199–200, 202–3, 210n.37; venereal disease (VD) control and, 192–98, 200–206, 209n.29, 210n.43, 211n.50, 277

protective custody, 120, 133, 136, 193, 202, 204, 219, 248, 269. *See also* police custody

protests: church protest on behalf of "non-Aryan Christians," 119, 144n.39; euthanasia, opposition to, 10–11, 37, 127, 156–57; German resistance to cultural purge of the Jews, 106; Jewish, 74, 76, 301; noncompliance of intermarried Germans, 117–19, 124–25, 128, 130, 141n.16; opposition to Nazi-run brothels, 195–97, 206n.1; Rosenstrasse Protest, 118, 134–35, 138–39

public defamation and punishment of crime, 260–62, 266, 268; Himmler's attitude towards, 261; Hitler and, 262. *See also* "lynch justice"

racial hygiene, 3–4, 10; communists and, 5; criminals and, 168, 170; in imperial Germany 31–32; and marriage health law, 150, 216, 279; against mentally ill and physically handicapped, 147–57; Nazis

Schandpfahl (pillar of shame), 22
Schlegelberger Minute, 129–30
Schmitt, Carl, 302
Schoenberg, Arnold, 111
Scholtz-Klink, Gertrud, 238
Schumann, Horst, 154–55
Section 175, 29, 107–9, 236, 240, 246–47, 250, 253n.16; homosexuals campaigning for the abolition of, 35; inconsistency of, 250
security confinement of criminals, 34, 166–83, 184n.6, 187nn.30,32, 188n.43; candidates for, 167–68; criticism of brutal condition of, 175; definition of, 166; increase in, 169; indefinite imprisonment and, 168; introduction of, 169; reasons for, 182; release from, 174–76, 188n.52; statistics on, 172–73, 178, 180, 190nn.74, 76; types of criminals in, 171
Sinti. See Roma and Sinti
Smyl, Stanislaus, 258–59
social democrats in the 19th century, 26, 29
social exclusion, 26, 35, 38–40, 145, 147; of criminals, 173; of Jews, 9, 46, 50, 52, 68, 123–26
social outsiders, 4, 145; attempted assimilation of ethnic minorities in Germany, 30; criminals as, 11; dishonorable status of, 21–24; in the early modern period, 21–25; in the early 20th century, 31–38; in the 18th century, 25; Himmler and, 5; Jews as, 8–9; Jews not as, 6; in the Nazi era, 38–39; Nazi ideology and, 4; in the 19th century, 25–31; police intervention and, 29; politicization of, 35–36; radicalization of Nazi policy towards, 39; sources of outsider status, 21–22; treatment of, in Germany compared to other countries, 30, 32, 38, 40; welfare payments to, 174, 225
social reform, 36
social work and welfare, 33–35, 38; payments, 174, 225
Sofsky, Wolfgang, 305
Sozialistengesetz, 29
SS, 39, 46, 48, 62n. 5, 77, 183, 195, 237,

249, 296; Leibstandarte Adolf Hitler, 133, 135, 244
Ständegesellschaft, 25, 38, 40
Stangl, Franz, 155
Star of David, 9, 58, 125–27
Stein, Gerhard, 218
sterilization, 10–11; of all undesirable races, 283–84; of criminals, 11, 32, 170, 176; Hitler and, 148; of homosexuals, 107, 248–49; of mentally ill and physically handicapped, 11, 146, 148–50; number of, 11; penalties against the sterilization of healthy couples, 150; popular opinion and, 10, 37; of Rhineland Bastards, 36, 145; of Roma and Sinti, 215, 218–22; statistics on, 149; in the USA, 146. See also eugenics; racial hygiene
Strauss, Richard, 104
Stravinsky, Igor, 111
Strength through Joy (KDF), 194
Stürmer, Der, 54–55
suicide, 61, 94n.74, 170, 174, 233, 267

Talmon, Jacob, 306
T4 killing operations, 152–56; recruitment of physicians, nurses, scientists, police officers, and other workers for, 152
Theresienstadt, 137
Theweleit, Klaus, 289n.9
Thierack, Otto-Georg, 39, 130–31, 179, 264–67
Todorov, Tzvetan, 305
Total War, 4, 131–32, 296

Untermenschen (subhumans), 118, 273, 283
urbanization, 27
utopianism, 303

vagrancy, vagrants: in 19th century, 27, 31; number of, 37; in 20th century, 33–34, 37; vagabundentreffen, 36
Vallat, Xavier, 222
Versailles, Treaty of, 4, 36
veterans: deportation and extermination of, 137, 144n.46; French, 295; German, 295; Jewish, 6, 57, 67, 137

Vichy regime, France, 222, 294, 296–98, 300

Volksdeutsche, 14, 274–75, 279–80, 283–85; identification of, 275

Volksgemeinschaft, 3–4, 47–48, 53, 60, 100, 120, 150, 198, 296

Wagner, Gerhard, 150–51
Walktor, Rosalie, 260
Walter, Bruno, 101–2
Warburg, Max, 52–53
Wehrmacht and collective war guilt, 297
Weimar Republic: anti-communism and anti-liberalism in, 4; antisemitism in, 6; art and culture in, 99–100; criminals in, 11, 167–69, 171–72; homosexuals in, 13, 34–35; mentally ill and physically handicapped in, 37; penal administrators in, 26; racial hygiene in, 32–35, 39; Roma and Sinti in, 38
Wends, 22
Widmann, Albert, 154
Wilhelm the Younger, Duke, 24
Wilhelm II, Kaiser, 25
Wippermann, Wolfgang, 19n.48, 41n.1, 44n.44

Wirth, Christian, 154–55
Wittgenstein, Ludwig, 233, 251n.1
Wolak, Thomas, 267
women, German: "Hausfrau," mother image of, 124, 194, 200; in Jewish households, 125; League of German Girls, 193; new gender roles in Nazi Germany, 125; in the 19th century, 26; protest and, 124–25, 134
women, non-German: "Aryan" households, 124–25; Nazi ideology and, 278, 289n.9; in Nazi occupied Europe, 274, 276–79, 283–88; as perpetrators, 289n.6; Polish, 14, 269, 283–88; racial identification and, 275, 280–81, 285–86; rape of, 276–77; reproduction control and, 280, 282–88; Roma and Sinti women, 218; sexual relations of, 275–79; as victims of Nazism, 289n.6. *See also* Jewish women
workers, foreign. *See* foreign workers and prisoners of war in Germany
World War I, Jewish veterans of. *See* Jews

Zimmermann, Michael, 13
Zionism, 70, 74, 299, 301, 306